D0729708

JUDICIAL POWER
AND
THE CONSTITUTION

JUDICIAL POWER AND THE CONSTITUTION

With an Introduction by Louis Fisher

Selections from the
Encyclopedia of the American Constitution
Edited by
Leonard W. Levy, Kenneth L. Karst, and
Dennis J. Mahoney

MACMILLAN PUBLISHING COMPANY

NEW YORK

Collier Macmillan Canada

TORONTO

Maxwell Macmillan International

NEW YORK   OXFORD   SINGAPORE   SYDNEY

Copyright © 1986, 1990 by Macmillan Publishing Company
A Division of Macmillan, Inc.

All rights reserved. No part of this book may be reproduced or transmitted in any form
or by any means, electronic or mechanical, including photocopying, recording, or by
any information storage and retrieval system, without permission in writing from the
Publisher.

Macmillan Publishing Company
866 Third Avenue, New York, NY 10022

Collier Macmillan Canada, Inc.
1200 Eglinton Avenue East, Suite 200, Don Mills, Ontario M3C 3N1

Library of Congress Catalog Card Number: 90-36086

Printed in the United States of America

printing number
1 2 3 4 5 6 7 8 9 10

Library of Congress Cataloging-in-Publication Data

Encyclopedia of the American Constitution. Selections
    Judicial power and the Constitution : selections from the
Encyclopedia of the American Constitution / edited by Leonard W.
Levy, Kenneth L. Karst, and Dennis J. Mahoney ; with an introduction
by Louis Fisher.
        p.   cm.
    Includes bibliographical references.
    ISBN 0-02-897148-5
    1. Judicial power—United States—Dictionaries.   2. Courts—United
States—Dictionaries.   I. Levy, Leonard Williams, 1923–
II. Karst, Kenneth L.   III. Mahoney, Dennis J.   IV. Title.
KF5130.A68E5325   1990
342.73′023′03—dc20
[347.3022303]   90-36086
                                                                  CIP

CONTENTS

The Jurisdiction of the Federal Courts

INTRODUCTION

In a sentence that mixes elegance with unsophistication, Justice Robert Jackson claimed that the Supreme Court is final "not because we are infallible, but we are infallible only because we are final." Jackson was too good a student of history to believe this beguiling account. The record plainly demonstrates that the Court, throughout its two centuries, has been neither infallible nor final. Instead, the Court successfully exercises judicial power only by recognizing the institutional and political limits within which it operates. Notwithstanding periodic announcements from the Court that it alone interprets the Constitution, constitutional law develops in ways far more complex and dynamic. The essays in this book describe the techniques used by the judiciary to accept and decide cases that form a part, but only a part, of the much larger process of shaping constitutional values.

The Constitution does not expressly empower the Court to review, for constitutionality, the actions of the Congress, the President, and the states. The power of judicial review might be drawn from suggestive language in Article III and Article VI, and there is some evidence from the Philadelphia Convention and the ratification debates that the Framers expected the federal courts to exercise judicial review. Yet the record is so maddeningly ambiguous, and John Marshall's decision in *Marbury v. Madison* more politically clever than legally convincing, that Edward S. Corwin offered this scholar's lament to the Senate Judiciary Committee in 1937: "These people who say the framers intended [judicial review] are talking nonsense; and the people who say they did not intend it are talking nonsense. There is evidence on both sides."

Having proclaimed the power of judicial review in *Marbury*, striking down a portion of the Judiciary Act of 1789, the Marshall Court never invalidated any other congressional statute. Judicial power was used instead to *uphold* congressional actions taken pursuant to the commerce clause, the necessary and proper clause, and other constitutional sources of legislative power. Rather than functioning as a nay-saying branch, the judiciary used its power affirmatively to add an important legitimacy to policy decisions reached by the executive and legislative branches. It was not until 1857, in its notorious decision in *Dred Scott v. Sandford*, that the Court invoked judicial review a second time to invalidate a congressional statute. That decision was later overturned by the Civil War Amendments, but by that time Congress had already acted through the regular legislative process to nullify part of *Dred Scott*, passing legislation in 1862 to prohibit slavery in the territories.

Thus, judicial power operated for almost a century with little constraint on Congress. The courts generally played a supportive role in helping to advance national power over the states. Under the leadership of John Marshall, the Supreme Court consistently gave broad support to congressional initiatives in exercising its powers. The Court did more than reinforce the express powers of Congress. It sanctioned the use of implied powers in *McCulloch v. Maryland* (1819) by upholding the authority of Congress to establish a national bank.

At the national and state level, courts upheld government regulation of business activities as a legitimate exercise of the "police power," allowing legislatures and municipalities broad discretion in protecting public health and safety. Following the Civil War, a variety of laws establishing maximum prices, maximum hours, and reasonable rates were sustained in the courts. At the turn of the twentieth century, however, courts began to invalidate state and federal laws designed to relieve the harsh effects of industrialization. In blocking these reform measures, judges manufactured a fictitious "liberty of contract" that depicted an employee as bargaining on equal terms with the employer, with no permissible intervention from the state. State labor legislation was regarded as "mere meddlesome interferences" by government.

Opposition to these judicial doctrines finally erupted in the court-packing proposal championed by President Franklin D. Roosevelt. His "reorganization" plan, submitted on February 5, 1937, was promptly unmasked as a clumsy and transparent effort to apply force to the judiciary. Although Roosevelt's party controlled both houses of Congress, his bill suffered an ignominious defeat in the Senate. Most senators sharply disagreed with the decisions of the Court, but they considered the principle of judicial independence to be more precious than pending legislative goals. A deep-seated suspicion of any attempt to concentrate political power provided sufficient reason to repudiate FDR's plan, regardless of the Court's unpopularity.

Other remedies, less radical than Roosevelt's proposal, enabled the political branches to overcome anachronistic Court doctrines. Congress passed legislation early in 1937 to provide full judicial pay during retirement. With that inducement, Justice Willis Van Devanter stepped down on June 2, 1937, giving Roosevelt his first opportunity to nominate a Justice to the Court. Within a few years Roosevelt placed other New Deal supporters on the Court, allowing the normal cycle of presidential appointments and Senate confirmations to bring the Court's composition in line with contemporary views.

The collision between the Court and the political institutions in the 1930s led to the abandonment of restrictive judicial doctrines. The Court upheld a price-setting statute in *Nebbia v. New York* (1934) and, in the midst of the court-packing fight, sustained a minimum wage law for women in *West Coast Hotel Co. v. Parrish* (1937). Other decisions in 1937 confirmed that the Court, even without wholesale changes by Roosevelt, could accommodate New Deal programs. The Court confessed in *Prudential Insurance Co. v. Benjamin* (1946) that the "history of judicial limitation of congressional power over commerce, when exercised affirmatively, has been more largely one of retreat than of ultimate victory."

Critics of the court-packing plan argued that an independent judiciary represented an essential means for protecting individual liberties and minority rights. However, the record of the courts over the previous century and a half provided meager evidence to support that proposition. Henry W. Edgerton, who later became a federal judge, wrote an article for the *Cornell Law Quarterly* in 1937 that reviewed the performance of the Supreme Court. The judicial track record was dismal. With few exceptions, the dominant theme consisted of judicial rulings that consistently favored governmental power over individual rights, lent support to harmful business activities, deprived blacks of protection, upheld business interests over labor interests, and defended private wealth against taxation. Judicial protection of individual liberties and minority rights, on any sustained basis, did not appear until the middle of the twentieth century.

During the years of the Warren Court, judicial activism was brought to bear on such areas as civil rights, reapportionment, and criminal law. Still, the courts encountered powerful constraints on their power. The desegregation case of 1954 yielded little progress toward the integration of public schools. The turning point required the leadership of President Lyndon B. Johnson, the determination of Congress, and public demands for decisive action. Within the space of a few years Congress passed such landmark statutes as the Civil Rights Act of 1964, the Voting Rights Act of 1965, and the Fair Housing Act of 1968. The struggle against racial discrimination needed the combined efforts of all three branches of the Federal Government, the states, and the private sector.

Chief Justice Earl Warren epitomized judicial activism, and yet he understood the limits of judicial power. In a 1962 article for the *New York University Law Review* he discussed the Court decisions during World War II that supported the detention of Japanese Americans. He cautioned: "The fact that the Court rules in a case like *Hirabayashi* that a given program is constitutional, does not necessarily answer the question whether, in a broader sense, it actually is." Warren believed that our political system mandated a limited role for the judiciary: "In our democracy it is still the Legislature and the elected Executive who have the primary responsibility for fashioning and executing policy consistent with the Constitution."

Judicial power is defined partly by specific grants of authority in the Constitution, including the case-or-controversy requirement and the Court's jurisdiction over appellate and original cases. The exercise of judicial power, however, relies on political and institutional judgments by the courts. Despite Chief Justice Marshall's declaration in *Cohens v. Virginia* that it is "most true that this Court will not take jurisdiction if it should not: but it is equally true, that it must take jurisdiction if it should," the reality of judicial power is quite different. Even when courts have jurisdiction they frequently duck a case for reasons of equity and prudence. To avoid conflicts with other branches of government, judges invoke rules of self-restraint. These thresholds, or "gatekeeping rules," determine who has access to the courts. Cases with constitutional dimensions are often sidestepped through the adroit use of various doctrines: justiciability, standing, mootness, ripeness, political questions, equitable discretion, and prudential considerations.

The use of these thresholds sends a constitutional issue back to the political branches for resolution. For example, a resident of Pennsylvania claimed that covert funding of the Central Intelligence Agency violated the statement and account clause, which requires that "a regular Statement and Account of the Receipts and Expenditures of all public Money shall be published from time to time." There is no public accounting for the CIA and other elements of the intelligence community. Nonetheless, the Supreme Court in *United States v. Richardson* (1974) ruled that the litigant had no standing to bring the suit. Unable to reach the merits through the courts, the meaning of the statement and account clause is left to the executive and legislative branches.

A similar lesson comes from *Schlesinger v. Reservists to Stop the War* (1974), a challenge to the constitutionality of members of Congress who serve in the military services. The litigants argued that these multiple duties in the legislative and executive branches conflicted with the ineligibility clause, which prohibits a member of Congress from holding any office under the United States. Once again the Court dismissed the case on standing. Another separation of power issue—the scope of the President's pocket-veto power—was avoided by the Court in *Burke v. Barnes* (1987) on grounds of mootness. As a result, the constitutional meaning of the pocket veto bounced back to the political branches for possible resolution.

The willingness of the courts to decide a constitutional issue does not eliminate participation by the other branches. At most, judicial decisions set a floor for constitutional rights; the political branches can protect rights above those minimum levels. In *Goldman v. Weinberger* (1986), the court upheld an Air Force regulation that prohibited an Orthodox Jew from wearing his yarmulke (skullcap) indoors while on duty. The Court accepted the judgment of the Air Force that obedience, discipline, and unity within the military services were crucial values that overrode religious freedom. In his dissent, Justice William J. Brennan objected that the Court had abdicated "its role as principal expositor of the Constitution and protector of individual liberties." Yet the individual liberties left unprotected by the Court were safeguarded a year later when Congress passed legislation telling the Air Force to change its regulation to permit military personnel to wear "neat and conservative" religious apparel indoors while on duty.

In addition to sharing with other branches of the national government the responsibility for protecting constitutional rights, the Court looks for assistance to state legislatures, state courts, and governors. In an effort to cultivate comity and respect between the national government and the states, federal courts relinquish jurisdiction under various circumstances in order to avoid "needless friction" with the administration of state affairs. By following this abstention doctrine, federal courts generally wait until the highest state court has disposed of a constitutional issue.

Many of the constitutional issues decided at the state level go no further. The Court has long made clear that if state courts based their decisions on "bona fide separate, adequate and independent grounds," the Court will not undertake a review. If state rulings rest exclusively on the state constitution and the laws of the state, the state decision is final and conclusive. This principle is illustrated by *Washington v. Chrisman,* a search and seizure case of 1982. The state supreme court had held that a police officer had exceeded his authority in seizing incriminating evidence in a student's room. The U.S. Supreme Court reversed, using its "plain view" doctrine to uphold the seizure and allow the introduction of the evidence in court. After the case had been remanded to the state, the supreme court of Washington, basing its opinion solely on the constitution and laws of the state, concluded that it was right the first time and excluded the evidence obtained by the officer.

In many areas of constitutional law, states have announced restrictions on the government that are more stringent than those followed in the federal courts. As the Court noted in *PruneYard Shopping Center v. Robins* in 1980, each state has the "sovereign right to adopt in its own Constitution individual liberties more expansive than those conferred by the federal government."

The Bill of Rights originally applied only to the federal government. Throughout the process of selective incorporation, most of the Bill of Rights has been incorporated in the due process clause of the Fourteenth Amendment, extending those protections to the states. It is a misconception, however, to believe that a national standard of individual rights and liberties is now imposed on the states. First, states may adopt standards higher than those of the federal government. Second, federal courts regularly push issues back to the states for specific resolution. Now that "community standards" are used to define obscenity, the meaning of obscenity can vary widely from one locale to another. Third, although the right to a jury trial applies to all states, the states may depart from standards for federal juries by establishing juries with less than twelve members and by accepting nonunanimous verdicts. Federalism still permits wide variations in individual rights.

The effective application of judicial power depends on discerning judgments by courts with regard to the cases accepted, the remedies selected, and the timing of decisions. The result is a sensitive combination of technical jurisdiction and political prudence, of principle and expedience, of assertiveness and self-restraint. Like all political power, judicial power is exercised safely by remaining alert to the potential for good and the danger of overreaching. Much depends on the good sense of judges. When that safeguard fails, there are adequate counterforces within the political system to restore the equilibrium needed for a constitutional order.

LOUIS FISHER

PUBLISHER'S NOTE

The essays in this volume form an overview of the development of the judicial power in the United States, from the framing of the Constitution up to and including the Burger Court. They are chosen from the four-volume set of the *Encyclopedia of the American Constitution*, which Macmillan published in 1986.

In these articles the reader will find certain words, names, and court cases set in small capital letters. This cross-referencing system was used in the *Encyclopedia* to refer to separate entries on those subjects. Readers of this volume who want to find out more about these topics will want to consult the *Encyclopedia of the American Constitution* for further information. In addition, each essay has a bibliography that will aid the reader in pursuing his or her own study of the subject.

This volume is the fifth in a series on topics of constitutional interest. We are publishing the series to make the contents of the *Encyclopedia of the American Constitution* more readily accessible to students. Other volumes in this series treat the subjects of American constitutional history, civil rights and equality, criminal justice, and the First Amendment.

ABOUT THE EDITOR

Louis Fisher is a Senior Specialist in the Separation of Powers at the Library of Congress in Washington, D.C. Among his many books are *Constitutional Dialogues* (1989) and *American Constitutional Law* (1990).

Role of the Judiciary in the Government System

JUDICIAL REVIEW

Gerald Gunther

Judicial review, in its most widely accepted meaning, is the power of courts to consider the constitutionality of acts of other organs of government when the issue of constitutionality is germane to the disposition of lawsuits properly pending before the courts. This power to consider constitutionality in appropriate cases includes the courts' authority to refuse to enforce, and in effect invalidate, governmental acts they find to be unconstitutional.

Judicial review is America's most distinctive contribution to CONSTITUTIONALISM. Although courts have exercised judicial review almost from the beginning of American constitutional government, the question of the legitimacy of that JUDICIAL POWER has often provoked controversy as well as recurrent charges that American judges usurped the authority. Nearly two centuries of exercises of and popular acquiescence in the power have quieted the storms over its basic justifiability in recent decades, but vehement controversy continues regarding the proper scope and authority of judicial rulings on constitutionality. Moreover, particular exercises of judicial review continue to stir passionate political debates, as they have from the beginning.

The classic justification for judicial review was set forth by Chief Justice JOHN MARSHALL in MARBURY v. MADISON (1803). Marshall relied on general principles and constitutional text. His arguments from principle are not compelling. For example, his unchallengeable assertion that the Constitution was designed to establish a limited government does not demonstrate that *courts* should enforce those limitations. Constitutions prescribing limits on government had been adopted before 1803, as many have been since; but relatively few look to the judiciary for enforcement. Similarly, the fact that judges take an oath to support the Constitution does not imply judicial review, for the Constitution requires the oath of all federal and state officers. Far more persuasive are Marshall's references to two passages of the constitutional text. First, Article III lists cases "arising under the Constitution" as one of the subjects included within the JUDICIAL POWER OF THE UNITED STATES, suggesting that constitutional questions can give rise to judicial rulings. Second, the SUPREMACY CLAUSE of Article VI lists the Constitution first as among the legal sources that "shall be the supreme Law of the Land."

Although the inferences derivable from the constitutional text are not unchallengeable, they provide the strongest available support for Marshall's justification for judicial review. True, Article VI is specifically addressed only to state judges, for the "supreme Law of the Land" clause is followed by the statement that "Judges in every State shall be bound thereby, any Thing in the Constitution or Laws of any State to the Contrary notwithstanding." Still, the CONSTITUTIONAL CONVENTION debates and federal LEGISLATION, ever since Section 25 of the JUDICIARY ACT OF 1789, have contemplated Supreme Court review of state court rulings on constitutional questions, and it is surely plausible to argue that the Supreme Court's authority on review would be no less than that of state judges obeying the command of the supremacy clause.

Federal court review of state court judgments is an especially plausible aspect of judicial review, for it is a typical policing technique to maintain the delineations of governing authority in federal systems. That strand of judicial review is common in other federal schemes as well, as in Switzerland and Australia. Yet even federal systems are conceivable without judicial review. Thus, nationalists at the Constitutional Convention initially urged reliance on the congressional veto and on military force to curb excesses by the states. The supremacy clause, and its reliance on routine judicial power to enforce federalistic restraints, stemmed from suggestions by states' rights forces at the convention.

Judicial review in the interest of FEDERALISM has played an important role in the United States; some observers, indeed, view it as the most essential function of judicial review. As Justice OLIVER WENDELL HOLMES once put it: "I do not think the United States would come to an end if we lost our power to declare an Act of Congress void. I do think the Union would be imperiled if we could not make that declaration as to the laws of the several States." The supremacy clause goes a long way toward assuring this protection of the Union; but it provides less compelling justification for judicial review of congressional acts.

The constitutional text cited by John Marshall supports judicial review in all its aspects in a more basic sense. Article III and Article VI both reflect the premise central to judicial review—the premise that the Constitution is to be considered a species of law and accordingly cognizable in courts of law. Judicial review is essentially the judicial enforceability of constitutional norms, and viewing the Constitution as law rather than mere policy or precatory adjuration is the keystone of the more persuasive argument that the American constitutional scheme was designed to rely on judges, not merely troops or political restraints, to enforce constitutional limits.

This view of the Constitution as law—the view central to the argument for giving courts a major role in constitutional enforcement—made it relevant for Marshall to state that it was "emphatically the province and duty of the judicial department to say what the law is," and to describe judicial review as an outgrowth of the normal task of judges: to adjudicate the cases before them on the basis of all relevant rules of law, rules that include those stemming from the Constitution. And that in turn made it plausible for him to say that, where a statute and the Constitution conflict, the courts must enforce the superior Constitution and "disregard" the statute. That, to Marshall, was "of the very essence of judicial duty."

Even if Marshall's views of the Constitution as law and of the "judicial duty" were unanswerable, charges of usurpation would not be stilled. Whatever the strength of the inferences from Articles III and VI, it is undeniable that the power of judicial review is not explicitly granted by the Constitution—in contrast to the constitutions of the nations that, in modern times, have embraced systems similar to the American scheme of judicial review, such as West Germany, Italy, India, and Japan. Defenders of judicial review have accordingly sought to find added support for Marshall's conclusion in historical understandings and practices. None of the sources relied on, however, conveys overwhelming force.

For example, it is true that Marshall's argument was to a considerable extent anticipated by ALEXANDER HAMILTON in THE FEDERALIST #78; but Hamilton's essay was after all only a propagandistic defense of the Constitution during the ratification debates. Similarly, the arguments from historical practice are inconclusive at best. The much invoked statement by EDWARD COKE in BONHAM'S CASE (1610)—that "the COMMON LAW will controul Acts of Parliament, [and] adjudge them to be utterly void" when they are "against common right and reason"—was inconsistent with British practice at the time and thus is not even respectable OBITER DICTUM. More relevant was the APPELLATE JURISDICTION of the PRIVY COUNCIL over colonial courts; but invalidation of legislation through that route was rare and unpopular. And the much debated alleged PRECEDENTS in the practice of state courts during the years immediately following independence hardly establish a well-entrenched practice of judicial review in the era of the ARTICLES OF CONFEDERATION. The preconstitutional examples that withstand scrutiny are few and controversial, and in any event it is not clear that many delegates at the Constitutional Convention knew about the scattered actual or alleged instances of invalidation of state laws by state judges.

Nor do the statements in the Constitutional Convention and the state ratification debates provide ironclad proof that judicial review was intended by the Framers. While it is true that most of the statements addressing the issue supported such a judicial power, it is equally true that only a minority of speakers at the Constitution framing and ratifying conventions expressed their views. The most important statements at the Constitutional Convention came during the discussion of the council of revision proposal—a proposal that the Justices join with the President in exercising the VETO POWER. That proposal was rejected, partly on grounds supporting the legitimacy of judicial review. Thus, LUTHER MARTIN, in criticizing "the association of the Judges with the Executive" as a "dangerous innovation," argued that, "as to the Constitutionality of laws, that point will come before the Judges in their proper official character. In this character they have a negative on the laws. Join them with the Executive in the Revision and they will have a double negative."

Some scholars have argued, questionably, that judicial review was so normal a judicial function that it was taken for granted by the Framers. HENRY M. HART and Herbert Wechsler claimed to find clear support in the Convention debates: "The grant of judicial power was to include the power, where necessary in the decision of cases, to disregard state or federal statutes found to be unconstitutional. Despite the curiously persisting myth of usurpation, the Convention's understanding on this point emerges from its records with singular clarity." But with regard to original intent, EDWARD S. CORWIN's Senate testimony on the 1937 Court-packing plan still represents a fair summary of the state of the record. Corwin stated that the "people who say the framers intended [judicial review] are talking nonsense," but he added that "people who say they did not intend it are talking nonsense." As Leonard W. Levy commented after noting Corwin's assessment that there is "great uncertainty" on the issue: "A close textual and contextual examination of the evidence will not result in an improvement on these propositions."

Most important in the search for preconstitutional bases for judicial review authority is probably the late-eighteenth-century prevalence of general ideas conducive to the acceptance of the power asserted in *Marbury v. Madison*. The belief in written CONSTITUTIONS to assure LIMITED GOVERNMENT was hardly an American invention, but Americans had an unusually extensive experience with basic, HIGHER LAW documents of government, from royal charters to state constitutions and the Articles of Confederation. Yet it is possible to have constitutions without judicial review: to say that a government cannot exceed constitutional limits does not demonstrate who is to decide. It bears reiterating, then, that viewing a constitution as a species of "law" was the vital link between constitutionalism and judicial competence to decide constitutional issues. Moreover, the view that the Constitution was an act of the people rather than of the state governments helped provide an ideology congenial to Marshall's insistence that the courts could, in the name of the people, refuse to enforce the acts of the people's representatives.

Accepting the persuasiveness of Marshall's core argument is not tantamount to endorsing all of the alleged implications of judicial review that are pervasive in the late twentieth century. Marshall's stated view of the role of courts in constitutional cases was a relatively modest one; after nearly two centuries of exercise of judicial review by courts, and especially the Supreme Court, the scope and binding effect of judicial rulings are far broader. Most of Marshall's argument was largely defensive, designed to undergird judicial competence and authority to adjudicate issues of constitutionality. He insisted that the Constitution is "a rule for the government of *courts* as well as the legislature" and concluded that "*courts,* as well as other departments, are bound by that instrument." Modern perceptions, by contrast, often view the courts as playing a superior or supreme role in CONSTITUTIONAL INTERPRETATION. Claims of JUDICIAL SUPREMACY and sometimes even exclusiveness are widespread in scholarly statements and popular understandings. The extent to which such impressions are justifiable continues to give rise to sharp controversy.

Marshall's claims about judicial competence and authority were closely tied to a tripartite theory of government reflecting the SEPARATION OF POWERS. He did not deny that other branches, including the President in the exercise of the veto power and Congress in enacting legislation, could and—under the oath to support the Constitution emphasized in *Marbury* itself—presumably must consider issues of constitutionality. Marshall's argument that courts *also* have competence to take the Constitution into account in their work was essentially a "me too" position. Modern variants on justifications for judicial review—and a number of statements from the modern Supreme Court itself—lend stronger support than anything in Marshall's reasoning to a "me superior" or even a "me only" view.

Nearly from the beginning, Presidents have taken issue with Supreme Court rulings. THOMAS JEFFERSON insisted that "nothing in the Constitution has given [the judges] a right to decide for the Executive, more than to the Executive to decide for them." And he argued that considering "the judges as the ultimate arbiters of all constitutional questions" was "a very dangerous doctrine indeed, and one which would place us under the despotism of an oligarchy." Similarly, ANDREW JACKSON insisted, in vetoing the bill to recharter the Bank of the United States in 1832, that McCULLOCH v. MARYLAND (1819) did not preclude his action: "Mere precedent is a dangerous source of authority, and should not be regarded as deciding questions of constitutional power except where the acquiescence of the people and the States can be considered as well settled." Similar statements are found in the utterances of later Presidents, from ABRAHAM LINCOLN to FRANKLIN D. ROOSEVELT and beyond.

John Marshall was no doubt unhappy with the political statements of Jeffersonians and Jacksonians. Clearly, he would have preferred ready acceptance of his Court's glosses on the Constitution by all governmental officials and the entire nation. But nothing in the stances of the leaders of his day or since was in sharp conflict with anything in *Marbury v. Madison.* Jefferson, Jackson, and their successors did not deny the binding effect of the judges' constitutional rulings in the cases before them. But the Presidents insisted on their right to disagree with the principles underlying the Court decision. As Lincoln said in the course of his debates with STEPHEN A. DOUGLAS, he did not propose that after Dred Scott had been held to be a slave by the Court—in DRED SCOTT v. SANDFORD (1857)—"we, as a mob, will decide him to be free." But, he added, "we nevertheless do oppose that decision as a political rule which shall be binding on the voter, to vote for nobody who thinks it wrong, which shall be binding on the members of Congress or the President to favor no measure that does not actually concur with the principles of that decision. [We] propose so resisting it as to have it reversed if we can, and a new judicial rule established upon this subject."

Does it follow that, if such presidential statements are consistent with *Marbury v. Madison,* the scheme sketched by Marshall in 1803 contemplated never-ending chaos—a state of chaos in which the political branches of the national government, and the states as well, might forever disagree with the principles of Supreme Court decisions, in which the only way to implement the Court's principles would be to bring the resisting parties to court in multiple lawsuits, in which no constitutional question would ever be settled? Not necessarily, and certainly not in American experience. Judicial review has not meant that the Supreme Court's reasoning ends all constitutional debate, but neither has it meant endless litigation and dispute over every constitutional issue. Yet the reasons for the growing role of the Supreme Court in settling constitutional issues rest less on any legal principle underlying judicial review than on considerations stemming from institutional arrangements and from prudence. The only arguable basis in *Marbury* itself for viewing the courts as the ultimate arbiters of constitutional issues is Marshall's ambiguous statement that it is "emphatically the province and duty of the judicial department to say what the law is." That statement establishes judicial competence, as noted; but its ambiguity also may provide the basis for arguments for a special judicial expertise in constitutional matters and for a de facto judicial supremacy. Marshall's statement is not so strong, however, as a similar one from Hamilton, in *The Federalist* #78: "The interpretation of laws is the proper and peculiar province of the courts."

The widely observable phenomenon that a Court interpretation of the Constitution has significance beyond the parties to a particular lawsuit rests on other, stronger bases. A central one is that, to the extent a disputed constitutional issue arises in a lawsuit, and to the extent that the Supreme Court is the highest court in the judicial hierarchy, a Supreme Court interpretation is final. Technically, it is final only with respect to the parties in the case, to be sure; but the Court gives general reasons in resolving specific controversies, and the Justices normally operate under a system of PRECEDENT and STARE DECISIS. Similarly situated parties not before the Court in the particular case ordinarily recognize that, other things being equal, the Court will adhere to precedent, will apply the same rule to them if litigation ensues, and accordingly choose not to engage in needless litigation.

Basically, then, the reason that the courts generally and the Supreme Court in particular wield such vast influence in Americans' understanding of their Constitution is that most constitutional issues can and do arise in lawsuits; and once they do, the courts, with the Supreme Court at the apex, do have the final say. As a result, most potential opponents of Court rulings follow the course implied in Lincoln's First Inaugural Address. Lincoln did not deny that Supreme Court decisions "must be binding in any case upon the parties to a suit as to the object of that suit" and "are also entitled to very high respect and consideration in all parallel cases by all other departments of the Government." He added: "And while it is obviously possible that such decision may be erroneous in any given case, still the evil effect following it, being limited to that particular case, with a chance that it may be overruled or never become a precedent for other cases, can better be borne than could the evil of a different practice." From that position, Herbert Wechsler's rhetorical question plausibly follows: When the chance that a judicial ruling "may be overruled and never become a precedent for other cases . . . has been exploited and has run its course, with reaffirmation rather than REVERSAL of decision, has not the time arrived when its acceptance is demanded, without insisting on repeated litigation? The answer here, it seems to me, must be affirmative, both as to a necessary implication of our constitutional tradition and to avoid the greater evils that will otherwise ensue." Wechsler's admonition, it should be noted, is one of prudence, not of any necessary legal mandate stemming from the *Marbury* rationale.

Beginning in the late twentieth century, however, the Supreme Court has repeatedly claimed a greater import for its exercises of judicial review than anything clearly set forth in *Marbury*. A major example came in one of the cases stemming from the school DESEGREGATION controversy, COOPER V. AARON (1958). The opinion in that case, signed by each of the Justices, provides the strongest judicial support for a view widely held by the public—that the Court is the ultimate, the supreme interpreter of the Constitution. Rejecting the premise of the actions of the legislature and of the governor of Arkansas in that case—that they were not bound by the ruling in BROWN V. BOARD OF EDUCATION (1954)—the Court purported to "recall some basic constitutional propositions which are settled doctrine." The Justices quoted Article VI and Marshall's "province and duty of the judicial department" passage in *Marbury* and added: "This decision declared the basic principle that the federal judiciary is supreme in the exposition of the law of the Constitution. [It] follows that the interpretation of the Fourteenth Amendment enunciated by this Court in the *Brown* case is the supreme law of the land, and Article VI of the Constitution makes it of binding effect on the States. [Every] state legislator and executive and judicial officer is solemnly committed by oath taken pursuant to Article VI, 3, 'to support this Constitution.' "

Similar statements have surfaced in other controversial cases in recent years, especially in BAKER v. CARR (1962) (referring to the "responsibility of this Court as ultimate interpreter of the Constitution") and POWELL v. McCORMACK (1969) ("[It] is the responsibility of this Court to act as the ultimate interpreter of the Constitution. *Marbury v. Madison.* "). The Court in these cases was no doubt marshaling all possible rhetorical force in efforts to ward off actual or potential resistance from the states or from other branches of the federal government; but these broad modern assertions no doubt also reflect widespread popular understandings of the "ultimate" role of the Court, understandings bolstered by the nation's general acceptance of that role, despite frequent and continuing disagreements with particular decisions.

From the relatively modest assertions of the judicial review power in *Marbury v. Madison,* nearly two centuries of history have brought the Court increasingly close to the self-announced dominant role in constitutional interpretation it set forth in *Cooper v. Aaron.* That does not mean that Supreme Court interpretations are entitled to immunity from criticism, popular or academic. Nor does it signify the end of all political restraints on the Court, restraints stemming from the same Constitution that Marshall relied on in defending judicial review. Judges may be subjected to congressional IMPEACHMENT and Congress may arguably curtail the federal courts' JURISDICTION in constitutional cases. (See JUDICIAL SYSTEM.) But both weapons, though frequently brandished, have rarely been used. Moreover, the constitutional AMENDING PROCESS, albeit difficult to invoke, is available to overturn unpopular Court rulings. More significant, the composition of the Court as well as its size rest with the political branches, and the President's nominating role, together with the Senate's in confirmation, have been major safeguards against judges deviating too far from the national consensus. Despite these potential and actual checks, however, the Supreme Court's role in American government has outgrown both the view that it is the weakest branch and Marshall's own delineation of the judicial review power. What ALEXIS DE TOCQUEVILLE recognized over a century and a half ago has become ever more true since he wrote: "Scarcely any question arises in the United States which does not become, sooner or later, a subject of judicial debate."

Even though historical exercises of judicial review and popular acquiescence have largely stilled the outcries that the federal courts usurped the power to consider the constitutionality of legislation, the core arguments on behalf of the legitimacy of judicial review, summarized by Marshall in *Marbury v. Madison,* continue to generate controversial implications. Two especially important and recurrent modern debates involve arguments reaching back all the way to *Marbury.* The first issue is whether courts should strain to avoid decisions on controversial constitutional issues by invoking such devices as the POLITICAL QUESTION doctrine. The second issue concerns the proper sources of constitutional adjudication: Must courts limit themselves to "interpretation" of the Constitution, or are "noninterpretive" decisions also legitimate?

Courts confident about the legitimacy of judicial review may tend to exercise that power assertively; judges in doubt about the underpinnings of that authority may shrink from exercising the power to invalidate legislative acts and may indeed seek to escape altogether from rulings on the merits in constitutional cases. The connection between views of legitimacy and modern exercises (or nonexercises) of judicial review is illustrated by an exchange between LEARNED HAND and Herbert Wechsler. Hand insisted that there was "nothing in the United States Constitution that gave courts any authority to review the decisions of Congress" and that the text "gave no ground for inferring that the decisions of the Supreme Court [were] to be authoritative upon the Executive and the Legislature." He found the sole justification for judicial review in the practical need "to prevent the defeat of the venture at hand"—to keep constitutional government from foundering. Wechsler retorted: "I believe the power of the courts is grounded in the language of the Constitution and is not a mere interpolation."

These contending positions have contrasting implications. Thus, Hand concluded that "since this power is not a logical deduction from the structure of the Constitution but only a practical condition upon its successful operation, it need not be exercised whenever a court sees, or thinks it sees, an invasion of the Constitution. It is always a preliminary question how importunately the occasion demands an answer." Wechsler countered that there was no such broad discretion to decline constitutional adjudication in a case properly before a court: "For me, as for anyone who finds the judicial power anchored in the Constitution, there is no such escape from the judicial obligation; the duty cannot be attenuated in this way." (That "duty," he cautioned, was "not that of policing or advising legislatures or executives," but rather simply "to decide the litigated case [in] accordance with the law.")

It is true that courts do often abstain from deciding constitutional questions pressed upon them. There is no question about the legitimacy of that phenomenon to the extent that courts rely on nonconstitutional, narrower grounds of decision in disposing of a case. Nor is there any doubt that courts need not—and under the *Marbury* rationale may not—decide constitutional issues if they are not properly presented in a case because, for example, the litigation does not square with the CASE AND CONTROVERSY requirement of Article III. But twentieth-century courts have occasionally gone beyond such justifiable ABSTENTIONS to claim a more general and more questionable authority to resort to considerations of prudence in refusing to issue rulings on the merits even though a case falls within the contours of Article III and even though congressional statutes appear to confer obligatory jurisdiction on the courts.

Some commentators have defended judicial resort to the "passive virtues"; others have attacked such refusals to adjudicate as often unprincipled and illegitimate. The controversy about the political question doctrine is illustrative. To the extent that the doctrine rests on constitutional interpretation, as it does under its strand regarding what the Court in *Baker v. Carr* (1962) called "a textually demonstrable constitutional commitment of the issue to a coordinate political department," it is undoubtedly legitimate. But the courts have often gone beyond that concern to refuse adjudication on the ground of a lack of judicially "manageable standards" and on the basis of even broader, wholly prudential considerations as well. Wechsler argued that, in political question cases, "the only proper judgment that may lead to an abstention from decision is that the Constitution has committed the determination of the issues to another agency of government than the courts. [What] is involved is in itself an act of constitutional interpretation, to be made and judged by standards that should govern the interpretive process generally. That, I submit, is *toto caelo* [by all heaven] different from a broad discretion to abstain or intervene." ALEXANDER M. BICKEL strongly disagreed, insisting that "only by means of a play on words can the broad discretion that the courts have in fact exercised be turned into an act of constitutional interpretation." He saw the political question doctrine as something different from the interpretive process—"something greatly more flexible, something of prudence, not construction and not principle."

To the extent that the Supreme Court rests largely on discretionary, prudential concerns in refusing to adjudicate—as, for example, it appears to have done in holding federalistic restraints on congressional power largely nonjusticiable in GARCIA v. SAN ANTONIO METROPOLITAN TRANSIT AUTHORITY (1985)—it raises questions of legitimacy under *Marbury v. Madison*. Courts deriving their authority from a premise that the Constitution is law, as the *Marbury* argument does, are not authorized to resort to discretionary abstention devices not justified by law. As Marshall himself pointed out in COHENS v. VIRGINIA (1821): "We have no more right to decline the exercise of jurisdiction which is given, than to usurp that which is not given." But discretionary devices of self-limitation have become commonplace in judicial behavior, as a result of glosses articulated by modern judges rather than because of anything in the Constitution itself or in Marshall's reasoning. (See COMITY.)

There is a second modern issue, especially pervasive and controversial, in which the rationale of *Marbury v. Madison* affects debates about judicial review: Are the courts bound to limit themselves to "interpretations" of the Constitution in exercising judicial review? Marshall's reasoning in *Marbury* suggests that "noninterpretive" rulings are illegitimate. A justification that derives judicial review from the existence of a written constitution and from the premise that the Constitution is a species of law implies that the courts are confined by the Constitution in delineating constitutional norms. And courts indeed almost invariably purport to rest their constitutional rulings on "interpretations" of the basic document.

But modern academic commentary is sharply divided on this issue. Most scholars who insist on "interpretation" as the sole legitimate ingredient of constitutional rulings do not argue for a narrow, strict interpretation based solely on a literal reading of the constitutional text or a specific basis in the Framers' intent. But their "broad interpretivist" position does insist that constitutional rulings must rest on a clear nexus to—and plausible inference from—the Constitution's text, history, or structure. The "noninterpretivist" critics of that position emphasize the many opaque and open-ended phrases in the Constitution and the changing interpretations of these phrases over the years. They claim that the Court's behavior cannot be squared with even a broad interpretivist position and argue that the Court has always relied on extraconstitutional norms. These critics insist that "noninterpretivist" decision making is justified not only by the history of the Court's elaborations of such vague yet pervasive concepts as SUBSTANTIVE DUE PROCESS but also by the appropriate role of courts in American constitutional democracy. The noninterpretivist literature accordingly abounds with suggestions of sources courts might rely on in the search for fundamental, judicially enforceable values—sources that range from moral philosophy to contemporary political consensus and analogies to literary and scriptural analyses.

The interpretivist arguments that draw in part on Marshall's justification for judicial review have difficulty explaining the Court's performance in "reinterpreting" the Constitution in light of changing societal contexts. The noninterpretivist position has difficulty squaring its arguments with the *Marbury* view of the Constitution as a species of law. That position has difficulty as well in articulating limits on the legitimate ingredients of constitutional decision making that safeguard adequately against excessive judicial subjectivism—against the specter reflected in Learned Hand's fear of being "ruled by a bevy of Platonic Guardians." Whether constitutional decision making by judges can continue to contribute to the flexibility and durability of the Constitution without deteriorating into merely politicized and personalized rulings that risk subverting the legitimacy of constitutional government is the central and unresolved challenge confronting modern judicial review.

Bibliography

BICKEL, ALEXANDER M.   1962   *The Least Dangerous Branch: The Supreme Court at the Bar of Politics.* Indianapolis: Bobbs-Merrill.

ELY, JOHN H.   1980   *Democracy and Distrust: A Theory of Judicial Review.* Cambridge, Mass.: Harvard University Press.

GREY, THOMAS   1975   Do We Have an Unwritten Constitution? *Stanford Law Review* 27:703–718.

GUNTHER, GERALD   1964   The Subtle Vices of the "Passive Virtues": A Comment on Principle and Expediency in Judicial Review. *Columbia Law Review* 64:1–25.

HAND, LEARNED   1958   *The Bill of Rights.* Cambridge, Mass.: Harvard University Press.

HART, HENRY M., JR. and WECHSLER, HERBERT   1973   Pages 1–241 in Paul Bator, Paul Mishkin, David Shapiro, and Herbert Wechsler, eds., *The Federal Courts and the Federal System,* 2nd ed. Mineola, N.Y.: Foundation Press.

LEVY, LEONARD W.   1967   Judicial Review, History, and Democracy: An Introduction. Pages 1–42 in Leonard W. Levy, ed., *Judicial Review and the Supreme Court: Selected Essays.* New York: Harper & Row.

McCLOSKEY, ROBERT G.   1960   *The American Supreme Court.* Chicago: University of Chicago Press.

McLAUGHLIN, ANDREW C.   1935   *A Constitutional History of the United States.* New York: Appleton-Century-Crofts.

PERRY, MICHAEL J.   1982   *The Constitution, the Courts, and Human Rights: An Inquiry into the Legitimacy of Constitutional Policymaking by the Judiciary.* New Haven, Conn.: Yale University Press.

WECHSLER, HERBERT   1961   *Principles, Politics, and Fundamental Law.* Cambridge, Mass.: Harvard University Press.

——   1965   The Courts and the Constitution. *Columbia Law Review* 65:1001–1014.

MARBURY v. MADISON

Leonard W. Levy

Marbury has transcended its origins in the party battles between Federalists and Republicans, achieving mythic status as the foremost precedent for JUDICIAL REVIEW. For the first time the Court held unconstitutional an act of Congress, establishing, if only for posterity, the doctrine that the Supreme Court has the final word among the coordinate branches of the national government in determining what is law under the Constitution. By 1803 no one doubted that an unconstitutional act of government was null and void, but who was to judge? What *Marbury* settled, doctrinally if not in reality, was the Court's ultimate authority over Congress and the President. Actually, the historic reputation of the case is all out of proportion to the merits of Chief Justice JOHN MARSHALL's unanimous opinion for the Court. On the issue of judicial review, which made the case live, he said nothing new, and his claim for the power of the Court occasioned little contemporary comment. The significance of the case in its time derived from its political context and from the fact that the Court appeared successfully to interfere with the executive branch. Marshall's most remarkable accomplishment, in retrospect, was his massing of the Court behind a poorly reasoned opinion that section 13 of the JUDICIARY ACT OF 1789 was unconstitutional. Though the Court's legal craftsmanship was not evident, its judicial politics—egregious partisanship and calculated expediency—was exceptionally adroit, leaving no target for Republican retaliation beyond frustrated rhetoric.

Republican hostility to the United States courts, which were Federalist to the last man as well as Federalist in doctrine and interests, had mounted increasingly and passed the threshold of tolerance when the Justices on circuit enforced the Sedition Act. (See ALIEN AND SEDITION ACTS.) Then the lame-duck Federalist administration passed the JUDICIARY ACT OF 1801 and, a week before THOMAS JEFFERSON's inauguration, passed the companion act for the appointment of forty-two justices of the peace for the DISTRICT OF COLUMBIA, prompting the new President to believe that "the Federalists have retired into the Judiciary as a stronghold . . . and from that battery all the works of republicanism are to be beaten down and erased." The new Circuit Court for the District of Columbia sought in vain to obtain the conviction of the editor of the administration's organ in the capital for the common law crime of SEDITIOUS LIBEL. The temperate response of the new administration was remarkable. Instead of increasing the size of the courts, especially the Supreme Court, and packing them with Republican appointees, the administration simply repealed the Judiciary Act of 1801. (See JUDICIARY ACTS OF 1802.) On taking office Jefferson also ordered that the commissions for the forty-two justices of the peace for the district be withheld, though he reappointed twenty-five, all political enemies originally appointed by President JOHN ADAMS.

Marbury v. Madison arose from the refusal of the administration to deliver the commissions of four of these appointees, including one William Marbury. The Senate had confirmed the appointments and Adams had signed their commissions, which Marshall, the outgoing secretary of state, had affixed with the great seal of the United States. But in the rush of the "midnight appointments" on the evening of March 3, the last day of the outgoing administration, Marshall had neglected to deliver the commissions. Marbury and three others sought from the Supreme Court, in a case of ORIGINAL JURISDICTION, a WRIT OF MANDAMUS compelling JAMES MADISON, the new secretary of state, to issue their commissions. In December 1801 the Court issued an order commanding Madison to show cause why the writ should not be issued.

A congressman reflected the Republican viewpoint when saying that the show-cause order was "a bold stroke against the Executive," and JOHN BRECKINRIDGE, the majority leader of the Senate, thought the order "the most daring attack which the annals of Federalism have yet exhibited." When the debate began on the repeal bill, Federalists defended the show-cause order, the independence of the judiciary, and the duty of the Supreme Court to hold void any unconstitutional acts of Congress. A Republican paper declared that the "mandamus business" had first appeared to be only a contest between the judiciary and the executive but now seemed a political act by the Court to deter repeal of the 1801 legislation. In retaliation the Republicans passed the repealer and altered the terms of the Court so that it would lose its June 1802 session and not again meet until February 1803, fourteen months after the show-cause order. The Republicans hoped, as proved to be the case, that the Justices would comply with the repealer and return to circuit duty, thereby averting a showdown and a constitutional crisis, which the administration preferred to avoid.

By the time the Court met in February 1803 to hear arguments in *Marbury*, which had become a political sensation, talk of IMPEACHMENT was in the air. A few days before the Court's term, Federalists in Congress moved that the Senate should produce for Marbury's benefit records of his confirmation, provoking Senator James Jackson to declare that the Senate would not interfere in the case and become "a party to an accusation which may end in an impeachment, of which the Senate were the constitutional Judges." By no coincidence, a week before the Court met, Jefferson instructed the House to impeach a U.S. District Court judge in New Hampshire, and already Federalists knew of the plan to impeach Justice SAMUEL CHASE. Jefferson's desire to replace John Marshall with SPENCER ROANE was also public knowledge. Right before Marshall delivered the Court's opinion in *Marbury*, the Washington correspondent of a Republican paper wrote: "The attempt of the Supreme Court . . . by a mandamus, to control the Executive functions, is a new experiment. It seems to be no less than a commencement of war. . . . The Court must be defeated and retreat from the attack; or march on, till they incur an impeachment and removal from office."

Marshall and his Court appeared to confront unattractive alternatives. To have issued the writ, which was the expected judgment, would have been like the papal bull against the moon; Madison would have defied it, exposing the Court's impotence, and the Republicans might have a pretext for retaliation based on the Court's breach of the principle of SEPARATION OF POWERS. To have withheld the writ would have violated the Federalist principle that the Republican administration was accountable under the law. ALEXANDER HAMILTON's newspaper reported the Court's opinion in a story headed "Constitution Violated by President," informing its readers that the new President by his first act had trampled on the charter of the peoples' liberties by unprincipled, even criminal, conduct against personal rights. Yet the Court did not issue the writ; the victorious party was Madison. But Marshall exhibited him and the President to the nation as if they were arbitrary Stuart tyrants, and then, affecting judicial humility, Marshall in obedience to the Constitution found that the Court could not obey an act of Congress that sought to aggrandize judicial powers in cases of original jurisdiction, contrary to Article III of the Constitution.

The Court was treading warily. The statute in question was not a Republican measure, not, for example, the repealer of the Judiciary Act of 1801. Indeed, shortly after *Marbury*, the Court sustained the repealer in STUART v. LAIRD (1803) against arguments that it was unconstitutional. In that case the Court ruled that the practice of the Justices in sitting as circuit judges derived from the Judiciary Act of 1789, and therefore derived "from a contemporary interpretation of the most forcible nature," as well as from customary acquiescence. Ironically, another provision of the same statute, section 13, was at issue in *Marbury*, not that the bench and bar realized it until Marshall delivered his opinion. The offending section, passed by a Federalist Congress after being drafted by OLIVER ELLSWORTH, one of the Constitution's Framers and Marshall's predecessor, had been the subject of previous litigation before the Court without anyone having thought it was unconstitutional. Section 13 simply authorized the Court to issue writs of *mandamus* "in cases warranted by the principles and usages of law," and that clause appeared in the context of a reference to the Court's APPELLATE JURISDICTION.

Marshall's entire argument hinged on the point that section 13 unconstitutionally extended the Court's original jurisdiction beyond the two categories of cases, specified in Article III, in which the Court was to have such jurisdiction. But for those two categories of cases, involving foreign diplomats or a state as a litigant, the Court has appellate jurisdiction. In quoting Article III, Marshall omitted the clause that directly follows as part of the same sentence: the Court has appellate jurisdiction "with such exceptions, and under such regulations as the Congress shall make." That might mean that Congress can detract from the Court's appellate jurisdiction or add to its original jurisdiction. The specification of two categories of cases in which the Court has original jurisdiction was surely intended as an irreducible minimum, but Marshall read it, by the narrowest construction, to mean a negation of congressional powers.

In any event, section 13 did not add to the Court's original jurisdiction. In effect it authorized the Court to issue writs of *mandamus* in the two categories of cases of original jurisdiction and in all appellate cases. The authority to issue such writs did not extend or add to the Court's jurisdiction; the writ of *mandamus* is merely a remedial device by which courts implement their existing jurisdiction. Marshall misinterpreted the statute and Article III, as well as the nature of the writ, in order to find that the statute conflicted with Article III. Had the Court employed the reasoning of *Stuart v. Laird* or the rule that the Court should hold a statute void only in a clear case, giving every presumption of validity in doubtful cases, Marshall could not have reached his conclusion that section 13 was unconstitutional. That conclusion allowed him to decide that the Court was powerless to issue the writ because Marbury had sued for it in a case of original jurisdiction.

Marshall could have said, simply, this is a case of original jurisdiction but it does not fall within either of the two categories of original jurisdiction specified in Article III; therefore we cannot decide: writ denied, case dismissed. Section 13 need never have entered the opinion, although, alternatively, Marshall could have declared: section 13 authorizes this Court to issue such writs only in cases warranted by the principles and usages of law; we have no jurisdiction here because we are not hearing the case in our appellate capacity and it is not one of the two categories in which we possess original jurisdiction: writ denied, case dismissed. Even if Marshall had to find that the statute augmented the Court's original jurisdiction, the ambiguity of the clause in Article III, which he neglected to quote, justified sustaining the statute.

Holding section 13 unconstitutional enabled Marshall to refuse an extension of the Court's powers and award the judgment to Madison, thus denying the administration a pretext for vengeance. Marshall also used the case to answer Republican arguments that the Court did not and should not have the power to declare an act of Congress unconstitutional, though he carefully chose an inoffensive section of a Federalist statute that pertained merely to writs of mandamus. That he gave his doctrine of judicial review the support of only abstract logic, without reference to history or precedents, was characteristic, as was the fact that his doctrine swept way beyond the statute that provoked it.

If Marshall had merely wanted a safe platform from which to espouse and exercise judicial review, he would have begun his opinion with the problems that section 13 posed for the Court; but he reached the question of constitutionality and of judicial review at the tail-end of his opinion. Although he concluded that the Court had to discharge the show-cause order, because it lacked jurisdiction, he first and most irregularly passed judgment on the merits of the case. Everything said on the merits was OBITER DICTA and should not have been said at all, given the judgment. Most of the opinion dealt with Marbury's unquestionable right to his commission and the correctness of the remedy he had sought by way of a writ of mandamus. In his elaborate discourse on those matters, Marshall assailed the President and his cabinet officer for their lawlessness. Before telling Marbury that he had initiated his case in the wrong court, Marshall engaged in what EDWARD S. CORWIN called "a deliberate partisan *coup.* " Then Marshall followed with a "judicial *coup d'état,* " in the words of ALBERT J. BEVERIDGE, on the constitutional issue that neither party had argued.

The partisan *coup* by which Marshall denounced the executive branch, not the grand declaration of the doctrine of judicial review for which the case is remembered, was the focus of contemporary excitement. Only the passages on judicial review survive. Cases on the REMOVAL POWER of the President, especially concerning inferior appointees, cast doubt on the validity of the dicta by which Marshall lectured the executive branch on its responsibilities under the law. Moreover, by statute and by judicial practice the Supreme Court exercises the authority to issue writs of mandamus in all appellate cases and in the two categories of cases of original jurisdiction. Over the passage of time *Marbury* came to stand for the monumental principle, so distinctive and dominant a feature of our constitutional system, that the Court may bind the coordinate branches of the national government to its rulings on what is the supreme LAW OF THE LAND. That principle stands out from *Marbury* like the grin on the Cheshire cat; all else, which preoccupied national attention in 1803, disappeared in our constitutional law. So too might have disappeared national judicial review if the impeachment of Chase had succeeded.

Marshall himself was prepared to submit to review of Supreme Court opinions by Congress. He was so shaken by the impeachment of Chase and by the thought that he himself might be the next victim in the event of Chase's conviction, that he wrote to Chase on January 23, 1804: "I think the modern doctrine of impeachment should yield to an appellate jurisdiction in the legislature. A reversal of those legal opinions deemed unsound by the legislature would certainly better comport with the mildness of our character than a removal of the judge who has rendered them unknowing of his fault." The acquittal of Chase meant that the Court could remain independent, that Marshall had no need to announce publicly his desperate plan for congressional review of the Court, and that *Marbury* remained as a precedent. Considering that the Court did not again hold unconstitutional an act of Congress until 1857, when it decided DRED SCOTT V. SANDFORD, sixty-eight years would have passed since 1789 without such a holding, and but for *Marbury*, after so long a period of congressional omnipotence, national judicial review might never have been established.

Bibliography

BEVERIDGE, ALBERT J.   1916–1919   *The Life of John Marshall*, 4 vols. Vol. III:50–178. Boston: Houghton Mifflin.

CORWIN, EDWARD S.   1914   *The Doctrine of Judicial Review*. Pages 1–78. Princeton, N.J.: Princeton University Press.

HAINES, CHARLES GROVE   1944   *The Role of the Supreme Court in American Government and Politics, 1789–1835*. Pages 223–258. Berkeley: University of California Press.

VAN ALSTYNE, WILLIAM W.   1969   A Critical Guide to Marbury v. Madison. *Duke Law Journal* 1969:1–47.

WARREN, CHARLES   1923   *The Supreme Court in United States History*, 3 vols. Vol. I:200–268. Boston: Little, Brown.

UNCONSTITUTIONALITY

Kenneth L. Karst

The American concept of unconstitutionality was born before the Constitution was adopted. The STAMP ACT CONGRESS of 1765, for example, declared that acts of Parliament imposing TAXATION WITHOUT REPRESENTATION were unconstitutional and need not be obeyed. Then as now, of course, the British constitution was an unwritten collection of customs and usages, only partly reflected in statutes and COMMON LAW principles. Since the adoption of the earliest state constitutions, however, the statement that a governmental action is unconstitutional has been taken as an assertion that the action violates a written constitution. In common speech, "unconstitutional" normally refers to an action's invalidity under the United States Constitution, but in law the term also refers to invalidity under a state constitution. Legislation is not the only form of governmental action that may be unconstitutional. When police officers conduct unreasonable SEARCHES AND SEIZURES, for example, they act unconstitutionally. Similarly, a state court acts unconstitutionally when it enforces a racially RESTRICTIVE COVENANT.

An assertion of unconstitutionality can be made by anyone: a citizen making a complaint, a newspaper editorial writer, a lawyer arguing a case. The assertion may take on a more authoritative character when it is made by a public officer acting in a governmental capacity. Thus, the President might veto a bill passed by Congress on the ground that it is unconstitutional. (See CIVIL RIGHTS ACT OF 1866; JACKSON'S VETO OF THE BANK BILL.) Or, the President might refuse to enforce an act of Congress on similar grounds. Such a presidential refusal led the House of Representatives to adopt ARTICLES OF IMPEACHMENT against ANDREW JOHNSON, thus registering its view that Johnson's conduct was itself unconstitutional. An executive officer may decline to enforce a law for the purpose of allowing others to frame a TEST CASE, thus allowing the courts to rule on the law's validity. BOARD OF EDUCATION v. ALLEN (1968) resulted from one such refusal.

The official in *Allen* thought it important to get a judicial ruling on the constitutionality of the law in question. In fact, Americans have become accustomed to identifying the idea of unconstitutionality with a judicial declaration of unconstitutionality—and, in particular, with such a declaration by the Supreme Court. A lawyer, asked by a client whether a law is or is not constitutional, ordinarily will respond with a prediction of what the courts will hold.

From MARBURY V. MADISON (1803) forward, American courts have assumed that they have the power to disregard a statute that violates a constitutional norm. When a court holds a statute unconstitutional it refuses to give effect to the law in the case before it. Indeed, the *Marbury* opinion grounded the principle of JUDICIAL REVIEW in the need for a court to decide the case before it according to law, including the Constitution as the supreme law. Federal courts are not permitted to give ADVISORY OPINIONS on the law but make their constitutional rulings only in the context of concrete CASES AND CONTROVERSIES. Yet there is a sense in which any opinion is, in part, advisory. The statement of a reason for decision requires a court to move from the particulars of the case before it to the more abstract level of a rule or principle which can be applied later as a PRECEDENT in deciding another appropriate case. Occasionally, particularly in the area of the FREEDOMS OF SPEECH and of the PRESS, a court may hold a law INVALID ON ITS FACE. But even if the court merely says it is holding the law "invalid as applied," the ruling becomes a precedent for other applications to similar facts.

In a statement now famous for its inaccuracy, the Supreme Court said in *Norton v. Shelby County* (1886) that an unconstitutional law "is not a law; it confers no rights; it imposes no duties; it affords no protection; it creates no office; it is, in legal contemplation, as inoperative as though it had never been passed." The statement is misleading in two respects. First, courts are no better than anyone else at undoing the past. A great many actions may be taken on the basis of a statute in the time between its enactment and its judicial invalidation. Justice often requires that those actions be given effect: a corporation organized under an invalid statute will be bound under its contracts; an official who enforces a law in good faith before the law is held invalid will not be liable in damages for the action. In *Lemon v. Kurtzman II* (1973), the Supreme Court allowed Pennsylvania to reimburse church schools for educational services performed under a statute before the Court had held the law invalid in LEMON V. KURTZMAN I (1971).

Second, the *Norton* statement is misleading in the context of an OVERRULING of a previous decision that has held a statute invalid. In ADKINS V. CHILDREN'S HOSPITAL (1923) the Supreme Court had held the DISTRICT OF COLUMBIA MINIMUM WAGE LAW unconstitutional, but in WEST COAST HOTEL CO. V. PARRISH (1937), the Court overruled *Adkins*. Was it then necessary for Congress to reenact the law for it to be effective? The attorney general issued an opinion answering this question negatively, and no one now challenges that opinion's soundness.

Determining whether a court has actually held a law unconstitutional may prove more difficult than identifying the court's HOLDING on the underlying constitutional law. In dealing with a federal statute, for example, the Supreme Court may make clear its view of the Constitution's command, but it may not make clear whether it has held the statute invalid or construed the statute narrowly to avoid holding it unconstitutional. Such an ambiguity still bemuses collectors of antique trivia when they contemplate HODGSON v. BOWERBANK (1809).

Ultimately, the notion of unconstitutionality refers not so much to a fact—or even an opinion, judicial or otherwise—as to a decisional process. In that process courts play the most prominent role, but now and then they yield the center of the stage to other actors. (See ABRAHAM LINCOLN; THOMAS JEFFERSON; WATERGATE AND THE CONSTITUTION.)

Bibliography

BICKEL, ALEXANDER M.   1962   *The Least Dangerous Branch: The Supreme Court at the Bar of Politics.* Indianapolis: Bobbs-Merrill.
FIELD, OLIVER P.   1935   *The Effect of an Unconstitutional Statute.* Minneapolis: University of Minnesota Press.

JUDICIAL REVIEW AND DEMOCRACY

Robert H. Bork

The American ideal of democracy lives in constant tension with the American ideal of JUDICIAL REVIEW in the service of individual liberties. It is a tension that sometimes erupts in crisis. THOMAS JEFFERSON planned a campaign of IMPEACHMENTS to rid the bench, and particularly the Supreme Court, of Federalist judges. The campaign collapsed when the impeachment of Associate Justice SAMUEL CHASE failed in the Senate. FRANKLIN D. ROOSEVELT, frustrated by a Court majority that repeatedly struck down New Deal economic measures, tried to "pack" the Court with additional Justices. That effort was defeated in Congress, though the attempt may have persuaded some Justices to alter their behavior. In recent years there have been movements in Congress to deprive federal courts of JURISDICTION over cases involving such matters as abortion, SCHOOL BUSING, and school prayer (see RELIGION IN PUBLIC SCHOOLS)—topics on which the Court's decisions have angered strong and articulate constituencies.

The problem is the resolution of what Robert Dahl called the Madisonian dilemma. The United States was founded as a Madisonian system, one that allows majorities to govern wide and important areas of life simply because they are majorities, but that also holds that individuals have some freedoms that must be exempt from majority control. The dilemma is that neither the majority nor the minority can be trusted to define the proper spheres of democratic authority and individual liberty.

It is not at all clear that the Founders envisaged a leading role for the judiciary in the resolution of this dilemma, for they thought of the third branch as relatively insignificant. Over time, however, Americans have come to assume that the definition of majority power and minority freedom is primarily the function of the judiciary, most particularly the function of the Supreme Court. This assumption places a great responsibility upon constitutional theory. America's basic method of policymaking is majoritarian. Thus, to justify exercise of a power to set at naught the considered decisions of elected representatives, judges must achieve, in ALEXANDER BICKEL's phrase, "a rigorous general accord between JUDICIAL SUPREMACY and democratic theory, so that the boundaries

of the one could be described with some precision in terms of the other."
At one time, an accord was based on the understanding that judges
followed the intentions of the Framers and ratifiers of the Constitution,
a legal document enacted by majorities, though subject to alteration
only by supermajorities. A conflict between democracy and judicial review
did not arise because the respective areas of each were specified and
intended to be inviolate. Though this obedience to original intent was
occasionally more pretense than reality, the accord was achieved in theory, and that theory stated an ideal to which courts were expected to
conform. That is no longer so. Many judges and scholars now believe
that the courts' obligations to intent are so highly generalized and remote
that judges are in fact free to create the Constitution they think appropriate to today's society. The result is that the accord no longer stands
even theoretically. The increasing perception that this is so raises the
question of what elected officials can do to reclaim authority they regard
as wrongfully taken by the judiciary.

There appear to be two possible responses to a judiciary that has
overstepped the limits of its legitimate authority. One is political, the
other intellectual. It seems tolerably clear that political responses are
of limited usefulness, at least in the short run. Impeachment and Court-
packing, having failed in the past, are unlikely to be resorted to again.
Amending the Constitution to correct judicial overreaching is such a
difficult and laborious process (requiring either two-thirds of both houses
of Congress or an application for a convention by the legislatures of
two-thirds of the states, followed, in either case, by ratification by three-
fourths of the states) that it is of little practical assistance. It is sometimes
proposed that Congress deal with the problem by removing federal
court jurisdiction, using the exceptions clause of Article III of the Constitution in the case of the Supreme Court. The constitutionality of this
approach has been much debated, but, in any case, it will often prove
not feasible. Removal of all federal court jurisdiction would not return
final power either to Congress or to state legislatures but to fifty state
court systems. Thus, as a practical matter, this device could not be used
as to any subject where national uniformity of constitutional law is necessary or highly desirable. Moreover, jurisdiction removal does not vindicate democratic governance, for it merely shifts ultimate power to different groups of judges. Democratic responses to judicial excesses probably
must come through the replacement of judges who die or retire with
new judges of different views. But this is a slow and uncertain process,
the accidents of mortality being what they are and prediction of what
new judges will do being so perilous.

The fact is that there exist few, if any, usable and effective techniques
by which federal courts can be kept within constitutional bounds. A
Constitution that provides numerous CHECKS AND BALANCES between Pres-

ident and Congress provides little to curb a judiciary that expands its powers beyond the allowable meaning of the Constitution. Perhaps one reason is that the Framers, though many of them foresaw that the Supreme Court would review laws for constitutionality, had little experience with such a function. They did not remotely foresee what the power of judicial review was capable of becoming. Nor is it clear that an institutional check—such as Senator ROBERT LA FOLLETTE's proposal to amend the Constitution so that Congress could override a Supreme Court decision by a two-thirds majority—would be desirable. Congress is less likely than the Court to be versed in the Constitution. La Follette's proposal could conceivably wreak as much or more damage to the Court's legitimate powers as it might accomplish in restraining its excesses. That must be reckoned at least a possibility with any of the institutional checks just discussed and is probably one of the reasons that they have rarely been used. In this sense, the Court's vulnerability is one of its most important protections.

If a political check on federal courts is unlikely to succeed, the only rein left is intellectual, the widespread acceptance of a theory of judicial review. After almost two centuries of constitutional adjudication, we appear to be further than ever from the possession of an adequate theory.

In the beginning, there was no controversy over theory. JOSEPH STORY, who was both an Associate Justice of the Supreme Court and the Dane Professor of Law at Harvard, could write in his *Commentaries on the Constitution of the United States,* published in 1833, that "I have not the ambition to be the author of any new plan of interpreting the theory of the Constitution, or of enlarging or narrowing its powers by ingenious subtleties and learned doubts." He thought that the job of constitutional judges was to interpret: "The first and fundamental rule in the interpretation of all instruments is, to construe them according to the sense of the terms and the intention of the parties."

The performance of the courts has not always conformed to this interpretivist ideal. In the last decade or so of the nineteenth century and the first third of the twentieth the Supreme Court assiduously protected economic liberties from federal and state regulation, often in ways that could not be reconciled with the Constitution. The case that stands as the symbol of that era of judicial adventurism is LOCHNER v. NEW YORK (1905), which struck down the state's law regulating maximum hours for bakers. That era ended when Franklin D. Roosevelt's appointments remade the Court, and *Lochner* is now generally regarded as discredited.

But, if the Court stopped defending economic liberties without constitutional justification in the mid-1930s, it began in the mid-1950s to make other decisions for which it offered little or no constitutional argument. It had been generally assumed that constitutional questions were to be answered on grounds of historical intent, but the Court began to make decisions that could hardly be, and were not, justified on that basis. Existing constitutional protections were expanded and new ones created. Sizable minorities on the Court indicated a willingness to go still further. The widespread perception that the judiciary was recreating the Constitution brought the tension between democracy and judicial review once more to a state of intellectual and political crisis.

Much of the new judicial power claimed cannot be derived from the text, structure, or history of the Constitution. Perhaps because of the increasing obviousness of this fact, legal scholars began to erect new theories of the judicial role. These constructs, which appear to be accepted by a majority of those who write about constitutional theory, go by the general name of noninterpretivism. They hold that mere interpretation of the Constitution may be impossible and is certainly inadequate. Judges are assigned not the task of defining the meanings and contours of values found in the historical Constitution but rather the function of creating new values and hence new rights for individuals against majorities. These new values are variously described as arising from "the evolving morality of our tradition," our "conventional morality" as discerned by "the method of philosophy," a "fusion of constitutional law and moral theory," or a HIGHER LAW of "unwritten NATURAL RIGHTS." One author has argued that, since "no defensible criteria" exist "to assess theories of judicial review," the judge should enforce his conception of the good. In all cases, these theories purport to empower judges to override majority will for extraconstitutional reasons.

Judges have articulated theories of their role no less removed from interpretation than those of the noninterpretivist academics. Writing for the Court in GRISWOLD v. CONNECTICUT (1965), Justice WILLIAM O. DOUGLAS created a constitutional RIGHT OF PRIVACY that invalidated the state's law against the use of contraceptives. He observed that many provisions of the BILL OF RIGHTS could be viewed as protections of aspects of personal privacy. These provisions were said to add up to a zone of constitutionally secured privacy that did not fall within any particular provision. The scope of this new right was not defined, but the Court has used the concept in a series of cases since, the most controversial being ROE v. WADE (1973). (See JUDICIAL ACTIVISM AND SELF RESTRAINT.)

A similar strategy for the creation of new rights was outlined by Justice WILLIAM J. BRENNAN in a 1985 address. He characterized the Constitution as being pervasively concerned with human dignity. From this, Justice Brennan drew a more general judicial function of enhancing human dignity, one not confined by the clauses in question and, indeed, capable of nullifying what those clauses reveal of the Framers' intentions.

Thus, the address states that continued judicial tolerance of CAPITAL PUNISHMENT causes us to "fall short of the constitutional vision of human dignity." For that reason, Justice Brennan continues to vote that capital punishment violates the Constitution. The potency of this method of generalizing from particular clauses, and then applying the generalization instead of the clauses, may be seen in the fact that it leads to a declaration of the unconstitutionality of a punishment explicitly assumed to be available three times in the Fifth Amendment to the Constitution and once again, some seventy-seven years later, in the FOURTEENTH AMENDMENT. By conventional methods of interpretation, it would be impossible to use the Constitution to prohibits that which the Constitution explicitly assumes to be lawful.

Because noninterpretive philosophies have little hard intellectual structure, it is impossible to control them or to predict from any inner logic or principle what they may require. Though it is regularly denied that a return to the judicial function as exemplified in *Lochner v. New York* is underway or, which comes to the same thing, that decisions are rooted only in the judges' moral predilections, it is difficult to see what else can be involved once the function of searching for the Framers' intent is abandoned. When constitutional adjudication proceeds in a noninterpretive manner, the Court necessarily imposes new values upon the society. They are new in the sense that they cannot be derived by interpretation of the historical Constitution. Moreover, they must rest upon the moral predilections of the judge because the values come out of the moral view that most of us, by definition (since we voted democratically for a different result), do not accept.

This mode of adjudication makes impossible any general accord between judicial supremacy and democratic theory. Instead, it brings the two into head-on conflict. The Constitution specifies certain liberties and allocates all else to democratic processes. Noninterpretivism gives the judge power to invade the province of democracy whenever majority morality conflicts with his own. That is impossible to square either with democratic theory or the concept of law. Attempts have, nonetheless, been made to reconcile, or at least to mitigate, the contradiction. One line of argument is that any society requires a mixture of principle and expediency, that courts are better than legislatures at discerning and formulating principle, and hence may intervene when principle has been inadequately served by the legislative process. Even if one assumes that courts have superior institutional capacities in this respect, which is by no means clear, the conclusion does not follow. By placing certain subjects in the legislative arena, the Constitution holds that the tradeoff between principle and expediency we are entitled to is what the legislature provides. Courts have no mandate to impose a different result merely because they would arrive at a tradeoff that weighed principle more heavily or that took an altogether different value into account.

A different reconciliation of democracy and noninterpretive judicial review begins with the proposition that the Supreme Court is not really final because popular sentiment can in the long run cause it to be overturned. As we know from history, however, it may take decades to overturn a decision, so that it will be final for many people. Even then an overruling probably cannot be forced if a substantial minority ardently supports the result.

To the degree, then, that the Constitution is not treated as law to be interpreted in conventional fashion, the clash between democracy and judicial review is real. It is also serious. When the judiciary imposes upon democracy limits not to be found in the Constitution, it deprives Americans of a right that is found there, the right to make the laws to govern themselves. Moreover, as courts intervene more frequently to set aside majoritarian outcomes, they teach the lesson that democratic processes are suspect, essentially unprincipled and untrustworthy.

The main charge against a strictly interpretive approach to the Constitution is that the Framers' intentions cannot be known because they could not foresee the changed circumstances of our time. The argument proves too much. If it were true, the judge would be left without any law to apply, and there would be no basis for judicial review.

But that is not what is involved. From the text, the structure, and the history of the Constitution we can usually learn at least the core values the Framers intended to protect. Interpreting the Constitution means discerning the principle the Framers wanted to enact and applying it to today's circumstances. As John Hart Ely put it, interpretivism holds that "the work of the political branches is to be invalidated only in accord with an inference whose starting point, whose underlying premise, is fairly discoverable in the Constitution. That the complete inference will not be found there—because the situation is not likely to have been foreseen—is generally common ground."

This, of course, requires that constitutional DOCTRINE evolve over time. Most doctrine is merely the judge-made superstructure that implements basic constitutional principles, and, because circumstances change, the evolution of doctrine is inevitable. The FOURTH AMENDMENT was framed by men who did not foresee electronic surveillance, but judges may properly apply the central value of that amendment to electronic invasions of personal privacy. The difference between this method and that endorsed by Justices Douglas and Brennan lies in the level of generality employed. Adapting the Fourth Amendment requires the judge merely to recognize a new method of governmental search of one's property. The Justices, on the other hand, create a right so general that it effectively becomes a new clause of the Constitution, one that gives courts no guidance in its application. Modifying doctrine to preserve a value already embedded in the Constitution is an enterprise wholly different in nature from creating new values.

The debate over the legitimate role of the judiciary is likely to continue for some years. Noninterpretivists have not as yet presented an adequate theoretical justification for a judiciary that creates rather than interprets the Constitution. The task of interpretation is often complex and difficult, but it remains the only model of the judicial role that achieves an accord between democracy and judicial review.

Bibliography

AGRESTO, JOHN   1984   *The Supreme Court and Constitutional Democracy.* Ithaca, N.Y.: Cornell University Press.

BICKEL, ALEXANDER M.   1962   *The Least Dangerous Branch: The Supreme Court at the Bar of Politics.* Indianapolis: Bobbs-Merrill.

BORK, ROBERT H.   1985   Styles in Constitutional Theory. *South Texas Law Journal* 26:383–395.

CHOPER, JESSE   1980   *Judicial Review and the National Political Process.* Chicago: University of Chicago Press.

ELY, JOHN HART   1980   *Democracy and Distrust: A Theory of Judicial Review.* Cambridge, Mass.: Harvard University Press.

LEVY, LEONARD W., ed.   1967   *Judicial Review and the Supreme Court.* New York: Harper & Row.

SUPREME COURT (History)

Paul A. Freund

The only court whose existence is mandated by the Constitution is the Supreme Court. Article III states: "The judicial power of the United States shall be vested in one supreme court, and in such inferior courts as the Congress may from time to time ordain and establish." Besides its existence, a few attributes are constitutionally entrenched by Article III. The tenure of the judges is to be "during GOOD BEHAVIOR," and their compensation "shall not be diminished during their continuance in office." These provisions, modeled on English law and made applicable to all federal judges, were obviously intended to assure the independence of a judiciary appointed, pursuant to Article II, by the President with the ADVICE AND CONSENT of the Senate.

Other features having a bearing on the character and independence of the Court were not addressed, presumably to be left at large or determined from time to time by Congress. Qualifications for membership on the Court were not specified; nor were the size of the Court, the period of its TERMS, or the level of the judges' compensation. The Court was to have both ORIGINAL JURISDICTION and APPELLATE JURISDICTION, but the latter was subject to "such exceptions, and under such regulations, as the Congress shall make." Nothing was said concerning the relation of the Supreme Court to the courts of the STATES.

Thus from the outset the Court was only partially sheltered from the politics of republican government. The status of the Court was one of those creative ambiguities that have marked the Constitution as no less an organism than a mechanism, Darwinian as well as Newtonian. The position of the Court may have been in the mind of an eminent modern foreign-born mathematician who, contemplating American CITIZENSHIP, regretted that he could not swear allegiance to the Constitution because "it is full of inconsistencies." In a self-governing nation, to be sure, the Court is detached but not disengaged, distant but not remote. Therein lay its potential either for popular neglect and scorn or for power and prestige.

The need for a federal judiciary, and so for an ultimate tribunal, was felt by the Framers as part of the transition from a confederation to a federal union. The ARTICLES OF CONFEDERATION supplied no such institution, except a supreme tribunal for prize and admiralty cases. A system of federal courts, parallel to those of the states, was one of the innovative conceptions of 1787. Their function was to serve as impartial tribunals, free of local bias, in suits between states, or controversies involving citizens of different states or a foreign country; to establish a uniform interpretation of federal laws; and to maintain the supremacy of federal law in cases where a state law conflicted with the Constitution, federal statutes, or treaties of the United States. In sum, the JURISDICTION OF THE FEDERAL COURTS could rest on the nature of the parties or of the question presented. Only in cases where a state, or a foreign country or its diplomatic representative, was a party was the Supreme Court given original (nonappellate) jurisdiction.

These skeletal provisions of Article III were fleshed out by Congress in the JUDICIARY ACT OF 1789. That act set the number of Supreme Court Justices at five associate Justices and one CHIEF JUSTICE, with salaries of $3,500 and $4,000, respectively. (The monetary differential remained at $500 until 1969, when it was increased to $2,500.) Three provisions of the act led to developments that proved to be of seminal importance for the prestige and power of the Supreme Court: a requirement that the Justices serve on regional CIRCUIT COURTS ("circuit riding"); a provision in section 13 that seemed to grant original jurisdiction to the Court to issue WRITS OF MANDAMUS; and a grant of power in section 25 to review the decisions of state supreme courts in cases turning on the Constitution, laws, or treaties of the United States. Each of these merits attention.

The circuit duties meant sitting with a federal district judge to form a circuit court, which heard appeals from district courts and had original jurisdiction in diversity of citizenship cases. In the early years circuit riding consumed the greater part of a Justice's time and surely his energy; travel by carriage or horseback over rough roads and stopovers at uncomfortable inns resulted in a weariness of flesh and spirit, against which the Justices complained bitterly, but which they forbore to resist. Yet these excursions into the local courthouses brought them into touch with lawyers, journalists, and townspeople, and gave a reality to the Supreme Court that its functioning in the capital city could not match. Moreover, the assignment of each Justice to a particular circuit affected significantly the appointments to the Court, for a vacancy on the Court would normally be filled by an appointment from the same circuit, and so at any time the practical range of nominees was limited and the influence of a small group of senators was proportionately great. Not until 1891, with the passage of the CIRCUIT COURTS OF APPEALS ACT, were the Justices fully relieved of circuit-riding duties. Thereafter geography played a decreasing role in appointments. A striking instance was the widely acclaimed appointment by President HERBERT C. HOOVER in 1932 of Judge BENJAMIN N. CARDOZO of New York to succeed Justice OLIVER WENDELL HOLMES of Massachusetts, although two New Yorkers,

Chief Justice CHARLES EVANS HUGHES and Justice HARLAN FISKE STONE, were already on the Court. A comparable instance was the appointment by President Reagan in 1981 of Judge SANDRA DAY O'CONNOR of Arizona to succeed Justice POTTER STEWART of Ohio even though another Arizonan, Justice WILLIAM H. REHNQUIST, was already serving.

As circuit riding was a cardinal factor in gaining popular recognition of the Court (at considerable cost to the Justices) and in determining appointments, so did the practice furnish an early opportunity for the Court to judge the validity of an act of Congress. In the waning days of the Federalist administration, Congress passed the JUDICIARY ACT OF 1801, compounded of partisanship and principle, which created new judgeships and abolished circuit riding. When the Jeffersonians took office, however, they countered with the JUDICIARY ACT OF 1802, which abolished the judgeships and restored circuit riding. Chief Justice JOHN MARSHALL, sensing a political crisis for the Court, solicited the opinions of his brethren on the question of complying with the law or treating it as beyond the authority of Congress. The Justices had serious doubts about the law's validity, and a strong distaste for the resumption of the burden it imposed, yet a majority counseled compliance, in accord with Marshall's own inclination. But a private litigant, defeated in a circuit court in Virginia at which Marshall himself presided, appealed to the Supreme Court, arguing the unconstitutionality of the 1802 act. The Congress, fearing a judgment voiding the act, had abolished the 1802 term of the Supreme Court. When the case, STUART v. LAIRD, was decided, in February of 1803, the Court, with Marshall not participating, surprised and gratified the Jeffersonians by upholding the act, in a brief opinion which simply declared that acquiescence by the Court in circuit duty for twelve years under the Judiciary Act of 1789 had given a practical construction of the Constitution that would not now be disturbed. That the Court would at least consider the validity of an act of Congress had been resolved just six days earlier in the landmark case of MARBURY v. MADISON (1803).

That case, establishing the power of JUDICAL REVIEW of acts of Congress, marked the second of the three germinal developments from the Judiciary Act of 1789. Section 13, which gave the Court power to issue mandamus and other writs, might have been read simply as conferring the power where the jurisdiction of the Court rested on one of the grounds specified in Article III. But the Court was not of a mind for so narrow a reading. When William Marbury of Maryland invoked the original jurisdiction of the Court to enforce a right to an office of justice of the peace pursuant to an appointment by President JOHN ADAMS, and sought a mandamus to compel Secretary of State JAMES MADISON to deliver his commission, the Court regarded section 13 as conferring jurisdiction, and as so construed beyond the ambit of original jurisdiction defined in Article III. The suit for mandamus was therefore dismissed, again to the gratification of the Jeffersonians, but in the process the Court had declared the far more significant principle that in the decision of a case where a federal law was arguably incompatible with the Constitution, the Court, in deciding what "the law" was, must, if necessary, vindicate the HIGHER LAW and treat the legislative act as ineffectual.

Despite some provocative language in Marshall's opinion (the executive branch cannot "sport away" the rights of others), the Jeffersonians focused on the immediate result and regarded it as a victory at the hands of a still-Federalist Court. Indeed, judicial review was not then the divisive party issue; the Jeffersonians would have welcomed a Supreme Court decision holding the Sedition Act of 1798 unconstitutional. Whether Marshall's doctrine of judicial review was a usurpation later became a subject of heated debate, scholarly and unscholarly. Although the Constitution contains no specific mention of the power, and although Marshall's opinion, resting on the logic of the decisional process, can be said to beg the question of who is to decide, the debates in the CONSTITUTIONAL CONVENTION do indicate obliquely an acceptance of the power, in explaining the rejection of attempts to involve judges in an extrajudicial power of veto of legislation. But the debates were not cited in *Marbury;* MADISON'S NOTES, the most authoritative source, pursuant to the policy of secrecy, were not published until fifty years after the Convention.

The third of the salient projections from the Judiciary Act of 1789, involving section 25, produced more immediate partisan repercussions. Section 25 empowered the Court to review decisions of state courts that denied rights claimed under the federal Constitution, statutes, or treaties. Again, no constitutional provision explicitly conferred such power on the Supreme Court, although Article VI does declare the supremacy of federal law: "the judges in every state shall be bound thereby." By their silence, the Framers may have sought to avoid confrontations in the ratifying process, as in forbearing to be explicit about a national power to issue paper money or to establish a national bank.

The storm over the Court's power to review state court decisions was precipitated by its decision in MARTIN v. HUNTER'S LESSEE (1816) sustaining the validity of section 25. The case was a contest over title to the extensive Fairfax estate in the northern neck of Virginia, turning on the intricate interrelations of Virginia land law and treaties of the United States with Great Britain concerning ownership of land by British nationals. Holding that the Virginia court had misapplied both Virginia and federal law, the Supreme Court in 1813, through Justice JOSEPH STORY, reversed the state court's judgment and remanded the case to that court. A number of factors weakened the force of the decision.

Story's opinion controverted the state court's even on points of the interpretation of state law, although section 25 itself limited review to federal
questions. At a time when seven Justices constituted the Court, only
four participated in the decision; the vote was 3–1, and the mandate
to the Virginia court was unfortunately in the traditional form addressed
to an inferior court, "you are hereby commanded, etc." The Virginia
court was outraged and refused to obey the mandate. On a new WRIT
OF ERROR to the Supreme Court, Story elaborated the justification of
Supreme Court review in terms of the need for uniformity and supremacy
of national law. The nature of the cause, not the court, was determinative
of the Supreme Court's power to review (though critics wondered, no
doubt unfairly, if the Supreme Court could then be given authority to
review certain decisions of the House of Lords). John Marshall could
not have uttered a pronouncement more nationalistic than that of the
New England Republican appointed by President JAMES MADISON. (Marshall had excused himself because of his family's ownership of part of
the land. Story, appointed in 1811 at the age of thirty-two, one of the
most learned and powerful of Justices and a firm ally of Marshall, had
been Madison's fourth choice to succeed WILLIAM CUSHING of Massachusetts: LEVI LINCOLN declined the nomination, Alexander Wolcott was
rejected by the Senate, and JOHN QUINCY ADAMS also declined. Thus
are the inevitabilities of history determined.)

In a sequel to the decision, the Court took the further step of sustaining its power to review even criminal judgments of state courts where
a federal question, such as the interpretation of a federal law, was impli-
cated. The opinion by Chief Justice Marshall in COHENS v. VIRGINIA
(1821) was the climactic realization of the Court's vision of a uniform
federal law and a Constitution that was supreme in reality as well as in
principle.

Reaction to the *Cohens* decision by Jeffersonians, particularly in
Virginia, was intense. Judge SPENCER ROANE, who instead of Marshall
would probably have become Chief Justice if OLIVER ELLSWORTH had
not resigned before Jefferson took office, published a series of bitter
letters under pseudonyms, paying his respects to "A most monstrous
and unexampled decision. It can only be accounted for from that love
of power which all history informs us infects and corrupts all who possess
it, and from which even the upright and eminent Judges are not exempt."
The Court's "extravagant pretension" reached "the zenith of despotic
power." In the following years a series of bills were introduced in Congress
to repeal, in whole or in part, the appellate jurisdiction of the Supreme
Court. Under these genial auspices was thus established a particularly
sensitive and probably the most crucial power of the highest court in
our federal union: the review of decisions of state courts in the interest
of vindicating rights secured by the Constitution.

Conflicts between the Supreme Court, on the one hand, and the executive or legislative branches, or both, on the other, have occurred continually. The other branches have utilized the full spectrum of measures made available by the constitution. The most drastic of these, IMPEACHMENT, was the first to be tried; indeed it was designed as a trial run by Jefferson to prepare the way for a similar attack on Chief Justice Marshall. The immediate target was Justice SAMUEL CHASE, ardent Federalist, whose partisan outbursts in charges to the grand jury in Maryland furnished the occasion. The attempt misfired, however; Chase was narrowly acquitted in the Senate, owing probably to comparable overreaching by the fiery JOHN RANDOLPH, who managed the case for the Jeffersonians.

A milder form of resistance to the Court was the doctrine of departmental independence, whereby the President was as free to act on his view of constitutional authority as the Court was to act on its own. Despite the prospect of endless oscillation that this theory implied, it was espoused in some form by Jefferson, ANDREW JACKSON, and ABRAHAM LINCOLN. President JACKSON'S VETO OF THE BANK BILL (1832) was based partly on grounds of unconstitutionality, although the earlier law creating the bank had been sustained by the Supreme Court. In his message justifying the veto, Jackson had the advice and aid of his attorney general, ROGER B. TANEY. By an irony of history, when President Lincoln in his first inaugural address dealt with Taney's opinion in DRED SCOTT v. SANDFORD (1857), he adopted something of the Jackson-Taney philosophy, maintaining that although he offered no resistance to the decision as a settlement of the lawsuit he could not regard it as binding on the political branches for the future.

The indeterminate size of the Court became a weapon in the contest between President ANDREW JOHNSON and Congress over Reconstruction. By successive statutory changes, following the admission of new states and the creation of new circuits, the authorized membership of the Court had been increased to ten. A radical Congress, distrustful of Johnson and wishing to deprive him of the power to make new appointments to the Court, reduced the number of seats prospectively to seven. (Contributing to the move was a plan of Chief Justice SALMON P. CHASE to induce a reluctant Congress to increase the Justices' salaries in return for a decrease in the number to be compensated. That plan failed, but Chase did succeed in having the title of his office changed from Chief Justice of the Supreme Court to Chief Justice of the United States.) The actual number of Justices did not fall below eight, and in 1869 the number was fixed at nine.

More famous is the action of the same Congress in withdrawing the appellate jurisdiction of the Supreme Court in cases under a HABEAS CORPUS act, giving rise to the decision in EX PARTE McCARDLE in 1869.

While the immediate issue in the case was whether a military commission in Mississippi could try a newspaper editor for inflammatory writings urging citizens not to cooperate with the military government, Congress was fearful that a politically minded majority on the Court would hold the entire plan of Reconstruction unconstitutional. The Court, which had already heard argument in the case, bowed to the withdrawal of jurisdiction, but carefully pointed out that another appellate route remained unaffected by the repealing statute. Consequently the value of *McCardle* as a PRECEDENT, which is the centerpiece of constitutional argument on the extent of congressional power to limit the Court's jurisdiction, is at best doubtful.

The post-Reconstruction Court alienated labor and progressives by decisions taking a narrow view of state power to regulate and tax business; the COMMERCE CLAUSE and FREEDOM OF CONTRACT protected by SUBSTANTIVE DUE PROCESS served as shields for industry. The Progressive party platform in 1912, under the aegis of THEODORE ROOSEVELT, advocated the RECALL of judges and judicial decisions by popular vote. Although this thrust was aimed at state courts rather than the Supreme Court, the latter had set a tone for judicial review in a triad of decisions in 1895. UNITED STATES V. E. C. KNIGHT CO. held that a combination of sugar refiners controlling ninety percent of sugar production in the nation was not subject to the SHERMAN ANTITRUST ACT because processing is not commerce. IN RE DEBS held that a labor leader could be imprisoned for violating a federal court's INJUNCTION in a railroad labor strike, without judicial reliance on any statutorily defined offense. POLLOCK V. FARMERS LOAN AND TRUST CO. held the federal income tax law unconstitutional as applied to income from real property, stocks, and bonds, though valid as applied to wages, because an income tax is tantamount to a tax on its source, and where the source is property in some form the tax is a DIRECT TAX which under the constitution is forbidden to Congress unless apportioned according to population.

The most serious conflict with the Court, certainly since Marshall's time, culminated in President FRANKLIN D. ROOSEVELT's Court reorganization plan in early 1937. The Court had held unconstitutional a series of major New Deal measures designed for economic recovery and reform: the NATIONAL INDUSTRIAL RECOVERY ACT; AGRICULTURAL ADJUSTMENT ACT; Railway Pension Act; Farm Mortgage Act; Guffey-Snyder Bituminous Coal Act; Municipal Bankruptcy Act; and a state minimum wage law for women. Still to be decided was the validity of the WAGNER NATIONAL LABOR RELATIONS ACT, the SOCIAL SECURITY ACT, the PUBLIC UTILITY HOLDING COMPANY ACT, and the TENNESSEE VALLEY AUTHORITY ACT in its full scope. The administration was persuaded that the barrier did not inhere in the Constitution but was the handiwork of Justices who were out of sympathy both with the New Deal and with the best traditions of constitutional decision. Apparently accepting the validity of this analysis, Chief Justice Hughes, appointed by President Hoover, though he greatly disliked 5–4 decisions, nevertheless joined Justices Louis D. Brandeis, Stone, and Cardozo as dissenters in the last five of the cases listed above as holding measures invalid. During his first term President Roosevelt had no opportunity to make an appointment to the Court.

The reorganization plan, which was formulated by Attorney General Homer S. Cummings, called for the appointment of an additional member of the Court for each Justice who did not retire at the age of seventy, up to a maximum membership of fifteen. Despite the President's sweeping electoral victory in 1936, and intensive political efforts by the administration for four months, the plan failed to pass the Senate. A number of factors contributed to the result. The argument based on age and inefficiency, stressed by proponents at the outset, was transparently disingenuous. A letter from Chief Justice Hughes, joined by Justices Willis Van Devanter and Brandeis, to Senator Burton K. Wheeler, at the latter's request, effectively refuted the charge that the Court needed additional members to keep abreast of its docket. The Court itself, while the bill was pending, sustained a state minimum wage law, the National Labor Relations Act, an amended Farm Bankruptcy Act, and the Social Security Act. As one senator remarked, "Why keep on running for the bus after you've caught it?" Moreover, Congress enacted a new retirement act for Supreme Court Justices, which made retirement more acceptable. Since 1869 a full pension had been provided for, but as retirement was equivalent to resignation under the statute, the pension was subject to the will of Congress and in 1932, as an economy measure, it had been reduced by half and was later restored. The act of 1937, by enabling retired Justices to serve on the lower federal courts, placed their retirement compensation under constitutional protection against diminution. Justice Van Devanter availed himself of this new law, giving the President his first opportunity to make an appointment and lessening further the need for enactment of his plan. But perhaps the most powerful factor leading to its defeat was a pervasive feeling, even among groups holding grievances against particular decisions, that the independence of the judiciary was too important a principle to be sacrificed, even under the extreme provocation furnished by a majority of the Court itself.

The appellate jurisdiction of the Court became a target of attack in 1958, as it had been in the early nineteenth century. Senator William E. Jenner of Indiana, reacting against decisions curtailing governmental actions in the field of loyalty investigations, introduced a series of bills withdrawing Supreme Court jurisdiction in this and related classes of cases. Passage was narrowly averted by the efforts of the then majority leader, Senator LYNDON B. JOHNSON. Comparable bills were introduced in 1982 to preclude review of decisions concerning abortion and school prayers. Such efforts, if successful, would produce chaotic results. In the name of the federal Constitution, varying decisions, for and against local laws, would stand unreconciled; the Supreme Court would have no opportunity to reconsider or modify its precedents; state and federal judges would be left to take different positions on the binding effect of prior Supreme Court decisions.

It is apparent that in the recurrent clashes of party, section, and class that have marked American history, the Court, whose role, in principle, is that of an arbiter, has not escaped the role of participant. In these judicial involvements, extraordinary force on one side has induced similar force on the other. A dramatic example is the contest over the production of the White House tapes for use as evidence in the prosecutions growing out of the Watergate break-in. President RICHARD M. NIXON refused to comply with a subpoena issued by the district court, on the ground of EXECUTIVE PRIVILEGE. The tension between the rule of law and presidential immunity from suit had been resolved in part by bringing suit against a subordinate who was carrying out presidential orders, as in the steel seizure case, YOUNGSTOWN SHEET AND TUBE CO. v. SAWYER (1952), where the named defendant was the secretary of commerce. President Nixon, however, forced the issue by taking sole custody of the tapes. On appeal, the Supreme Court responded with the countervailing measure of holding the President amenable to the process of a court where the need of EVIDENCE in a criminal trial outweighs a generalized claim of privilege. The unanimity of the decision (with one abstention) was doubtless a factor impelling the President to yield, thus avoiding an ultimate confrontation.

That the supreme judicial tribunal, without the power of purse or sword, should have survived crises and vicissitudes and maintained its prestige can be ascribed partly to its own resourcefulness and partly to the recognition by a mature people of the Court's necessary functions in the American constitutional democracy. The Court's resourcefulness owes much to the central paradox of its work: it decides issues of great political moment, yet it does so in the context of a controversy between ordinary litigants in a conventional lawsuit. That setting provides a test of concreteness in the formulation of DOCTRINE, allows flexibility of development, and enables the Court to adapt and refine doctrine as new factual and procedural settings may suggest.

The Supreme Court's essential functions, performed within the framework of conventional lawsuits, are fourfold: to resolve controversies between states; to assure the uniform application of national law; to maintain a common market in a continental union; and to enforce the guarantees of liberty and equality embodied in the BILL OF RIGHTS, the post-Civil War Amendments, and other provisions of the Constitution.

Although the Court's jurisdiction over suits between states is statistically insignificant, the function is of practical and symbolic importance, serving as a substitute for diplomacy and war in disputes over boundaries, allotment of waters, and the like. Because these cases originate in the Supreme Court, factual disputes are referred to a SPECIAL MASTER for hearings, findings, and recommendations, which are then presented to the Court for argument and decision.

The uniform interpretation and application of national law has become increasingly important with the proliferation of federal regulatory statutes and administrative rules. For almost a century, until 1938, the Supreme Court essayed a broader concept of uniformity in the COMMON LAW itself, in fields such as commercial law and torts, under the doctrine of SWIFT V. TYSON (1842), which empowered the federal courts to pronounce a FEDERAL COMMON LAW without regard to the common law of particular states. Sweeping as it was, the doctrine was truncated, for the federal common law could have no binding authority in state courts, and thus a bifurcated system of common law developed, along with a practice of forum shopping by lawyers as between federal and state courts. The doctrine was repudiated by the Court in ERIE RAILWAY V. TOMPKINS (1938) in an opinion by Justice Brandeis that branded as unconstitutional the course theretofore pursued by the federal courts. With the demise of *Swift v. Tyson* the rationale for retaining DIVERSITY OF CITIZENSHIP JURISDICTION in the federal courts, for the decision of matters of state law, was materially weakened.

The maintenance of a common market is a modern description of a historic function of the Court, exercised since Marshall and his colleagues decided in GIBBONS V. OGDEN (1824) that the constitutional power of Congress over commerce among the states implied a negative on state power, even when Congress has not acted, and that the Supreme Court would enforce that implied prohibition. For a generation these commerce clause cases elicited a series of decisions upholding or setting aside state regulations—of quarantine, pilotage, intoxicating liquors, entry fees—by classifying them as either regulations of commerce, and so invalid, or regulations of local health or safety, and so valid as POLICE POWER measures. This effort at classification obscured the process of judgment by treating a conclusory label as if it were a premise for reasoning. A pivotal change in methodology occurred in COOLEY V. BOARD OF WARDENS (1852), a pilotage case where the opinion by Justice BENJAMIN CURTIS recognized that commercial regulation and police power were not mutually exclusive categories, and that decision should turn on an empirical judgment, weighing the necessity of the local law, the seriousness of the impact on commerce, the need for uniformity of treatment, and the possible discriminatory impact on out-of-state enterprise. This kind of scrutiny, and comparable analysis of local taxation when challenged by multistate business, have been staples of Supreme Court adjudication and exemplars for other economic federations struggling to accommodate local interests and those of a union.

The most intensive, acclaimed, and in some quarters questioned, aspects of the Court's work has been the elaboration of fundamental human rights. While in England the great expressions of these rights are found in the writings of philosophers and poets—the secular trinity of John Milton, JOHN LOCKE, and John Stuart Mill—in America the pronouncements are embodied—Jefferson apart—in the judicial opinions of Holmes, Brandeis, Hughes, Stone, ROBERT H. JACKSON, HUGO L. BLACK, and other Justices. The development of a body of CIVIL LIBERTIES guarantees, mainly under the Bill of Rights and the FOURTEENTH AMENDMENT, reached its fullest flowering during the Chief Justiceship of EARL WARREN (1953–1969), though the seeds were planted in the HUGHES COURT.

During the 1930s, while public attention was focused on the Court's struggle with national power over the economy, path-breaking advances were made in a series of decisions applying federal constitutional guarantees against the states. It is more than coincidence that this development occurred at a time of rising totalitarianism abroad. FREEDOM OF THE PRESS and FREEDOM OF ASSOCIATION AND ASSEMBLY were unmistakably put under the protection of the liberty secured by the Fourteenth Amendment in NEAR V. MINNESOTA (1931) and DEJONGE V. OREGON (1937), respectively. The principle that a conviction in a state court following the use of a coerced confession is a violation of DUE PROCESS OF LAW was announced for the first time BROWN V. MISSISSIPPI (1936). A state's duty to afford racial equality in education was sharpened in MISSOURI EX REL. GAINES V. CANADA (1938): it could not be satisfied by resort to a neighboring state. Mayors and governors were subjected to the reach of federal judicial process in HAGUE V. CIO (1939) and *Sterling v. Constantin* (1932), an accountability that came to be important in later contests over desegregation.

If the drama of these seminal developments was largely overlooked, the same cannot be said of the great expansion of civil liberties and CIVIL RIGHTS by the WARREN COURT. The leading decisions have become familiar landmarks. BAKER V. CARR (1962), requiring substantial equality of population in electoral districts within a state, asserted judicial power over what had previously been deemed a POLITICAL QUESTION; Chief Justice Warren regarded it as the most important decision of his tenure, because of its potential for redistributing basic political power. BROWN V. BOARD OF EDUCATION (1954, 1955) was both the culmination and the beginning in the long drive against RACIAL DISCRIMINATION: doctrinally a climax, practically a starting point in the devising of remedies. MIRANDA v. ARIZONA (1966), limiting POLICE INTERROGATION of suspects in custody and giving suspects the RIGHT TO COUNSEL during interrogation, has become a symbol of the Court's intense concern for standards of CRIMINAL PROCEDURE, a concern that has sometimes been viewed as an index to a society's civilization. The EQUAL PROTECTION guarantee, which Justice Holmes in 1927 could call the last refuge of a constitutional lawyer, was revitalized in the service not only of racial minorities but of other stereotyped groups: ALIENS, illegitimates, and women. Freedom of the press was extended well beyond freedom from restraint on publication: In actions for LIBEL brought by PUBLIC FIGURES following NEW YORK TIMES v. SULLIVAN (1964), the defendant publisher would be liable only if he acted with legal malice, that is, with knowledge of the publication's falsity or with reckless disregard for its truth or falsity.

A constitutional RIGHT OF PRIVACY, of uncertain scope, extending beyond the explicit SEARCH AND SEIZURE guarantee to encompass at least certain conjugal intimacies, was established in GRISWOLD v. CONNECTICUT (1965). The religion clauses of the FIRST AMENDMENT were given new vitality in decisions rejecting organized prayer in the public schools, such as ENGEL v. VITALE (1962).

On any measure, it is an impressive performance. The momentum was somewhat slackened during the first decade and a half of Chief Justice WARREN E. BURGER's tenure, particularly in the areas of criminal procedure and nonestablishment of religion; yet during this period the Court reached the high-water mark of constitutionally protected autonomy in ROE v. WADE (1973), upholding freedom of choice respecting abortion in the first two trimesters of pregnancy.

Criticism of the modern Court has taken diverse directions. Some critics have complained that the Court has been unfaithful to the historic meaning of constitutional provisions. But the argument begs the question of "meaning." If the term signifies denotative meaning, the particular instances that the Framers envisioned as comprehended in the text, the original meaning has indeed been departed from. If, however, the purposive meaning is accepted, and the application does not contradict the language of the text, there is no infidelity. Such an analysis will not disapprove, for example, the "meaning" ascribed to the freedom of the press in the First Amendment.

Another criticism charges defenders of the Court with a double standard: the modern Court is a mirror image of the pre-1937 Court, the judicial vetoes coming now from the left instead of the right. The asserted parallel, however, is inexact. The problem is to identify the appropriate role for judicial review in a representative democracy. The older Court set aside such products of the political process as minimum wage, price control, and tax legislation. The modern Court, by and large, has given its intensive scrutiny to two areas of law that are of peculiarly legitimate concern to the judiciary. One is the field of procedure, in a large sense, civil and criminal. The other is the set of issues concerning representation of interests in the formation of public opinion and lawmaking. This category would include FREEDOM OF SPEECH and press and association, VOTING RIGHTS, education, and the interests of groups underrepresented in the formulation of public policy. This approach gives a certain coherence to constitutional theory: as the commerce clause protects out-of-state enterprise against hostility, open or covert, the Bill of Rights and the Civil War amendments especially protect the political, social, or ethnic "outsider" against official neglect or ostracism.

A more qualified criticism is addressed to two tendencies of the modern Court. One is a perceived disposition to carry a constitutional safeguard to excessive lengths, as in BUCKLEY v. VALEO (1976), which held invalid, in the name of freedom of expression, statutory limits on expenditures by or on behalf of candidates for federal offices. The other, illustrated by the abortion and police interrogation cases, is an inclination, when holding a state law or practice invalid, to prescribe only a single form of corrective that will not offend constitutional standards.

A problem faced by the Court throughout much of its history, one that has again become acute, is the burden of an expanding caseload. In the last hundred years two statutory jurisdictional revisions brought temporary relief. The Circuit Courts of Appeals Act of 1891, by establishing a system of regional appellate courts, assured litigants of one opportunity for review without resort to the Supreme Court. The JUDICIARY ACT OF 1925, sponsored by the Justices themselves and promoted by Chief Justice WILLIAM HOWARD TAFT, made discretionary review by WRIT OF CERTIORARI, instead of APPEAL as of right, the normal mode of access to the Supreme Court.

Each solution, however, has in time become part of the problem. With thirteen courts of appeals, and the burgeoning of federal statutory law, there is a growing incidence of conflicting decisions calling for review. Moreover, the disposition of petitions for certiorari has occupied an increasing amount of the Justices' time, with more than 4,000 filed each term. Of these, approximately 175 are granted and the cases decided with full opinion after oral argument.

A study group appointed under the auspices of the Federal Judicial Center reported in 1972 that the caseload was reaching the saturation point. Certain ameliorative measures had already been taken. The normal time allowed for oral argument had been reduced from an hour to a half hour for each side. The number of law CLERKS had been increased in stages from one to four for each Justice. The study group expressed disquiet at what it viewed as a bureaucratic movement, and recommended the creation of a national court of appeals to review decisions that warranted review but not necessarily by the Supreme Court. Others proposed variations on this plan, notably one or more courts of appeals having specialized jurisdiction, in tax or criminal or regulatory cases. Sixty years after the 1925 act, the problem has not been resolved. And yet without adequate time for reflection, collegial discussion, critical scrutiny, mutual accommodation, and persuasive exposition, the Court cannot function at its best.

At its best, the Court can recall the legal profession and the people to an appreciation of their constitutional heritage, by translating the ideals and practices embodied in an eighteenth-century charter of the Enlightenment into the realities of a modern industrial democracy.

Bibliography

BICKEL, ALEXANDER M.   1962   *The Least Dangerous Branch*. Indianapolis: Bobbs-Merrill.

CONGRESSIONAL QUARTERLY   1981   *The Supreme Court and Its Work*. Washington, D.C.: Congressional Quarterly.

FREUND, PAUL A.   1961   *The Supreme Court of the United States*. Cleveland and New York: Meridian Books.

FREUND, PAUL A. and KATZ, STANLEY N.   1971–   The Oliver Wendell Holmes Devise History of the Supreme Court of the United States. 11 Vols. New York: Macmillan. The following volumes have been published: vol. I, GOEBEL, JULIUS, JR.   1971   *Antecedents and Beginnings to 1801;* vol. II, HASKINS, GEORGE L. AND JOHNSON, HERBERT A.   1981   *Foundations of Power: John Marshall, 1801–1815;* vol. V, SWISHER, CARL B.   1974   *The Taney Period, 1836–1864;* vols. VI and VII, FAIRMAN, CHARLES   1971   *Reconstruction and Reunion, 1864–1888, Part One;* 1986 *Part Two;* vol. IX, BICKEL, ALEXANDER M. and SCHMIDT, BENNO C., JR.   1984   *The Judiciary and Responsible Government, 1910–1921.*

FRIEDMAN, LEON and ISRAEL, FRED L., eds.   1969–1978   *The Justices of the United States Supreme Court, 1789–1969.* 5 Vols. New York: Chelsea House.

LEWIS, ANTHONY   1964   *Gideon's Trumpet*. New York: Random House.

POLLAK, LOUIS H., ed.   1966   *The Constitution and the Supreme Court: A Documentary History.* 2 Vols. Cleveland: World Publishing Co.

SWINDLER, WILLIAM F.   1970   *Court and Constitution in the Twentieth Century: The New Legality, 1932–1968.* Indianapolis: Bobbs-Merrill.

WARREN, CHARLES   1926   *The Supreme Court in United States History.* 2 Vols. Boston: Little, Brown.

WESTIN, ALAN, ed.   1961   *The Supreme Court: Views from Inside.* New York: Norton.

SUPREME COURT
(in American Government)

William Van Alstyne

The Supreme Court is the only court in the United States whose existence is mandated by the Constitution, yet the Constitution designates no number of judges for the Supreme Court and sets no qualifications for judicial service. So far as the Constitution is concerned, the Supreme Court could as readily consist of two or of twenty-two judges, rather than of nine as has been the case since 1870. And so undemanding is the Constitution in setting qualifications for appointment to the Supreme Court that its members could consist entirely of persons not qualified to serve in either House of Congress, for which at least a few minimum standards of eligibility (of age and of CITIZENSHIP) are constitutionally prescribed. The Constitution speaks simply to the vesting of the JUDICIAL POWER OF THE UNITED STATES in "one supreme court, and in such inferior Courts as the Congress may from time to time ordain and establish," but it leaves much else to discretion and a great deal to chance.

The role of the Supreme Court in American government is much like this overall. Some impressions of what the Court's role was meant to be can be gained from what the Constitution says and from the immediate history of 1789, as well as from the categories of JURISDICTION assigned to the Court by Article III. But much of that role is also the product of custom and of practice about which the Constitution itself is silent.

The constitutional text itself suggests several ways of describing the Supreme Court's role, in conformity with Article III's prescriptions of the Court's jurisdiction. The useful jurisdictional distinctions are of four principal kinds, each providing some insight into what the Court was originally expected to do.

First mentioned is the Supreme Court's jurisdiction as a trial court, an ORIGINAL JURISDICTION invocable by certain parties in particular (states and representatives of foreign states) but by no one else. Second is that branch of its appellate jurisdiction applicable also solely because of who the parties are, irrespective of the nature of the dispute between them. Third is the Court's appellate jurisdiction that attaches solely because the case involves a federal statute or treaty of the United States, or arises under ADMIRALTY AND MARITIME LAW, without regard to who the parties may be and whether or not any constitutional question may be involved. Finally, the Court may exercise an appellate jurisdiction over "all cases arising under [the] Constitution," a phrase construed broadly to include any case in which the outcome may be affected by a question of constitutional law. It is the application of this phrase, of course, that tends to fix the Supreme Court's most important role, but as can be seen from the foregoing larger enumeration, it is not by any means the sole business to which the Court was expected to attend.

The role of the Supreme Court as a court of original jurisdiction has been useful but minor. Ordinarily, the Court's small complement of original jurisdiction has merely expedited its speedy examination of certain legal issues raised by states against other states (typically involving boundary or interstate river claims) or against the national government, as in OREGON V. MITCHELL—a 1970 decision holding unconstitutional one portion of an act of Congress that sought to override state voting age restrictions. Because Congress can provide for expedited Supreme Court review of cases originating in other courts, however, it is doubtful whether this feature of Article III has been terribly vital. Its one theoretical importance may be that the original jurisdiction it provides to the states is guaranteed against elimination by Congress—for unlike the Court's appellate jurisdiction, its original jurisdiction is not subject to the "exceptions" clause of Article III.

Dwarfing the Court's role as a court of original jurisdiction is its much larger and more familiar role as the ultimate appellate court in the United States for a vastly greater number and variety of disputes, although the Court is not obliged to review all such cases and in fact hears but a small fraction of those eligible for review. The cases eligible for review, some on APPEAL and a larger number on petition for a WRIT OF CERTIORARI, are divisible into two principal categories: those in which the character of the contesting parties makes the case reviewable, and those in which the nature of the legal issue raised by the case makes the case reviewable.

In the first category of cases within the Court's appellate jurisdiction there are many that raise no constitutional questions and indeed need not raise any kind of federal question. As these cases are within the Court's power of review solely because of the parties, regardless of the subject in dispute between them, they may involve very ordinary legal issues (for example, of contract, tort, or property law) as to which there is no special expertise in the Supreme Court and no obvious reason why they need be considered there. And in practice, they are not reviewed.

Part of the original interest in providing the Supreme Court as the ultimate appellate tribunal in the United States reflected the Framers' desire to provide an appellate court for litigants likely to be sued in hostile jurisdictions—cases, for instance, arising in state courts which nonresident defendants might fear would be inclined to favor local parties as against outsiders. Since the furnishing of lower federal courts (to hear such cases) was left entirely optional with Congress to provide or not provide as it liked, the Supreme Court's appellate jurisdiction even from state court diversity cases was directly provided for in Article III. Nonetheless, in the course of 200 years the felt need for such cases to be heard in the Supreme Court has never materialized—although such cases remain a staple of lower federal court jurisdiction. (Efforts in Congress to repeal this entire category of lower federal court jurisdiction are more than a half-century old, but they have been only partly successful, largely in restricting such cases to those involving sums in excess of $10,000.) In the meantime, however, the Supreme Court does not review such cases and, by act of Congress, it is under no obligation to take them. This particular anticipated role of the Supreme Court, as an active court in hearing appeals in ordinary diversity cases presenting no federal question and implicating no general interest of the United States, has never been significant in fact.

In contrast, the second branch of the Supreme Court's appellate jurisdiction—identified not by the parties but by the nature of the legal questions—remains intensely active. Indeed, the principal role the Court plays today as an appellate court undoubtedly arises almost entirely from this subject matter assignment of appellate jurisdiction of cases involving disputes of national law. In these cases the Court interprets acts of Congress and treaties of the United States as well as the Constitution as the ultimate source of governing law in the United States.

Specifically, these cases may raise any of the following four kinds of basic conflicts: conflicts between claims relying upon mutually exclusive interpretations of concededly valid acts of Congress or treaties of the United States; between constitutional claims of state power and claims of federal power (FEDERALISM conflicts); between constitutional claims by Congress and claims by the President or claims by the judiciary (SEPARATION OF POWERS conflicts); or between constitutional claims of personal right and claims of either state or of national power (personal rights conflicts). A principal function of Article III was to establish the Supreme Court as the ultimate national court of appeals to provide finality and consistency of result in the interpretation and application of all federal and constitutional law in the United States, within the full range of these four fundamental and enduring concerns.

For nearly the first hundred years (1789–1875), almost all appeals to the Supreme Court on such federal questions as these came from state courts rather than from lower federal courts. Not until 1875, in the aftermath of the Civil War, were lower federal courts given any significant original (trial) jurisdiction over private civil cases arising under acts of Congress or treaties of the United States. Since 1875, moreover, many federal question cases still proceed from state courts to the Supreme Court, because reliance on some federal law or on the Constitution often arises only in answer to some claim filed in a state court and thus emerges only by way of defense rather than as the basis of complaint.

The fact that this arrangement of the Court's appellate jurisdiction places the Supreme Court in appellate command over all other courts in the United States in all federal question cases is exactly what makes the Supreme Court supreme. In constitutional matters, for instance, this fact is the basis of Justice ROBERT H. JACKSON's observation, in speaking of the Court, that "[w]e are not final because we are infallible, but we are infallible only because we are final," that is, superior in constitutional authority to review the determinations of other courts and in turn unreviewable by any other court. It likewise animates the 1907 observation by CHARLES EVANS HUGHES (later Chief Justice of the United States). "We are under a Constitution," Hughes acknowledged, "but the Constitution is what the judges say it is," since it is their view and, most important, the Supreme Court's view, that ultimately controls in each case. And even when no constitutional issue is present, but the issue is how an act of Congress shall be interpreted and applied, the finality of the Supreme Court's appellate jurisdiction is equally pivotal; it is the Americanized version of Bishop Hoadley's observation in 1717, in reference to the power of the English courts in interpreting acts of Parliament. "Whoever hath an absolute authority to interpret any written or spoken laws," Hoadley observed, "it is he who is truly the lawgiver, to all intents and purposes, and not the person who first spoke or wrote them." From an early time Americans seem to have believed in the wisdom of reposing in the courts—and ultimately in the Supreme Court— the responsibility of substantive constitutional review, and it seems clear (despite some scholars' qualified doubts) that the Supreme Court was indeed meant to exercise that responsibility. (See JUDICIAL REVIEW.) It is unquestionably this role of substantive constitutional review that marks the special position of the Supreme Court.

The Supreme Court's decisions in constitutional cases may be roughly divided into three kinds, according to which its role in American government is occasionally assessed or described. The three kinds of decisions are these: legitimizing, braking, and catalytic.

A decision is said to be legitimizing whenever the Court examines any act of government on constitutional grounds and finds it not wanting. In holding that the act as applied is in fact authorized by the Constitution and not offensive to any of its provisions (for example, the BILL OF RIGHTS or the FOURTEENTH AMENDMENT), the Court thus vouches for its constitutional legitimacy. A decision may be called a braking decision whenever its immediate effect is necessarily to arrest the further applica- tion of an act of Congress because the Court holds the act either inapplicable or unconstitutional, or whenever OBITER DICTA accompanying the decision serve notice of constitutional barriers in the way of similar legislation. Finally, a decision may be called catalytic when its immediate practical effect is to compel highly significant action of a sort not previously forthcoming from national or state government.

A significant and controversial example of the legitimizing sort is PLESSY V. FERGUSON (1896), the case sustaining certain state racial SEGREGATION laws as not inconsistent with the Fourteenth Amendment, despite intense argument to the contrary. A modern example of the same sort may be FULLILOVE V. KLUTZNICK (1980), a case sustaining a limited form of RACIAL DISCRIMINATION in favor of certain minority contractors as not inconsistent with the Fifth Amendment, despite intense argument as well. In each case, the Court considered a previously untested kind of race-related law. In each, the Supreme Court's decision could be said effectively to have impressed the operative law with a judicial imprimatur of constitutional legitimacy, given that in each case the challenged statute was sustained.

Examples of the braking sort may be found in the Court's early New Deal decisions holding Congress unauthorized by the COMMERCE CLAUSE to supplant state laws with its own much more sweeping and detailed ECONOMIC REGULATIONS. In this instance, the critical decisions of the Court forced a momentary pause in the onrush of legislation, compelling more deliberate attention to what the nation had been and what it meant to become. As it happened, the braking effect of these cases was eventually overcome, but it is nonetheless true that in the meantime the position taken by the Court played a sobering role. In a few other instances, the braking effect of equivalent cases was overcome by formal amendment of the Constitution itself: the SIXTEENTH AMENDMENT, for instance, was adopted principally to overcome the effect of the Court's decision in POLLOCK V. FARMERS' LOAN & TRUST (1895); the Thirteenth Amendment and Fourteenth Amendment displaced the Court's decision in DRED SCOTT V. SANDFORD (1857); and the TWENTY-SIXTH AMENDMENT displaced the decision in *Oregon v. Mitchell.* These reactions are by themselves not an indication that the Court has erred, of course, since the Constitution itself separates the role of the Court from the formal processes of constitutional modification. (See AMENDING PROCESS.) Any decision in the Supreme Court holding a statute unconstitutional may provide occasion to activate the AMENDING PROCESS provided for in Article V. Amendments by themselves are not proof that the decisions they effectively overrule were necessarily poorly conceived. They may, rather, but mark new Cambrian rings in what is meant to be a living constitution.

An example of a catalytic decision would be one holding certain prison conditions to be so inadequate as to constitute a form of CRUEL

AND UNUSUAL PUNISHMENT, such that either the prisoners must be released (which public authorities are loath to do), or large sums must be raised and less congested prisons must be built. The change-forcing nature of the Court's catalytic decision is but descriptive of its practical implications. By itself it thus carries no suggestion that the Court acted from impulse rather than from obligation, in ruling as it did. The same observation may apply equally to the other two categories of decisions.

Thus, in the "legitimizing" decision there is no necessary insinuation that the measure that has been sustained is on that account also necessarily desirable or well-taken legislation; such questions are ordinarily regarded as no proper part of the judicial business. Adjudicated constitutionality properly vouches solely for an act's consistency with the Constitution, which consistency may still leave much to be desired, depending upon one's own point of view and one's feeling of constitutional adequacy. Similarly, it does not follow that an act's adjudicated unconstitutionality necessarily implies its undesirability or, indeed, that there would be anything terribly wrong were the Constitution amended so that similar legislation might subsequently be reenacted and sustained. It means merely that the act does not pass muster under the Constitution as it is and as the judges are oath-bound to apply it until it is altered.

So also with catalytic decisions: such forced change as a particular decision may produce is required simply to bring the conduct of government back within constitutional lines as they are, and not as they need be. As conscientiously applied by the Court, the Constitution thus speaks to such constitutional boundaries as were put in place sometime in the past, from a considered political judgment of the time that such boundaries would be important. The judgment is wholly an inherited one, however, and contemplates the possibility of amendment to cast off such restraints as subsequent extraordinary majorities may find unendurable. Viewed in this way, the Constitution is a device by means of which past generations signal to subsequent generations their cumulative assessment of what sorts of restraints simple majoritarianism needs most. The Supreme Court is the ultimate judicial means by which the integrity of those restraints is secured against the common tendency to think them ill-conceived or obsolete, sustaining them when pressed by proper litigants with suitable standing, until instructed by amendment to acknowledge the change. It is a signal responsibility and an unusual power— one which few other national supreme courts have been given.

On the other hand, the phrases "legitimizing," "braking," and "catalytic" are not always used so descriptively, however well they capture the by-products of the Court's work. Rather, they are sometimes used prescriptively, and thus in an entirely different sense. In this different usage they presume to provide a more jurisprudential blueprint for the role of the Supreme Court: that it is appropriate for the Court actively to serve these three functions politically as it were, and to involve the Constitution only instrumentally in their service. Employed in this different locution, they are phrases used to express faith in a specific kind of judicial activism, according to which the right role of the Court is to identify the needs of efficient and humane government and to adjust its own adjudications accordingly.

In this view, it is in fact the proper role of the Supreme Court to legitimate (by holding constitutional) such laws as circumstances persuade it ought not be disapproved, to brake (by adverse construction or by holding unconstitutional) such developments as it determines to have been precipitously taken or otherwise to have been ill-advised, and to catalyze (by artful action) such changes it deems highly desirable but unlikely to be forthcoming from government unless the Court so requires. The persuasive justification for the Supreme Court lies in what it can do best as a distinct institution, in this view, and only secondarily in adhering to the Constitution. And what the Supreme Court can do better than others is to compensate for such gaps as it finds in the Constitution or in the political process, and to take such measured steps as it can to repair them. Accordingly, the more appropriate role of the Supreme Court is to conduct itself institutionally as best it can to contribute actively to a better political quality of life in the United States: in deciding which cases to hear, when to hear them, on what grounds to decide them, and how to make them come out in ways most in keeping with these three vital functions of granting legitimacy to the good, putting brakes on the bad, and compelling such changes as are overdue.

As an original jurisprudence of proposed judicial role, this perspective on the Supreme Court has had considerable occasional support. In the concrete, moreover, there is good reason to believe that certain Justices—probably a nontrivial number—have embraced it in selected aspects of their own work. At the least, there are a large number of constitutional decisions that appear to reflect its view of what judges should seek to do, as indeed some Justices have virtually absorbed it as an articulate feature of proper judicial review; their decisions seem sometimes to be based on little else.

Still, and for obvious reasons, it remains deeply problematic, for at bottom it would have the judges struggle against the obligation of their oaths. Insofar as cases such as *Plessy* or *Fullilove* were to any extent self-conscious efforts by a Supreme Court majority simply to legitimate race-based arrangements it thought desirable, and not decisions reporting a difficult judicial conclusion respecting the lack of constitutional restrictions on the legislative acts at issue, for instance, it is doubtful whether the "legitimacy" thus established was appropriate or, indeed, constitutionally authorized. Likewise, insofar as the early New Deal cases were to any extent simply a deliberate institutional attempt by the majority Justices to arrest what they thought to be ill-advised varieties of market intervention, and not decisions reflecting an attentive interpretation respecting the limits of Congress's commerce power, it is debatable whether the "braking" thus applied was appropriate or authorized. So, too, with such decisions as may be catalytic, but which may be driven more by a judicial desire to see changes made than by a mere firm resolve that the Constitution shall be obeyed.

Without doubt, however, the tendency to urge the Supreme Court to compose its interpretations of the Constitution in subordination to allegedly significant social tasks remains widespread. Moreover, the malleability of many constitutional clauses invites it, and the political staffing mechanism (provided by Article III) for selecting the judges may appear obliquely to legitimate it. The tendency to rationalize its propriety is deeply entrenched.

Even so, the conscious treatment of constitutional clauses as but textual or pretextual occasions for judicial legitimation, braking, or social catalysis, does tend to pit the Court against itself in its disjunction of fundamentally incompatible roles. The resulting tension has split the Court virtually from the beginning. It divides it even now: between these two visions of the Court, as a professional court first of all or as a political court first of all, lie two centuries of unsteady swings of actual judicial review. The history of the Supreme Court in this respect but reiterates a classic antinomy in American constitutional law. It doubtless reflects the conflicts Americans tend to sense within themselves—as to what role they genuinely wish this Court to fulfill.

With certain highly notable exceptions (including West Germany, Japan, Australia, and most recently Canada), the written CONSTITUTIONS of most modern nation-states serve merely as each nation's explanation of itself as a government. Such a constitution typically presents a full plan of government, a statement of its purposes and powers, and an ample declaration of rights. Yet, unlike the Constitution of the United States, such a constitution cannot be invoked by litigants and does not require or even permit courts of law to use it as against which all other laws may be examined. It is, rather, a nonjusticiable document. It is intended to be taken seriously (at least this is the case generally), but only in the political sense that legislative and executive authorities are meant to reconcile their actions with the constitution at the risk of possible popular disaffection should they stray too far from what the constitution provides. Whether the authorities have thus strayed, however, and what consequences shall follow if they have, is not deemed to be the appropriate business of courts of law.

The enormous distinction of American constitutional law has thus rested in the very different and exceptional role of the judiciary, from the most unprepossessing county courts through the hierarchy of the entire federal court system. The unique role of the Supreme Court has been its own role as the ultimate appellate court in reference to that judiciary, most critically in all constitutional cases. The arrangement thus established does not lessen the original obligation of other government officials separately to take care that their own actions are consistent with the Constitution, but it is meant to provide—as effectively as human institutions can arrange—an additional and positive check. When official action is not consistent with the Constitution, as ultimately determined under the Supreme Court's authority, the courts are given both the power and the obligation to intercede: to interpose such authority as they have and to provide such redress as appears to be due. Judged even by international standards, this is an ample role. It is not this role that now appears fairly open to question, moreover, but rather the definition of role that would assume something more or accept something less.

Bibliography

ABRAHAM, HENRY J. 1986 *The Judicial Process.* 5th ed. New York: Oxford University Press.

AGRESTO, JOHN 1984 *The Supreme Court and Constitutional Democracy.* Ithaca, N.Y.: Cornell University Press.

BICKEL, ALEXANDER M. 1962 *The Least Dangerous Branch: The Supreme Court at the Bar of Politics.* Indianapolis, Ind.: Bobbs-Merrill.

COX, ARCHIBALD 1976 *The Role of the Supreme Court in American Government.* New York: Oxford University Press.

ELY, JOHN HART 1980 *Democracy and Distrust: A Theory of Judicial Review.* Cambridge, Mass.: Harvard University Press.

FREUND, PAUL 1961 *The Supreme Court of the United States.* Cleveland, Ohio: World Publishing Company.

HOROWITZ, DONALD L. 1977 *The Courts and Social Policy.* Washington, D.C.: The Brookings Institution.

JACKSON, ROBERT H. 1955 *The Supreme Court in the American System of Government.* New York: Harper & Row.

MASON, ALPHEUS THOMAS 1979 *The Supreme Court from Taft to Burger.* 3d ed. Baton Rouge: Louisiana State University Press.

MCCLOSKEY, ROBERT G. 1960 *The American Supreme Court.* Chicago: University of Chicago Press.

WOLFE, CHRISTOPHER 1986 *The Rise of Modern Judicial Review.* New York: Basic Books.

JUDICIAL SUPREMACY

Walter F. Murphy

Stripped of the partisan rhetoric that usually surrounds important decisions of the Supreme Court, debate about judicial supremacy raises a fundamental question: Who is the final, authoritative interpreter of the Constitution? The response of judicial supremacy is that courts perform that function and other officials are bound not only to respect judges' decisions in particular cases but also, in formulating future public policy, to follow the general principles judges have laid down.

JUDICIAL REVIEW does not necessarily entail or logically imply judicial supremacy. One can, as THOMAS JEFFERSON did, concede the legitimacy of courts' refusing on constitutional grounds to enforce statutes and EXECUTIVE ORDERS and still deny either that officials of a coordinate branch must obey a decision or follow its rationale in the future. This view, called "departmentalism," sees the three branches of the national government as equal in CONSTITUTIONAL INTERPRETATION: Each department has authority to interpret the Constitution for itself, but its interpretations do not bind the other two.

There are other possible answers to the basic question: Congress, the President, the states, or the people. A claim for the states presupposes the Constitution to be a compact among sovereign entities who reserved to themselves authority to construe their obligations. Such was Jefferson's assertion in the KENTUCKY RESOLUTIONS (1798), and it echoed down decades of dreary debates on NULLIFICATION and SECESSION. The Civil War settled the matter, though some southern states briefly tried to resurrect nullification to oppose BROWN V. BOARD OF EDUCATION (1954).

A claim for the President as the ultimate, authoritative interpreter smacks too much of royalty for the idea to have been seriously maintained. On the other hand, Presidents have frequently and effectively defended their independent authority to interpret the Constitution for the executive department.

A case for the people as the final, authoritative interpreter permeates the debate. American government rests on popular consent. The people can elect officials to amend the Constitution or create a new constitution and so shape basic political arrangements as well as concrete public policies. Jefferson advocated constitutional conventions as a means of popular judging between conflicting departmental interpretations.

Although even JAMES MADISON rejected Jefferson's solution, indirect appeals to the people as the ultimate interpreters are reflected in claims to the supremacy of a popularly elected legislature. On the other hand, in THE FEDERALIST #78, ALEXANDER HAMILTON rested his argument for judicial review on the authority of the people who have declared their will in the Constitution. Judicial review, he argued, does not imply that judges are superior to legislators but that "the power of the people is superior to both."

Although JOHN MARSHALL partially incorporated this line of reasoning in MARBURY v. MADISON (1803), neither he nor Hamilton ever explicitly asserted that the Supreme Court's interpretation of the Constitution was binding on other branches of the federal government. One might, however, infer that conclusion from Marshall's opinions in *Marbury* and in *McCulloch v. Maryland* (1819), where he expressly claimed supremacy as far as state governments were concerned.

We know little of the Framers' attitudes toward judicial supremacy. In *The Federalist* #51, Madison took a clear departmentalist stand, as he did in the First Congress. In 1788 Madison wrote a friend that the new Constitution made no provision for settling differences among departments' interpretations: "[A]nd as ye Courts are generally the last in making the decision, it results to them by refusing or not refusing to execute a law, to stamp it with its final character. This makes the Judiciary Dept paramount in fact to the Legislature, which was never intended and can never be proper."

In the Senate in 1802, however, GOUVERNEUR MORRIS argued that the judges derived their power to decide on the constitutionality of laws "from authority higher than this Constitution. They derive it from the constitution of man, from the nature of things, from the necessary progress of human affairs. The decision of the Supreme Court is and, of necessity, must be final."

What turns a brief for judicial review into one for judicial supremacy is, of course, the claim of finality. Partially, that claim rests on the notion that interpretation of law is a uniquely judicial function (and, by its own terms, the Constitution is "the supreme law"); partially, on the ambiguity of the Constitution about the interpretive authority of other branches; and partially on the need for a supreme arbiter to assure the supremacy and uniform interpretations of the Constitution. The claim also rests on the belief that judges, because they are protected from popular pressures, are more apt to act fairly and coherently than elected officials. "It is only from the Supreme Court," CHARLES EVANS HUGHES once asserted, "that we can obtain a sane, well-ordered interpretation of the Constitution." The Court itself has seldom explicitly claimed judicial supremacy and has never articulated a full argument for it vis-à-vis Congress or the President. Indeed, through such DOCTRINES as the presumption of constitutionality and POLITICAL QUESTIONS, the Court often defers to interpretations by other departments.

The first modern, categorical claim by the Court to supremacy came in COOPER V. AARON (1958), where the Justices said that "the federal judiciary is supreme in the exposition of the law of the Constitution," and thus that *Brown v. Board of Education* was "the supreme law of the land." But *Cooper* involved state officials as did BAKER V. CARR (1962), where the Court first referred to itself as the "ultimate interpreter of the Constitution." Still, it was not until POWELL V. MCCORMACK (1969) that the Court so designated itself in a dispute involving Congress, an assertion the Justices repeated about the President in UNITED STATES V. NIXON (1974) and about both in IMMIGRATION AND NATURALIZATION SERVICE V. CHADHA (1983). *Powell,* however, addressed only the authority of the House to exclude a duly elected member and it did not require that he be readmitted or be given back pay. *Nixon* upheld a SUBPOENA to a President whose political situation was already desperate. What would have happened to the Court's claim as "ultimate interpreter" had it faced a politically secure chief executive in *Nixon* or tried to force Congress to take action in *Powell* might well have produced examples of departmentalism, as did Jefferson's refusal to obey Marshall's subpoena in UNITED STATES V. BURR (1807). And early congressional reactions to *Chadha's* declaring the LEGISLATIVE VETO unconstitutional have been mixed. Formally as well as informally, Congress has continued the practice, though in a more guarded fashion and on a smaller scale.

Although the constitutional text does not require judicial supremacy, Congress and the President have usually gone along with the Court's constitutional interpretations. Yet the exceptions have been sufficiently frequent and important that it is difficult to demonstrate a firm tradition requiring coordinate federal branches to accept the Court's doctrines. In matters strictly judicial—whether or not courts will enforce particular statutes—judges have been supreme, though subject to checks regarding, JURISDICTION and appointment of new personnel. The other branches, however, have frequently denied that they have an obligation, when setting policy, to follow the Court's constitutional interpretations.

There is a stronger argument for a duty of enforcing a judicial decision in a particular case. Certainly where the government has brought the case to the courts, an obligation to obey is obvious, as even Jefferson admitted. Where, however, the government is the defendant, the matter is much more complicated, especially when a court commands an official to perform a positive action. Jefferson and ANDREW JACKSON said they had no duty to obey such orders; ABRAHAM LINCOLN acted as if he did not; and FRANKLIN D. ROOSEVELT was prepared to ignore the GOLD CLAUSE CASES (1934) had they been decided against the government.

Typically, Congress and the President acquiesce in judicial interpretations of the Constitution because they agree with the results of judicial decisions, or fear public opinion, or recognize the difficulty of securing a congressional response. Often, too, the Justices reinforce Congress's tendency toward inertia by not pressing a claim to supremacy. Always hovering in the background of any department's assertion of supremacy is the possibility of an appeal to "the people" through the AMENDING PROCESS. Yet even such an appeal, when directed against the Court's jurisprudence, implies an admission of the tactical if not theoretical superiority of the Court as constitutional interpreter.

Bibliography

CORWIN, EDWARD S.   1914   *Marbury v. Madison* and the Doctrine of Judicial Review. *Michigan Law Review* 12:538–572.

FISHER, LOUIS   1985   Constitutional Interpretation by Members of Congress. *North Carolina Law Review* 63:701–741.

MIKVA, ABNER J.   1983   How Well Does Congress Support and Defend the Constitution? *North Carolina Law Review* 61:587–611.

MURPHY, WALTER F.; FLEMING, JAMES E.; and HARRIS, WILLIAM F., II   1986   *American Constitutional Interpretation.* Chaps. 6–7. Mineola, N.Y.: Foundation Press.

JUDICIAL ACTIVISM AND JUDICIAL RESTRAINT

William Van Alstyne

"Judicial activism" and "judicial restraint" are terms used to describe the assertiveness of judicial power. In no sense unique to the Supreme Court or to cases involving some construction of the Constitution, they are editorial summations of how different courts and different judges conduct themselves.

The user of these terms ("judicial activism" and "judicial restraint") presumes to locate the relative assertiveness of particular courts or individual judges between two theoretical extremes. The extreme model of judicial activism is of a court so intrusive and ubiquitous that it virtually dominates the institutions of government. The antithesis of such a model is a court that decides virtually nothing at all: it strains to find reasons why it lacks JURISDICTION; it avows deference to the superiority of other departments or agencies in construing the law; it finds endless reasons why the constitutionality of laws cannot be examined. It is a model of government virtually without useful recourse to courts as enforcers of constitutional limits.

The uses of "judicial activism" and "judicial restraint," however, are not entirely uniform. Often the terms are employed noncommittally, that is, merely as descriptive shorthand to identify some court or judge as more activist or more restrained than some other, or more than the same court formerly appeared to be. In this sense, the usage is neither commendatory nor condemnatory. Especially with reference to the Supreme Court, however, the terms are also used polemically. The user has a personal or professional view of the "right" role of the Court and, accordingly, commends or condemns the Court for conforming to or straying from that right role. Indeed, an enduring issue of American constitutional law has centered on this lively controversy of right role; procedurally and substantively, how activist or how restrained ought the Supreme Court to be in its use of the power of constitutional JUDICIAL REVIEW?

Ought that Court to confront the constitutionality of the laws as speedily as opportunity affords, the better to furnish authoritative guidance and settle political controversy in keeping with its unique competence and function as the chief constitutional court of the nation? Or ought it, rather, to eschew any unnecessary voluntarism, recognizing that all participants in government are as bound as the Court to observe the Constitution and that the very insularity of the Supreme Court from representative government is a powerful reason to avoid the appearance of constitutional arrogance or constitutional monopoly? In brief, what degree of strict necessity should the Supreme Court require as a condition of examining the substantive constitutionality of government acts or government practices?

Substantively, the issues of "proper" activism or proper restraint are similar. When the constitutionality of governmental action is considered, what predisposition, if any, ought the Supreme Court to bring to bear? Should it take a fairly strict view of the Constitution and, accordingly, hold against the constitutionality of each duly contested governmental act unless the consistency of that act with the Constitution can be demonstrated virtually to anyone's satisfaction? Or, to the contrary, recognizing its own fallibility and the shared obligation of Congress (and the President and every member of every state legislature) fully to respect the Constitution as much as judges are bound to respect it, should the Court hold against the constitutionality of what other departments of government have enacted only when virtually no reasonable person could conclude that the act in question is consistent with the Constitution?

Disputes respecting the Supreme Court's procedural judicial activism (or restraint) and substantive judicial activism (or restraint) are thus of recurring political interest. Most emphatically is this the case with regard to judicial review of the constitutionality of legislation, as distinct from nonconstitutional judicial review. For here, unlike activism on nonconstitutional issues (such as the interpretation of statutes), the consequences of an adverse holding on the merits are typically difficult to change. An act of Congress, held inapplicable to a given transaction, need only be approved in modified form to "reverse" the Supreme Court's impression. On the other hand, a holding that the statute did cover the transaction but in presuming to do so was unconstitutional is a much more nearly permanent boundary. It may be overcome only by extraordinary processes of amending the Constitution itself (a recourse successfully taken during two centuries only four times), or by a reconsideration and overruling by the Supreme Court itself (an eventuality that has occurred about 130 times). Thus, the special force of adjudication of constitutionality, being of the greatest consequence and least reversibility, has made the proper constitutional activism (or proper restraint) of the Supreme Court itself a central question.

An appraisal of the Supreme Court in these terms involves two problems: the activism (or restraint) with which the Court rations the judicial process in developing or in avoiding occasions to decide constitutional claims; and the activism (or restraint) of its STANDARDS OF REVIEW when it does decide such claims.

The Supreme Court's own description of its proper role in interpreting the Constitution is one of strict necessity and of last resort. In brief, the Court has repeatedly held that the Constitution itself precludes the Court from considering constitutional issues unless they are incidental to an actual CASE OR CONTROVERSY that meets very stringent demands imposed by Article III. In addition, the Court holds that prudence requires the complete avoidance of constitutional issues in any case in which the rights of the litigants can be resolved without reference to such an issue.

In 1982, in VALLEY FORGE CHRISTIAN SCHOOLS v. AMERICANS UNITED, Justice WILLIAM H. REHNQUIST recapitulated the Court's conventional wisdom. Forswearing any judicial power generally to furnish advice on the Constitution, and denying that the Supreme Court may extend its jurisdiction more freely merely because constitutional issues are at stake, he declared: "The constitutional power of federal courts cannot be defined, and indeed has no substance, without reference to the necessity to 'adjudge the legal rights of litigants in actual controversies.'" Even when the stringent prerequisites of jurisdiction have been fully satisfied, moreover, "[t]he power to declare the rights of individuals and to measure the authority of governments, this Court said 90 years ago, 'is legitimate only in the last resort, and as a necessity in the determination of real, earnest, and vital controversy.'" For emphasis, he added, "The federal courts were simply not constituted as ombudsmen of the general welfare. [Such a philosophy] has no place in our constitutional scheme."

In so declaring, Justice Rehnquist was relying substantially upon a similar position adopted by Chief Justice JOHN MARSHALL in MARBURY v. MADISON (1803). Explaining that the Court's determination of constitutional questions was but an incident of its duty to pass upon legal questions raised in the due course of litigation, in no respect different from its duty when some statutory issue or COMMON LAW question might likewise be presented in a case, Marshall had insisted: "The province of the Court is, solely, to decide on the rights of individuals," and not to presume any larger role.

Accordingly, though a constitutional issue may be present, if the dispute in which it arises does not otherwise meet conventionally strict standards of STANDING, RIPENESS, genuine adverseness of parties, or sufficient factual concreteness to meet the demands of a justiciable case or controversy as required by Article III, the felt urgency or gravity of the constitutional question can make no difference. In steering a wide course around the impropriety of deciding constitutional questions except as incidental to a genuine adversary proceeding, moreover, the Court has also declared that it will not entertain COLLUSIVE SUITS. As

Marshall declared in *Marbury*, "it never was the thought that, by means of a friendly suit, a party beaten in the legislature could transfer to the courts an inquiry as to the constitutionality of a legislative act." Similarly, if during the course of genuine litigation the grievance has become moot in light of subsequent events, it must then be dismissed insofar as there remains no necessity to address the original issue.

When, moreover, all requisites of conventional, genuine litigation remain such that adjudication of the parties' rights is an unavoidable judicial duty, the Court has still insisted that it should determine whether the case can be disposed of without addressing any issue requiring it to render an interpretation of the Constitution itself. Accordingly (within the conventional wisdom), even with respect to disputes properly before it, well within its jurisdiction and prominently featuring a major, well-framed, well-contested constitutional question, the Supreme Court may still refuse to address that question. In his famous concurring opinion in ASHWANDER v. TENNESSEE VALLEY AUTHORITY (1936), Justice LOUIS D. BRANDEIS insisted that constitutional questions were to be decided only as a last resort: "When the validity of an act of Congress is drawn in question, and even if a serious doubt of constitutionality is raised, it is a cardinal principle that this Court will first ascertain whether a construction of the statute is fairly possible by which the question may be avoided." Indeed, Brandeis continued, the Court will not "pass upon a constitutional question although properly presented by the record, if there is also present some other ground upon which the case may be disposed of." Moreover, though there may be no other ground, if the constitutional question arises at the instance of a public official, "the challenge by a public official interested only in the performance of his official duty will not be entertained." Even when the issue is raised by a private litigant, his challenge to the constitutionality of a statute will not be heard "at the instance of one who has availed himself of its benefits."

Self-portrayals of the Court as a wholly reluctant constitutional tribunal that is not an oracle of constitutional proclamation but a court of law that will face constitutional questions only when a failure to do so would involve it as a tribunal in an unconstitutional oppression of a litigant go even further. A litigant may have much at stake, and nothing except his reliance upon some clause in the Constitution may remain to save him from jeopardy. Still, if the clause in the Constitution is deemed not to yield objective criteria adequate to guide its application by the Court, the Court may decline to attempt to fix any meaning for the clause on the basis that it is nonjusticiable. (See POLITICAL QUESTIONS.) Similarly, if the relief requested should require the Court to consider an order against the Congress itself, an order the Court cannot be confident would be obeyed and which it is without resources otherwise to enforce, it may refuse to consider the case. Identically, if an adjudication of the constitutional question, though otherwise imperative to the litigant's case, might involve conflict with the President respecting decisions already made, communicated to, and relied upon by other governments, the case may also be regarded as nonjusticiable.

In rough outline, then, these are the principal elements of the orthodoxy of extreme judicial restraint. Consistent with them, even when the Court does adjudicate a constitutional question, its decision is supposed to be "no broader than is required by the precise facts." Anything remotely resembling an advisory opinion or a gratuitous judicial utterance respecting the meaning of the Constitution is to be altogether avoided.

Although this combination of Article III requirements and policies has characterized a large part of the Court's history (most substantially when the constitutional questions involved acts of Congress or executive action), the Court's practice has not, in fact, been at all uniform. Collusive suits have sometimes been entertained, and the constitutional issues at once examined. Public officials sometimes have been deemed to have sufficient standing to press constitutional questions, though they have had no more than an official interest in the matter. Holdings on the Constitution occasionally have been rendered in far broader terms than essential to decide the case, often for the advisory guidance of other judges or for the benefit of state or local officials. When the constitutional issue seemed clear enough and strongly meritorious, parties placed in positions of advantage solely by force of the very condition of which they later complained on constitutional grounds have not always been estopped from securing a decision. On occasion when third parties would be unlikely or unable to raise a constitutional claim on their own behalf, moreover, other litigants deemed suitable to represent their claim have been allowed to proceed on the merits of the constitutional issues. And some utterly moot cases have been decided on the merits of their constitutional questions on the paradoxical explanation that unless the moot cases were treated as still lively, then conceivably the merits of the constitutional issues would forever elude judicial review. Indeed, the nation's most famous case, *Marbury v. Madison,* was in many respects an example of extreme procedural activism despite its disclaimer of strict necessity.

At issue in Marbury's case was the question of the Supreme Court's power to hear the case in the first instance, within its ORIGINAL JURISDICTION, rather than merely on appeal. The statute William Marbury relied upon to demonstrate his right to commence his action in the Supreme Court was altogether unclear as to whether it authorized his suit to begin in the Supreme Court. Avoidance of the necessity of examining the constitutionality of the statute was readily available merely by construing the statute as not providing for original jurisdiction: an interpretation thus making clear that Marbury had sued in the wrong court, resulting in his case's being dismissed for lack of (statutory) jurisdiction and obviating any need to say anything at all about the constitutionality of an act of Congress.

Rather than pursue that course, however, Chief Justice Marshall "actively" interpreted the act of Congress, that is, he interpreted it to draw into issue its very constitutionality and then promptly resolved that issue by holding the act unconstitutional. Beyond that, rather than be content to dismiss the case for lack of either statutory or constitutional jurisdiction, the Chief Justice also (and quite gratuitously) addressed every other question raised by the complaint, including Marbury's right to the public office he sought, the appropriateness of the remedy he asked for, the illegality of the secretary of state's refusal to give it to him, and the lack of immunity from such suits by the secretary of state. Each of these other issues was of substantial controversy. Several of them raised substantial constitutional questions. Marshall resolved all in an opinion most of which was purely advisory, that is, of no necessity in light of the ultimate holding, which was that the Court was (constitutionally) without power (jurisdiction) to address the merits of the case at all. Marshall addressed all these questions on the basis of a factual record supplied principally on affidavit of his own brother. Still, Marshall, far from recusing himself on that account or on account of his own participation as the secretary of state who failed to deliver Marbury's commission, fully participated in the case, voted, and wrote the opinion for the Court. In these many respects, the case of *Marbury v. Madison* was an extraordinary example of extreme procedural activism. Its resemblance to what the Court has otherwise said (as in the Brandeis *Ashwander* guidelines or the *Valley Forge* case) is purely ironic. Indeed, the unstable actual practices of the Court which has so often described its institutional role in constitutional adjudication as one of the utmost procedural restraint, while not uniformly adhering to that description, have contributed to the Court's great controversiality in American government.

As we have seen, procedural activism (and restraint) has consisted principally of two parts. The first part is the rigor or lack of rigor with which the Court has interpreted the limitation in Article III of the Constitution, according to which the use of the judicial power can operate solely on "cases and controversies." The second part is the extent to which the Court has also adopted a number of purely self-denying ordinances according to which it will decline to adjudicate the merits of a constitutional claim in any case in which a decision can be reached on some other ground.

In contrast, substantive activism (and restraint) has consisted principally of three parts, each reflecting the extent to which the Court has interpreted the Constitution either aggressively to invalidate actions taken by other departments of government, or diffidently to acquiesce in these actions. The first part pertains to the Court's substantive interpretations of the ENUMERATED and IMPLIED POWERS of the other departments of the national government, that is, the powers vested by Article I in Congress and the powers vested by Article II in the President. The second part pertains to the Court's interpretation of the Constitution as implicitly withdrawing from state governments a variety of powers not explicitly forbidden to them by the Constitution. And the third part pertains to the Court's interpretations of those clauses in the Constitution that impose positive restrictions on the national and the state governments, principally the provisions in Article I, sections 9 and 10, in the BILL OF RIGHTS, and in the FOURTEENTH AMENDMENT. Although there may be no a priori reason to separate the substantive activism and restraint of the Supreme Court into these three particular categories, it is nonetheless practically useful to do so: overall, the Court has responded to them quite distinctly. Indeed, in practice, despite very great differences among particular Justices, the general tendency has been to develop a constitutional jurisprudence of selective activism and selective restraint.

In respect to constitutional challenges to acts of Congress for consistency with Article I's enumeration of affirmative powers, the Court's standard of review has generally been one of extraordinary restraint. With the exception of the first three and a half decades of the twentieth century, the Court has largely deferred to Congress's own suppositions respecting the scope of its powers. During the first seventy-five years of the Constitution, for instance, only two acts of Congress were held not to square with the Constitution. During the most recent forty years (a period of intense and extremely far-reaching national legislation), again but two acts have been held to fail for want of enumerated or implied constitutional authorization. Indeed, even when the comparison is enlarged to include cases challenging acts of Congress not merely for want of enacting authority but rather because they were alleged to transgress specific prohibitions (for example, the FIRST AMENDMENT restriction that Congress shall make no law abridging the FREEDOM OF SPEECH), still the record overall is one of general diffidence and restraint. Over the entirety of the Court's history, scarcely more than 120 acts of Congress have been held invalid.

An influential rationale for such restraint toward acts of Congress was set forth in 1893, in an essay by JAMES BRADLEY THAYER that Justice FELIX FRANKFURTER subsequently identified as uniquely influential on his own thinking as a judicial conservative. Thayer admonished the judiciary to bear in mind that the executive and legislative departments of the national government were constitutionally equal to the judiciary, that they were equivalently bound by oath of office to respect the Constitution, and that each was a good deal more representative of the people than the life-tenured members of the Supreme Court. Accordingly, Thayer urged, the Court should test the acts of coordinate national departments solely according to a rule of "clear error." In brief, such acts were to be examined not to determine whether their constitutionality necessarily conformed to the particular interpretation which the judges themselves might independently have concluded was the most clearly correct interpretation of the Constitution. Rather, such acts should be sustained unless they depended on an interpretation of constitutional power that was itself manifestly unreasonable, that is, an interpretation *clearly* erroneous.

Thayer's rule provided a strong political rationale for extreme judicial deference in respect to enumerated and implied national powers. Of necessity, however, it also tended practically to the enlistment of the judiciary less as an independent guardian of the Constitution (at least in respect to the scope of enumerated and implied powers) than as an institution tending to validate claims of national authority against state perspectives on the proper boundaries of FEDERALISM. It is a thesis that has periodically attracted criticism on that account, but it does not stand as the sole explanation for the general restraint reflected in the Supreme Court's permissive construction of national legislative and executive powers. Rather, without necessarily assuming that Congress and the President possess a suitably reliable detachment to be the presumptive best judges of their respective powers, decades before the appearance of Thayer's essay the Supreme Court had already expressed a separate rationale: a judicial rule of BROAD CONSTRUCTION respecting enumerated national powers.

The most durable expression of that rule is reported in a famous OBITER DICTUM by Chief Justice John Marshall. In McCULLOCH v. MARYLAND (1819), Marshall emphasized to his own colleagues, the federal judges: "We must never forget, that it is a *constitution* we are expounding." In full context, Marshall plainly meant that it was a Constitution for the future as well as for the present, for a nation then quite small and new but expected to become much more considerable. To meet these uncertain responsibilities, Congress would require flexibility and legislative latitude. Thus, powers granted to it by the Constitution should be read generously.

The point was expanded upon more than a century later by Justice OLIVER WENDELL HOLMES, in MISSOURI v. HOLLAND (1920), defending the judiciary's predisposition to interpret the TREATY POWER very deferentially: "When we are dealing with words that also are a constituent act, like the Constitution of the United States, we must realize that they have called into life a being the development of which could not have been foreseen completely by the most gifted of its begetters. . . . [I]t has taken a century and has cost their successors much sweat and blood to prove that they created a nation." This rule of generous construction, like Thayer's rule of "clear error," tends to support a judicial policy of substantive interpretative restraint. And while not free of criticism on its own account (as federalism critics will tend to fault it as unfaithful to their view of the extent to which substantive legislative authority was meant to be reserved to the states), it is not contingent upon doubtful assumptions respecting the capacity of the President or of the Congress fairly to assess the scope of powers they are given by the Constitution. Arguably, it is as well that this policy of judicial restraint not be made to rest on such assumptions. Although reference to the early constitutional history of the United States tends to support Thayer's thesis (early members of Congress included many persons who had participated in the shaping of the Constitution and who frequently debated proposed legislation in terms of its consistency with that Constitution), two centuries of political change have weakened its suppositions considerably. Persons serving in Congress are far removed from the original debates over enumerated powers; the business of Congress is vastly greater than it once was; the electorate is itself vastly enlarged beyond the limited numbers of persons originally eligible to vote; and such attention as may be given within Congress to issues of constitutionality is understandably likely to be principally political in its preoccupations rather than cautious and detached. Thus, the Marshall rule of generous construction in respect to national powers, rather than the Thayer proposal (of yielding to not-unreasonable interpretations by Congress), tends more strongly to anchor the general policy of judicial restraint in this area. (When the issue had been one of conflict between Congress and the President, on the other hand, the Court has tended to defer to the position of Congress as first among equals.)

In contrast, there is less evidence of a consistent policy of substantive judicial restraint in the Supreme Court's examination of state laws and state acts. Here, to the contrary, the role of the Court has emphatically been significantly more activist, procedurally as well as substantively. The Court will more readily regard the review of governmental action as within the JUDICIAL POWER OF THE UNITED STATES in the litigation of state laws. A principal example is the ease with which state TAXPAYER SUITS impugning state laws on federal constitutional grounds will be deemed reviewable in the Supreme Court, when in most instances an equivalently situated federal taxpayer is deemed to have inadequate standing in respect to an act of Congress. In addition, the Court has interpreted the Constitution to create a judicial duty to determine the constitutionality of certain kinds of state laws, though the clauses relied upon do not themselves expressly confer such a judicial duty (or power) and speak, rather, solely of some preemptive power in Congress to determine the same matter. For instance, the COMMERCE CLAUSE provides merely that Congress shall have power to regulate commerce among the several states. But in the absence of congressional regulation, the Court has actively construed the clause as directing the federal courts themselves to determine, by their own criteria, whether state statutes so unreasonably or discriminatorily burden INTERSTATE COMMERCE that they should be deemed invalid by the courts as an unconstitutional trespass upon a field of regulation reserved to Congress.

Here also the rationales have differed, and indeed not every Supreme Court Justice has embraced either rationale. (Justice HUGO L. BLACK, for instance, preferring a constitutional jurisprudence of "literal" interpretation, generally declined to find any basis in the commerce clause for judicial intervention against state statutes.) In part, the substantive activism of the Court has been explained by a "political marketplace" calculus that is the obverse of Thayer's rule for deference to Congress. According to this view, as the state legislatures are not equal departments to the Supreme Court (in the sense that Congress is an equal department), and as national interests are not necessarily as well represented in state assemblies as state interests are said to be represented in Congress (insofar as members of Congress are all chosen from state-based constituencies), there are fewer built-in political safeguards in state legislatures than in Congress. To the extent of these differences, it is said that there is correspondingly less reason for courts to assume that state legislatures will have acted with appropriate sensitivity to federal constitutional questions and, accordingly, that there is more need for closer judicial attention to their acts. The sheer nonuniformity of state legislation may be of such felt distress to overriding needs for greater uniformity in a nation with an increasingly integrated economy that a larger measure of judicial activism in adjudicating the constitutional consistency of state legislation may be warranted in light of that fact. Something of this thought may lie behind Justice Holmes's view respecting the relative importance of constitutional review itself: "I do not think the United States would come to an end if we lost our power to declare an Act of Congress void. I do think the Union would be imperiled if we could not make that declaration as to the laws of the several states." Finally, more activist substantive review of state laws has been defended on the view that, assuming Congress itself may presume to substitute a uniform rule or otherwise forbid states to legislate in respect to certain matters, the frequency with which state statutes may be adopted and the resulting interference they may impose upon matters of national importance prior to any possibility of corrective congressional action require that the federal courts exercise an interim and activist responsibility of their own. In any event, this much is clear. In respect to substantive standards of constitutional review and challenges to state laws on grounds that they usurp national authority, the overall position of the Supreme Court has been that of an activist judiciary in umpiring the boundaries of federalism.

Finally, and most prominently within the last half-century, selective judicial activism has made its strongest appearance in the judicial review of either federal or state laws that, in the Court's view, bear adversely on one or more of the following three subjects: participation in the political process, specific personal rights enumerated in the Bill of Rights, and laws adversely affecting "DISCRETE AND INSULAR MINORITIES." The scope of these respective activist exceptions (to the general rule of procedural and substantive restraint) is still not entirely settled. Indeed, each is itself somewhat unstable. Nonetheless, the indication of more aggressive, judicially assertive constitutional intervention in all three areas was strongly suggested in a footnote to UNITED STATES v. CAROLENE PRODUCTS Co. (1938). There, the Court suggested that the conventional "presumption of constitutionality" would not obtain, and that "searching judicial inquiry" would be applied to the review of laws that, on their face, appeared "to be within a specific prohibition of the Constitution," or to "restrict those political processes which can ordinarily be expected to bring about the repeal of undesirable legislation," or to bear heavily on "discrete and insular minorities" suffering from prejudice likely to lead to their neglect in the legislative process.

In respect to the first of these categories, however, it is doubtful whether the standards applied by the Supreme Court should be defined as unconventionally activist at all. To the extent that a constitutional provision explicitly forbids a given kind of statute, its mere application by the Court scarcely seems exceptional. To the contrary, it would require an extreme version of "restraint" to do otherwise.

The second category (principally concerned with limitations on voting eligibility or with varieties of unfairness in REPRESENTATION) is differently reasoned. The Court has assumed generally that deference is ordinarily due the constitutional interpretations of legislative bodies because they are themselves representatives of the people (who have the greatest stake in the Constitution). But if the law in question itself abridges the representative character of the legislatures, it tends by that fact to undermine the entire foundation of judicial restraint in respect to all other legislative acts. As it tends thereby also to reduce the efficacy of the legislative process to repeal improvident legislation, such representation-reducing statutes ought to be severely questioned.

The third category (such legislation as bears adversely on insular and discrete minorities) has emerged as by far the most controversial and unstable example of modern judicial activism. Its theory of justification is one of rationing the activism of constitutional review inversely, again in keeping with the perceived "market failure" of representative government. And, up to a point, it is quite straightforward in keeping with that theory. Thus, when the numbers of a particular class are few and their financial resources insignificant, and when the class upon whom a law falls with great force is not well-connected but, to the contrary, seems left out of account in legislative processes (by prejudices entrenched within legislatures), the resulting market place failure of political power or ordinary empathy is felt to leave a gap to be filled by exceptional judicial solicitude.

The paradigm case for such activism is that of legislation adversely affecting blacks, when challenged on grounds of inconsistency with the EQUAL PROTECTION clause of the Fourteenth Amendment. On its face, the equal protection clause provides no special standards of justification that race-related legislation must satisfy that other kinds of adverse legislative classifications need not meet. Nonetheless, on quite sound historical grounds, race-related legislation was singled out for exceptional judicial activism by the WARREN COURT. Although many of the Warren Court decisions remain of enduring controversy, it is generally conceded that the Court's STRICT SCRUTINY of such race-based laws was itself consistent with the special preoccupation of the Fourteenth Amendment with that subject. Thus, as early as 1873, in the SLAUGHTERHOUSE CASES, the Court had observed: In the light of the history of [the THIRTEENTH, Fourteenth, and FIFTEENTH] AMENDMENTS, and the pervading purpose of them, [it] is not difficult to give a meaning to [the equal protection clause]. The existence of laws in the states where the newly emancipated negroes resided, which discriminated with gross injustice and hardship against them as a class, was the evil to be remedied by this clause, and by it such laws are forbidden."

As this historical Civil War basis for that one exception was left behind, the Supreme Court plied an increasingly complicated sociology of political marketplace failure to explain an equivalent interventionism on a much broader front. Thus, gender-based laws, laws restricting ALIENS vis-à-vis citizens, and laws restricting minors vis-à-vis adults came also to be examined much more stringently under the equal protection clause than laws adversely affecting particular businesses, particular classes of property owners, certain groups of taxpayers, or others. The determination of "adequate representation" (whether direct or vicarious), the conjecture as to whether such legislative classifications were based on "stereotypes" rather than real differences, and ultimately the tentative extension of equal protection activism even to require a variety of state support for poor persons, produced unstable and largely unsustainable pluralities within the Supreme Court.

Indeed, the difficulties of selective activism in this area have been the principal object of contemporary criticism in American constitutional law. The most serious questions have been addressed to the apparent tendency of the Court to adjust its own interpretations of the Constitution not according simply to its own best understanding of that document, but rather according to its perceptions respecting the adequacy of representative government. Given the fact that far more cases compete for the opportunity to be determined by the Supreme Court than its own resources can permit it to hear, the Court might be expected to pursue a course of selective procedural activism according to which it would more readily entertain cases and more readily reach the merits of constitutional claims it should consider not to have been adequately considered elsewhere because of built-in weaknesses of representative government. On the other hand, it remains much more problematic why the Court should utilize its impressions respecting the adequacies of representative government twice over: once to determine which cases to review, and again to determine whether the Constitution has in fact been violated.

Descriptions of judicial activism and judicial restraint in constitutional adjudication are, of course, but partial truths. In two centuries of judicial review, superintended by more than one hundred Justices who have served on the Supreme Court and who have interpreted a Constitution highly ambiguous in much of its text, consistency has not been institutional but personal. Individual judges have maintained strongly diverse notions of the "proper" judicial role, and the political process of APPOINTMENT OF SUPREME COURT JUSTICES has itself had a great deal to do with the dominant perspectives of that role from time to time. Here, only the most prominent features of judicial activism and judicial restraint have been canvassed.

It is roughly accurate to summarize that in respect to interpreting the Constitution, procedurally the Supreme Court has usually exercised great restraint. Subject to some notable exceptions, it has eschewed addressing the constitutional consistency of acts of government to a dramatically greater degree of self-denial than it has exercised in confronting other kinds of legal issues seeking judicial resolution. Substantively, the Court has been predisposed to the national government in respect to the powers of that government: except for the early twentieth century, Thayer's law, requiring a showing of "clear error," has been the dominant motif. In respect to the states, on the other hand, the Court has been actively more interventionist, construing the Constitution to enforce its own notions of national interest in the absence of decisions by Congress. And, most controversially in recent decades, it has been unstably activist in deciding whether it will interpret the Constitution more as an egalitarian set of imperatives than as a document principally concerned with commerce, federalism, the SEPARATION OF POWERS, and the protection of explicitly protected liberties.

Bibliography

BICKEL, ALEXANDER M. 1962 *The Least Dangerous Branch: The Supreme Court at the Bar of Politics.* Indianapolis: Bobbs-Merrill.

ELY, JOHN H. 1980 *Democracy and Distrust: A Theory of Judicial Review.* Cambridge, Mass.: Harvard University Press.

JACKSON, ROBERT H. 1941 *The Struggle for Judicial Supremacy.* New York: Knopf.

THAYER, JAMES B. 1893 "The Origin and Scope of the American Doctrine of Constitutional Law." *Harvard Law Review* 7:129.

WECHSLER, HERBERT 1959 "Toward Neutral Principles of Constitutional Law." *Harvard Law Review* 73:1.

JUDICIAL POLICYMAKING

Howard E. Dean

Judicial policymaking and related terms—JUDICIAL ACTIVISM, judicial creativity, and JUDICIAL LEGISLATION—emphasize that judges are not mere legal automatons who simply "discover" or "find" definite, preexisting principles and rules, as the declaratory or oracular conception of the judicial function insisted, but are often their makers. As Justice OLIVER WENDELL HOLMES remarked, they often exercise "the sovereign prerogative of choice," and they "can and do legislate." Indeed, that is why the Supreme Court has often been viewed as "a continuing constitutional convention."

Policymaking is deciding what is to be done by choosing among possible actions, methods, or principles for determining and guiding present and future actions or decisions. Courts, especially high appellate courts such as the SUPREME COURT, often make such choices, establishing new rules and principles, and thus are properly called policymakers. That was emphasized by CHARLES EVANS HUGHES's famous rhetorical exaggeration, "The Constitution is what the judges say it is," and by his remark that a federal statute finally means what the Court, as ultimate interpreter of congressional LEGISLATION, says it means.

The persistent "declaratory" conception of the judicial role, a view critics derided as MECHANICAL JURISPRUDENCE, and simplistic notions of the SEPARATION OF POWERS principle long obscured the reality of judicial policymaking. Today it is widely recognized that, as C. Herman Pritchett has explained, "judges are inevitably participants in the process of public policy formulation; that they do in fact 'make law'; that in making law they are necessarily guided in part by their personal conceptions of justice and public policy; that written law requires interpretation which involves the making of choices; that the rule of STARE DECISIS is vulnerable because precedents are typically available to support both sides in a controversy."

As a system of social control, law must function largely through general propositions rather than through specific directives to particular persons. And that is especially true of the Constitution. The Framers did not minutely specify the national government's powers or the means for executing them: as Chief Justice JOHN MARSHALL said, the Constitution "is one of enumeration, rather than of definition." Many of its most important provisions are indeterminate and open-textured. They are not self-interpreting, and thus judges must read specific meanings into them and determine their applicability to particular situations, many of which their authors could not have anticipated.

Among the Constitution's many ambiguous, undefined, pregnant provisions are those concerning CRUEL AND UNUSUAL PUNISHMENT; DOUBLE JEOPARDY; DUE PROCESS OF LAW; EQUAL PROTECTION OF THE LAWS; ESTABLISHMENT OF RELIGION; excessive BAIL and fines; EX POST FACTO LAWS; FREEDOM OF SPEECH, press, assembly, and religion; life, liberty, and property; the power to regulate commerce among the several states; and unreasonable SEARCHES AND SEIZURES. Also undefined by the Constitution are such fundamental conceptions as FEDERALISM, JUDICIAL REVIEW, the RULE OF LAW, and the separation of powers. Small wonder, then, that Justice ROBERT H. JACKSON plaintively remarked that the Court must deal with materials nearly as enigmatic as the dreams of Pharaoh which Joseph had to interpret; or that Chief Justice EARL WARREN emphasized that the Constitution's words often have "an iceberg quality, containing beneath their surface simplicity submerged complexities which go to the very heart of our constitutional form of government."

Because the Constitution embodies in its ambiguous provisions both common and conflicting community ideals, the Supreme Court serves, as Edward H. Levi has said, as "a forum for the discussion of policy in the gap of ambiguity," which allows the infusion into constitutional law of new meanings and new ideas as situations and people's ideas change. That is the process which Justice FELIX FRANKFURTER described as "the evolution of social policy by way of judicial application of the Delphic provisions of the Constitution." Brief accounts of some notable Supreme Court decisions reveal their policymaking features.

Although the Constitution nowhere explicitly grants Congress the power to incorporate a national bank, the Supreme Court in McCULLOCH v. MARYLAND (1819) held that power to be implied by the Constitution's NECESSARY AND PROPER CLAUSE. That clause empowers Congress, in executing its various enumerated powers, to make all laws for that purpose which are "necessary and proper." But those ambiguous words are not further defined by the Constitution.

In making its *McCulloch* decision, the Court chose between two historic, diametrically opposed interpretations. The narrow, STATES' RIGHTS, STRICT CONSTRUCTION, Jeffersonian interpretation of the clause was restrictive and limited Congress to legislation that was "absolutely necessary," that is, literally indispensable. The opposing interpretation, which the Court adopted, was the broad, nationalist, loose constructionist, Hamiltonian view that "necessary and proper" were equivalent to "convenient and useful" and thus were facilitative, not restrictive. The bank, declared the Court, was a convenient and useful means to legitimate ends and thus was constitutional.

Viewed broadly as the great implied powers case and the "fountainhead of national powers," *McCulloch* laid down the Hamiltonian doctrine as the authoritative rule of construction to be followed in interpreting Congress's various undefined powers. Subsequently, on that foundation, Congress erected vast superstructures of regulatory and social service legislation. The profound policy considerations underlying the Court's choices are highlighted by the contrast between Jefferson's warning that the dangerous Hamiltonian doctrine would give Congress a boundless field of undefined powers, and Chief Justice Marshall's emphasis upon the "pernicious, baneful," narrow construction which would make the national government's operations "difficult, hazardous, and expensive" and would reduce the Constitution to "a splendid bauble."

The RIGHT TO PRIVACY was recognized by the Supreme Court in GRISWOLD v. CONNECTICUT (1965). There, and in other cases, the Court variously discerned the "roots" of that right, which is not explicitly mentioned in the Constitution, in the FIRST, FOURTH, Fifth, NINTH, and FOURTEENTH AMENDMENTS and in "the penumbras of the BILL OF RIGHTS." Later, in ROE v. WADE (1973), the Court included a woman's right to an abortion in the right of privacy, and, in the detailed manner characteristic of legislation, divided the pregnancy term into three periods and prescribed specific rules governing each. Balancing a woman's interests against a state's interests during these three periods, the Court held that any decision regarding abortion during the first was solely at the discretion of the woman and her physician. But it further ruled that a state's interests in protecting maternal health, maintaining medical standards, and safeguarding potential human life—interests growing in substantiality as the pregnancy term extended—justified greater state regulation later. Thus, state regulations relating to maternal health and medical standards would be permissible in the second period, and more stringent state regulations, even extending to prohibition of abortion, would be permissible in the third period in the interest of safeguarding potential life.

The protests by dissenting Justices in the *Griswold* and *Roe* cases emphasized the judicial policymaking which those decisions revealed. The *Griswold* dissenters objected that no right of privacy could be found "in the Bill of Rights, in any other part of the Constitution, or in any case ever before decided by this Court." And dissenters in *Roe* complained that the Court's decision was "an improvident and extravagant exercise of the power of JUDICIAL REVIEW"; that the Court had fashioned "a new constitutional right for pregnant mothers"; and that the Court's "conscious weighing of competing factors" and its division of the pregnancy term into distinct periods were "far more appropriate to a legislative judgement than to a judicial one."

The Supreme Court's "REAPPORTIONMENT revolution" remedied long-standing discriminations against urban and metropolitan areas in favor of rural areas, by requiring states to reapportion their legislatures in conformity with the rule that legislative districts must be as nearly of equal population as is practicable.

That rule is not found in any constitutional provision specifically addressed to legislative apportionment, for none exists. It is a Court-created rule which clearly demonstrates the leeway for policymaking that open-ended constitutional provisions give the Court. Equal population, the Court said in WESBERRY V. SANDERS (1964), is required for congressional districts by "the command" of Article I, section 2, of the Constitution, that representatives "be chosen by the People" of the states; and is required for state legislative districts, the Court held in REYNOLDS v. SIMS (1964), by "the clear and strong command" of the FOURTEENTH AMENDMENT's equal protection clause, forbidding states to deny to any persons "the equal protection of the laws."

Courtesy may ascribe the Court's rule to CONSTITUTIONAL INTERPRETATION; but candor ascribes it to judicial policymaking. The dissenting Justices' objections in these cases made that clear. They included complaints that the Court had frozen one political theory of REPRESENTATION into the Constitution; had failed to exercise judicial self-restraint; had decided questions appropriate only for legislative judgment; had violated the separation of powers doctrine; and had excluded numerous important considerations other than population.

Supreme Court overruling decisions, in which it rejects its earlier positions for those later thought more fitting, often strikingly exemplify judicial policymaking. In MAPP v. OHIO (1961) the Court imposed upon state courts its judicially created EXCLUSIONARY RULE making illegally obtained evidence inadmissible in court. It overruled WOLF V. COLORADO (1949) which, in deference to state policies, had held an exclusionary rule not essential for due process of law.

Some overruling decisions illustrate "the victory of dissent," when earlier dissenting Justices' views in time became the law. Thus in GIDEON v. WAINWRIGHT (1963) the Court applied its rule that indigent defendants in all state felony trials must have court-appointed counsel. Overruling BETTS v. BRADY (1942), the Court adopted Justice Black's dissenting position from it, thus repudiating its *Betts* pronouncement that such appointment was "not a fundamental right, essential to a fair trial."

According to the Court in BARRON v. BALTIMORE (1833), the Bill of Rights—the first ten amendments—limits the national government but not the states. But the Court, by its INCORPORATION DOCTRINE, has read nearly all the specific guarantees of the Bill of Rights into the due process clause of the Fourteenth Amendment which provides simply that no state shall "deprive any person of life, liberty, or property, without due process of law." The incorporation has been called selective because the Court, proceeding case by case, has incorporated those guarantees which it considers "fundamental" and "of the very essence of a scheme of ORDERED LIBERTY."

Selective incorporation has involved two kinds of Supreme Court policymaking: adopting the FUNDAMENTAL RIGHTS standard for guiding incorporation, and making the separate decisions incorporating particular Bill of Rights guarantees. Thus the Court, applying its open-textured rule, has given specific meaning to "the vague contours" of the due process clause. And it has become "a perpetual censor" over state actions, invalidating those that violate fundamental rights and liberties.

Clearly the Supreme Court is more than just a legal body: the Justices are also "rulers," sharing in the quintessentially political function of authoritatively allocating values for the American polity. Representing a coordinate branch of the national government, they address their mandates variously to lawyers, litigants, federal and state legislative, executive, and judicial officials, and to broader concerned "publics." Concerning their role, no sharp line can be drawn between law and politics in the broad sense. They do not expound a prolix or rigid legal code, but rather a living Constitution "intended to be adapted to the various *crises* of human affairs," as Chief Justice Marshall said in the *McCulloch* case. And the Justices employ essentially COMMON LAW judicial techniques: they are inheritors indeed, but developers too—"weavers of the fabric of constitutional law"—as Chief Justice Hughes observed. The nature of the judicial process and the growth of the law are intertwined. The Constitution, itself the product of great policy choices, is both the abiding Great Charter of the American polity and the continual focus of clashing philosophies of law and politics among which the Supreme Court must choose: "We are very quiet there," said Justice Holmes plaintively, "but it is the quiet of a storm center, as we all know."

Bibliography

CARDOZO, BENJAMIN N.   1921   *The Nature of the Judicial Process.* New Haven, Conn.: Yale University Press.

LEVI, EDWARD H.   1948   *An Introduction to Legal Reasoning.* Chicago: University of Chicago Press.

MILLER, ARTHUR SELWYN   1978   *The Supreme Court: Myth and Reality.* Westport, Conn.: Greenwood Press.

MURPHY, WALTER F.   1964   *Elements of Judicial Strategy*. Chicago: University of Chicago Press.
PRITCHETT, C. HERMAN   1969   The Development of Judicial Research. Pages 27–42 in Joel B. Grossman and Joseph Tanenhaus, eds., *Frontiers of Judicial Research*. New York: Wiley.

JUDICIAL LEGISLATION

John Agresto

The term "judicial legislation" appears to be something of an oxymoron, as the Constitution clearly assigns the principal task of LEGISLATION to the Congress. The Constitution does, of course, give the President a role in the legislative process through the VETO POWER and through his power to recommend legislation to Congress that "he shall judge necessary and expedient." The Framers explicitly rejected, however, a similar role for the judiciary. Several attempts to create a council of revision, composed of the executive and members of the Supreme Court, to review the constitutionality of proposed legislation, were defeated in the CONSTITUTIONAL CONVENTION. The most effective arguments against including the Court in a council of revision were derived from considerations of the SEPARATION OF POWERS. ELBRIDGE GERRY, for example, remarked that including members of the Supreme Court in a revisory council "was quite foreign from the nature of the office," because it would not only "make them judges of the policy of public measures" but would also involve them in judging measures they had a direct hand in creating. Assigning ultimate legislative responsibility to the Congress apparently reflected the Framers' belief that, in popular forms of government, primary lawmaking responsibility should be lodged with the most representative branches of the government. In JAMES MADISON's words, "the people are the only legitimate fountain of power."

Justice FELIX FRANKFURTER expressed the same view in his concurring opinion in *American Federation of Labor v. American Sash and Door Co.* (1949). "Even where the social undesirability of a law may be convincingly urged," he said, "invalidation of the law by a court debilitates popular democratic government. . . . Such an assertion of JUDICIAL POWER deflects responsibility from those on whom in a democratic society it ultimately rests—the people." Frankfurter continued his brief for judicial restraint by arguing that because the powers exercised by the Supreme Court are "inherently oligarchic" they should "be exercised with rigorous self-restraint." The Court, Frankfurter laconically concluded, "is not saved from being oligarchic because it professes to act in the service of humane ends."

The modern Supreme Court is not so easily deterred as Frankfurter was by charges of oligarchy. Since the landmark BROWN v. BOARD OF EDUCATION decision in 1954, the Court has actively and overtly engaged in the kind of lawmaking and policymaking that in previous years was regarded as exclusively the province of the more political branches of government. William Swindler explained the Court's transition from judicial deference to judicial activisim in these terms: "If the freedom of government to act was the basic principle evolving from the Hughes-Stone decade, from 1937–1946, the next logical question—to be disposed of by the WARREN COURT—was the obligation created by the Constitution itself, to compel action in the face of inaction. This led in turn to the epochal decisions in *Brown v. Board of Education*, BAKER V. CARR, and GIDEON V. WAINWRIGHT."

Some scholars have argued that it was the identification of EQUAL PROTECTION rights as class rights and the attendant necessity of fashioning classwide remedies for class injuries that gave the real impetus to the Court's JUDICIAL ACTIVISM in the years immediately following *Brown*. The Court, in other words, effectively legislated under its new-molded EQUITY powers. (See INSTITUTIONAL LITIGATION.)

The Court's legislative role is usually justified in terms of its power of JUDICIAL REVIEW. But judicial review—even if it be regarded as a necessary inference from the fact of a written constitution—is not a part of the powers explicitly assigned to the Court by the Constitution. The Court made its boldest claim for the legitimacy of judicial legislation in COOPER V. AARON (1958). Justice WILLIAM J. BRENNAN, writing an opinion signed by all the members of the Court, outlined the basic constitutional argument for JUDICIAL SUPREMACY. Brennan recited "some basic constitutional propositions which are settled doctrine," and which were derived from Chief Justice JOHN MARSHALL's argument in MARBURY V. MADISON (1803). First is the proposition, contained in Article VI of the Constitution, that the Constitution is the supreme law of the land (see SUPREMACY CLAUSE); second is Marshall's statement that the Constitution is "the fundamental and paramount law of the nation"; third is Marshall's declaration that "[i]t is emphatically the province and duty of the judicial department to say what the law is." Justice Brennan concluded that *Marbury* therefore "declared the basic principle that the federal judiciary is supreme in the exposition of the law of the Constitution, and that principle has ever since been respected by this Court and the Country as a permanent and indispensable feature of our constitutional system. It follows that the interpretation of the FOURTEENTH AMENDMENT enunciated by this Court in the Brown Case is the supreme law of the land. . . ." The defect of Brennan's argument, of course, is that it confounds the Constitution with constitutional law.

Marshall did indeed say that the Constitution was "the fundamental and paramount law of the nation," and that any "ordinary legislative acts" "repugnant to the constitution" were necessarily void. But when Marshall wrote the famous line relied upon by Brennan that "it is emphatically the province and duty of the judicial department to say what the law is," he was referring not to the Constitution but to "ordinary legislative acts." In order to determine the law's conformity with the Constitution it is first necessary to know what the law is. And once the law is ascertained it is also necessary to determine whether the law is in conformity with the "paramount law" of the Constitution. This latter, of course, means that "in some cases" the Constitution itself "must be looked into by the judges" in order to determine the particular disposition of a case. But Marshall was clear that the ability of the Court to interpret the Constitution was incident to the necessity of deciding a law's conformity to the Constitution, and not a general warrant for CONSTITUTIONAL INTERPRETATION or judicial legislation. Marshall was emphatic in his pronouncement that "the province of the court is, solely, to decide on the rights of individuals."

"It is apparent," Marshall concluded, "that the framers of the constitution contemplated that instrument as a rule for the government of courts, as well as of the legislature." As he laconically noted in the peroration of his argument, "it is also not entirely unworthy of observation, that in declaring what shall be the supreme law of the land, the constitution itself is first mentioned; and not the laws of the United States generally, but those only which shall be made in pursuance of the constitution, have that rank." For Marshall, Brennan's assertion that the Court's decision in *Brown* was "the supreme law of the land" would indeed make "written constitutions absurd" because it would usurp the "original right" of the people to establish their government on "such principles" that must be "deemed fundamental" and "permanent." If the Supreme Court were indeed to sit as a "continuing constitutional convention," any written Constitution would certainly be superfluous since, under the circumstances there would be no "rule for the government of courts." After all, by parity of reasoning, if one were to accept Brennan's argument, it would also be necessary to hold that the Court's decision in DRED SCOTT V. SANDFORD (1857) was the supreme law of the land. But *Dred Scott* gave way because forces other than the Supreme Court decided that it was a decision not "pursuant" to the "fundamental and paramount law" of the nation. As John Agresto has cogently remarked; "If Congress can mistake the meaning of the text [of the Constitution], which is what the doctrine of judicial review asserts, so, of course, can the Court. And if it be said that it is more dangerous to have interpretive supremacy in the same body that directs the nation's public policy—that is, Congress—then (especially in this age of pervasive judicial direction of political and social life) an independent judicial interpretive power is equally fearsome for exactly the same reasons."

In SWANN V. CHARLOTTE-MECKLENBURG BOARD OF EDUCATION (1971) the Court was confronted with the question of the federal judiciary's equity powers under the equal protection clause of the Fourteenth Amendment. At issue was whether the Court could uphold SCHOOL BUSING as a "remedy for state-imposed segregation in violation of Brown I." As part of the CIVIL RIGHTS ACT OF 1964 the Congress had included in Title IV a provision that "nothing herein shall empower any official or court . . . to issue any order seeking to achieve a racial balance in any school by requiring the transportation of pupils or students from one school to another . . . or otherwise enlarge the existing power of the court to insure compliance with constitutional standards." Chief Justice WARREN E. BURGER, writing for a unanimous Court, remarked that on its face this section of Title IV is only "designed to foreclose any interpretation of the Act as expanding the *existing* powers of federal courts to enforce the Equal Protection Clause. There is no suggestion of an intention to restrict those powers or withdraw from courts their historic equitable remedial powers." According to Burger these equity powers flow directly from the Fourteenth Amendment—despite the fact that section 5 of the Amendment gives Congress explicit enforcement authority, an authority that was mistakenly restricted by the Court in the SLAUGHTERHOUSE CASES (1873) and the CIVIL RIGHTS CASES (1883).

A serious question arises, however, concerning Burger's claim that forced busing is one of the "historic" equity powers of the Court. It was never asserted as such by the Court prior to 1964, and as late as two years *after* the *Swann* decision it was still being described by Justice LEWIS F. POWELL as "a novel application of equitable power—not to mention a dubious extension of constitutional doctrine." Congress's response to *Swann,* the Equal Educational Opportunity and Transportation of Students Act of 1972, contained restrictions similar to those included in Title IV. These provisions suffered the same fate as the Title IV provisions, only now the Court was able to use *Swann* as authority for its ruling.

The *Swann* rationale derives equity powers directly from the Constitution. But the way in which the Court exercises its equity powers is indistinguishable from legislation. Thus, in effect, the Court now derives what is tantamount to legislative power from the Constitution. Because this power rests upon an interpretation of the Constitution, no act of Congress can overturn or modify the interpretation. Many scholars argue that if the Congress were to attempt to curtail the Court's power to order forced busing under the exceptions clause, the Court would be obligated, under the *Swann* reasoning, to declare such an attempt unconstitutional, because the Court's obligation to require busing as a remedy for equal protection violations is derived directly from the Constitution.

Judicial legislation incident to statutory interpretation is less controversial, for the Congress can overturn any constructions of the Court by repassing the legislation in a way that clarifies congressional intent.

The interpretation of statutes necessarily involves the judiciary in legislation. In many instances the courts must engage in judicial legislation in order to say what the law is. In years past the Court's sense of judicial deference confined such judicial legislation to what Justice OLIVER WENDELL HOLMES called the "interstices" of the law. It was generally believed that the plain language of the statute should be the controlling factor in statutory construction and that extrinsic aids to construction such as legislative history should be used only where they were necessary to avoid a contradictory or absurd result.

The courts are not always the aggressive agents in the process of judicial legislation. In recent years courts have acted to fill the void created by Congress's abdication of legislative responsibility. Many statutes passed by Congress are deliberately vague and imprecise; indeed, the Congress in numerous instances charges administrative agencies and courts to supply the necessary details. This delegation of authority to administrative agencies with provisions for judicial oversight of the administrative process has contributed to the judiciary's increased participation in judicial legislation. This tendency was intensified by the Court's decision in IMMIGRATION AND NATURALIZATION SERVICE v. CHADHA (1983), holding the LEGISLATIVE VETO unconstitutional. Congress had for years used the single-house legislative veto as a device for overseeing the activities of administrative agencies. But, as Judge Carl McGowan has noted, "the question inevitably recurs as to whether judicial review is an adequate protection against the abdication by Congress of substantive policy making in favor of broad delegation of what may essentially be the power to make laws and not merely to administer them."

The volume of litigation calling for "legislation" on the part of the courts also increases in proportion with the liberalization of the rules of STANDING. In previous years the Court's stricter requirements for standing were merely a recognition that the province of the judiciary, in the words of John Marshall quoted earlier, "was solely to decide on the rights of individuals, not to inquire how the executive, or executive officers, perform duties in which they have a discretion." Liberalized rules of standing tend to produce what Court of Appeals Judge Atonin Scalia has called "an overjudicialization of the process of self-governance." Judge Scalia reminds us of the question posed by Justice Frankfurter—whether it is wise for a self-governing people to give itself over to the rule of an oligarchic judiciary. James Bradley Thayer wrote more than eighty-five years ago that "the exercise of [judicial review], even when unavoidable, is always attended with a serious evil, namely, that the correction of legislative mistakes comes from the outside, and the people thus lose the political experience, and the moral education and stimulus that comes from fighting the question out in the ordinary way, and correcting their own errors. The tendency of a common and easy resort to this great function, now lamentably too common, is to dwarf the political capacity of the people, and to deaden its sense of moral responsibility."

If, on the other hand, the processes of democracy are unsuited for protecting democratic ends—if, that is, in the words of Jesse Choper, it is necessary for the Supreme Court generally to act "contrary to the popular will" to promote "the precepts of democracy"—then the question whether the American people can be a self-governing people is indeed a serious one. It was once thought that constitutional majorities could rule safely in the interest of the whole of society—that constitutional government could avoid the formation of majority faction. Today many scholars—and often the Supreme Court itself—simply assume that the majority will always be a factious majority seeking to promote its own interest at the expense of the interest of the minority. This requires that the judiciary intervene not only in the processes of democracy but also as the virtual representatives of the interest of those who are said to be permanently isolated from the majoritarian political process. If American politics is indeed incapable of forming nonfactious majorities— and America has never had such a monolithic majority—then the American people should give itself over honestly and openly to "government by judiciary," for if constitutional government is impossible, then so too is the possibility of self-governance.

Bibliography

AGRESTO, JOHN   1984   *The Supreme Court and Constitutional Democracy.* Ithaca, N.Y.: Cornell University Press.

ERLER, EDWARD J.   1985   Sowing the Wind: Judicial Oligarchy and the Legacy of *Brown v. Board of Education. Harvard Journal of Law and Public Policy* 8:399–426.

LEVY, LEONARD W.   1967   Judicial Review, History, and Democracy. Pages 1–42 in Leonard W. Levy, ed., *Judicial Review and the Supreme Court.* New York: Harper & Row.

SWINDLER, WILLIAM   1969   *Court and Constitution in the 20th Century.* Indianapolis: Bobbs-Merrill.

JUDICIAL STRATEGY

Walter F. Murphy

That judges shape much public policy is a fact of political life. The significant questions are how, how often, how effectively, and how wisely they influence policy. Each of these inquiries poses normative as well as empirical problems. Here we shall be concerned only with legitimate strategies that a Justice of the United States Supreme Court can employ to maximize his or her influence. We shall focus mainly on marshalling the Court.

A Justice, like any strategist, must coordinate limited resources to achieve goals. He or she must make choices—about goals and priorities among goals and also about means to achieve those goals. Intelligent choices among means depend in part on accurate assessments of the resources the Justice controls and of the limitations that others may impose on use of those resources.

The Justices can order litigants, including government officials, to act or not act in specified ways. Less tangibly, judges also have the prestige of their office, supported by a general cultural ethos of respect for the RULE OF LAW. In particular, a Justice has a powerful weapon, an opinion—a document that will be widely distributed by the Government Printing Office and several private firms. That opinion will justify—well or poorly—a particular decision and, explicitly or implicitly, the public policy it supports.

A Justice's power is limited by the nature of judicial institutions. Judges lack self-starters. Someone has to bring a case to them. Furthermore, while they can hold acts of other public officials constitutional or unconstitutional and so allow or forbid particular policies, it is much more difficult for judges to compel government to act. The Supreme Court can rule that blacks are entitled to vote, but it cannot force Congress to pass a CIVIL RIGHTS law to make that right effective. Moreover, the Court can hear only a limited number of cases. It depends on thousands of state and federal judges to carry out its jurisprudence. And no Justice plays an *official* role in selecting, retaining, or promoting judges.

Second, a Supreme Court Justice needs the agreement of at least four colleagues. And each Justice can write a separate opinion, dissenting or concurring, in any case.

Third, and more broadly, the Court is dependent on Congress and the President for appropriations and enforcement of decisions. Each of these branches has other important checks: The House can impeach and the Senate can then remove a Justice. Congress can increase the size of the Court, remove at least part of its APPELLATE JURISDICTION, propose constitutional amendments to erase the effects of decisions or strike at judicial power itself, and use its access to mass media to challenge the Court's prestige. The President can even more effectively attack the Court's prestige, and he can persuade Congress to use any of its weapons against the Justices. He can also choose new judges who, he hopes, will change the course of CONSTITUTIONAL INTERPRETATION.

Fourth, state officials can influence public opinion to pressure Congress and the President. State officers can also drag their heels in carrying out judicial decisions and select judges who are hostile to the Court's jurisprudence.

Fifth, leaders of interest groups can pressure elected officials at all levels of government. And when judicial decisions threaten or support their values, these people seldom hesitate to apply whatever political leverage is in their self-interest.

Commentators—journalists and social scientists as well as law professors—constitute a sixth check. If judges make law, EDWARD S. CORWIN said, so do commentators. Justices who want their jurisprudence to endure must look not only to immediate reactions but also to the future. What commentators write may influence later generations of voters, lawyers, and public officials.

A Justice confronts these limitations simultaneously, and each of these groups will include a range of opinion. Any ruling will elate some and infuriate others, and the political power of various factions is likely to vary widely. In short, problems of synchronizing activities are always present and are typically complex.

The first audience a Justice must convince is composed of other Justices. The most obvious way of having one's views accepted by one's colleagues is to have colleagues who agree with one's views. Thus ability to influence the recruiting process is a difficult but fruitful means of maximizing influence. (See APPOINTMENT OF SUPREME COURT JUSTICES.) Justices who cannot choose their colleagues must consider how to persuade them.

Although treating others with courtesy may never change a vote or modify an opinion, it does make it more likely that others will listen. When others listen, intellectual capacity becomes critical. The Justice who knows "the law," speaks succinctly, writes clearly, and analyzes wisely gains distinct advantages.

Practical experience can be a valuable adjunct. Logic is concerned with relations among propositions, not with their desirability or social utility. According to WILLIAM O. DOUGLAS, several Justices were converted to Chief Justice EARL WARREN's position in BROWN V. BOARD OF EDUCATION

(1954) because of his vast political experience. Strength of character is also crucial. Although neither learned nor gifted as a writer, Warren led the Court and the country through a constitutional revolution. It was his "passion for justice," his massive integrity, Douglas also recalled, that made Warren such a forceful leader. "Is it right?" was his typical question, not "Do earlier decisions allow it?"

In another sense, intellect alone is unlikely to suffice. Justices are all apt to be intelligent, strong-willed people with divergent views about earlier rulings as well as public policy. They are also apt to differ about the Court's proper roles in the political system—in sum, about fundamentals of jurisprudence. At that level of dispute, it is improbable that one Justice, no matter how astute and eloquent, will convert another.

Facing disagreements that cannot be intellectually reconciled, a Justice may opt for several courses. Basically, he can negotiate with his colleagues or go it alone. Most often, it will be prudent to negotiate. Like policymaking, negotiation, even bargaining, is a fact of judicial life. Writing the opinion of the Court requires "an orchestral, not a solo performance." All Justices can utilize their votes and freedom to write separate opinions. The value of each depends upon the circumstances. If the Court divides 4–4, the ninth Justice, in effect, decides the case. On the other hand, when the Court votes 8–0, the ninth Justice's ability to negotiate will depend almost totally on his capacity to write a separate opinion that, the others fear, would undermine their position.

To be effective, negotiations must be restrained and sensitive. Justices are likely to sit together for many years. Driving a hard bargain today may damage future relations. The mores of the Court forbid trading of votes. The Justices take their oaths of office seriously; and, while reality pushes them toward accommodation, they are not hagglers in a market, peddling their views.

The most common channels of negotiating are circulation of draft opinions, comments on those drafts, and private conversations. A Justice can nudge others, especially the judge assigned the task of producing the OPINION OF THE COURT, by suggesting additions, deletions, and rephrasings. In turn, to retain a majority, the opinion writer must be willing to accede to many suggestions, even painful ones, as he tries to persuade the Court to accept the core of his reasoning. OLIVER WENDELL HOLMES once complained that "the boys generally cut one of the genitals" out of his drafts, and he made no claim to have restored their manhood.

Drafts and discussions of opinions can and do change votes, even outcomes. Sometimes those changes are not in the intended direction. After reading FELIX FRANKFURTER's dissent in BAKER V. CARR (1961), TOM C. CLARK changed his vote, remarking that if those were the reasons for dissenting he would join the majority.

Although the art of negotiation is essential, a Justice should not wish to appear so malleable as to encourage efforts to dilute his jurisprudence. He would much prefer a reputation of being reasonable but tough-minded. He thus might sometimes find it wise to stand alone rather than even attempt compromise. It is usually prudent for a Justice, when with the majority, to inject as many of his views as possible into the Court's opinion, and when with the minority to squeeze as many hostile ideas as possible out of the Court's opinion. There are, however, times when both conscience and prudence counsel standing alone, appealing to officials in other governmental processes or to future judges to vindicate his jurisprudence.

Although Justices have very limited authority to make the other branches of government act, they are not powerless. Judges can often find more in a statute than legislators believe they put there. OBITER DICTA in an opinion can also prod other officials to follow the "proper" path. The Court might even pursue a dangerous course that might push a reluctant President to carry out its decisions lest he seem either indifferent to the rule of law or unprotective of federal power against state challenges.

Lobbying with either branch is also possible. Indeed, judicial lobbying has a venerable history running back to JOHN JAY. Advice delivered through third parties may have been even more common. Over time, however, expectations of judicial conduct have risen so that even a hint of such activity triggers an outcry. Thus a judge must heavily discount the benefits of direct or indirect contacts by the probability of their being discovered.

The most obvious weapon that a Justice has against unwelcome political action is the ability to persuade his colleagues to declare that action unconstitutional or, if it comes in the shape of a federal statute or EXECUTIVE ORDER, to disarm it by interpretation. These are the Court's ultimate weapons, and their overuse or use at the wrong time might provoke massive retaliation.

A Justice must therefore consider more indirect means. Delay is the tactic that procedural rules most readily permit. The Justices can deny a WRIT OF CERTIORARI, dismiss an APPEAL, REMAND the case for clarification, order reargument, or use a dozen other tactics to delay deciding volatile disputes until the political climate changes.

Under other circumstances, it might be more prudent for a Justice to move the Court step by step. Gradual erosion of old rules and accretion of new ones may win more adherents than sudden statements of novel DOCTRINES. The Court's treatment of segregation provides an excellent illustration. If MISSOURI EX REL. GAINES V. CANADA (1938) had struck down SEPARATE BUT EQUAL, the Court could never have made the decision stick. Indeed, years later, when it excommunicated Jim Crow, enforcement created a generation of litigation that still continues.

Strategy is concerned with efficient utilization of scarce resources to achieve important objectives. Its domain is that of patience and prudence, not of wisdom in choosing among goals nor of courage in fighting for the right. The messages that a study of judicial strategy yields are: A web of checks restrains a judge's power; and If he or she wishes to maximize his or her ability to do good, a judge must learn to cope with those restrictions, to work within and around them, and to conserve available resources for the times when he or she must, as a matter of conscience, directly challenge what he or she sees as a threat to the basic values of constitutional democracy.

Bibliography

BICKEL, ALEXANDER M.   1957   *The Unpublished Opinions of Mr. Justice Brandeis.* Cambridge, Mass.: Harvard University Press.
_____   1961   The Passive Virtues. *Harvard Law Review* 75:40–79.
DOUGLAS, WILLIAM O.   1980   *The Court Years, 1939–1975.* New York: Random House.
KLUGER, RICHARD   1976   *Simple Justice.* New York: Knopf.
MURPHY, BRUCE   1982   *The Brandeis/Frankfurter Connection.* New York: Oxford University Press.
MURPHY, WALTER F.   1964   *Elements of Judicial Strategy.* Chicago: University of Chicago Press.
O'BRIEN, DAVID M.   1986   *Storm Center: The Supreme Court in American Politics.* New York: Norton.

IMPACT OF SUPREME COURT DECISIONS

Stephen L. Wasby

The Supreme Court's decisions have regularly embroiled it in controversy. Its rulings have considerable impact. In its early years, the Court, over strenuous objection from the states, shaped our federal system and helped establish the national government's supremacy. The Court also had substantial effects on the economy, aiding in the creation of an American economic common market and providing opportunities for the private sector to develop. The Court's major effects on FEDERALISM and the economy subsided after the 1930s. However, its effect on CIVIL RIGHTS, visible earlier with respect to slavery and its emasculation of Reconstruction civil rights statutes, again became apparent as questions such as school DESEGREGATION came to the fore in the 1950s.

The Supreme Court's impact includes ways in which federal and state agencies and lower federal and state courts carry out the Court's decisions, but it also includes the ways in which the agencies and courts delay, circumvent, misunderstand, and erode them. It includes the response to decisions by different "populations"—those who explain or elaborate its rulings, those supposed to apply or implement them, those for whom the rulings are intended, and the general population. Because the Court, "the least dangerous branch," lacks the capacity to enforce its rulings directly, assistance from those at whom a ruling is directed or from others (legislatures, executive agencies, courts) is required. The Court is now recognized to be a political actor, but one must abandon the tacit assumption held by earlier scholars that Supreme Court decisions are self-executing and recognize that the law is what the judges say it is only after all others have had their say.

Impact and compliance are not identical but are related. Compliance, the process by which individuals accept a decision prior to its impact or effect, cannot occur unless a person knows of the ruling and is required to take or abstain from a certain action. Compliance means an individual's intentionally conforming behavior to the ruling's dictates, that is, doing what the decision commands because of the ruling. Because noncompliance, or refusal to obey, occurs relatively seldom despite the attention it receives, it is important to pay heed to implementation of decisions, the process by which they are put into effect. Short-run resistance may blend into longer-run obedience, as resulted in the aftermath of the REAPPORTIONMENT decisions.

Impact includes all effects, direct and indirect, resulting from a ruling of the Court, regardless of whether those affected knew about the decision; it includes the results of rulings permitting but not requiring the adoption of certain policies. When effects of a ruling indirectly induce behavior congruent with the ruling, that behavior is better viewed as impact than as compliance. Impact encompasses actions neither directly defiant nor clearly obedient, such as attempts at evasion coupled with technical obedience and efforts to anticipate the Court's decisions ("anticipatory compliance"). Impact also includes both short-term and long-run consequences of a decision, for example, massive resistance to school desegregation rulings and the rulings' arguable contribution to "white flight" to the suburbs. There will also be situations in which no response occurs, that is, where there is an absence of obvious impact.

The Supreme Court's effect on the President has generally been one of support and reinforcement. The Court has been least willing to overturn his acts in time of war, when presidential resistance to Court decisions would be most likely. Although limiting somewhat the President's authority to remove certain government employees, the Court, since the New Deal, has sustained DELEGATIONS OF POWER to the President and the executive branch and has generally been deferential to the REGULATORY COMMISSIONS since World War II. Confrontations between Court and President have been relatively infrequent; when the Court invalidates policies the President had espoused, for example, WIRETAPPING, it is not attacking the presidency as an institution. Presidents may have been reluctant to assist in enforcing the Court's decisions, but direct defiance is rare indeed. Both President HARRY S. TRUMAN and President RICHARD M. NIXON complied with orders when their actions (seizure of the steel mills and withholding of tapes) were ruled improper. In those situations, as with IMPOUNDMENT of appropriated funds, the Court insisted that the President follow the law as interpreted by the courts rather than determine for himself whether he should be subject to it; in the case of the STEEL SEIZURE, the Court insisted that he follow a course of action legislated by Congress.

The Court has had considerable impact on Congress's internal processes—its authority to exclude members, LEGISLATIVE INVESTIGATIONS, and the CONTEMPT POWER. Congressional reaction to the Court's decisions has been manifested in a number of ways. After the Court has engaged in statutory interpretation or, less frequently, has invalidated statutes for VAGUENESS, Congress has often rewritten or reenacted the laws to reestablish its "legislative intent," in effect establishing a continuing dialogue between Court and Congress. Congress has also shown negative reaction to the Court's ruling through proposals to eliminate APPELLATE

JURISDICTION in particular classes of cases, for example, internal security, abortions, and school prayer, but these attempts have been less frequent and far less successful than those to rewrite statutes. Efforts to overturn the Court's rulings have also resulted in introduction of numerous proposals to amend the Constitution, but most such proposals die. Only a few—the ELEVENTH AMENDMENT, Civil War Amendments, SIXTEENTH AMENDMENT, and TWENTY-SIXTH AMENDMENT—have been both submitted and ratified.

The impact of the Supreme Court's decisions extends well beyond the other branches of the national government. Controversial Supreme Court rulings have affected public opinion and have produced divided editorial reaction on a wide range of decisions. Changes in the public's feelings of trust or confidence in the Court have paralleled changes in feeling about the presidency and Congress but generally have been somewhat more positive. Such ratings have changed rapidly, but shifts in the Court's doctrine on controversial topics (such as CRIMINAL PROCEDURE) in the direction of public opinion usually are not immediately reflected in changed public opinion ratings.

The public generally supports the Court's work. Those giving the Court general (or "diffuse") support, however, outnumber those giving the Court specific support (for particular rulings) by a large ratio. The proportion of the public that feels the Court may legitimately produce structural political change is quite small. Acquiescence in the Court's rulings, which helps produce compliance, has been more common than active approval of the decisions.

The public also has little information about the Court. Even many controversial decisions fail to penetrate the general public's consciousness. The greater the knowledge, however, the greater the *dis*approval, but those reporting negative views on specific cases outnumber those whose general view of the Court is negative. Those with negative views also tend to hold them more intensely, but seldom would most members of the public do more than write letters of protest; demonstrations and other overt protest are atypical. Negative views about the Court are usually accounted for by reactions to the few specific decisions that catch the attention of large proportions of the public. Those salient decisions change with considerable rapidity, shifting in the 1960s from civil rights and school prayer to criminal procedure.

The Supreme Court's impact on the states and local communities is varied. Effectuating many decisions involves little controversy, and implementation may be prompt and complete, particularly if actions of only a few public officials are necessary. Other rulings, such as those on school DESEGREGATION, school prayer, and criminal procedure, produce a disproportionate amount both of resistance or attempts to evade and of critical rhetoric—rhetoric at times not matched by reality. Despite claims that the warnings required by MIRANDA V. ARIZONA (1966) would have a negative impact on police work, suspects and defendants often talk to police after being "read their rights." However, even these criticized rulings have definite impacts, for example, more professional police work as a result of criminal procedure rulings. Although opponents of the rule that improperly seized evidence should be excluded (the EXCLUSIONARY RULE of MAPP V. OHIO, 1961) have claimed that the rule does not deter illegal seizures and is too costly because guilty defendants are set free, some studies have suggested that the rule might be having some of its intended effect. At least in some cities, few cases were dropped after motions to suppress evidence and a higher proportion of searches conducted after the rule was promulgated were constitutional.

If people are to comply with Supreme Court rulings or if the rulings are to have an impact, they must be communicated to those expected to implement or adhere to them. One cannot, however, assume that effective communication takes place. A ruling may have to be transmitted through several levels, at each of which distortion can be introduced, before reaching its ultimate audience. Lawyers may be accustomed to easy access to the Court's published opinions, but many others, such as police or school officials, often do not receive the opinions or have such direct access to them and must therefore rely on other means of communication through which to learn of them.

The mass media, with the exception of a few newspapers, provide only sketchy information about the Court's decisions. Specialized media, for example, trade publications, provide only erratic coverage even of decisions relevant to the groups for which they are published. Most newspapers and radio and television stations must rely on the wire services for information about Supreme Court rulings. Disproportionate nationwide emphasis is given to decisions the wire services emphasize, with little or no coverage given to other rulings. The media also have different patterns of coverage ("profiles"). Newspapers, for example, give more attention to postdecision events, while the wire services and television pay more attention to cases before they are decided. All the media, however, generally convey much information about immediate reaction to, or impact of, decisions instead of emphasizing the content of, or rationale for, the Court's rulings.

The lower courts do not constitute a bureaucratic structure through which decisions are fully communicated downward. Lawyers thus become particularly important in transmitting the Court's rulings, as they are in transmitting any law. Lower court judges who do not routinely follow the Court's decisions may find out about them only if lawyers arguing cases cite the decisions, which they do not always do accurately. Lawyers, either individually or through their bar associations, do little to inform the general public about developments in the law. Some state attorneys general and local prosecutors undertake to inform state and local officials of recent rulings affecting their work. The failure of these officials to do so in most locations has led some local agencies, which can afford to do so, to hire their own lawyers, for example, police department "police legal advisers," to monitor the Court's rulings, provide appropriate information to the agency, and arrange for implementation.

Training programs—effective because they combine printed materials with oral presentation—can be particularly important in the transmission of rulings. They are especially necessary because the educational system has generally done little to educate students, later to be members of the general public, about the Court's functioning or its rulings. Training programs are, however, not available to all those expected to be cognizant or familiar with the Court's rulings. Many members of some important occupational groups such as the police do not receive adequate legal training about the Court's decisions. Even if initially well-trained, they are less likely to receive adequate follow-up through in-service training.

The impact of the Court's decisions is, of course, affected by far more than deficiencies and distortions in the lengthy, often convoluted process by which the decisions are communicated. Numerous other factors affect both the communication process, thus indirectly affecting impact, and impact itself. One is the legitimacy attributed to the Court and its work. If a particular audience, for example, the police during the WARREN COURT's "criminal procedure revolution," feels that the Court is not acting fairly or lacks appropriate information on which to base its decisions, that audience will heed the Court's word less carefully even when the opinions are fully communicated. Characteristics of the Court's rulings, such as their relative unanimity and relative clarity or ambiguity, are also important, as both unanimity and clarity are thought to produce greater compliance. In new and sensitive areas of policy such as civil rights and criminal procedure, the lower courts can exercise power over the Supreme Court by their resistance. Rulings by lower court judges applying and extending (or narrowing) the Court's decisions are particularly important in such situations and in those where gaps in doctrinal development—a result of case-by-case development of the law—leave unanswered questions. In many, perhaps most, areas of the law, however, lower court judges enforce Supreme Court rulings because those rulings are a matter of relative personal indifference for the judges, because they have been socialized to follow those rulings, and because they wish to avoid being reversed.

Whether someone follows up a decision, who that "someone" is, and how they act, also affect a decision's impact. Elites' support for a decision may be able to calm negative public reaction. The likelihood that desegregation would be accepted in either the short or long run was decreased because southern elites were not favorably disposed toward either the result of BROWN v. BOARD OF EDUCATION (1954) or the Court's opinion. Because most rulings of the Court are not self-enforcing, follow-up by government agencies is often crucial for effective implementation. Officials not committed to the values in the Court's rulings are less likely to be assiduous in their follow-up; thus the attitudes of individual decision makers, particularly those in key policymaking or enforcement positions, are of considerable importance.

The situation into which a Supreme Court ruling is "injected"— whether in a crisis or in normal times—also affects the ruling's impact. A local community's belief system and its past history both are part of that situation. So are community pressures on the individuals expected to carry out the Court's dictates. Often a wide variety of enforcement mechanisms must be used before compliance is achieved. Incentive systems in organizations can lead individuals either to follow the Court's rulings or to continue existing practices. Because organizations have considerable interest in maintaining such practices, externally imposed penalties may be insufficient to produce required change.

To overcome problems of communicating Supreme Court rulings so that they reach the appropriate audience might seem insuperable. The Court's rulings are, however, often complied with and do have widespread impact. Were it otherwise, we should not hear so much about the problems occurring in particularly sensitive areas of the law such as civil rights and CIVIL LIBERTIES. The difficulties in implementing the Court's decisions to achieve their greatest impact should remind us that, as an active policymaker, the Supreme Court faces many of the same problems faced by other policymaking institutions.

Bibliography

BECKER, THEODORE L. and FEELEY, MALCOLM, EDS.   1973   *The Impact of Supreme Court Decisions: Empirical Studies,* 2nd ed. New York: Oxford University Press.

JOHNSON, CHARLES A. and CANON, BRADLEY C. 1984   *Judicial Policies: Implementation and Impact.* Washington D.C.: Congressional Quarterly Press.

KRISLOV, SAMUEL, ED.   1972   *Compliance and the Law: A Multidisciplinary Approach.* Beverly Hills, Calif.: Sage Publications.

WASBY, STEPHEN L.   1970   *The Impact of the United States Supreme Court: Some Perspectives.* Homewood, Ill.: Dorsey Press.

APPOINTMENT OF SUPREME COURT JUSTICES

Henry J. Abraham

Under Article II, section 2, of the Constitution, Supreme Court Justices, like all other federal judges, are nominated and, with the ADVICE AND CONSENT of the Senate, appointed by the President. No other textual mandate, either procedural or substantive, governs the Chief Executive's selection. However, section 1 of Article III—which deals exclusively with the judicial branch of the government—provides GOOD BEHAVIOR tenure for all federal judges; in effect, that means appointment for life. As additional security, that provision of the Constitution provides that the compensation of federal judges "shall not be diminished during their Continuance in Office." But neither the Constitution nor any federal statute provides any clue as to qualifications for office; neither a law degree nor any other proof of professional capability is formally required. But in practice none other than lawyers are appointable to the federal judiciary, in general, and the Supreme Court, in particular. All of the 102 individuals who sat on that highest tribunal through 1985 held degrees from a school of law or had been admitted to the bar via examination. Indeed, although all the Justices were members of the professional bar in good standing at the time of their appointment, it was not until 1922 that a majority of sitting Justices was composed of law school graduates, and not until 1957 that every Justice was a law school graduate. Once confirmed by the Senate, a Justice is removable only via IMPEACHMENT (by simple majority vote by the House of Representatives) and subsequent conviction (by two-thirds vote of the Senate, there being a quorum on the floor). Only one Justice of the Supreme Court has been impeached by the House—Justice SAMUEL CHASE, by a 72–32 vote in 1804—but he was acquitted on all eight charges by the Senate in 1805. To all intents and purposes, once appointed, a Supreme Court Justice serves as long as he or she wishes—typically until illness or death intervenes.

Theoretically, the President has *carte blanche* in selecting his nominees to the Court. In practice, three facts of political life inform and limit his choices. The first is that it is not realistically feasible for the

Chief Executive to designate a Justice and obtain confirmation by the Senate without the at least grudging approval by the two home state senators concerned, especially if the latter are members of the President's own political party. The time-honored practice of "Senatorial courtesy" is an omnipresent phenomenon, because of senatorial camaraderie and the "blue slip" approval system, under which the Judiciary Committee normally will not favorably report a nominee to the floor if an objecting home-state senator has failed to return that slip. (Senator Edward Kennedy, during his two-year tenure as head of the Committee, abandoned the system in 1979, but it was partly restored by his successor, Senator Strom Thurmond, in 1981.) Although nominations to the Supreme Court are regarded as a personal province of presidential choice far more than the appointment of other judges, the Senate's "advice and consent" is neither routine nor perfunctory, to which recent history amply attests. In 1968, despite a favorable Judiciary Committee vote, the Senate refused to consent to President Johnson's promotion of Justice ABE FORTAS to the Chief Justiceship; in 1969 it rejected President RICHARD M. NIXON's nomination of Judge Clement Haynsworth, Jr., by 55 to 45; and in 1970 it turned down that same President's selection of Judge G. Harrold Carswell by 51 to 45. Indeed, to date the Senate, for a variety of reasons, has refused to confirm twenty-seven Supreme Court nominees out of the total of 139 sent to it for its "advice and consent" (twenty-one of these during the nineteenth century).

The second major factor to be taken into account by the President is the evaluative role played by the American Bar Association's fourteen-member Committee on the Federal Judiciary, which has been an unofficial part of the judicial appointments process since 1946. The committee scrutinizes the qualifications of all nominees to the federal bench and normally assigns one of four "grades": Exceptionally Well Qualified, Well Qualified, Qualified, and Not Qualified. In the rare instances of a vacancy on the Supreme Court, however, the committee has in recent years adopted a different, threefold, categorization: "High Standards of Integrity, Judicial Temperament, and Professional Competence"; "Not Opposed"; and "Not Qualified."

The third consideration incumbent upon the Chief Executive is the subtle but demonstrable one of the influence, however *sub rosa* and *sotto voce,* of sitting and retired jurists. Recent research points convincingly to that phenomenon, personified most prominently by Chief Justice WILLIAM HOWARD TAFT. If Taft did not exactly "appoint" colleagues to vacancies that occurred during his nine-year tenure (1921–1930), he assuredly vetoed those unacceptable to him. Among others also involved in advisory or lobbying roles, although on a lesser scale than Taft, were Chief Justices CHARLES EVANS HUGHES, HARLAN F. STONE, FRED VINSON, EARL WARREN, and WARREN E. BURGER and Associate

Justices John Marshall Harlan I, Samuel F. Miller, Willis Van Devanter, Louis D. Brandeis, and Felix Frankfurter.

A composite portrait of the 101 men and one woman who have been Justices of the Supreme Court provides the following cross-section: native-born: 96; male: 101 (the first woman, Sandra Day O'Connor, was appointed by President Ronald Reagan in the summer of 1981); white: 101 (the first black Justice, Thurgood Marshall, was appointed by President Lyndon B. Johnson in 1967); predominantly Protestant: 91 (there have been six Roman Catholic and five Jewish Justices—the first in each category were Andrew Jackson's appointment of Chief Justice Roger B. Taney in 1836 and Woodrow Wilson's of Louis D. Brandeis in 1916, respectively); 50–55 years of age at time of appointment (the two youngest have been Joseph Story, 33, in 1812 and William O. Douglas, 41, in 1939); of Anglo-Saxon ethnic stock (all except fifteen); from an upper middle to high social status (all except a handful); reared in a nonrural but not necessarily urban environment; member of a civic-minded, politically aware, economically comfortable family (all except a handful); holders of B.A. and, in this century, LL.B. or J.D. degrees (with one-third from "Ivy League" institutions); and a background of at least some type of public or community service (all except Justice George Shiras). Contemporary recognition of egalitarianism and "representativeness" may alter this profile, but it is not likely to change radically.

Only the President and his close advisers know the actual motivations for the choice of a particular Supreme Court appointee. But a perusal of the records of the thirty-five Presidents who nominated Justices (four—W. H. Harrison, Zachary Taylor, Andrew Johnson, and Jimmy Carter—had no opportunity to do so) points to several predominating criteria, most apparent of which have been: (1) objective merit; (2) personal friendship; (3) considerations of "representativeness"; (4) political ideological compatibility, what Theodore Roosevelt referred to as a selectee's "real politics"; and (5) past judicial experience. Appropriate examples of (1) would be Benjamin N. Cardozo (Herbert Hoover) and John Marshall Harlan (Dwight D. Eisenhower); of (2) Harold H. Burton (Harry S. Truman) and Abe Fortas (Lyndon Johnson); of (4) Hugo Black (Franklin D. Roosevelt) and William Howard Taft (Warren G. Harding); of (5) Oliver Wendell Holmes (Theodore Roosevelt) and David J. Brewer (Benjamin Harrison). Deservedly most contentious is motivation (3), under which Presidents have been moved to weigh such "equitable" factors as geography, religion, gender, race, and perhaps even age in order to provide a "representative" profile of the Court. Of uncertain justification, it is nonetheless a fact of life of the appointive process. Thus geography proved decisive in Franklin D. Roosevelt's selection of Wiley Rutledge of Iowa ("Wiley, you have

geography," Roosevelt told him) and ABRAHAM LINCOLN's selection of
STEPHEN J. FIELD of California. But given the superb qualifications of
Judge Cardozo, despite the presence of two other New Yorkers (Hughes
and Stone), the former's selection was all but forced upon Hoover. The
notion that there should be a "Roman Catholic" and "Jewish" seat has
been present ever since the appointments of Taney and Brandeis. Although there have been periods without such "reserved" seats (for example, 1949–1956 in the former case and since 1965 in the latter), Presidents
are aware of the insistent pressures for such "representation." These
pressures have increased since the "establishment" of a "black" seat (Marshall in 1967, by Johnson) and a "woman's seat" (O'Connor, by Reagan,
in 1981). It has become all but unthinkable that future Supreme Court
lineups will not henceforth have "representatives" from such categories.
That the Founding Fathers neither considered nor addressed any of
these "representative" factors does not gainsay their presence and significance in the political process.

Whatever may be the merits of other criteria motivating presidential
Supreme Court appointments, the key factor is the Chief Executive's
perception of a candidate's "real" politics—for it is the nominee's likely
voting pattern as a Justice that matters most to an incumbent President.
To a greater or lesser extent, all Presidents have thus attempted to
"pack" the bench. Court-packing has been most closely associated with
Franklin D. Roosevelt. Failing a single opportunity to fill a Court vacancy
during his first term (and five months of his second), and seeing his
domestic programs consistently battered by "the Nine Old Men," Roosevelt moved to get his way in one fell swoop with his "Court Packing
Bill" of 1937; however, it was reported unfavorably by the Senate Judiciary Committee and was interred by a decisive recommittal vote. Ultimately, the passage of time enabled him to fill nine vacancies between
1937 and 1943. Yet GEORGE WASHINGTON was able to nominate fourteen,
of whom ten chose to serve, and his selectees were measured against a
sextet of criteria: (1) support and advocacy of the Constitution; (2) distinguished service in the revolution; (3) active participation in the political
life of the new nation; (4) prior judicial experience on lower tribunals;
(5) either a "favorable reputation with his fellows" or personal ties with
Washington himself; and (6) geographic "suitability." Whatever the specific predispositions may be, concern with a nominee's "real" politics
has been and will continue to be crucial in presidential motivations. It
even prompted Republican President Taft to award half of his six nominations to the Court to Democrats, who were kindred "real politics" souls
(HORACE H. LURTON, EDWARD D. WHITE's promotion to Chief Justice,
and JOSEPH R. LAMAR). In ten other instances the appointee came from
a formal political affiliation other than that of the appointer, ranging
from Whig President JOHN TYLER's appointment of Democrat SAMUEL

NELSON in 1845 to Republican Richard M. Nixon's selection of Democrat LEWIS F. POWELL, JR., in 1971.

But to predict the ultimate voting pattern or behavior of a nominee is to lean upon a slender reed. In the characteristically blunt words of President Truman: "Packing the Supreme Court simply can't be done. . . . I've tried and it won't work. . . . Whenever you put a man on the Supreme Court he ceases to be your friend. I'm sure of that." There is indeed a considerable element of unpredictability in the judicial appointment process. To the question whether a judicial robe makes a person any different, Justice Frankfurter's sharp retort was always, "If he is any good, he does!" In ALEXANDER M. BICKEL's words, "You shoot an arrow into a far-distant future when you appoint a Justice and not the man himself can tell you what he will think about some of the problems that he will face." And late in 1969, reflecting upon his sixteen years as Chief Justice of the United States, Earl Warren pointed out that he, for one, did not "see how a man could be on the Court and not change his views substantially over a period of years . . . for change you must if you are to do your duty on the Supreme Court." It is clear beyond doubt that the Supreme Court appointment process is fraught with imponderables and guesswork, notwithstanding the carefully composed constitutional obligations of President and Senate.

Bibliography

ABRAHAM, HENRY J.   1985   *Justices and Presidents: A Political History of Appointments to the Supreme Court,* 2nd ed. New York: Oxford University Press.

———   1986   *The Judicial Process: An Introductory Analysis of the Courts of the United States, England and France,* 5th ed. New York: Oxford University Press.

DANELSKI, DAVID J.   1964   *A Supreme Court Justice Is Appointed.* New York: Random House.

SCHMIDHAUSER, JOHN R.   1960   *The Supreme Court: Its Politics, Personalities and Procedures.* New York: Holt, Rinehart & Winston.

———   1979   *Judges and Justices: The Federal Appellate Judiciary.* Boston: Little, Brown.

CONGRESS AND THE SUPREME COURT

Gary L. McDowell

The delegates to the CONSTITUTIONAL CONVENTION OF 1787 confronted two fundamental problems in their quest to correct the political defects of the ARTICLES OF CONFEDERATION. First, they needed to bolster the powers of government at the national level so as to transform the "league of friendship" created by the Articles into a government with all the coercive powers requisite to government. Second, the Framers sought to create energetic but limited powers that would enable the new national government to govern, but in ways safe to the rights of the people. As JAMES MADISON put it in THE FEDERALIST #51, the task was to "enable the government to control the governed, but in the next place oblige it to control itself."

Their successful solution to this political problem was to separate the powers of government. Because the primary source of trouble in a popular form of government would be the legislative branch, the object was to bolster the coordinate executive and judicial branches, to offer "some more adequate defence . . . for the more feeble, against the more powerful members of the government." The arrangement of checked and balanced institutions would at once avoid "a tyrannical concentration of all the powers of government in the same hands" while rendering the administration of the national government more efficient.

When the Framers examined the existing federal system under the Articles to determine precisely what it was that rendered it "altogether unfit for the administration of the affairs of the Union," the want of an independent judiciary "crown[ed] the defects of the confederation." As ALEXANDER HAMILTON put it in *The Federalist* #22, "Laws are a dead letter without courts to expound and define their true meaning and operation." Thus the improved science of politics offered by the friends of the Constitution prominently included provision for "the institution of courts composed of judges, holding their offices during good behavior."

But to some Anti-Federalist critics of the Federalist-backed Constitution, the judiciary was too independent and too powerful. To the New York Anti-Federalist "Brutus," the proposed judiciary possessed such independence as to allow the courts to "mould the government into

100

almost any shape they please." The "Federal Farmer" was equally critical: his fellow citizens were "more in danger of sowing the seeds of arbitrary government in this department than in any other." With such unanticipated criticism, the Federalists were forced to defend the judicial power more elaborately than had been done in the early pages of *The Federalist*.

So compelling were the Anti-Federalist arguments that Hamilton saw fit to explain and defend the proposed judicial power in no fewer than six separate essays (#78–83) in *The Federalist*. His task was to show how an independent judiciary was not only *not* a threat to safe popular government but was absolutely essential to it. In making his now famous argument in *The Federalist* #78 that the judiciary would be that branch of the new government "least dangerous to the political rights of the Constitution," Hamilton made the case that the courts were "designed to be an intermediate body between the people and the legislature, in order, among other things, to keep the latter within the limits assigned to their authority." By exercising neither force nor will but merely judgment, the courts would prove to be the "bulwarks of a limited constitution." Such an institution, Hamilton argued, politically independent yet constitutionally rooted, was essential to resist the overwhelming power of the majority of the community. Only with such a constitutional defense could the rights of individuals and of minor parties be protected against majority tyranny; only an independent judiciary could allow the powers of the national government to be sufficiently enhanced, while simultaneously checking the unhealthy impulses of majority rule that had characterized politics at the state level under the Articles.

To counter the Anti-Federalist complaint that the courts would be imperiously independent, Hamilton reminded them that the courts would not be simply freewheeling sources of arbitrary judgments and decrees. The Constitution, in giving Congress the power to regulate the APPELLATE JURISDICTION of the Supreme Court "with such exceptions, and under such regulations, as the Congress shall make," hedged against too expansive a conception of judicial power. "To avoid an arbitrary discretion in the courts," Hamilton noted, "it is indispensable that they should be bound down by strict rules and precedents, which serve to define and point out their duty in every particular case that comes before them." Thus the stage was set for a history of political confrontation between the Congress and the Court.

The tension between Congress and the Court has been a constant part of American politics at least since CHISHOLM V. GEORGIA (1793) led to the ELEVENTH AMENDMENT. Each generation has seen dramatic Supreme Court rulings that have prompted political cries to curb the courts. JOHN MARSHALL's now celebrated opinions in MARBURY V. MADISON (1803) and McCULLOCH V. MARYLAND (1819), for example, caused him a good bit of political grief when he wrote them; the decision in

DRED SCOTT V. SANDFORD (1857) soon came to be viewed as a judicially "self-inflicted wound" that weakened the Court and exacerbated the conflict that descended into civil war; and more recently, protests against the rulings in BROWN V. BOARD OF EDUCATION (1954) and ROE V. WADE (1973) have caused not only political demands for retaliation against the Court but social conflict and even violence as well. But through it all the Court has weathered the hostility with its independence intact.

Only once were the critics successful in persuading Congress to act against the Court, and the Court validated that move. In EX PARTE MCCARDLE (1869) the Court confirmed Congress's power to withdraw a portion of the Court's appellate jurisdiction. Fearing that the Court would use William McCardle's petition for a writ of HABEAS CORPUS under the HABEAS CORPUS ACT OF 1867 as a vehicle for invalidating the Reconstruction Acts *in toto,* the Congress repealed that portion of the act under which McCardle had brought his action—and after the Court had heard arguments in the case. The Court upheld the constitutionality of Congress's action in repealing this particular part of the Court's JURIS-DICTION. The extent of Congress's power to withdraw the Court's appellate jurisdiction remains a matter of constitutional controversy.

The constitutional relationship between Congress and the Court is one thing; their political relationship is another matter. Although there are often loud cries for reaction against the Court, the critics usually lack sufficient force to achieve political retribution. The reason is most often explained as a matter of political prudence. The courts by their decisions frequently irritate a portion of the community—but usually only a portion. For most decisions will satisfy certain public constituencies that are as vociferous as the critics. Even the most errant exercises of judicial decision making are rarely sufficient to undermine the public respect for the idea of an independent judiciary.

The reason for this is simple enough: an independent judiciary makes good political sense. To make the judiciary too much dependent upon "popularity" as that popularity may be reflected in Congress would be to lower the constitutional barriers to congressional power, barriers generally agreeable to most people most of the time. The arguments of Hamilton in *The Federalist* still carry considerable weight.

Thus in the constitutional design of separating the powers of government through the device of "partial agency"—mingling the powers enough to give each branch some control over the others—is to be found the inevitable gulf between legitimate power and prudent restraint. For Congress to be persuaded to restrict judicial power, the case must first be made that such restrictions are both necessary and proper.

Despite the dangers of legislative power, it was still considered by the Framers to be the cardinal principle of POPULAR SOVEREIGNTY. Basic to this principle is the belief that it is legitimate for the people through the instrumentality of law to adjust, check, or enhance certain institutions of the government. This belief embraces the power of the legislature to exert some control over the structure and administration of the executive and judicial branches.

The qualified power of the legislature to tamper with the judiciary is not so grave a danger to the balance of the Constitution as some see it. For even when a judicial decision runs counter to particular—and perhaps pervasive—political interests, the institutional arrangements of the Constitution are such as to slow down the popular outrage and give the people time for "more cool and sedate reflection." And given the distance between the people and LEGISLATION afforded by such devices as REPRESENTATION (with its multiplicity of interests), BICAMERALISM, and the executive VETO POWER, an immediate legislative backlash to judicial behavior is unlikely. Experience demonstrates that any backlash at all is likely to be "weak and ineffectual." But if the negative response is not merely transient and is widely and deeply felt, then the Constitution wisely provides well-defined mechanisms for a deliberate political reaction to what the people hold to be intolerable judicial excesses.

But ultimately the history of court-curbing efforts in America, from the failed IMPEACHMENT of Justice SAMUEL CHASE to the Court-packing plan of FRANKLIN D. ROOSEVELT, teaches one basic lesson: the American political system generally operates to the advantage of the judiciary. Presidential court-packing is ineffective as a means of exerting political influence, and impeachment is too difficult to use as an everyday check against unpopular decisions. Not since John Marshall saw fit pseudonymously to defend his opinion in *McCulloch v. Maryland* (1819) in the public press has any Justice or judge felt obliged to respond to public outrage over a decision.

Political responses to perceived excesses of judicial power tend to take one of two forms: either a policy response against a particular decision or an institutional response against the structure and powers of the courts. In either event, the response may be either partisan or principled. Usually a policy response will take the form of a proposed constitutional amendment or statute designed to overrule a decision. An institutional response will generally seek to make jurisdictional exceptions, to create special courts with specific jurisdiction, or to make adjustments regarding the personnel, administration, or procedures of the judicial branch. Whatever the response, court-curbing is difficult. Although a majority of one of the houses of Congress may object to particular cases of "judicial impertinence," as one congressman viewed Justice DAVID DAVIS's controversial opinion in EX PARTE MILLIGAN (1866), a variety of objections will issue in different views of what should be done.

On the whole, there has consistently been a consensus that tampering with judicial independence is a serious matter and that rash reprisals against the Court as an institution may upset the constitutional balance. Underlying the occasional outbursts of angry public sentiment against the court is that "moral force" of the community of which ALEXIS DE TOCQUEVILLE wrote. On the whole, the American people continue to view the judiciary as the "boast of the Constitution."

For any political attempt to adjust or limit the judicial power to be successful it is necessary that it be—and be perceived to be—a principled rather than a merely partisan response. Only then will the issue of JUDICIAL ACTIVISM be met on a ground high enough to transcend the more common—and generally fruitless—debates over judicial liberalism and conservatism. The deepest issue is not whether a particular decision or even a particular court is too liberal for some and too conservative for others; the point is whether the courts are exercising their powers capably and legitimately. Keeping the courts constitutionally legitimate and institutionally capable benefits both the liberal and the conservative elements in American politics.

The system the Framers devised is so structured that the branch the Framers thought "least dangerous" is not so malleable in the hands of Congress as to be powerless. Yet the threat of congressional restriction of the Court remains, a threat that probably helps to keep an otherwise largely unfettered institution within constitutional bounds.

Bibliography

BERGER, RAOUL 1969 *Congress versus the Supreme Court.* Cambridge, Mass.: Harvard University Press.

BRECKENRIDGE, A. C. 1971 *Congress Against the Court.* Lincoln: University of Nebraska Press.

MORGAN, DONALD L. 1967 *Congress and the Constitution.* Cambridge, Mass.: Harvard University Press.

MURPHY, WALTER F. 1962 *Congress and the Courts.* Chicago: University of Chicago Press.

LEGISLATION

Paul Brest

In addition to the separation of powers, there are at least two intersections of the Constitution and the legislative process. One concerns the obligation and capacity of legislatures to assess the constitutionality of their proposed enactments. The other concerns the federal judiciary's role in inducing legislatures to meet their constitutional obligations. Within this context there are issues common to state and congressional lawmaking.

The American constitutional scheme obligates legislatures to assess the constitutionality of proposed enactments and to enact only legislation they deem constitutionally permissible. Although this proposition may seem obvious, it has often been contradicted by respectable lawmakers, who assert that legislatures should engage in policymaking without regard to the Constitution and leave constitutional questions exclusively to the courts. Therefore the reasons that legislatures are obligated, no less than courts, to determine the constitutionality of proposed enactments deserve explanation.

If, as Chief Justice JOHN MARSHALL asserted in MARBURY V. MADISON (1803), the Constitution is a law paramount to ordinary legislation, then to assert that legislatures need not consult the Constitution is the equivalent of asserting that individuals need not consult the law before acting. To be sure, people sometimes act in disregard of the law, subject only to the risk of sanctions if they are caught and a court holds their actions to be unlawful. But it would be perverse to conclude from this observation that we are not obligated to obey the law.

The structure and text of the Constitution certainly imply that legislatures must initially determine the legality of their enactments. For example, how would Congress know whether it had the authority to enact a bill without consulting Article I and the other provisions that delegate limited powers to the national government? Indeed, some provisions of the Constitution are explicitly addressed to legislators. Article I, section 9, provides, "No bill of attainder or ex post facto law shall be passed." The FIRST AMENDMENT says, "Congress shall make no law," and the FOURTEENTH AMENDMENT's prohibitions begin with the words, "No state shall make or enforce any law. . . ." Article VI binds legislators and officials "by Oath or Affirmation to support this Constitution. . . ." Although this command does not entail that all constitutional questions are open to all institutions at all times, it does imply that a legislator must vote only for legislation that he or she believes is authorized by the Constitution. If history matters, the obligation of legislatures to interpret the Constitution was affirmed and acted on by various of the Framers and by early legislators and Presidents—some of whom, indeed, expressed this duty or prerogative even in the face of contrary judicial interpretations.

The existence of JUDICIAL REVIEW is sometimes thought to relieve legislatures of the obligations to determine the constitutionality of their enactments. But Chief Justice Marshall's classic justifications for judicial review in *Marbury* do not necessarily imply a privileged judicial function. As Herbert Wechsler wrote: "Federal courts, including the Supreme Court, do not pass on constitutional questions because there is a special function vested in them to enforce the Constitution or police the other agencies of government. They do so rather for the reason that they must decide a litigated issue that is otherwise within their jurisdiction and in doing so they must give effect to the supreme law of the land. That is, at least, what *Marbury v. Madison* was all about." (Wechsler, 1965, p. 1006.) Other arguments for judicial review have accorded the judiciary a special role, and in COOPER V. AARON (1958) the modern Court claimed that it was "supreme in the exposition of the law of the Constitution." But the Court has never implied that JUDICIAL SUPREMACY implies judicial exclusively, or that its privileged position relieves other institutions of the responsibility for making constitutional judgments.

Indeed, some constitutional issues—so-called POLITICAL QUESTIONS— may be committed to the legislative and executive branches to the exclusion of the judiciary. For example, it is widely assumed that the Senate's judgment in an IMPEACHMENT proceeding is not reviewable by the courts even though the decision may involve controverted constitutional questions, and even though the Senate's role in cases of impeachment is more judicial than legislative. In such cases, at least, if the legislature does not consider the constitutional questions, no one will.

If legislatures are obligated to consider constitutional questions, what deference, if any, should they accord prior judicial interpretations of the Constitution? In what might be called the judicial supremacy view, a legislature is in essentially the same position as a state or lower federal court: it must treat the Supreme Court's rulings as authoritative and binding. This was the view expressed by the Court in *Cooper v. Aaron*. Quoting Marshall's assertion in *Marbury* that "[i]t is emphatically the province and the duty of the judicial department to say what the law is," the Justices continued: "This decision declared the basic principle that the federal judiciary is supreme in the exposition of the law of the Constitution, and that principle has ever since been respected by this Court and the Country as a permanent and indispensable feature of our constitutional system."

The polar view is that legislators and other officials may, or must, apply the Constitution according to their best lights. This position was asserted by THOMAS JEFFERSON, ANDREW JACKSON, and ABRAHAM LINCOLN, among others. In vetoing the bill to recharter the Bank of the United States in 1832, Jackson wrote:

It is maintained by advocates of the bank that its constitutionality in all its features ought to be considered settled by the decision of the Supreme Court [in McCULLOCH v. MARYLAND (1819)]. To this conclusion I can not assent. . . . The Congress, the Executive, and the Court must each for itself be guided by its own opinion of the Constitution. Each public officer who takes an oath to support the Constitution swears that he will support it as he understands it, and not as it is understood by others. It is as much the duty of the House of Representatives, of the Senate, and of the President to decide upon the constitutionality of any bill or resolution which may be presented to them for passage or approval as it is of the supreme judges when it may be brought before them for judicial decision. The opinion of the judges has no more authority over Congress than the opinion of Congress has over the judges, and on that point the President is independent of both. The authority of the Supreme Court must not, therefore, be permitted to control the Congress or the Executive when acting in their legislative capacities, but to have only such influence as the force of their reasoning may deserve.

The issues presented by these opposed positions are of more than theoretical or historical interest. They have surfaced in recent years in debates over Congress's authority under section 5 of the Fourteenth Amendment to interpret or apply the amendment differently from the Court, and over Congress's power to limit the JURISDICTION OF FEDERAL COURTS over particular issues. For present purposes, I will assume that Congress, as well as state legislatures, must operate within the constitutional doctrines exposited by the United States Supreme Court. What does this obligation entail?

The dimensions of legislative responsibility and some of the difficulties in meeting it are illustrated by considering a bill introduced in the 89th Congress to punish the destruction of draft cards. The bill was enacted in 1965, seemingly in response to public DRAFT CARD BURNING to protest the VIETNAM WAR. It was challenged on First Amendment grounds and upheld by the Court in UNITED STATES v. O'BRIEN (1968).

The governing constitutional standard (as the Court later recapitulated it in O'Brien) was that "a governmental regulation is sufficiently justified . . . if it furthers an important or substantial governmental interest; if the governmental interest is unrelated to the suppression of free expression; and if the incidental restriction on alleged First

Amendment freedoms is not greater than is essential to the furtherance of that interest."

Because this area of judicial doctrine was already well developed in 1965, legislators considering the draft card destruction law did not have to engage in much independent constitutional interpretation. They were, however, required to apply existing doctrine to the situation that faced them.

First, a legislator had to determine that his or her reasons for supporting the bill were "unrelated to the suppression of free expression." This obligation meant that he could not vote for the bill if his dominant, or causative, reason for favoring it was to suppress antiwar protests (rather than, say, to facilitate the administration of the selective service). The obligation demanded only introspection, a modicum of self-awareness, and the courage or will to follow the law.

It is worth pausing for a moment to ask why the Constitution should be concerned with a legislator's motivation in voting for a measure rather than simply with the legislation itself. The answer begins with the observation that the First Amendment is designed to protect citizens' freedom to protest against government policies. The Amendment does not, however, forbid all laws that inhibit protests to any extent. For example, the Congress surely may prohibit burning anything, including draft cards, if the activity poses a fire hazard to property that Congress has the power to protect. Thus, legislators have discretion to compromise constitutional values in the pursuit of other legitimate ends of government. However, as the Court's reference to "important or substantial" interests suggests, the First Amendment demands that a legislator treat a law's inhibition of expression as a cost, indeed a cost that should not be lightly imposed. But a legislator who votes for the bill in order to suppress protest, treats the inhibition as a benefit, not a cost. He has confused the credits and debits column on the constitutional balance sheet, for he seeks to bring about the very result that the First Amendment seeks to avert.

The second factual determination—actually a mixture of law, fact, and judgment—stems from the requirement that the law further an "important or substantial governmental interest." In *O'Brien* the Court was required to speculate about the nature and importance of the interests furthered by the draft card law. As happens frequently in matters concerning the national defense, the Court gave Congress the benefit of the doubt. But, of course, the legislators know what ends they intend a law to serve. Judgments about the importance of those ends, and how well a proposed law will actually accomplish them, are among the core responsibilities of legislators—who do not owe themselves any benefit of the doubt. It would be ironic, to say the least, if the Court deferred to Congress's judgments in these matters when Congress had not actually considered the issues carefully and in good faith.

The preceding paragraphs have not distinguished between the responsibilities of "legislators" and the "legislature." How, in fact, is responsibility for constitutional decision making allocated within the lawmaking process?

The answer seems easiest with respect to motivation. Granting that not even psychoanalysis can always reveal our deepest motivations, a conscientious legislator usually knows why he or she supports or opposes a law. (A contrary position would call into doubt the very foundations of the legislative process.) The Constitution demands that legislators assure themselves that illicit motivations, such as suppressing expression or disadvantaging racial minorities, play no role in their decisions to support the legislation. A legislator who "personally" does not care to pursue an illicit end but who supports a measure to satisfy her constituents' or colleagues' desires for those ends must be taken to have incorporated their ends as her own.

However intimately legislators know their own minds, they often lack the expertise and time to assimilate the complex factual and legal information bearing on the constitutionality of a proposed law. In the ordinary run of cases, these issues must be addressed and resolved through institutional mechanisms. A number of such mechanisms exist and are actually employed.

Federal legislation is typically drafted by lawyers and other specialists—either in an executive agency or department or in a congressional committee—who are familiar with any potential constitutional issues presented by the legislation. The committee to which a bill is referred can call upon its own legal staff or on the American Law Division of the Congressional Research Service of the Library of Congress for assistance with constitutional questions. Individual legislators can also seek advice from the research service and from their own staffs, and constitutional issues may be raised in debates on the floor of the House and Senate. Before signing a bill, the President can consult with the Office of Legal Counsel or seek an opinion from the attorney general. Although most state legislators cannot avail themselves of such rich resources, all have analogous methods for assessing the constitutionality of proposed legislation.

It is sometimes said that legislators have too little time and too much political interest to take constitutional issues seriously. Surely, however, this remark cannot justify legislative inattention to questions of constitutionality—unless one believes that legislators should be held to a lower standard of law-abidingness than individuals or enterprises, who may also lack the time or inclination to follow the law. To the extent that the observation is accurate, it is a source of concern to anyone committed to constitutional democracy.

The principal deterrent against unconstitutional legislative action is the threat of judicial invalidation of a law on the ground of its substantive unconstitutionality. From time to time, courts have also engaged in what might be called "procedural review" of legislative decisions—review that focuses on the process by which the law was enacted.

Procedural review encompasses two different inquiries. One is whether the legislators acted out of unconstitutional motives; the other is whether the legislators adequately considered the factual and legal bases for the law. Chief Justice Marshall alluded to both inquiries in *McCulloch v. Maryland* (1819). With respect to unconstitutional motivation, he wrote: "Should Congress, . . . under the pretext of executing its powers, pass laws for the accomplishment of objectives not entrusted to the government, it would become the painful duty of this tribunal . . . to say that such an act was not the law of the land." And he invoked the Executive's and Congress's attention to the underlying constitutional issues as a basis for judicial deference to their decision:

The bill for incorporating the [first] bank of the United States did not steal upon an unsuspecting legislature, and pass unobserved. Its principle was completely understood and was opposed with equal zeal and ability. After being resisted, first in the fair and open field of debate, and afterwards in the executive cabinet, with as much persevering talent as any measure has ever experienced, and being supported by arguments which convinced minds as pure and as intelligent as this country can boast, it became law. . . . It would require no ordinary share of intrepidity to assert that a measure adopted under these circumstances was a bold and plain usurpation, to which the constitution gives no countenance.

Judicial inquiry into legislative motivation has had a checkered career. The Court in HAMMER V. DAGENHART (1918) and BAILEY V. DREXEL FURNITURE COMPANY (1922) relied on Marshall's "pretext" statement to strike down federal child labor legislation, and the Court in LOCHNER V. NEW YORK (1905) expressed doubt whether the maximum hours law had been adopted for permissible motives.

Inquiries into legislative motivation declined with the judicial modesty of the late 1930s, but it reappeared with the WARREN COURT's resurgence of activism. The Court in ABINGTON SCHOOL DISTRICT V. SCHEMPP (1963) articulated this standard for assessing establishment of religion claims: "[W]hat are the purpose and primary effect of the enactment? If either is the advancement or inhibition of religion then the enactment exceeds the scope of legislative power as circumscribed by the Constitution." EPPERSON V. ARKANSAS (1968) applied the "purpose" aspect of this test to strike down a law forbidding the teaching of evolutionary theory. GOMILLION V. LIGHTFOOT (1960) struck down the Alabama legislature's redrawing of the boundaries of Tuskeegee on the ground that it was designed to exclude black citizens from the city limits. And GRIFFIN V. PRINCE EDWARD COUNTY SCHOOL BOARD (1964) held that the county could not constitutionally close its public schools with the motive of avoiding integration.

In contrast to these decisions, *United States v. O'Brien* (1968) refused to consider the defendant's contention that Congress enacted the draft-card destruction law in order to suppress antiwar protest rather than for any legitimate administrative purposes. And PALMER V. THOMPSON (1971) dismissed the plaintiff's claim that Jackson, Mississippi, had closed its swimming pools in order to avoid integrating them. Writing for the Court in *Palmer,* Justice HUGO L. BLACK emphasized that it was extremely difficult to determine an official's motivation and especially difficult "to determine the 'sole' or 'dominant' motivation behind the choices of a group of legislators." Black also remarked that "there is an element of futility in a judicial attempt to invalidate a law because of the bad motives of its supporters. If a law is struck down for this reason, rather than because of its facial contents or effect, it would presumably be valid as soon as the legislature . . . repassed it for different reasons."

More recently, the Court has repudiated the broadest implications of *O'Brien* and *Palmer.* In ARLINGTON HEIGHTS V. METROPOLITAN HOUS-ING DEVELOPMENT CORPORATION (1977) Justice LEWIS F. POWELL noted the importance of "[p]roof of racially discriminatory intent or purpose" to claims under the EQUAL PROTECTION clause. The Court held that the complainant was entitled—indeed, required—to prove that the town's refusal to rezone an area to permit multiple-family housing was discrimi-natorily motivated. The relevent standard was not whether the decision was solely or even dominantly motivated by racial considerations. Rather, proof that racial motivation played any part in the decision shifts to the decision maker "the burden of establishing that the same decision would have resulted even had the impermissible purpose not been consid-ered." In *Mt. Healthy City Board of Education v. Doyle* (1977) the Court applied a similar standard in reviewing an employee's claim that he had been discharged for exercising First Amendment rights.

The current doctrine is correct. Legislative motives are not always obscure; nor does judicial review usually require inquiring into and aggregating the motives of individual legislators. As Justice Powell noted in *Arlington Heights,* the bizarrely shaped boundaries of Tuskeegee in *Gomillion* revealed "a clear pattern, unexplainable on grounds other than race." Sometimes, as in the school- and pool-closing cases, the historical background and sequence of actions leading up to the contested event may reveal invidious purposes. Placing a substantial burden on the complainant and permitting the respondent to show that the decision was in fact overdetermined by legitimate purposes amply protect against judicial invalidation of legislative policies that were based on legitimate considerations.

Indeed, this objective might be better achieved simply by invalidating a law where unconstitutional motives played any substantial role and permitting the legislature to consider the measure anew. Justice Black's concern to the contrary, such a course is not inevitably futile. Although a legislature may disguise its motivation and reenact the law for illicit reasons, it may also choose to reenact the law for entirely legitimate reasons—or the legislature may have lost whatever interest motivated it to act in the first instance. The Alabama legislature did not attempt to gerrymander Tuskeegee again, nor did Prince Edward County try to close its schools again for a "better" reason.

Judicial inquiry into unconstitutional motivation is sometimes said to be especially intrusive because it requires the judiciary to concern itself directly with the legislative process. In an important sense, however, any form of procedural review is less intrusive than substantive review. The Court leaves to the legislature its assigned task of weighing the costs and benefits of proposed legislation, and requires only that the legislature not count a constitutionally illicit objective as a benefit.

When a law is challenged on the ground that it does not further any valid interests, or does not further them sufficiently, the Supreme Court typically does not ask what ends the legislature actually sought to achieve, but hypothesizes possible objectives and asks whether the law can be upheld in terms of them. For example, in *United States v. O'Brien,* lacking any information about what legitimate objectives Congress actually sought to achieve through the draft card destruction law, the Court upheld the law on the basis of several administrative objectives that the Justices thought the law might serve.

In a widely cited 1972 article Gerald Gunther urged that the Court should be "less willing to supply justifying rationale by exercising its imagination. . . . [It] should assess the means in terms of legislative purposes that have substantial basis in actuality, not mere conjecture." Gunther asserted that a court need not delve into "actual legislative motivation" but can rely on legislative materials such as debates and reports or on a "state court's or attorney general office's description of purpose."

The Court has sometimes taken this approach. For example, in GRISWOLD V. CONNECTICUT (1965) the Court held that the state's anticontraceptive law was not justified as a means of deterring illicit sexual intercourse—the only purpose urged by the state attorney general. The Court did not consider whether the law might be upheld on the more plausible (though constitutionally problematic) ground that the Connecticut legislature believed that contraception was immoral. Whatever the justification for this judicial strategy, it is not likely to identify the legislature's actual purposes: state courts and attorneys general have no privileged access to actual legislative purposes but must rely on the same public materials available to the Supreme Court.

In recent years some Justices, and occasionally a majority of the Court, have limited the objectives that can be considered in support of a challenged regulation to the decision maker's (supposed) actual objectives. This course is easiest for a court to follow when statutory limitations on an agency's mandate foreclose it from pursuing a broad range of objectives. For example, HAMPTON V. MOW SUN WONG (1976) invalidated a United States Civil Service regulation barring resident ALIENS from federal civil service jobs. Writing for the Court, Justice JOHN PAUL STEVENS assumed that Congress or the President might constitutionally have adopted such a requirement for reasons of foreign policy, but held that the commission's jurisdiction was limited to adopting regulations to "promote the efficiency of the federal service." Similarly, in REGENTS OF THE UNIVERSITY OF CALIFORNIA V. BAKKE (1978), Justice Powell refused to consider whether the university's preferential admissions policy was justified as a remedy for past discrimination, holding that the regents were empowered only to pursue educational objectives.

The Supreme Court has sometimes relied on legislative history to refuse to uphold legislation on the basis of objectives that were not intended. For example, in *Weinberger v. Wiesenfeld* (1975), in assessing the constitutionality of the "mother's insurance benefit" provision of the SOCIAL SECURITY ACT, Justice WILLIAM J. BRENNAN wrote for the Court that "the mere recitation of a benign, compensatory purpose is not an automatic shield which protects against an inquiry into the actual purposes underlying a statutory scheme." Although the provision might have been designed to compensate for past economic discrimination against women, the legislative history belied this purpose and the Court refused to uphold the law on a false basis.

Legislative history is often sparse or nonexistent, however. A complex legislative scheme may make a myriad of classifications; the chances are slight that legislative materials will illuminate the classification challenged in any particular case; and the absence of legislative history does not mean that the legislators did not intend to pursue a particular objective. Partly because of these complexities, judicial efforts to limit the purposes on the basis of which laws can be justified have not followed a consistent pattern. The current state of the law is captured in *Kassell v. Consolidated Freightways Corporation* (1981), which struck down a state's highway regulation prohibiting double trailers as an undue burden on INTERSTATE COMMERCE. In a concurring opinion, Justice Brennan wrote that he would give no deference to the state's arguments based on safety because the law was not actually designed to promote safety but to

protect local industries. Justice WILLIAM H. REHNQUIST, dissenting, asserted that there was "no authority for the proposition that possible
legislative purposes suggested by a state's lawyers should not be considered in COMMERCE CLAUSE cases." The plurality avoided the issue by
rejecting the state's safety claims on the merits.

In *McCulloch* Marshall implied that the BANK OF THE UNITED STATES
ACT was entitled to special deference because of the attention paid to
the constitutional issues within the executive and legislative branches.
Because of the difficulty of such an inquiry, however, and perhaps because of its perceived impropriety, the court has seldom conditioned
deference on the extent to which the legislature actually considered
the factual and legal issues bearing on the constitutional questions at
stake. In *Textile Workers Union v. Lincoln Mills* (1957) the Court gave a
strained interpretation to a federal statute in order to avoid a difficult
constitutional question of federal jurisdiction, to which Congress had
apparently paid no attention. In a separate opinion, Justice FELIX FRANK-
FURTER noted that "this Court cannot do what a President sometimes
does in returning a bill to Congress. We cannot return this provision
to Congress and respectfully request that body to assume the responsibility placed upon it by the Constitution."

In an article on the *Lincoln Mills* case, ALEXANDER M. BICKEL and
Harry Wellington responded that the Court could properly perform
such a "remanding function" and that it had sometimes done so, albeit
surreptitiously. KENT V. DULLES (1958) is often cited as an example.
Rather than decide whether the secretary of state could constitutionally
refuse to issue passports to members of the Communist party, the Court
held that Congress had not delegated the secretary this authority, thus
in effect returning the matter to Congress. More recently, Justice Stevens,
dissenting in FULLILOVE V. KLUTZNICK (1980), explicitly urged such a
"remand." *Fullilove* upheld a congressional provision requiring that ten
percent of the federal funds allocated to public work projects be used
to procure services from minority contractors. Justice Stevens's dissent
started from the premise that the Constitution disfavors all racial classifications. Noting that the challenged provision was scarcely discussed in
committee or on the floor of the Congress, he wrote:

Although it is traditional for judges to accord the same presumption of regularity
to the legislative process no matter how obvious it may be that a busy Congress
has acted precipitately, I see no reason why the character of their procedures
may not be considered relevant to the decision whether the legislative product
has [violated the Constitution]. A holding that the classification was not adequately
preceded by a consideration of less drastic alternatives or adequately explained
by a statement of legislative purpose would be far less intrusive than a final
decision [of unconstitutionality]. . . . [T]here can be no separation-of-powers
objection to a more tentative holding of unconstitutionality based on a failure

to follow procedures that guarantee the kind of deliberation that a fundamental constitutional decision of this kind obviously merits.

"Procedural" judicial review, which takes account of the legislature's consideration of relevant constitutional issues, has two objectives. First, it may foster legislative attention to the Constitution in the first instance. Second, it prevents constitutional concerns from falling between two stools—which happens when a court blindly defers to a judgment that the legislature did not in fact make.

Procedural review seems appropriate where a legislature evidently has ignored issues of law or fact that bear on the constitutionality of an enactment. It is questionable whether a general practice of procedural review would prove workable, however. Among other things, a court will have difficulty in assessing the adequacy of constitutional deliberation from external indicia. Justice Powell, concurring in *Fullilove*, thus responded to the argument that the legislation was not adequately supported by factual findings or debate:

The creation of national rules for the governance of our society simply does not entail the same concept of recordmaking that is appropriate to a judicial or administrative proceeding. Congress has no responsibility to confine its vision to the facts and evidence adduced by particular parties. One appropriate source [of facts] is the information and expertise that Congress acquires in the consideration and enactment of earlier legislation. After Congress has legislated repeatedly in an area of national concern, its Members gain experience that may reduce the need for fresh hearings or prolonged debate when Congress again considers action in that area.

In addition to the specific powers and limitations found in the Constitution, the Court has interpreted the DUE PROCESS and equal protection clauses to impose general requirements of "rationality" on the outcome of the legislative process. As stated in *F. S. Royster Guano Company v. Virginia* (1920), the equal protection STANDARD OF REVIEW requires that "the classification must be reasonable, not arbitrary, and must rest upon some ground of difference having a fair and substantial relation to the object of the legislation. . . ." The modern Court has usually articulated an even less demanding RATIONAL BASIS requirement: the law, and any classifications it makes, must plausibly promote some permissible ends to some extent.

The rationality standards may provide a minimal judicial safeguard against laws whose only purpose is constitutionally illicit, without requiring a direct inquiry into legislative motivation. But they may also impose a broader requirement on the legislative process. They may imply what Frank Michelman has described as a "public interest" rather than a "public choice" model of the legislative process.

The public interest model is premised on the possibility of shared public values or ends. "[T]he legislature is regarded as the forum for identifying or defining, and acting towards those ends. The process is one of mutual search through joint deliberation, relying on the use of reason supposed to have persuasive force" (Michelman, 1977, p. 149). The public choice model regards "all substantive values and ends . . . as strictly private. . . . There is no public or general social interest, there are only concatenations of particular interests or private preferences. There is no reason, only strategy. . . . There are no good legislators, only shrewd ones; no statesmen; only messengers" (ibid., p. 148).

The constitutional implications of the two models can be illustrated by the city ordinance challenged in RAILWAY EXPRESS AGENCY v. NEW YORK (1949). The ordinance prohibited advertisements on the side of vehicles but exempted business delivery vehicles advertising their own business. The most obvious beneficiaries of the exemption were the city's newspapers.

If the Court had adopted a "public choice" model, it would have been pointless to subject the New York ordinance to a rationality requirement: the exemption would be permissible even if its only rationale were to "buy off" the newspapers to get the ordinance enacted or, indeed, to favor the newspapers over other advertisers. Under a "public interest" model, however, the Court would at least ask whether the exemption was related to some extrinsic purpose—and this it did. Justice WILLIAM O. DOUGLAS wrote for the Court that the "local authorities may well have concluded that those who advertise their own wares on their trucks do not present the same traffic problem in view of the nature or extent of the advertising which they use." In a concurring opinion, Justice ROBERT H. JACKSON pointed to "a real difference between doing in self-interest and doing for hire."

Thus, the Court seems nominally to adhere to a public interest model. But the weakness of the rationality standards, and the Court's generosity in imagining possible rationales for classifications (exemplified by *Railway Express Agency* itself), suggest some judicial ambivalence about the extent to which this model should be treated as a constitutional norm. There is some academic controversy about both the norm itself and its judicial enforceability.

JAMES BRADLEY THAYER asserted in his 1901 biography of John Marshall that judicial review implies a distrust of legislatures and that the legislatures "are growing accustomed to this distrust, and more and more readily incline to justify it, and to shed the consideration of constitutional restraints, . . . turning that subject over to the courts; and what is worse, they insensibly fall into a habit of assuming that whatever they can constitutionally do they may do. . . . The tendency of a common and easy resort to this great function is to dwarf the political capacity of the people, and to deaden its sense of moral responsibility." Assessing

Thayer's argument is practically impossible, but it seems at least as plausible that the practice of judicial review is a necessary reminder to legislators that their actions are constrained by fundamental public law and not only by their constituents' interests or even their own moral principles.

Thayer's argument nonetheless underscores the point that the Constitution speaks directly to legislatures. In a properly functioning constitutional system, judicial review should be just that—the review of the legislature's considered judgment that the challenged act is constitutionally permissible. Whether this position is "realistic" is another matter. Surely, however, one cannot expect legislators to take their constitutional responsibilities seriously if they and the citizenry at large assume that they have none.

Bibliography

BENNETT, ROBERT   1979   "Mere" Rationality in Constitutional Law: Judicial Review and Democratic Theory. *California Law Review* 67:1049–1103.

BICKEL, ALEXANDER and WELLINGTON, HARRY 1957   Legislative Purpose and the Judicial Function: The Lincoln Mills Case. *Harvard Law Review* 71:1–39.

BREST, PAUL   1971   An Approach to the Problem of Unconstitutional Legislative Motive. *Supreme Court Review* 1971:95–146.

ELY, JOHN H.   1970   Legislative and Administrative Motivation in Constitutional Law. *Yale Law Journal* 79:1205–1341.

GUNTHER, GERALD   1982   In Search of Evolving Doctrine on a Changing Court: A Model for a Newer Equal Protection. *Harvard Law Review* 86:1–48.

LINDE, HANS   1976   Due Process of Lawmaking. *Nebraska Law Review* 55:197–255.

MICHELMAN, FRANK   1977   Political Markets and Community Self-Determination: Competing Judicial Models of Local Government Legitimacy. *Indiana Law Journal* 53:145–206.

MORGAN, DONALD G.   1966   *Congress and the Constitution: A Study in Responsibility.* Cambridge, Mass.: Belknap Press.

THAYER, JAMES BRADLEY   1901   *John Marshall.* Boston: Houghton Mifflin.

WECHSLER, HERBERT   1965   The Courts and the Constitution. *Columbia Law Review* 65:1001–1014.

POLITICAL QUESTION

Philippa Strum

As early as MARBURY V. MADISON (1803) the Supreme Court recognized that decisions on some governmental questions lie entirely within the discretion of the "political" branches of the national government—the President and Congress—and thus outside the proper scope of JUDICIAL REVIEW. Today such questions are called "political questions."

Among the clauses of the federal Constitution held to involve political questions, the one most frequently cited has been Article IV, section 4, under which the federal government "shall guarantee to every State in this Union a REPUBLICAN FORM OF GOVERNMENT." Federal courts, and particularly the Supreme Court, have argued that as the definition of "republican" is at the heart of the American political system, only the "political branches," which are accountable to the sovereign people, can make that definition. The electorate can ratify or reject the definition by reelecting or defeating their representatives at the next election. The choice of definition, Justice FELIX FRANKFURTER said, dissenting in BAKER V. CARR (1962), entails choosing "among competing theories of political philosophy," which is not a proper judicial function.

Thus the Supreme Court has refused to review political decisions in cases involving two governments, each claiming to be the legitimate one of a state (LUTHER V. BORDEN, 1849); the question whether the post-Civil War Reconstruction governments in southern states were republican (*Georgia v. Stanton* and MISSISSIPPI V. JOHNSON, 1867); the "republican" nature of the INITIATIVE and REFERENDUM (*Pacific Telephone & Telegraph Co. v. Oregon*, 1912; *Hawke v. Smith*, 1920); lack of REAPPORTIONMENT by state legislatures (COLEGROVE V. GREEN, 1946); contested elections (*Taylor & Marshall v. Beckham*, 1900); certain presidential actions (*Mississippi v. Johnson*, 1867); certain cases arising in Indian territory (CHEROKEE INDIAN CASES, 1831–1832); and FOREIGN AFFAIRS (*Foster v. Neilson*, 1829; *Charlton v. Kelly*, 1913).

The Supreme Court has never successfully differentiated those questions proper for judicial interpretation from those that are reserved to the "political" branches. A plurality of the Justices having held in *Colegrove v. Green* (1946) that a state legislature's failure to reapportion itself after the decennial federal census was a political question, for example, the Court in *Baker v. Carr* decided that such inaction raised a question under the equal protection clause of the FOURTEENTH AMENDMENT rather than the guarantee clause, and therefore raised an issue proper for judicial decision. After having handed down a line of cases holding that contested elections were matters in which the final decision could come only from the relevant legislative body, the Court overturned the refusal by the House of Representatives (POWELL V. MCCORMACK, 1969) to seat a member who, in the Court's view, had been excluded unconstitutionally.

The Court has been relatively consistent in holding various foreign relations issues to constitute political questions, because of the necessity for the country to speak with one voice, the inability of courts to develop a body of principles to govern such issues, and what Justice Frankfurter described in *Perez v. Brownell* (1958) as the "constitutional allocation of governmental function" concerning foreign affairs to the President and Congress. Matters such as the existence of a state of war, the relevance of a treaty, the boundaries of the nation, and the credentials of foreign diplomats have been left to congressional and presidential diplomats. But the Court stated in REID V. COVERT (1957) that even the provisions of a treaty or EXECUTIVE AGREEMENT are reviewable if citizens assert violations of their rights. And, in the face of government claims that the travel of Americans abroad raises diplomatic issues fit only for executive discretion, the Court has enunciated the RIGHT TO TRAVEL abroad and has made substantive rulings for and against claims of that right (KENT V. DULLES, 1958; APTHEKER V. SECRETARY OF STATE, 1964; ZEMEL V. RUSK, 1965).

The Supreme Court's variable commitment to the political question doctrine may be explained by reasons that are nondoctrinal. The Court appears to resort to the doctrine when only two substantive judgments are possible, the first being unacceptable to the Court because it would likely go unenforced and the second being equally unacceptable because it would violate a major tenet of American political ideology. In *Colegrove v. Green,* for example, the plurality suggested that the Illinois legislation might ignore a HOLDING that the legislature's refusal to redesign badly malapportioned congressional districts was unconstitutional—and the House of Representatives might take no action. Yet upholding such a malapportionment, which gave some citizens a vote of far greater weight than that of others, would have run contrary to the American belief that all citizens are equal in the electoral process. Similarly, the Court in *Mississippi v. Johnson* had the choice of deciding that the Reconstruction state governments were illegitimate, a ruling that the President and Congress surely would have ignored; or that the governments, which had been imposed by the federal government on citizens denied the right to participate in the election process, were legitimate—which would have offended the basic American idea of SOVEREIGNTY of the people. In both cases the Court invoked the political question doctrine and left decision in the hands of the "political branches."

The very notion of "political branches," however, is untenable. Article III of the Constitution makes the federal judiciary indirectly accountable insofar as it may enable the people's representatives in Congress to strip the courts of JURISDICTION over matters the people believe the courts to have mishandled. Federal judges, too, are liable to IMPEACHMENT—although this resource has never been taken for purely political purposes since the earliest days of the nineteenth century.

Court decisions necessarily affect power. The decision in PLESSY V. FERGUSON (1896) legitimizing SEPARATE BUT EQUAL railroad cars for black and white passengers encouraged southern states to establish racially segregated schools; the holding of BROWN V. BOARD OF EDUCATION (1954) that "separate but equal" schools violated the equal protection clause stripped the states of that power, transferring the power to define SEGREGATION and integration to the federal courts, the Congress, and, in some cases, to the President. The Court's upholding of ECONOMIC REGULATION affecting wages, hours, unionization, social security, job safety, and competition shifted power from employers to state and federal legislatures, executives, and REGULATORY AGENCIES, as well as to unions, and enabled the United States to consolidate a system of welfare capitalism under which privately owned property is systematically regulated by governmental bodies.

The Court nonetheless insists that the judicial branch is apolitical, because its own institutional power depends on the electorate's belief that the Court is above politics. As JAMES MADISON pointed out in THE FEDERALIST #51, the Court possesses neither the power of the purse nor that of the sword. It is entirely dependent for the enforcement of its decisions on the willingness of the population and public officials to carry them out. Were the Court's decisions to be ignored, the Court's prestige would suffer; in a circular fashion, the loss of prestige would increase the possibility that subsequent decisions would go unheeded.

The Court's decisions find ready compliance when the decisions reflect a societal consensus. The difference between the Court's 1946 *Colegrove* decision that malapportionment was a political question and its contrary 1962 *Baker* decision can be linked to the large-scale movement of population to urban areas underrepresented in the legislatures. By 1962 a majority of the nation's population could be expected to concur in a decision that enhanced its political power. Promise of additional support from the President was implicit in the appearance of Attorney General ROBERT F. KENNEDY before the Court to argue as AMICUS CURIAE for reapportionment, for Kennedy was, of course, the brother of President JOHN F. KENNEDY, who owed his office to urban votes.

The political question device derives its legitimacy from the necessity to preserve an independent judiciary in the American political system. The device is justifiable because it enables the judiciary to maintain its independence by withdrawing from no-win situations. In addition, it prevents the courts from usurping the role of the ballot box. The Supreme Court, declaring the presence of a political question, tacitly admits that it cannot find and therefore cannot ratify a social consensus that does not violate basic American beliefs. The Court has no moral right to impose rules upon a country not yet ready for them. The political question doctrine, which permits the Court to restrain itself from precipitating impossible situations that might tear the social fabric, gives the electorate and its representatives time to work out their own rules, which can ultimately be translated into constitutional doctrine through judicial decision. The doctrine of political questions is more than a self-saving mechanism for the Court; it is also an affirmation of a governmental system based on popular sovereignty.

Bibliography

BICKEL, ALEXANDER M.   1962   *The Least Dangerous Branch*. Indianapolis: Bobbs-Merrill.

SCHARPF, FRITZ W.   1966   Judicial Review and the Political Question: A Functional Analysis. *Yale Law Journal* 75:517–546.

STRUM, PHILIPPA   1974   *The Supreme Court and "Political Questions."* University: University of Alabama Press.

JUDICIAL SYSTEM, FEDERAL

Paul M. Bator

The charter of the federal judicial system is Article III of the Constitution, authorizing the creation of federal tribunals vested with the JUDICIAL POWER OF THE UNITED STATES, that is, the authority to adjudicate a specifically enumerated set of CASES AND CONTROVERSIES. Article III also specifies the method of appointment of federal judges and lays down rules designed to guard their independence.

The Framers, mindful of the problems that the absence of a national judiciary had caused under the ARTICLES OF CONFEDERATION, easily agreed that there must be a national Supreme Court with power to assure the uniformity and supremacy of federal law. But the Framers were divided over the question whether further provision should be made for national courts. Some favored the creation of a complete system of federal courts. Some thought that this would unnecessarily narrow the preexisting general JURISDICTION of the state courts; they argued that national interests could be sufficiently protected by providing for Supreme Court review of state court decisions involving questions of federal law. This division was settled by a compromise: Article III itself mandates that there shall be "one Supreme Court"; but beyond this the federal judicial power is simply vested in "such inferior Courts as the Congress may from time to time ordain and establish."

Article III specifies that the Supreme Court (and whatever inferior federal courts Congress may establish) are to be courts of a strictly limited jurisdiction: they may adjudicate only nine enumerated categories of cases. Some of these were included because they touch on issues of national interest: most important, cases "arising under" the Constitution and laws of the United States (the FEDERAL QUESTION JURISDICTION); cases of ADMIRALTY AND MARITIME JURISDICTION; and cases to which the United States is a party. Federal courts were also empowered to decide certain controversies implicating the nation's FOREIGN AFFAIRS (for example, disputes affecting ambassadors and other alien parties; cases arising under treaties). The remaining categories authorize the federal courts to engage in interstate umpiring in cases where it was feared that parochial interests would prevail in the state courts. Examples are controversies between states, between a state and a citizen of another state, and between citizens of different states.

Article III's specification that the judicial power consists of adjudicating "cases" or "controversies" itself embodies a fundamental political decision: the national courts were to exercise only a judicial power. Thus the CONSTITUTIONAL CONVENTION OF 1787 repeatedly and explicitly rejected a variety of proposals to allow federal courts or judges to participate as advisers or revisers in the legislative process or to render ADVISORY OPINIONS; their authority was to be limited to "cases of a judiciary nature." On the other hand, the historical evidence establishes the Framers' understanding that the grant of the judicial power was to include the authority, where necessary to the lawful decision of a case properly within a court's jurisdiction, to disregard federal or state statutes found to be unconstitutional. This power of JUDICIAL REVIEW, occasionally challenged as a usurpation because it is not explicitly mentioned in Article III, has been settled since MARBURY V. MADISON (1803).

Besides defining the outer bounds of the federal judicial power, Article III protects federal judges from political pressures by guaranteeing tenure during GOOD BEHAVIOR without reduction in compensation.

Article III is not self-executing; it needs LEGISLATION to bring it to life, most particularly because Congress must determine whether there should be "inferior" federal courts and what should be the scope of their jurisdiction. It is to this task that the First Congress turned in its twentieth enactment: the seminal JUDICIARY ACT OF 1789. Obeying the Constitution's command, the act constituted a Supreme Court, consisting of a CHIEF JUSTICE and five associates. Next, the act, establishing a tradition persisting without interruption to this day, took up the constitutional option to create a system of federal courts of ORIGINAL JURISDICTION. The structure created was curious, but survived for a century. The country was divided into districts (at least one for each state), with a district court manned by a district judge. In addition, the country was divided into circuits (originally three), each with another trial court—a CIRCUIT COURT—manned not by its own judges but by two supreme COURT JUSTICES (sitting "on circuit") and a district judge.

Only a fraction of the constitutional potential for original federal court jurisdiction was exploited by the first Judiciary Act, attesting to the clear contemporaneous understanding of the Constitution that it is for Congress to determine which (if any) of the cases and controversies encompassed by the federal judicial power should be adjudicated in the first instance in a lower federal (rather than a state) court. (The modest original jurisdiction of the Supreme Court, limited to controversies where a state is a party and certain cases involving foreign diplomats, is thought to flow "directly" from the Constitution and thus represents a special case.) The district courts were given the jurisdiction most clearly felt to be a national one: authority to adjudicate admiralty cases. In a controversial decision, the First Congress set a precedent by opening the circuit courts to some cases involving controversies between citizens of different states and involving ALIENS. The federal trial courts were also granted jurisdiction over most civil suits brought by the United States and over the then negligible federal criminal caseload. Notably, the act did not give the federal trial courts jurisdiction over cases "arising under" federal law, leaving these to be adjudicated in the state courts.

The appellate structure of the new court system was rudimentary. Federal criminal cases were left without direct review (and remained so for a century). The circuit courts were given a limited APPELLATE JURISDICTION over the district courts, and the Supreme Court was authorized to review civil cases decided by the circuit courts involving more than $2,000.

Finally, in its famous section 25, the act—consistent with the Framers' intention to assure the supremacy of federal law—gave the Supreme Court power to review final state court judgments rejecting claims of right or immunity under federal law. (State court judgments upholding claims of right under federal law were not made reviewable until 1914.) Supreme Court review of state judgments involving questions of federal law has been a feature of our judicial FEDERALISM ever since 1789, and has served as a profoundly significant instrument for consolidating and protecting national power.

The institutional structure created by the first Judiciary Act proved to be remarkably stable; major structural change did not come until 1891. The Supreme Court has had a continuous existence since 1789, with changes only in the number of Justices. So also have the district courts (though their number has of course undergone major change). Even the circuit courts—architecturally the weakest feature of the system—survived for more than a century.

As to the jurisdiction of the federal courts, changes were incremental in the pre-Civil War period, with the state courts acting as the primary enforcers of the still rudimentary corpus of national law. But the Civil War brought a sea change: Congress was no longer prepared to depend on the state judiciaries to enforce rights guaranteed by the new FOUR-TEENTH AMENDMENT and by the Reconstruction legislation. By the HABEAS CORPUS ACT of 1867 and the various CIVIL RIGHTS ACTS, Congress extended the lower federal courts' jurisdiction to include claims against state officials for invasion of federal constitutional and statutory rights. These extensions were in turn overtaken by the JUDICIARY ACT OF 1875, giving the federal courts a general jurisdiction to adjudicate civil cases arising under federal law, subject only to a minimum amount-in-controversy. These expansions, supplemented by subsequent numerous specific extensions of federal trial jurisdiction over various sorts of actions involving national law, signaled the transformation of the federal courts from narrow forums designed to resolve maritime and certain interstate disputes into catholic tribunals playing a principal role in enforcing the growing body of national rights, privileges, and immunities.

The growth of the federal judicial business in the post-Civil War era placed an ever-growing pressure on the federal judicial system. The Supreme Court was especially burdened by the duties of circuit riding and by an increasing caseload. By 1890 the Court had a backload of 1800 cases; in the same year, 54,194 cases were pending in the lower federal courts. Congress responded to the crisis in the CIRCUIT COURTS OF APPEALS ACT (Evarts Act) of 1891, which fixed the outline of the contemporary federal judicial system. The act established a system of intermediate appellate courts called Circuit Courts of Appeals (not to be confused with the old circuit courts, which were finally abolished in 1911), one for each of (the then) nine circuits and staffed with its own judges. Although a narrow category of district court decisions continued (and continue) to be reviewed directly by the Supreme Court, the Evarts Act created the standard modern practice: appeals went normally from the district courts to the new courts of appeals; the judgments of the latter were in turn reviewable by the Supreme Court.

The second major and seminal innovation of the Evarts Act related to appellate review in the Supreme Court: the act introduced the principle of review at the Court's own discretion (by writ of CERTIORARI) of judgments in the lower courts. This principle was in turn greatly expanded in the so-called Judges' Bill of 1925, which sharply reduced the availability of Supreme Court review as of right of decisions of state and federal courts and substituted for it discretionary review on certiorari—the method of review that, to this day, dominates the Court's docket.

Changes in the structure of the federal judicial system have been few and minor since 1925, although both the statutory jurisdiction and the business of the courts have undergone major transformations. In essence the system remains a three-tier system, with the district courts serving as the trial courts, the courts of appeals as the appellate tribunals of first instance, and the Supreme Court as the court of final review (having also the power to review state court decisions involving issues of federal law). The picture is completed by the existence of special federal tribunals empowered to decide particular categories of cases, and by numerous federal administrative tribunals; the decisions of all of these are typically subject to review in the regular federal courts.

The most important component of the contemporary statutory jurisdiction of the UNITED STATES DISTRICT COURTS encompasses diversity cases involving more than $10,000, criminal prosecutions and civil actions brought by the United States, a large range of actions against the United States and its agencies and officials, federal HABEAS CORPUS, and—most significant—all civil cases in which a plaintiff sues on a claim arising under the Constitution and laws of the United States. The latter, all-encompassing rubric includes not only cases brought pursuant to the hundreds of federal statutes specifying a right to sue but also the numerous cases where that right is a judge-created ("implied") right to enforce a federal statutory or—(of profound significance)—constitutional provision not itself explicitly containing a right of action. In addition, the statutes allow certain diversity and federal question cases brought in the state courts to be removed for trial to a federal district court. Finally, the district courts exercise a significant jurisdiction to review the work of many federal administrative agencies and to review and supervise the work of the system of bankruptcy courts. The jurisdiction of the district courts is occasionally specified as exclusive of the state courts (for example, admiralty, COPYRIGHT, and PATENT); most of their civil jurisdiction is, however, concurrent with that of the state courts.

The country is, in the mid-1980s, divided into ninety-seven districts (including the DISTRICT OF COLUMBIA and Puerto Rico). Each state has at least one district; districts have never encompassed more than one state. The district courts are staffed by 576 active district judges—almost three times the 1950 figure (182 new district judgeships were created between 1978 and 1984 alone). The growth in number of judges has, nevertheless, failed to keep pace with the explosive increase in the caseload that has occurred since the 1960s. In 1940 about 70,000 criminal and civil (nonbankruptcy) cases were filed in the federal courts; in 1960, about 80,000; by 1980, the figure was almost 200,000, and in 1984 it exceeded 275,000. (The compound annual rate of increase in the federal district court case load was under one percent between 1934 and 1960; it has been five percent since 1960.) The increase is due primarily and naturally to the vast growth in the total corpus of federal (constitutional, statutory, common, and administrative) law applied in turn to a growing country with an expansive and mobile economy. It has also been fed, however, in the past twenty-five years by congressional and court-initiated changes in substantive and remedial rules that have made the federal courts into powerful litigation-attracting engines for the creation and expansion of rights and the redistribution of entitlements and powers in our society. Thus open-ended constitutional and statutory formulas have been used to fuel aggressive judicial review of the validity of federal and state legislative and administrative action and to create an expansive system of remedies against federal and state government (including affirmative claims on the resources of these governments). JUSTICIABILITY requirements (such as STANDING) that previously narrowed the scope of jurisdiction over public law actions have been significantly eroded. And federal court litigation has become increasingly attractive to plaintiffs as a result of provisions for attorneys' fees, the elimination (or inflation-caused erosion) of amount-in-controversy requirements, and the increasing use of CLASS ACTIONS.

These developments are reflected in the changing content of the federal district courts' workload. There were 6,000 suits against the United States in 1960, and almost 30,000 in 1983. There were only 300 CIVIL RIGHTS cases in 1960, almost 20,000 in 1983; 2,100 prisoner postconviction cases in 1960, more than 30,000 in 1983; 500 social security law cases in 1960, more than 20,000 in 1983. In general, about thirty-five to forty percent of the mid-1980s district court civil caseload involve the United States or its officials as a plaintiff or defendant; sixty to sixty-five percent of the civil caseload is "private" (including, however, litigation against state and local governments and officials). Diversity cases have contributed about twenty percent of the caseload since the 1970s. The number of criminal prosecutions has, historically, fluctuated widely in response to special federal programs (peaking during PROHIBITION); since the mid-1970s the criminal caseload has been quite stable and in the mid-1980s contributed about fifteen to twenty percent of the total.

In response to the explosive caseload Congress has acted to allow the district courts to rely substantially on the work of so-called federal magistrates—officials appointed by district judges with wide powers (subject to review by the district judge) to issue warrants, conduct preliminary hearings, try minor criminal offenses, supervise civil discovery, rule on preliminary motions and prisoner petitions, and (with the consent of the parties) even to hear and enter judgment generally in civil cases. The conferring of additional powers on magistrates has evoked controversy as well as some (so far unsuccessful) constitutional attacks.

The UNITED STATES COURTS OF APPEALS (as they are now called) have jurisdiction to review all final (and some interlocutory) decisions of the district courts. Pursuant to special statutory provisions they also review some cases coming directly from federal administrative agencies (this being an especially significant component of the business of the Court of Appeals for the District of Columbia Circuit). About fifteen percent of their cases are criminal cases, and another fifteen percent are federal and state prisoner postconviction and civil rights cases; only fourteen percent of their docket consists of diversity cases.

The caseload of the courts of appeals has increased dramatically in the last twenty-five years and is, in the mid-1980s, commonly described as constituting a crisis. In the forty years before 1960 that caseload hovered between 1,500 and the peak of 3,700 reached in 1960. In 1970 the figure was almost 11,500, and in 1980 it was over 21,000. From 1980 to 1983 the caseload jumped again to 29,580. From 1960 to 1983 there was an increase of almost 800 percent in the number of appeals from the district courts; the compound annual rate of increase for all cases from 1960 to 1983 was 9.4 percent (compared to 0.5 percent in the preceding twenty-five years).

To manage this workload there exist (in the mid-1980s) twelve courts of appeals assigned to geographical circuits (eleven in the states and one for the District of Columbia) and an additional one (described below) for certain special categories of subject matter. The number of judges in each circuit ranges from six (First) to twenty-eight (Ninth). There are 156 authorized circuit judgeships; in 1960 there were sixty-eight (and as recently as 1978 only ninety-seven). Cases are typically heard by panels of three judges; a few cases of special importance are in turn reheard by the court sitting EN BANC. The increase in number of judges has by no means kept pace with the expansion of the caseload since 1960. As a result, there have been substantial changes in the procedures of these courts: opportunities for oral argument (and even for briefing) have been sharply curtailed and an increasing proportion of cases is disposed of summarily, without opinion. Central staff attorneys (as well as a growing army of conventional law clerks) assist the judges.

From the beginning of our national history Congress has perceived a need to create special tribunals for the adjudication of cases falling outside the traditional areas of federal court jurisdiction. Military tribunals have, from the outset, administered a special body of law through special procedures. The administration of justice in the TERRITORIES in transition toward statehood was perceived as requiring special temporary federal tribunals that would become state courts upon statehood; the District of Columbia and the territories and dependencies of the United States also require a full panoply of special federal courts to administer local law. Beginning in 1855, with the establishment of a rudimentary Court of Claims, Congress has created a series of special tribunals to adjudicate money claims against the United States. And, particularly with the advent in this century of the modern administrative state, Congress has created numerous administrative agencies and tribunals whose business includes adjudication.

Unlike the ordinary federal courts, the institutional hallmark of most of these tribunals has been specialization. Further, the transitory nature of some of these tribunals, the perceived need to allow some of them to function inexpensively with expeditious or informal procedures, and (in the case of the administrative agencies) the equally strongly perceived need to endow them with a range of policymaking functions in addition to adjudicative functions, has typically led Congress to create them not as tribunals constituted under Article III (with lifetime judges performing an exclusively judicial function) but as special LEGISLATIVE COURTS or administrative tribunals. Their judges typically serve temporary terms and are removable for misfeasance without IMPEACHMENT. The constitutional authority for such tribunals has been much discussed and litigated; Congress's authority to constitute them has virtually always been upheld.

The most important specialized tribunals in the current federal judicial system are: the local courts of the District of Columbia, Puerto Rico, and the territories and dependencies; the system of military courts; the system of bankruptcy courts; the TAX COURT and the CLAIMS COURT, adjudicating certain tax refund claims and certain damage actions against the federal government; the Court of International Trade, adjudicating certain customs disputes; and a large and variegated array of administrative tribunals and agencies. The work of all of these tribunals is typically subject to review, through various forms of proceedings, in the regular federal courts.

In addition, in 1982 Congress created a thirteenth court of appeals, the UNITED STATES COURT OF APPEALS FOR THE FEDERAL CIRCUIT. This is a regular Article III court, whose jurisdiction is not territorial but is defined in terms of subject matter, including appeals from the Claims Court and the Court of International Trade and many patent and trademark cases.

Continuously since 1789 the Supreme Court has been the single institution with nationwide authority to supervise the inferior federal courts and to give voice to a uniform national law. The Court's size has varied from five to ten Justices; since 1869 it has consisted of a Chief Justice and eight associate Justices. The Supreme Court acts *en banc,* not in panels, though individual Justices have the conventional authority to issue stays and take emergency action. The Court acts by majority, but in this century the practice has been to grant a certiorari petition (setting the case for plenary review) if four Justices are in favor.

The caseload explosion in the lower federal courts has imposed major burdens on the Court. The Court disposed of over 4,000 cases in its 1983 term (compared to about 3,300 in 1970, 1,900 in 1960, and 1,200 in 1950). The task is possible because only a small number of cases (usually about 150) are decided on the merits by full opinion after plenary briefing and oral argument. Another 100 to 150 cases are decided on the merits by MEMORANDUM ORDER. The remaining dispositions consist of summary denials of petitions for certiorari (or other writs); there were almost 3,900 of these in 1983–1984. In 1960 there were just under 2,000 new cases docketed in the Court; in 1970, about 3,400; in 1983, about 4,200. The increase in cases docketed means more and more resources devoted to "screening" cases for decision and less to the hearing and disposition of cases on the merits. Thus the time devoted to oral argument has shrunk steadily in this century and now almost never exceeds one hour per case. The length of briefs is limited; and an ever-growing battery of law CLERKS assists in legal research and in the drafting of opinions.

The content of the Court's work reflects the scope and content of the national law. In the 1983 term the Court's decisions by full opinion included three cases within the original jurisdiction; ninety-six civil cases coming from the lower federal courts (of which forty-six involved the federal government, twenty-eight involved state and local governments, and twenty-two were private cases); sixteen federal habeas corpus cases; and thirty-two cases from the state courts (eighteen civil and fourteen criminal). Diversity cases are rarely reviewed. The Court is, increasingly, a constitutional court; about half of its cases tend to involve a constitutional question as the (or a) principal issue. The United States (as party or AMICUS CURIAE) participates in over half of the cases that the Court decides on the merits.

Although the federal judicial system has grown substantially in its 200 years, the federal courts continue to constitute only a small—though disproportionately powerful—component of the American judicial system. (Fewer than three percent of the country's judges are federal Article III judges; the biggest states have judicial systems larger than the federal system.)

The relations between state and federal courts are multifarious and exceedingly complex. Except where Congress has specified that federal court jurisdiction is exclusive, state courts of general jurisdiction exercise a normal competence to adjudicate cases involving issues of federal law (particularly in that many such issues arise by way of defense in civil and criminal cases arising under state law). Their decisions of these cases are subject to Supreme Court review, usually on certiorari; but that Court's jurisdiction in such a case is limited to the federal question in the case and may not be exercised at all if the judgment rests on a valid and dispositive state-law ground. State court judgments on issues of federal law (unless reversed by the Supreme Court) have normal RES JUDICATA effect.

The federal district courts, in turn, adjudicate many questions of state law, not only in diversity cases but also in cases arising under federal law where state law governs one or more issues. No provision for review by the state courts of the correctness of federal court decisions on issues of state law has ever existed; but in a narrow class of cases federal courts will abstain from exercising an otherwise proper federal jurisdiction in order to allow a state law issue to be determined in the state courts. (See ABSTENTION DOCTRINE.) Under the decision in ERIE RAILROAD v. TOMPKINS (1938), on issues of state law (including issues of state common law) state court precedents are accepted as authoritative by the federal courts.

Special problems are presented by the politically sensitive role of the federal courts in controlling the legality of the actions of state and local governments and their officials. Although the ELEVENTH AMENDMENT bars the federal courts from asserting jurisdiction over actions against a state as such, a wide range of remedies against state and local governments and their officials exist in the federal courts. Federal courts routinely review the constitutional validity of state criminal convictions through the writ of habeas corpus. Since the adoption of the Civil Rights Act of 1871, they have exercised jurisdiction to grant INJUNCTIONS and DAMAGES against state and local officials (and, more recently, against local governmental entities as such) for conduct under color of state law—including conduct by officials asserting official power even where the conduct is prohibited by state law—that infringes on the ever-growing corpus of federal constitutional and statutory rules governing STATE ACTION. Federal courts may enjoin state officials from enforcing unconstitutional state statutes and administrative schemes; moreover, the courts' injunctive remedial powers are frequently exercised to assume broad managerial supervision over state agencies and bureaucracies (for example, schools, mental hospitals, prisons). And the ever-burgeoning array of federal conditions and restrictions that accompany federal economic and social programs available to the states are, as a matter of routine, enforceable in the federal courts.

The political sensitivities aroused by the federal courts' jurisdiction to control the validity of state and local government action has led to some statutory and judge-made restrictions on the exercise of this jurisdiction. For over half a century federal court actions to enjoin the enforcement of state statutes on constitutional grounds had to be litigated before THREE-JUDGE COURTS and were subject to direct review by APPEAL to the Supreme Court. (The institution of the three-judge district court was virtually abolished in 1976.) During the New Deal, statutory restrictions were placed on the jurisdiction of the federal courts to interfere with state tax statutes and public utility rate orders. Statutory and judge-made rules restrict the power of the federal courts to enjoin or interfere with pending state court proceedings; and state prisoners who fail to exhaust state court remedies or fail to comply with state procedural rules do not have access to federal habeas corpus.

The federal judicial system appears to operate on one-hundred-year cycles. The structure created in 1789 became increasingly unwieldy after the Civil War and was—after some twenty years of pressure for reform—finally transformed by the Evarts Act of 1891. That act created a stable system which has, in turn, come under increasing pressure from the caseload explosion that began in the 1960s. Relief could come in the form of diminutions in the district courts' original jurisdiction (such as a long-discussed abolition of or reduction in the diversity jurisdiction); but the need for architectural revision has also become increasingly clear in the 1970s and 1980s.

Structural problems center on the appellate tiers. Further substantial increases in the number of circuit judges is an uncertain remedy. Some circuits are already unwieldy and are finding it increasingly difficult to maintain stability and uniformity in the intracircuit law. Increasing the number of circuits would increase intercircuit instability and disuniformity and place further pressure on the finite appellate capacity of our "one Supreme Court"—the latter constituting the obvious structural bottleneck in the system.

More generally, a judicial system administering an enormous and dynamic corpus of national law and adjudicating a rising caseload (approaching 300,000 cases a year) cannot operate forever on an appellate capacity that is limited to some 150–200 judicial opinions with nationwide authority. There is rising concern, too, about the quality of federal justice as the growing caseload leads to an increasing bureaucratization of the federal judicial process, with the judges reduced to an oversight capacity in managing a growing array of magistrates, central staff, and law clerks.

Since the 1970s, two methods of increasing the system's capacity to provide authoritative and uniform judicial pronouncements on issues of national law have been discussed. One consists of greater subject-matter specialization at the appellate level, with special courts of appeals having nationwide authority to deal with specified subjects of federal litigation (for instance, tax cases, administrative appeals); such courts would remove pressure from the regional courts of appeals and the Supreme Court. The alternative (or additional) possibility is to create an additional appellate "tier": a national court of appeals with power to render decisions of nationwide authority, receiving its business by assignment from the Supreme Court or by transfer from the regional courts of appeals. In addition, if the number of certiorari petitions continues to mount, the Supreme Court will eventually have to make some adjustments in its screening procedures (perhaps dealing with these petitions in panels).

Behind these structural problems lie more fundamental questions about the enormous power that the federal courts have come to exercise over the political, economic, and social policies of the nation. Throughout our history intense controversy has surrounded the question whether (and to what extent) a small corps of appointed life-tenured officials should exercise wide-ranging powers to supervise and invalidate the actions of the political branches of federal, state, and local governments. From time to time these debates have threatened to affect the independence of the federal judicial system. Thus, in the 1930s, facing wholesale invalidations of the New Deal program by a "conservative" Supreme Court, President FRANKLIN D. ROOSEVELT proposed to "pack" the Court with additional judges; his plan was widely perceived to be contrary to the spirit of the Constitution and was defeated in Congress. (Shortly thereafter a Court with a new membership and a new judicial philosophy in effect accomplished Roosevelt's purposes.)

In the second half of the twentieth century retaliatory proposals have mostly consisted of attempts to strip a "liberal" Supreme Court of appellate jurisdiction in certain categories of constitutional litigation (for example, REAPPORTIONMENT or abortion), leaving the state courts to be the final arbiters of federal law in these areas. Intense controversy surrounds the question whether Congress has constitutional power to divest the Supreme Court of appellate jurisdiction over specific categories of constitutional litigation. (The one explicit Supreme Court pronouncement on the question, the celebrated EX PARTE McCARDLE [1869], in sweeping language upheld this power pursuant to the explicit provision of Article III providing that the Court's appellate jurisdiction is subject to "such Exceptions" and "such Regulations" as "the Congress shall make.") Even if Congress has jurisdiction-stripping power, however, its exercise—much like the exercise of the power to "pack" the Court— would be widely perceived as anticonstitutional in spirit. In fact, no such legislation has come near to achieving acceptance, attesting to the vast reservoir of ideological and political strength that the ideal of an independent federal judiciary continues to possess.

The more important and authentic debate that continues to rage as the federal court system enters its third century relates to the proper role of an independent federal judiciary in a nation that is democratic but also committed to the ideal of fidelity to law. The federal courts have come to exercise a power over the political, economic, and social life of this nation that no other independent judicial system in the history of mankind has possessed. Whether that power is wholly benign—or whether it should and can be reduced—is one of the great questions to which the twenty-first century will have to attend.

Bibliography

AMERICAN LAW INSTITUTE   1969   Study of the Division of Jurisdiction Between State and Federal Courts. Washington D.C.: American Law Institute.

BATOR, PAUL M.; MISHKIN, PAUL J.; SHAPIRO, DAVID L.; and WECHSLER, HERBERT   1973   *The Federal Courts and the Federal System,* 2nd ed., with 1981 Supplement. Mineola, N.Y.: Foundation Press.

CARRINGTON, PAUL D.; MEADOR, DANIEL J.; AND ROSENBERG, MAURICE   1976   *Justice on Appeal.* St. Paul, Minn.: West Publishing Co.

DIRECTOR OF THE ADMINISTRATIVE OFFICE OF THE UNITED STATES COURTS   [annually]   *Annual Reports.* Washington, D.C.: United States Government Printing Office.

FRANKFURTER, FELIX and LANDIS, JAMES M.   1928   *The Business of the Supreme Court: A Study in the Federal Judicial System.* New York: Macmillan.

FRIENDLY, HENRY J.   1973   *Federal Jurisdiction: A General View.* New York: Columbia University Press.

POSNER, RICHARD A.   1985   *The Federal Courts: Crisis and Reform.* Cambridge, Mass.: Harvard University Press.

WRIGHT, CHARLES ALAN   1983   *The Law of Federal Courts.* St. Paul, Minn.: West Publishing Co.

CHIEF JUSTICE, ROLE OF THE

Kenneth F. Ripple

The title "Chief Justice" appears only once in the Constitution. That mention occurs not in Article III, the judicial article, but in connection with the Chief Justice's role as presiding officer of the Senate during an IMPEACHMENT trial of the President. With such a meager delineation of powers and duties in the Constitution, the importance of the office was hardly obvious during the early days of the Republic. Despite President GEORGE WASHINGTON's great expectations for the post, his first appointee, JOHN JAY, left disillusioned and convinced that neither the Supreme Court nor the chief justiceship would amount to anything. Yet, a little over a century later, President WILLIAM HOWARD TAFT stated that he would prefer the office to his own. During that intervening century, an office of considerable power and prestige had emerged from the constitutional vacuum. Since then, the Chief Justice's role has continued to evolve. Today, the office is the product of both the personalities and the priorities of its incumbents and of the institutional forces which have become stronger as the Supreme Court's role in our government has expanded and matured.

Like the other Justices of the Supreme Court, the Chief Justice of the United States is appointed by the President with the ADVICE AND CONSENT of the Senate. He enjoys, along with all other full members of the federal judiciary, life tenure "during his GOOD BEHAVIOR." With respect to the judicial work of the Court, he has traditionally been referred to as *primus inter pares* —first among equals. He has the same vote as each Associate Justice of the Court. His judicial duties differ only in that he presides over the sessions of the Court and over the Court's private CONFERENCE at which the cases are discussed and eventually decided. When in the majority, he assigns the writing of the OPINION OF THE COURT. Like an Associate Justice, the Chief Justice also performs the duties of a circuit Justice. A circuit Justice must pass upon various applications for temporary relief and BAIL from his circuit and participate, at least in a liaison or advisory capacity, in the judicial administration of that circuit. By tradition, the Chief Justice is circuit Justice for the Fourth and District of Columbia Circuits.

In addition to his judicial duties, the Chief Justice has, by statute, responsibility for the general administration of the Supreme Court. While the senior officers of the Court are appointed by the entire Court, they perform their daily duties under his general supervision. Other employees of the Court must be approved by the Chief Justice.

The Chief Justice also serves as presiding officer of the Judicial Conference of the United States. The Conference, composed of the chief judge and a district judge from each circuit, has the statutory responsibility for making comprehensive surveys of the business of the federal courts and for undertaking a continuous study of the rules of practice and procedure. The Chief Justice, as presiding officer, must appoint the various committees of the Conference which undertake the studies necessary for the achievement of those statutory objectives. He must also submit to the Congress an annual report of the proceedings of the Conference and a report as to its legislative recommendations. Other areas of court administration also occupy the Chief Justice's attention regularly. He has the authority to assign, temporarily, judges of the lower federal courts to courts other than their own and for service on the Panel on Multidistrict Litigation. He is also the permanent Chairman of the Board of the Federal Judicial Center which develops and recommends improvements in the area of judicial administration to the Judicial Conference.

From time to time, Congress has also assigned by statute other duties to the Chief Justice. Some are related to the judiciary; others are not. For instance, he must appoint some of the members of the Commission on Executive, Legislative, and Judicial Salaries; the Advisory Corrections Council; the Federal Records Council; and the National Study Commission on Records and Documents of Federal Officials. He also serves as Chancellor of the Smithsonian Institution and as a member of the Board of Trustees of both the National Gallery of Art and the Joseph H. Hirshhorn Museum and Sculpture Garden.

In addition to these formal duties, the Chief Justice is considered the titular head of the legal profession in the United States. He traditionally addresses the American Bar Association on the state of the judiciary and delivers the opening address at the annual meeting of the American Law Institute. He is regularly invited to other ceremonial and substantive meetings of the bar. Finally, as head of the judicial branch, he regularly participates in national observances and state ceremonies honoring foreign dignitaries.

The foregoing catalog of duties, while describing a burdensome role, does not fully indicate the impact of the Chief Justice on the Supreme Court's work. For instance, with respect to his judicial duties, the Chief Justice, while nominally only "first among equals," may exercise a significant influence on the Court's decision-making process and, consequently, on its final judicial work product. His most obvious opportunity to influence that process is while presiding at the Court's conference. He presents each case initially and is the first to give his views. Thus, he has the opportunity to take the initiative by directing the Court's inquiry to those aspects of the case he believes are crucial. Moreover, although the Justices discuss cases in descending order of seniority, they vote in the opposite order. Therefore, while speaking first, the "Chief," as he is referred to by his colleagues, votes last and commits himself, even preliminarily, only after all of the associates have explained their positions and cast their votes. If he votes with the majority, he may retain the opinion for himself or assign it to a colleague whose views are most compatible with his own. In cases where there is significant indecision among the Justices, it falls to the "Chief" to take the initiative with respect to the Court's further consideration of the case. He may, for instance, suggest that further discussion be deferred until argument of other related cases or he may request that several Justices set forth their views in writing in the hope that such a memorandum might form the basis of a later opinion.

There are also more indirect but highly significant ways by which the "Chief" can influence the decision-making process. As presiding officer during open session, he sets a "tone" which can make ORAL ARGUMENT either a formal, stilted affair or a disciplined but relaxed, productive dialogue between the Court and counsel. Even the Chief Justice's "administrative" duties within the Court can have a subtle influence on the Court's decision-making processes. The efficient administration of the Court's support services as well as the employment of adequate staff personnel can nurture an ambiance conducive to harmonious decision making.

While occupancy of the Court's center chair no doubt gives the incumbent an enhanced capacity to influence jurisprudential developments, there are clear limitations on the exercise of that power. The Court is a collegial institution; disagreement on important issues is a natural phenomenon. In such a context, as Justice WILLIAM H. REHNQUIST put it in a 1976 article: "The power to calm such naturally troubled waters is usually beyond the capacity of any mortal chief justice. He presides over a conference not of eight subordinates, whom he may direct or instruct, but of eight associates who, like him, have tenure during good behavior, and who are as independent as hogs on ice. He may at most persuade or cajole them." Political acumen is often as important as intellectual brilliance. Whatever the Chief's view of his power, he must remember that, in the eyes of the associates, "the Chief Justice is not entitled to a presumption that he knows more law than other members of the Court . . .," as Justice Rehnquist said in chambers in CLEMENTS v. LOGAN (1981). Other institutional concerns further constrain the Chief's ability to guide the Court's decisions. All Chief Justices have recognized, although to varying degrees, a responsibility to see not only that the Court gets its business done but also that it does so in a manner which maintains the country's confidence. Sometimes, those objectives require that the Chief refrain from taking a strong ideological stance and act as a mediator in the formation of a majority. Similarly, while the assignment power can be a powerful tool, it must be exercised to ensure a majority opinion that advances, not retards, growth in the law. Even the prerogative of presiding over the conference has a price. The Chief Justice must spend significant additional time reviewing all the petitions filed with the Court. As the performance of Chief Justice CHARLES EVANS HUGHES demonstrated, perceiving those areas of ambiguity and conflict that are most troublesome in the administration of justice is essential to leading effectively the discussion of the conference. For the same reason, the Chief must take the time to master the intricacies of the Court's procedure.

The extrajudicial responsibilities of the Chief Justice can also place him at a distinct disadvantage in influencing the Court's jurisprudential direction. The internal decision-making process of the Court is essentially competitive. There is nothing so humble as a draft opinion with four votes and nothing so arrogant as one with six. Such a process does not easily take into account that one participant must regularly divert his attention because of other official responsibilities. Moreover, there is a special intellectual and physical cost in shifting constantly between the abstract world of the appellate judge and the pragmatic one of the administrator. A Chief Justice who takes all his responsibilities seriously must experience the fatiguing tension that inevitably results from such bifurcation of responsibilities. Here, however, there may be compensating considerations. Whatever advantage the Chief may lose in the judicial bargaining because of administrative distractions may well be partially recovered by the prestige gained by his accomplishments beyond the Court. The Court has benefited from a strong Chief Justice's defense against specific political threats such as President FRANKLIN D. ROOSEVELT's Court-packing plan. It has also benefited when the Chief's efforts have resulted in legislation making its own workload more manageable. Chief Justice Taft's support of the JUDICIARY ACT OF 1925, for instance, gave the Court more control over its own docket and, consequently, increased capacity to address, selectively, the most pressing issues. In modern times, the tremors of the litigation explosion that has engulfed the lower courts have been felt on the Supreme Court. The accomplishments of a Chief Justice in alleviating these problems cannot be overlooked by his associates.

Certainly, with respect to nonjudicial matters, a Chief Justice's special responsibility for institutional concerns has commanded respect from the associates. Even such greats as Justice LOUIS D. BRANDEIS regularly consulted the Chief on matters that might have an impact on the reputa-tion of the Court as an institution. This same identification of the Chief Justice with the Supreme Court as an institution has made some Chief Justices the acknowledged spokesperson for both the Supreme Court and the lower federal courts before the other branches of government and, indeed, before the public.

With no specific constitutional mandate to fulfill, early Chief Justices, most especially JOHN MARSHALL, molded the office in which they served just as they molded the courts over which they presided. In those forma-tive periods, the dominance of personal factors was understandable. Today, however, significant institutional forces also shape the office. In addition to the extrajudicial duties imposed by Congress, the Court, now a mature institution of American government, exerts through its traditions a powerful influence over every new incumbent of its bench—including the person in the center chair.

Bibliography

FRANKFURTER, FELIX 1953 Chief Justices I Have Known. *Virginia Law Review* 39:883–905.

FREUND, PAUL A. 1967 Charles Evans Hughes as Chief Justice. *Harvard Law Review* 81:4–43.

REHNQUIST, WILLIAM H. 1976 Chief Justices I Never Knew. *Hastings Constitutional Law Quarterly* 3:637–655.

SWINDLER, WILLIAM F. 1971 The Chief Justice and Law Reform. *The Supreme Court Review* 1971:241–264.

SOLICITOR GENERAL

Erwin N. Griswold

The solicitor general is a senior officer of the United States Department of Justice with special responsibilities in the representation of the United States and its officers and agencies before the Supreme Court, and in the administration of justice in the federal appellate courts.

The title—solicitor general—like that of ATTORNEY GENERAL is derived from English usage, but the functions of the offices are quite different in the United States. In England, both offices are political in the sense that they are filled by members of Parliament. In the United States, neither the attorney general nor the solicitor general is a member of Congress. The attorney general is a member of the Cabinet. He advises the President, works with members of Congress on legislative matters and judicial appointments, holds press conferences and is otherwise responsible for governmental and public relations. He is also charged with administering a large department which includes the Federal Bureau of Investigation, the Bureau of Prisons, the Immigration and Naturalization Service, and other important agencies. Though he has policy and administrative responsibilities of great importance, he has virtually no time to be a lawyer in the traditional sense.

Until 1870, the attorney general functioned alone with only a small staff, and in association with the United States attorneys in the various states, over whom he had little authority. In 1870, apparently as an economy device (to eliminate the cost of retaining private lawyers in the increasing number of cases), Congress established the Department of Justice, with the attorney general as its head. The statute provided that there should be in the Department "an officer learned in the law, to assist the Attorney-General in the performance of his duties, to be called the solicitor-general." Under the statute the solicitor general was authorized in the attorney general's discretion to argue "any case in which the government is interested" before the Supreme Court, or in any federal or state court." These statutory provisions remain to the present day, essentially unchanged.

In the years since 1870, the duties of the Department of Justice have greatly increased. Until 1953 the solicitor general was the second officer in the Department of Justice and served as acting attorney general in the attorney general's absence. The responsibilities of the attorney general have made it necessary to add a deputy attorney general and an associate attorney general, so that the solicitor general is now the fourth ranking officer in the department. But the solicitor general's responsibilities have remained essentially unchanged in substance—though greatly increased in volume—over the past sixty years. He remains the leading officer in the department functioning primarily as a lawyer.

As the pattern has developed, the solicitor general is not a politician, and he has only a minimum of political responsibility. His function is to be the government's top lawyer in the courts, particularly the Supreme Court, and by well-established tradition he is allowed considerable independence in carrying out this role. Bent and Schloss, describing the office as "the bridge between the Executive and the Judiciary," have said that "[t]he Solicitor General must often choose between incongruous roles and differing loyalties. He is still the government's lawyer, and he most frequently acts as an advocate. On the other hand, he also functions as a reviewer of government policies, an officer of the Court, and . . . a protector of the public interest."

In more specific terms, the organization of the Department of Justice assigns to the solicitor general four areas of responsibility. Two of these are of primary importance. First, the solicitor general is responsible for the representation of the United States and its officers and agencies in all cases before the Supreme Court of the United States. The BRIEFS which are filed on behalf of the government in the Supreme Court are prepared by him or under his direction. He argues the most important cases himself, and assigns the argument in other cases to members of his staff, to other lawyers in the Department of Justice or to lawyers for the agencies which may be involved in the cases before the Court. Second, the Solicitor General decides whether the United States will APPEAL in any case which it loses in any court, state or federal, or indeed in foreign courts. This function is not widely known, even in the legal profession. It is, however, a very important means of coordinating and controlling the government's litigation, so that cases of little importance are not taken to the appellate courts. It also serves to minimize the taking of inconsistent positions before the various appellate courts.

This function includes determining whether any case will be taken by the government to the Supreme Court. This is probably the most important responsibility assigned to the solicitor general. With few exceptions, no case can now be taken to the Supreme Court except on application for review—called a petition for a WRIT OF CERTIORARI. In recent years, some four thousand such applications are made to the Court by all parties each year. Yet the Court can hear on the merits only about a hundred and fifty cases a year. This means that it is of great importance for the solicitor general to select with care the relatively small number of cases in which the government will file petitions. A high proportion of the solicitor general's petitions are in fact granted by the Court, which means that he has, as part of his responsibility, carried out an important part of the selection process necessarily confronting the Court.

In addition to the two functions just outlined, the solicitor general has two other responsibilities. These assist him in carrying out his role as overall controller of Government APPELLATE JURISDICTION. First his authorization must be obtained before the United States or one of its officers or agencies files a brief as friend of the court—AMICUS CURIAE— in any appellate court. Second his authorization must be obtained before a petition for REHEARING *en banc* —before the whole court—is filed in any UNITED STATES COURT OF APPEALS. The courts of appeals are overburdened, and hearings EN BANC present serious logistical problems. Requiring authority from the solicitor general means that such petitions are rarely filed, and only in the most important cases.

The solicitor general's office is a relatively small one, though it has grown slowly in recent years. At the present time it numbers about twenty lawyers in addition to the solicitor general himself; and, including secretaries and aides, the total number of personnel in the office is about fifty. Thus it can operate in much the same way as a moderate-sized law firm. There is considerable pressure in the office as the cases keep coming in, from all parts of the country, and almost all of them are subject to relatively short deadlines.

In the nature of things, the solicitor general cannot be a specialist. The cases coming to his desk involve every field of law—constitutional law, ADMINISTRATIVE LAW, criminal law, tax law, antitrust law, labor law, international law, ENVIRONMENTAL PROTECTION, energy, and every other field with which the government is concerned. Inevitably, the staff in the office specialize to some extent, and there are four deputy solicitors general, each of whom has special responsibilities for particular areas. But there are no rigid lines, and all lawyers in the office are available to handle the various types of cases as they come in.

The solicitor general's role in the Supreme Court is limited to the representation of the United States, its officers, and its agencies. Other cases which may be of great importance involve private parties, or states or their subsidiaries. Thus, the cases involving BIRTH CONTROL (GRISWOLD v. CONNECTICUT, 1965) and abortion (ROE v. WADE, 1973) were not handled by the solicitor general. But more than half of the cases before the Supreme Court (particularly those heard by the Court on the merits) are "government cases," that is, cases in which the United States, or its officers or agents, are parties. It is important to the Court to have these cases handled in competent fashion, and the research and ideas, and policy decisions, lying behind the solicitor general's advocacy before the Supreme Court can influence the decisions reached by the Court.

Much of the government's litigation before the Supreme Court, though important, does not attract wide public attention. From time to time, though, cases coming before the Court are rather spectacular in terms of public interest. Reference may be made, for example, to YOUNGSTOWN SHEET & TUBE CO. v. SAWYER (1952), where the Court invalidated the action of President HARRY S. TRUMAN in seizing the steel industry during the KOREAN WAR, the Pentagon Papers case (NEW YORK TIMES CO. v. UNITED STATES, 1971), and UNITED STATES v. NIXON (1974), where the Court held that the White House tapes made under the direction of President RICHARD M. NIXON must be turned over in response to a SUBPOENA from a GRAND JURY. For the most part, though, the work of the solicitor general and his staff is rather straightforward professional work.

It is important to recognize that in all cases the solicitor general is an advocate and not a judge. However, he is a very special sort of advocate. There are some positions which he will not support because he thinks the government's position is clearly wrong in law. On rare occasions, in such cases, he "confesses error" before the Court. The Court is not bound by such a confession, but it usually accepts the solicitor general's conclusion. There are other cases where the solicitor general will not himself defend the government's position, but he thinks a "respectable" defense can be made, and he assigns another government lawyer who is willing to do so to present that defense. Illustration of this may be found in *Peters v. Hobby* (1955), involving the LOYALTY-SECURITY PROGRAM during the 1950s, and in *Gutknecht v. United States* (1970), involving "delinquency reclassification" under the SELECTIVE SERVICE ACT. But the solicitor general will frequently advocate a position which he believes to be worthy of presentation to the Court even though he might not decide in favor of that position if he were a judge. Laymen sometimes have difficulty in accepting this, but, within limits, it is inherent in the role of a lawyer, and it is inherent in the position of the solicitor general. For he is the government's chief advocate. The function of deciding cases is assigned to others.

In this situation, the solicitor general's role is sometimes a difficult one. Whenever he decides not to take a case before the Supreme Court, he is in effect depriving the Court of the opportunity to decide it. This is, indeed, an important part of his function, in view of the fact that many more applications come to the Court than it can possibly accept. The solicitor general's judgment that the chances of success in a particular case are slim is obviously a relevant consideration. Yet there are cases of such importance that he should take the case to the Court, in order to obtain a definitive decision, even though he has little faith in the government's position.

An illustration is found in UNITED STATES v. UNITED STATES DISTRICT COURT (1972). This involved the validity of so-called national security WIRETAPS, made on executive authority (the President or the attorney general) alone, without a judicial warrant. As the cases before the Supreme Court developed, it seemed unlikely that the Court would uphold such wiretaps, at least in cases of domestic security. Yet the attorney general needed to know. If he had such authority, cases might develop where he would need to use it. If he did not have the authority, he should have the definitive decision of the Supreme Court, by which he would, of course, abide. A petition was filed with the Court in order that the question might be definitively settled, and the Court granted the petition. In due course, the Court held that domestic "national security" wiretaps are illegal under the FOURTH AMENDMENT, when made without a court warrant. Thus the solicitor general, though himself dubious about the government's case, played his appropriate role in obtaining a definitive decision on an important public question.

In the daily routine of his office the solicitor general has many decisions to make. In making these decisions, he may be subject to various pressures. These pressures may be wholly legitimate professional pressures from other lawyers in the government seeking to persuade him to accept their view. He frequently gives hearings, too, to opposing lawyers. There may also be various forms of political pressure—rarely presented as such—from Capitol Hill, or from other officers of the government. The solicitor general should be able to receive such representations and come to his own conclusions. Attorneys general have usually been firm in their support of the solicitor general. And, indeed, the fact that the decision is assigned to the solicitor general may serve to protect the attorney general from such pressures. But the attorney general and the President are the solicitor general's superiors, and if he receives an order from above he must decide whether the matter is one of principle for him; if it is, he must resign. As far as is known, no solicitor general has ever resigned for such a reason. But this is what happened to Attorney General Elliott Richardson and Deputy Attorney General William Ruckelshaus, when they refused to comply with President Nixon's order to discharge Archibald Cox as Special Prosecutor in 1973.

Special problems arise when officers or agencies differ from the position of the solicitor general, and especially when two or more agencies have different interests or points of view which they present vigorously to the solicitor general or his staff. A situation of this sort arose in the case of *Fortnightly Corp. v. United Artists Television, Inc.* (1968), involving cable television. The Copyright Office in the Library of Congress had one view about the case. The Federal Communications Commission had another. And the Antitrust Division in the Department of Justice had still a third. All views were strongly advocated. The solicitor general negotiated separately with the lawyers for each office concerned. None would yield. Then he held a meeting at which all interested lawyers were present, hoping that some sort of a consensus would emerge. Unfortunately, none did, and the solicitor general concluded that he had no alternative but to formulate his own view, which he submitted to the Court.

This case exemplifies one of the important roles of the solicitor general, in resolving differences within the government, so that a single position may be presented to the Court. When these differences arise within the Justice Department, or between the several executive departments, the solicitor general seeks to persuade but eventually may have to make his own decision. The situation is somewhat more difficult when the difference is with one of the "independent agencies," such as the Federal Trade Commission or the Securities and Exchange Commission.

For historical reasons, it has long been settled that the Interstate Commerce Commission and the Maritime Commission can appear before the Supreme Court through their own lawyers. With respect to the other agencies, however, the statutory provisions are not explicit. Though there is occasionally some tension, the solicitor general has been able to maintain effective control over agency cases in the Supreme Court. In this process, various devices are used. He sometimes advises the Court that the agency has a different view. He sometimes authorizes the agency to file a brief stating its view. By and large, the agencies believe that the solicitor general's support is important and helpful, and this belief is reinforced by the standing of the solicitor general before the Court. Cases of this sort are carefully considered in the solicitor general's office, and full hearings are given to the lawyers from the agencies involved. In this way problems of real difficulty have been resolved with substantial satisfaction on the part of all concerned.

There is a final role of the solicitor general which, though long an important one, has been of increasing significance in recent years. This is the preparation and filing of briefs in the Supreme Court as a friend of the Court—amicus curiae. Under the Rules of the Supreme Court, the solicitor general is authorized to file such a brief without consent of the parties or special leave of the Court. Frequently a case between private parties, or a state criminal prosecution, may raise a question of great interest to the federal government, though the latter is not a party. An example is TERRY v. OHIO (1968), involving the validity of a STOP AND FRISK by local police. The solicitor general filed an amicus brief in that case because of the great interest of the federal government in law enforcement. Through such briefs, the solicitor general protects the interests of the federal government, aids the Court by furnishing information and relevant legal materials, facilitates the handling of difficult questions with the "independent agencies" of the government, and, on occasion, presents his own views on novel constitutional questions.

In this way, the solicitor general has participated in cases involving

SCHOOL DESEGREGATION, legislative REAPPORTIONMENT, CAPITAL PUNISH-
MENT, CIVIL RIGHTS, and many other important questions of developing
constitutional and statutory law. Within wide limits, the solicitor general
has freedom to develop his own position in such briefs. The solicitor
general and his staff have great experience in Supreme Court cases,
and well-considered and carefully prepared briefs can be of considerable
assistance to the Court through impartial and informed analysis of novel
questions.

Indeed, a high proportion of briefs amicus filed by the solicitor
general are prepared because of direct invitation from the Court. Such
invitations are always treated as commands, and great care is taken in
determining the position to be taken and in developing the materials
to be included in the brief. In many ways, such briefs are the purest
expression of the relation of trust and confidence which has long been
established between the solicitor general and the Court.

It is this trust and confidence on which the position of the solicitor
general before the Court, and his effective representation of the United
States, in the long run depend.

Bibliography

NOTE   1969   Government Litigation in the Supreme Court: The Roles of the
    Solicitor General. *Yale Law Journal* 78:1442–1481.

UNITED STATES COURTS OF APPEALS

Judge Carl McGowan

The United States Courts of Appeals form the intermediate component of the three-tiered federal judiciary, lying between the UNITED STATES DISTRICT COURTS and the SUPREME COURT of the United States. As such, they normally serve as the first courts of review in the federal JUDICIAL SYSTEM. But because of the natural limitations upon the Supreme Court's capacity, the Courts of Appeals are often also the final courts of review.

Article III, section 1, of the Constitution provides: "The JUDICIAL POWER OF THE UNITED STATES, shall be vested in one supreme Court, and in such inferior Courts as the Congress may from time to time ordain and establish." Thus, in contrast to the Supreme Court, inferior federal courts were not required by the Constitution; rather, their creation was left to the discretion of Congress. Such treatment reflected a compromise between two views, one favoring the mandatory creation of inferior courts, and the other completely opposed to the existence of any such courts.

The Courts of Appeals are relative newcomers to the federal judicial system, having been born with the CIRCUIT COURTS OF APPEALS ACT (Evarts Act) of 1891. The Courts of Appeals were created to solve an acute crisis in the federal judiciary stemming from the limited capacity of the existing system, which had remained largely unchanged since the JUDICIARY ACT OF 1789. That act had established a bilevel system of inferior federal courts. There were, first of all, single-judge "district courts," generally one per state. The Union was also divided into several "circuits." CIRCUIT COURT was to be held twice a year in each of the districts encompassed by a given circuit. At these sittings, cases would be heard by a three-judge panel consisting of two Supreme Court Justices and the district judge for the district in which the circuit court was being held.

Having determined to avail itself of its constitutional prerogative to establish inferior federal courts, Congress faced the further issue of those courts' appropriate function and JURISDICTION. In the debates over Article III, there had been substantial support for giving Congress the power to create only admiralty courts, rather than inferior courts of general jurisdiction. No such limitation was adopted, however. It has therefore been generally assumed that Congress is constitutionally free to define the role of the inferior federal courts however it chooses.

The manner that Congress selected in the 1789 act is of some interest. The district courts were, and remain today, trial courts or courts of first instance. The circuit courts, in distinct contrast to today's middle-tier courts, also functioned primarily as trial courts. In the area of private civil law, the circuit courts' jurisdiction was largely concurrent with that of the district courts: it encompassed cases within the DIVERSITY JURISDIC-TION, but not FEDERAL QUESTION cases. (Original federal jurisdiction was not extended to federal question cases until 1875.) Similarly, with respect to civil suits by the United States, both circuit and district courts were given ORIGINAL JURISDICTION, the only difference being that the requisite amount in controversy was higher for circuit court jurisdiction.

The circuit courts even had certain original jurisdiction that the district courts lacked. The first removal jurisdiction was vested in the circuit courts alone. And the circuit courts had exclusive jurisdiction over most federal crimes.

Nonetheless, the seeds of the modern federal courts of appeals were planted by the first Judiciary Act. The early circuit courts had appellate jurisdiction in civil cases involving disputes over amounts exceeding $50, and in admiralty cases exceeding $300. (A district judge sitting as a circuit judge was not, however, permitted to vote on appeals from his own decisions.) Unlike the modern courts of appeals, however, the circuit courts were the final federal forum for many of these cases. In civil suits, circuit court judgments were reviewable only when the amount in dispute exceeded $2,000. Judgments in criminal cases were categorically unreviewable.

The early circuit courts proved problematic, in the main because of the burden that circuit riding placed on the Supreme Court Justices. Congress attempted to alleviate that hardship by reducing from two to one the number of Justices required to sit on a circuit court, but the benefit of the reduction was more than outweighed by several important augmentations of the High Court's jurisdiction that were enacted by Congress during the century following the 1789 Judiciary Act. Most notable of such legislation was the JUDICIARY ACT OF 1875, which granted the lower courts, as well as the Supreme Court, nearly the full scope of Article III jurisdiction, including original federal question jurisdiction in the district and circuit courts. The federal courts, already vastly over-loaded with cases, were virtually submerged after this act. Reform was inevitable.

Indeed, attempts to improve the judicial system had more than once been made. In 1801 Congress had enacted the JUDICIARY ACT OF 1801 (the "Law of the Midnight Judges"), which among other things had established permanent circuit judgeships, three to a circuit. When political tides shifted the following year, however, the act was repealed, and the system reverted essentially to its original condition, except that Congress permitted circuit court to be held by a single judge, rather than three. Much later, in 1869, Congress partially restored the plan of 1801 by creating a single permanent circuit judgeship for each of the nine circuits then in existence. And in 1887 and 1888 Congress passed a series of measures aimed at pruning the expanded jurisdiction of the lower federal courts.

But it was not until the Evarts Act that Congress provided structural reforms adequate to the crisis of judicial overload. The act established three-judge courts of appeals for each of the nine circuits, and increased the number of permanent circuit judgeships to two per circuit. The third appeals judge would in most instances be a district judge (though Supreme Court Justices remained eligible), but the act, following the rule set down by the Act of 1789, barred district judges from reviewing their own decisions.

Curiously, the Evarts Act left the old circuit courts standing, although it did remove their APPELLATE JURISDICTION. Until these courts were abolished in 1911, there thus functioned two sets of federal trial courts.

The Evarts Act provided for direct review by the Supreme Court of the decisions of the district courts and the old circuit courts, in some important cases. The new circuit courts of appeals would review the remainder. Under the act, a circuit court's decision in an admiralty or diversity case would be final, unless that court certified a question to the Supreme Court or the Supreme Court granted a WRIT OF CERTIORARI in order to review the circuit court's decision. In most other cases, circuit court decisions were appealable as of right.

Since the Evarts Act, only a few significant alterations have been made to the federal judicial system in general, and the courts of appeals in particular. The rules governing Supreme Court review are perhaps the most important arena of change. In 1925, Congress replaced appeal as of right with discretionary review for all circuit court judgments except those holding a state statute unconstitutional. In 1937, Congress passed a law permitting appeal to the Supreme Court from any judgment by a federal court holding an act of Congress unconstitutional in any civil case to which the United States is a party.

In 1948 the circuit courts established by the Evarts Act were renamed; each court is now known as the United States Court of Appeals for the_____Circuit. The number of circuits has also been increased; and there is now a "Federal Circuit" court to hear appeals from the CLAIMS COURT and from district courts in patent cases or in cases arising under the TUCKER ACT. Finally, procedures in the various courts of appeals were standardized in 1968 in the Federal Rules of Appellate Procedure. Each circuit, however, retains its own rule-making power for matters not covered by the Federal Rules.

The chief work of the courts of appeals is the review of final judgments of the United States district courts. The courts, however, are also empowered to review certain orders that are not strictly final, essentially when the benefit of such review clearly outweighs any attendant disruption and delay of district court proceedings. In addition, Congress has enabled the appeals courts to issue the extraordinary WRIT OF MANDAMUS and WRIT OF PROHIBITION in cases in which district courts may abuse their constitutional powers. Finally, the statutes governing many of the various federal administrative agencies provide for direct review of agency adjudication and rule-making in the court of appeals for the circuit in which the party seeking review resides, or in the Court of Appeals for the District of Columbia Circuit. The latter circuit court has been a frequent forum for challenges, constitutional and otherwise, to federal agency action.

To understand the role of the courts of appeals in the development of constitutional law, it is necessary to understand the relationship between the appeals courts and the Supreme Court. As was noted above, since the JUDICIARY ACT OF 1925, the "Judges Bill," the Supreme Court has had a discretionary power of review of most circuit court decisions. Again, however, appeal as of right lies in cases in which the appeals court has held a state statute to be repugnant to the Constitution, laws, or treaties of the United States, and in civil cases in which either a court of appeals or a district court has held an act of Congress unconstitutional and the United States is a party. Nonetheless, neither type of case in which appeal is of right bulks very large in the overall volume of appeals from circuit courts, and of those, many are denied Supreme Court review for want of a substantial federal question.

Accordingly, the Supreme Court has the discretion to review or not to review the vast majority of decisions by the courts of appeals. Not surprisingly, because of the limited capacity of the High Court, its discretion is much more often exercised to deny review than to grant it. As a general rule, in fact, the Supreme Court tends not to review appeals court decisions unless the issues involved either have an urgent importance or have received conflicting treatment by different circuits, or both.

One might conclude that, because the Supreme Court does review important cases, the appeals courts have no significant role in the development of constitutional law. Constitutional law, however, is not the product solely of the Supreme Court.

To begin, the Supreme Court can only review a decision that a party seeks to have reviewed; not every losing party in the court of appeals may do so. For example, in *Kennedy v. Sampson* (1974) the District of Columbia Circuit construed the POCKET VETO clause of the Constitution (Article 1, section 7, clause 2) to bar the President from exercising the pocket veto power during brief, intrasession adjournments of Congress. The President then declined to seek review in the Supreme Court; he chose instead to acquiesce in the rule laid down by the appeals court. The court's decision thus became a cornerstone of the law respecting the presentation of laws for presidential approval.

Of course, as a glance at any constitutional law textbook or casebook reveals, the vast majority of important constitutional PRECEDENTS are produced not by the courts of appeals but by the Supreme Court. Decisions like *Kennedy* are thus the exception, not the rule. Nonetheless, in several ways the appeals courts contribute significantly to the development of constitutional law.

Before a constitutional issue is decided by the Supreme Court, it will often have received a thorough ventilation by one or more circuit courts. The Supreme Court thus has the benefit of the circuit judges' consideration of difficult constitutional matters, and may sometimes explicitly adopt the reasoning of the court of appeals. For example, in *United States v. Dennis* (1950) the Second Circuit faced the difficult issue of whether, and if so, how, the CLEAR AND PRESENT DANGER test applied to a conspiracy to advocate the overthrow of the government by force and violence and to organize a political party for the purpose of such advocacy. The Court of Appeals, in an opinion by Judge LEARNED HAND, held that such advocacy was unprotected by the FIRST AMENDMENT even though the actual forceful overthrow of the government was not imminent. The Supreme Court affirmed the decision in DENNIS V. UNITED STATES (1951), and its opinion adopted much of Judge Hand's analysis, including Judge Hand's "clear and present danger" formula, namely, "whether the gravity of the 'evil,' discounted by its improbability, justifies such invasion of free speech as is necessary to avoid the danger."

The role of the courts of appeals in resolving novel issues of constitutional law, however, is only half of the picture. Equally important is the appeals courts' adjudication of cases raising issues on which the Supreme Court has already spoken. Because the High Court can only sketch the broad outlines of constitutional DOCTRINE, it remains for the lower courts to apply precedent, elaborate or clarify it, and extrapolate from it. Because appeal from the district courts to the appeals court is of right, and because most litigation never reaches the Supreme Court, it is in the courts of appeals that the Supreme Court's sketch is worked into a fully drawn landscape.

When the Supreme Court decides not to give plenary review to a case arising from an appeals court, what implication should be drawn concerning the value of the appeals court's opinion as a precedent? By denying a petition for certiorari or dismissing an appeal as of right for want of jurisdiction, the Court formally indicates no view of the merits or demerits of the appeals court's decision. Nonetheless, it is commonly thought that the Supreme Court generally does not decline to review an appeals court decision that it finds clearly incorrect. Similarly, when the Supreme Court summarily affirms an appeals court's decision, it is formally signaling its agreement with the result only, and not necessarily the reasoning of the lower court. Yet, such affirmances are popularly thought to indicate at least the Court's tentative agreement with the substance of the lower court's opinion.

Since the early 1960s, the federal courts at all three levels have experienced a dramatic and continuing increase in their workload. At the district and circuit levels, Congress has responded by adding judges to existing courts. When the number of judges in a circuit has become sufficiently great, Congress has divided the circuit into two. That course is not entirely satisfactory, however, because it tends to push the appeals courts in the direction of being regional, rather than national courts, and increases the likelihood of intercircuit conflict.

At the Supreme Court level, Congress has made no significant changes. Various proposals for reducing the Court's workload would also affect adjudication at the appeals court level. A frequent suggestion has been to establish a national court of appeals. In one version, the national court would sit only to resolve conflicts among the circuits, thereby eliminating a significant share of the Supreme Court's annual docket. In another version, the national court would screen cases to determine those worthy of Supreme Court review. Another proposal would reduce the Supreme Court's workload by eliminating appeal as of right. One effect of such a measure, of course, would be to increase the number of appeals court decisions that are effectively final.

Bibliography

BATOR, PAUL M.; MISHKIN, PAUL J.; SHAPIRO, DAVID L.; and WECHSLER, HERBERT 1973 *Hart and Wechsler's The Federal Courts and the Federal System,* 2nd ed. Mineola, N.Y.: Foundation Press.
WRIGHT, CHARLES A. 1983 *Handbook of the Law of Federal Courts.* St. Paul, Minn.: West Publishing Co.

UNITED STATES DISTRICT COURTS

Judge Robert L. Carter

In enacting Article III, the Framers of the Constitution authorized the establishment of a federal judicial system consisting of a SUPREME COURT and such inferior courts as Congress might decide to establish. In the JUDICIARY ACT OF 1789 Congress created a Supreme Court, divided the country into three circuits, authorized a CIRCUIT COURT to sit in each circuit, and established a federal district court in each of the states. The Supreme Court was the only truly appellate court in the system. Unlike the modern courts of appeal, the old circuit courts, while exercising some appellate jurisdiction, were intended to be the chief federal trial courts. A Supreme Court Justice riding the circuit and judges of the district courts in the circuit manned each of these circuit courts.

The federal district courts were empowered to sit at various times in specified locations within the states where they were located. They were tribunals of very limited JURISDICTION and originally had as their main function the adjudication of admiralty and maritime matters. It was anticipated that the state trial courts or federal circuit courts would handle, as trial courts, the most important legal issues facing the new nation. The federal district courts were empowered to try minor criminal cases. In addition, they had CONCURRENT JURISDICTION with the circuit courts over suits by ALIENS for tort violations of a treaty or the law of nations, suits against consuls, and disputes in which the federal government initiated the proceeding and the matter in controversy was $100 or less. However, district court jurisdiction was exclusive in admiralty, over seizures of land for violation of federal statutes, and over seizures under import, navigation, and trade statutes.

This limited and specialized jurisdiction has steadily expanded. Today the district court is the only federal nonspecialized court, handling both criminal and civil matters. Among the latter are admiralty cases, federal question cases, and cases within the DIVERSITY JURISDICTION (cases between different states). In a diversity case the matter in controversy must exceed $10,000. No jurisdictional amount is normally required for the other exercises of the district court's civil jurisdiction. Appeals from a district court go to the UNITED STATES COURT OF APPEALS.

The first district court to be organized was the district court of

New York. That court began functioning on November 3, 1789, and was the predecessor to the current district court for the Southern District of New York. Even today judges of the Southern District refer to theirs as the "Mother Court."

As the system was originally conceived, each state was to contain at least one federal district and one federal court. There has been no deviation from this pattern as the country has expanded from thirteen to fifty states. In addition, the DISTRICT OF COLUMBIA and the federal TERRITORIES (the Virgin Islands, PUERTO RICO, and Guam) are each organized as a federal district with a district court. In over half the states, although there may be a number of federal district judges who sit in separate locations throughout the state, there is only one federal district. Twelve states are divided into two federal districts; some states have three federal districts; and California, New York, and Texas are subdivided into four federal districts.

As the country has expanded, the number of federal district judges has increased. Since 1954 the roster of federal judges has grown through enactment of legislation authorizing additional judgeships for federal district courts nationwide. The Omnibus Judgeship Act of 1978 raised the number of authorized district judges from 399 to 516. The Southern District of New York has twenty-seven authorized judgeships, the largest number of any district in the country.

Federal district judges are nominated by the President and appointed with the ADVICE AND CONSENT of the Senate. The prevailing practice is for the selection of the nominee to come to the President from the Department of Justice. If one or both of the senators from the state in question belong to the President's party, the candidate for nomination is proposed by one or both senators and submitted to the Department of Justice for approval and recommendation to the President for nomination. Today few candidates are nominated and sent to the Senate for confirmation without first being found qualified by the American Bar Association. When the President decides to nominate a candidate, the Federal Bureau of Investigation undertakes a security check. If the candidate is cleared, the President announces the nomination and sends the name to the Senate. The Senate Judiciary Committee holds hearings, which are usually one-day affairs for candidates for federal district courts. If the Senate Judiciary Committee approves, the nomination is voted on by the full Senate.

An Article III judge has life tenure during GOOD BEHAVIOR, and his salary cannot be diminished while he is in office. The only way to remove a federal district judge from office is by IMPEACHMENT. Of course, a federal judge, like any other person, may be prosecuted for criminal law violations. Bribery has been the most frequent charge, but criminal prosecutions of federal judges are rare and attempts to remove them by impeachment have been infrequent.

When the first change of political power occurred in the United States at the national level, from the Federalist party to the Republican party of THOMAS JEFFERSON, the Jeffersonians commenced impeachment proceedings against two judges appointed by the Federalists and disliked by the Republicans: JOHN PICKERING, a judge of the district court in New Hampshire, and SAMUEL CHASE, an Associate Justice of the Supreme Court. Pickering was convicted by the Senate in 1803, but the requisite two-thirds Senate majority could not be mustered to convict Chase. Since that time impeachment to unseat a federal judge has not been a successful political weapon. Partisan politics has from time to time generated unsuccessful calls for impeachment of various judges.

A federal district court judgeship carries considerable prestige. It is a presidential appointment; it is a national rather than a local office; and federal district court judgeships are limited in number. District judges in the main have had prior careers as prominent or distinguished lawyers before going on the bench. They are drawn for the most part from the middle and upper strata of our society. They are generally alumni of the best known law schools of the nation or of the state in which they will serve. They have generally had successful careers in private practice, often with backgrounds as federal, state, or local prosecutors. A few are former academics, and some come to court from public service careers outside government.

Until the twentieth century, all federal district judges were white males. The first woman to be confirmed as a federal judge was Florence Allen, who was appointed to the Court of Appeals for the Sixth Circuit in 1934. The first woman appointed to the district court was Burneta Matthews, who was given an interim appointment to the District of Columbia bench in 1949. She was confirmed by the Senate in 1950 for a permanent appointment. Constance Baker Motley was the first black woman to be appointed to the federal bench. She was appointed to the District Court for the Southern District of New York in 1966, and in 1982 became chief judge of that court.

WILLIAM HASTIE was the first black to be made a federal judge. He was appointed to the District Court of the Virgin Islands in 1937 and in 1949 was named to the Court of Appeals for the Third Circuit. James Parsons, appointed judge of the Northern District of Illinois in 1961, was the first black named a district judge in the continental United States. Since these initial appointments the number of blacks, women, and members of other ethnic minorities has grown steadily.

The first Judiciary Act authorized each court to make rules for conducting its own business, and in 1842 the Supreme Court was empowered to regulate process, pleading, proof and DISCOVERY in EQUITY, admiralty, and law cases in the district and circuit courts. In 1938 uniform rules for conducting civil cases, entitled the FEDERAL RULES OF CIVIL PROCEDURE, were adopted for the federal system. In 1946 the FEDERAL RULES OF CRIMINAL PROCEDURE were enacted. These rules have achieved uniformity of procedure and practice in the federal district courts throughout the nation.

The typical calendar of civil cases in a federal district court contains a plethora of complex cases involving PATENT, trademark, and COPYRIGHT infringement claims; federal securities law violations; CIVIL RIGHTS infractions; private antitrust claims; shareholders' derivative suits; IMMIGRATION and NATURALIZATION cases; employment, age, and housing discrimination claims; and claims under a variety of other federal statutes, such as the FREEDOM OF INFORMATION ACT, Investment Advisers Act, Commodities Exchange Act, FAIR LABOR STANDARDS ACT, and Federal Employers' Liability Act. In addition, there are seamen's injury and cargo damage claims, HABEAS CORPUS petitions by both state and federal prisoners, and litigation based on diversity jurisdiction. The criminal case load involves a variety of infractions defined in the United States criminal code.

Among the primary functions of the federal district courts are the vindication of federal rights secured by the Constitution and laws of the United States. The federal district court is often called upon to hold a state law or act unconstitutional because it violates federal constitutional guarantees or has been preempted by federal legislation. Obviously, the exercise of this power by federal district courts has the potential for creating friction and disharmony between state and federal courts. A lower federal court's power to strike down a state law on federal constitutional grounds, in the face of a contrary ruling by the highest court of the state, is not an easy pill for state judges to swallow. Federal courts have devised doctrines of COMITY and ABSTENTION to ease the friction. A growing number of federal judges, recognizing that state judges, too, have a duty to protect and enforce federal rights, have been inclined to give increasing deference to state court determinations of federal constitutional questions.

A burgeoning federal caseload undoubtedly promotes this inclination toward accommodation and also promotes a tightening of limitations on federal habeas corpus review of state court criminal convictions. A habeas corpus petition enables a state prisoner, after unsuccessfully appealing his conviction through the state court system, to have the matter reviewed by the federal district court to determine whether the trial and conviction violated the defendant's federal constitutional rights. Not surprisingly, habeas corpus petitions have inundated the federal courts. While most are without merit, the few petitions of substance that succeed are another cause of federal–state court friction. Rules of limitations have been imposed requiring exhaustion of state remedies and forbidding review if the state court's denial of the appeal of the criminal conviction rests on the defendant's failure to conform to state governing procedure absent a showing of cause and prejudice. (See WAINWRIGHT V. SYKES, 1977.)

Diversity jurisdiction brings to the federal courts issues of state law that would ordinarily be tried in the state courts. The initial justification for giving federal courts jurisdiction over such cases was concern that parochialism would put the out-of-state complainant at a disadvantage in seeking redress in state court against a resident of the forum state.

Exercise of federal diversity jurisdiction was at one time a cause of federal–state confusion if not friction. The district courts in diversity cases have been required to follow applicable state statutes, but until 1938 they were free to disregard state decisional law and decide on the basis of their own notions of what the COMMON LAW was or should be. With the Supreme Court's decision in ERIE RAILROAD V. TOMPKINS (1938) federal courts were no longer free to disregard state court decisions. Federal courts may apply their own rules as to pleading and practice but on substantive issues must function as adjuncts of the state judiciary.

ERIE V. TOMPKINS has made clear that the diversity jurisdiction is a wasteful use of federal judicial resources. State court parochialism is no longer a justifiable basis for federal diversity jurisdiction. Because the federal court must apply state law, apart from federal procedural rules, the litigant is seldom better off in federal court than he would be if relegated to state courts, where increasing numbers of federal judges feel such cases belong. Congress, however, has shown little interest in divesting federal district courts of the diversity jurisdiction.

The federal district court is the place where litigation usually commences to test the constitutional validity of state or federal governmental action with national implication. These TEST CASES usually seek injunctive relief or DECLARATORY JUDGMENTS. These are suits in EQUITY; thus no jury is empaneled, and the district judge must determine both the facts and the law. The judge will articulate his or her findings of the facts and legal conclusions as to the constitutional validity of the governmental action being tested. The trial record and the district court's analysis are thus extremely important for appellate courts, particularly in cases of first impression.

It is the district court that decides in the first instance whether the government is violating a newspaper's FIRST AMENDMENT rights, an accused's RIGHT AGAINST SELF-INCRIMINATION, or a minority citizen's right to the equal protection of the laws. Organizations such as the AMERICAN CIVIL LIBERTIES UNION, the National Association for the Advancement of Colored People, Jehovah's Witnesses, environmental groups, corporations, and individuals initiate litigation in the district court to test the constitutionality of some federal, state, or local legislation or practice. (See TEST CASES.)

Such a case was *McLean v. Arkansas Board of Education* (D. Ark., 1982). The American Civil Liberties Union sought to challenge an Arkansas law requiring that creationism—a biblical story of man's and the world's creation, as opposed to Darwin's evolutionary theory for explaining the genesis of mankind—be taught in the public schools. The issue was tried first in the federal district court, which framed the issue in these terms: is creationism a religious doctrine or a valid scientific theory? The court heard and weighed testimony, chiefly from experts on both sides, and held that the Arkansas statute was an unconstitutional ESTABLISHMENT OF RELIGION.

Sometimes prior DOCTRINE has forecast the outcome. For instance, although the SEPARATE BUT EQUAL DOCTRINE on which school SEGREGATION had been founded was not overruled until BROWN V. BOARD OF EDUCATION (1954), earlier decisions such as SWEATT V. PAINTER (1950) and *McLaurin v. Oklahoma State Regents* (1950) pointed to that overruling. Nonetheless, the record amassed by several district courts, showing the psychological and education deprivation inflicted by segregation on black children, was crucial in enabling the Supreme Court to take the final step of overruling PLESSY V. FERGUSON (1896) and holding that segregated schools violated the right of minority school children to equal protection of the law.

Similarly, a federal district court facing a constitutional challenge to the HYDE AMENDMENT, a congressional provision largely denying Medicaid funds for the cost of abortions, held hearings for about a year. The trial record contained some 400 exhibits and 5,000 pages of testimony. The judge was required to digest this mountain of testimonial and documentary evidence and prepare cohesive findings of facts and conclusions of law. (See HARRIS V. MCRAE, 1980.)

The need for so long a trial and the condensation of so voluminous a record into a coherent decision is not commonplace. However, it is not unusual for a district judge to be required to master the facts in a complex trial lasting many months, and to set forth the facts found and legal conclusions in a comprehensive fashion.

In some cases the district court, as a supplement to its own adjudicative fact-finding, must make findings as to LEGISLATIVE FACTS as well. For instance, in FULLILOVE V. KLUTZNICK (1980) Congress had required at least ten percent of federal funds granted for local public works projects to be set aside for minority businesses. This legislation was attacked as unconstitutional racial discrimination. The district court framed the issue as the power of Congress to remedy past discrimination. The district judge relied on congressional findings that minorities had been denied access to entrepreneurial opportunities provided in building construction works financed by public funds. Based on this legislative finding and Congress's purpose to take remedial action, the district court found the set-aside to be a legitimate remedial act. The Supreme Court adopted this rationale, and upheld the quota.

At times, in a constitutional controversy, the district court, although adhering to judicial precedent requiring it to dismiss the constitutional challenge, may help to bring about a reversal of precedent by recognizing that a wrong exists which should be remedied. BAKER V. CARR (1962) was a challenge to Tennessee's malapportioned legislature. The district court, in its opinion, carefully and sympathetically tracked the contentions of the plaintiffs that the legislators had condoned gross inequality in legislative REPRESENTATION and debased the VOTING RIGHTS of a large number of citizens. The court, however, relied on COLEGROVE V. GREEN (1946) and dismissed the action. On review of this order, the Supreme Court ruled that the plaintiffs' allegations had stated a case within the district court's jurisdiction. Subsequently, REYNOLDS V. SIMS (1964) embodied the Supreme Court's famous ONE PERSON, ONE VOTE principle, requiring legislative districts to be constructed as nearly as possible of an equal number of voters. (See REAPPORTIONMENT.)

Issues of such magnitude are highly charged; it is not unusual, in these controversial circumstances, for the judge who decides a case contrary to the majority's view to face public criticism and in some cases even social ostracism.

Judge Waties Waring's unpopular decision in favor of blacks in voting and school cases led to his social ostracism in Charleston, South Carolina; Judge Skelly Wright became anathema to many whites in New Orleans for the same reason, and escaped that environment through appointment to the Court of Appeals of the District of Columbia Circuit. Similarly, Judge William Ray Overton, who decided the creationism case adversely to local sentiments, and Judge James B. MacMillan, who ordered a complex program of SCHOOL BUSING in Charlotte, North Carolina, were subjected to severe community criticism.

Although not so dramatic as the examples given, public criticism meets almost every district judge at one time or another for rendering an unpopular decision. Because most public controversies have a way of ending up in the federal courts, district judges must decide whether seniority systems must be modified to prevent the employment gains of minorities and women from being wiped out; whether regulations requiring physicians to report to parents abortions performed on teenagers are valid; whether the overcrowding and the rundown conditions of a prison require it to be closed; or whether permitting school authorities to provide for prayer or meditation violates the SEPARATION OF CHURCH AND STATE. The district judge normally sits alone, and does not share decision with others, as do federal appellate judges—and therefore is singularly exposed to abuse and pressure.

Life tenure helps secure the independence of the district judge in facing such issues. This independence is crucial, not only for the judge but also for a constitutional system that seeks to secure the rights of the unpopular and despised.

Bibliography

ADMINISTRATIVE OFFICE OF THE UNITED STATES COURT. *Annual Report of the Director*. Washington, D.C.: Government Printing Office.

CLARK, D. S. 1981 Adjudication to Administration: A Statistical Analysis of Federal District Courts in the 20th Century. *Southern California Law Review* 55:65–152.

HALL, KERMIT 1976 The Antebellum Lower Federal Judiciary, 1829–1861. *Vanderbilt Law Review* 29:1089–1129.

_____ 1981 California's Lower Federal First Judicial Appointments. *Hastings Law Journal* 32:819–837.

HENDERSON, DWIGHT F. 1971 *Courts for a New Nation.* Washington, D.C.: Public Affairs Press.

HOUGH, CHARLES M. 1934 *The U.S. District Court for the Southern District of New York.* New York: Maritime Law Association.

Management Statistic for United States Courts. 1981.

STECKLER, WILLIAM E. 1978 Future of the Federal District Courts. *Indiana Law Review* 11:601–620.

SURRENCY, ERWIN C. 1963 History of Federal Courts. *Missouri Law Review* 28:214–244.

THOMPSON, FRANK, JR. 1970 Impeachment of Federal Judges: A Historical Overview. *North Carolina Law Review* 49:87–121.

The Processes
of Judicial Review

CONSTITUTIONAL INTERPRETATION

Paul Brest

"Constitutional interpretation" comprehends the methods or strategies available to people attempting to resolve disputes about the meaning or application of the Constitution. The possible sources for interpretation include the text of the Constitution, its "original history," including the general social and political context in which it was adopted as well as the events immediately surrounding its adoption, the governmental structures created and recognized by the Constitution, the "ongoing history" of interpretations of the Constitution, and the social, political, and moral values of the interpreter's society or some subgroup of the society. The term "originalist" refers to interpretation concerned with the first three of these sources.

The extraordinary current interest in constitutional interpretation is partly the result of controversy over the SUPREME COURT's expansive readings of the FOURTEENTH AMENDMENT; it also parallels developments in literary theory and more generally the humanities. Received notions about the intrinsic meaning of words or texts, access to an author's intentions, and the very notion of "validity" in interpretation have been forcefully attacked and vehemently defended by philosophers, literary theorists, social scientists, and historians of knowledge. Legal writers have imported scholarship from these disciplines into their own, and some humanists have become interested in legal interpretation.

Issues of interpretive methodology have always been politically charged—certainly so in constitutional law. JOHN MARSHALL's foundational decisions asserting the power of the central government were met by claims that he had willfully misconstrued the document. In our own time, modernist interpretive theories tend to be invoked by proponents of JUDICIAL ACTIVISM, and more conventional views by its opponents. The controversy within the humanities and the social sciences is itself deeply political, for the modernist assertion that truth or validity is socially constructed and hence contingent is often perceived as destabilizing or delegitimating.

The Constitution is a political document; it serves political ends; its interpretations are political acts. Any theory of constitutional interpretation therefore presupposes a normative theory of the Constitution

itself—a theory, for example, about the constraints that the words and
intentions of the adopters should impose on those who apply or interpret
the Constitution. As Ronald Dworkin observed, "Some parts of any constitutional theory must be independent of the intentions or beliefs or indeed
the acts of the people the theory designates as Framers. Some part
must stand on its own political or moral theory; otherwise the theory
would be wholly circular."

The eclectic practices of interpreters and the continuing debate
over the appropriate methods or strategies of constitutional interpretation suggest that we have no unitary, received theory of the Constitution.
The American tradition of constitutional interpretation accords considerable authority to the language of the Constitution, its adopters' purposes,
and the implications of the structures created and recognized by the
Constitution. But our tradition also accords authority to precedents and
the judicial exegesis of social values and practices, even when these
diverge from plausible readings of the text and original understandings.

Any theory of constitutional interpretation must start from the fact
that we have a written Constitution. Why is the written Constitution
treated as binding? Because, as Chief Justice Marshall asserted in MAR-
BURY V. MADISON (1803), it is law—the supreme law of the land—and
because since 1789 public institutions and the citizenry have treated it
as an authoritative legal document. It is no exaggeration to say that
the written Constitution lies at the core of the American "civil religion."

Doubtless, the most frequently invoked canon of textual interpretation is the "plain meaning rule." Marshall wrote in STURGES V. CROWN-
INSHIELD (1819):

[A]lthough the spirit of an instrument, especially of a constitution, is to be
respected not less than its letter, yet the spirit is to be collected chiefly from its
words. . . . [I]f, in any case, the plain meaning of a provision, not contradicted
by any other provision in the same instrument, is to be disregarded, because
we believe the framers of that instrument could not intend what they say, it
must be one in which the absurdity and injustice of applying the provision to
the case, would be so monstrous that all mankind would, without hesitation,
unite in rejecting the application.

Marshall did not equate "plain" meaning with "literal" meaning,
but rather (as Justice OLIVER WENDELL HOLMES later put it) the meaning
that it would have for "a normal speaker of English" under the circumstances in which it was used. The distinction is nicely illustrated by
Chief Justice Marshall's opinion in McCULLOCH V. MARYLAND (1819),
decided the same year as *Sturges*. Maryland had argued that the NECES-
SARY AND PROPER clause of Article I authorized Congress only to enact
legislation "indispensable" to executing the ENUMERATED POWERS. Marshall responded with the observation that the word "necessary," as used
"in the common affairs of the world, or in approved authors, . . . fre-

quently imports no more than that one thing is convenient, or useful, or essential to another." He continued:

Such is the character of human language, that no word conveys to the mind, in all situations, one single definite idea; and nothing is more common than to use words in a figurative sense. Almost all compositions contain words, which, taken in their rigorous sense, would convey a meaning different from that which is obviously intended. It is essential to just construction that many words which import something excessive, should be understood in a more mitigated sense— in that sense which common usage justifies. . . . This word, then, like others, is used in various senses; and in its construction, the subject, the context, the intention of the person using them, are all to be taken into view.

To read a provision without regard to its context and likely purposes will yield either unresolvable indeterminacies or plain nonsense. An interpreter could not, for example, decide whether the FIRST AMENDMENT'S "FREEDOM OF SPEECH" encompassed singing, flag-waving, and criminal solicitation; or whether the "writings" protected by the COPYRIGHT clause included photographs, sculptures, performances, television broadcasts, and computer programs. She would not know whether the provision in Article II that "No person except a natural born Citizen . . . shall be eligible to the Office of President" disqualified persons born abroad or those born by Caesarian section. We can identify interpretations as compelling, plausible, or beyond the pale only because we think we understand the concerns that underlie the provisions.

One's understanding of a provision, including the concerns that underlie it, depends partly on the ideological or political presuppositions one brings to the interpretive enterprise. Marshall could so readily label Maryland's construction of the word "necessary" as excessive because of his antecedent conception of a "constitution" as essentially different from a legal code—as a document "intended to endure for ages to come"—and because of his beliefs about the structure of FEDERALISM implicit in the United States Constitution. A judge starting from different premises might have found Maryland's construction more plausible.

A meaning thus is "plain" when it follows from the interpreter's presuppositions and when these presuppositions are shared within the society or at least within the relevant "community of interpretation"— for example, the legal profession. Kenneth Abraham has remarked, "The plain is plain because it is constantly recurring in similar contexts and there is general agreement about the meaning of language that may be applied to it. In short, meaning is a function of agreement. . . ."

When a provision is interpreted roughly contemporaneously with its adoption, an interpreter unconsciously places it in the social and linguistic context of her society. Over the course of several centuries, however, even a relatively stable nation will undergo changes—in social and economic relations, in technology, and ultimately in values—to an extent that a later interpreter cannot readily assume that she has direct access to the contexts in which a constitutional provision was adopted. This poses both a normative and a methodological question for the modern interpreter: should she attempt to read provisions in their original social and linguistic contexts, or in a modern context, or in some way that mediates between the two? And, to the extent that the original contexts are relevant, how can she ascertain them?

Original history includes "legislative history"—the debates and proceedings in the conventions and legislatures that proposed and adopted constitutional provisions—and the broader social, economic, and political contexts surrounding their adoption. Although it is widely acknowledged that original history should play a role in constitutional interpretation, there is little agreement over the aims and methods of historical inquiry. The controversy centers on the level of generality on which an interpreter should try to apprehend the adopters' intentions. On the highest or broadest level, an interpreter poses the questions: "What was the general problem to which this provision was responsive and how did the provision respond to it?" On the most specific level, she inquires: "How would the adopters have resolved the particular issue that we are now considering?"

The first or "general" question elicits answers such as: "The purpose of the COMMERCE CLAUSE was to permit Congress to regulate commerce that affects more than one state, or to regulate where the states are separately incompetent to regulate." Or: "The purpose of the EQUAL PROTECTION clause was to prohibit invidious discrimination." These characterizations do not purport to describe the scope of a provision precisely. On the contrary, they are avowedly vague or open-ended: the claim is not that the equal protection clause forbids every conceivable invidious discrimination (it may or may not) but that it is generally concerned with preventing invidious discriminations.

The general question is an indispensable component of any textual interpretation. The interpreter seeks a "purpose" that she can plausibly attribute to everyone who voted for the provision, and which, indeed, must have been understood as their purpose even by those who opposed its adoption. The question is often couched in objective-sounding terms: it seeks the "purpose of the provision" rather than the "intent of the framers." And its answer is typically sought in the text read in the social and linguistic context in which it was adopted. As Marshall wrote in *McCulloch*, "the spirit of an instrument . . . is to be collected chiefly from its words." If the status of the written Constitution as "law" demands textual interpretation, it also entails this general inquiry, without which textual interpretation cannot proceed.

The second inquiry, which can be called "intentionalist," seeks very specific answers, such as: "Did the adopters of the Fourteenth Amendment intend to prohibit school SEGREGATION?" or "Did they intend to prohibit 'reverse' discrimination?" One rationale for this focus was asserted by Justice GEORGE H. SUTHERLAND, dissenting in HOME BUILDING & LOAN ASSOCIATION v. BLAISDELL (1934): "[T]he whole aim of construction, as applied to a provision of the Constitution, is . . . to ascertain and give effect to the intent of its framers and the people who adopted it." Another rationale is that recourse to the adopters' intentions constrains the interpreter's discretion and hence the imposition of her own values. Some methodological problems are presented by any interpretive strategy that seeks to specify the adopters' intentions.

The procedures by which the *text* of a proposed constitutional provision is adopted are usually straightforward and clear: a text becomes a law if it is adopted by the constitutionally prescribed procedures and receives the requisite number of votes. For example, an amendment proposed in Congress becomes a part of the Constitution when it is approved by two-thirds of the members of each House and ratified by the legislatures in three-fourths of the states, or by conventions in three-fourths of the states, as Congress may prescribe.

How does an *intention* acquire the status of law? Some interpreters assume, without discussion, that by ratifying the framers' language, the thousands of people whose votes are necessary to adopt a constitutional provision either manifest their intent to adopt, or are somehow bound by, the intentions of certain of the drafters or framers—even if those intentions are not evident from the text itself. This view is not supported by anything in the Constitution, however, or by eighteenth- or nineteenth-century legal theory or practice.

If one analogizes the adoption of "an intention" concerning the text of the Constitution to the adoption of a text, an intention would become binding only when it was held by the number and combination of adopters prescribed by Article V. This poses no particular difficulty for an interpreter who wishes to understand the general aims or purposes of a provision. Statements by framers, proponents, and opponents, together with the social and political background against which the provision was adopted, often indicate a shared understanding. But these sources cannot usually answer specific questions about the adopters' intentions. The intentionalist interpreter thus often engages in a degree of speculation that undermines the very rationale for the enterprise.

The adopters of a provision may intend that it prohibit or permit some activity, or that it *not* prohibit or permit the activity; or they may have no intentions at all regarding the matter. An intentionalist interpreter must often infer the adopters' intentions from opaque sources, and must try to describe their intentions with respect to situations that they probably never thought about.

The effort to determine the adopters' intentions is further complicated by the problem of identifying the intended specificity of a provision. This problem is nicely illustrated by an example of Ronald Dworkin's. Consider the possible intentions of those who adopted the CRUEL AND UNUSUAL PUNISHMENT clause of the Eighth Amendment. They might have intended the language to serve only as a shorthand for the Stuart tortures which were their exemplary applications of the clause. Somewhat more broadly, they might have intended the clause to be understood to incorporate the principle of *ejusdem generis* —to include their exemplary applications and other punishments that they found, or would have found, equally repugnant.

More broadly yet, they might have intended to delegate to future decision makers the authority to apply the clause in light of the general principles underlying it. To use Dworkin's terms, they might have intended future interpreters to develop their own "conceptions" of cruel and unusual punishment within the framework of the adopters' general "concept" of the clause. If so, then the fact that they viewed a certain punishment as tolerable does not imply that they intended the clause "not to prohibit" such punishments. Like parents who instill values in their children both by articulating and applying a moral principle, the adopters may have accepted the eventuality that the principle would be applied in ways that diverged from their own particular views.

Whether or not such a motivation seems likely with respect to applications of the clause in the adopters' contemporary society, it may be more plausible with respect to applications by future interpreters, whose understandings of the clause would be affected by changing knowledge, values, and forms of society. On the other hand, the adopters may have thought of themselves as more virtuous or less corruptible than unknown future generations, and for that reason may have intended this and other clauses to be construed narrowly.

How can an interpreter determine the breadth of construction intended by the adopters of any particular provision? Primarily, if not exclusively, from the language of the provision itself. Justice FELIX FRANKFURTER wrote in *National Mutual Insurance Company v. Tidewater Transfer Company* (1949):

The precision which characterizes [the jurisdictional provisions] . . . of Article III is in striking contrast to the imprecision of so many other provisions of the Constitution dealing with other very vital aspects of government. This was not due to chance or ineptitude on the part of the Framers. The differences in subject-matter account for the drastic difference in treatment. Great concepts like "Commerce among the several states," "due process of law," "liberty," "property," were purposely left to gather meaning from experience. For they relate to the whole domain of social and economic fact, and the statesmen who founded this nation knew too well that only a stagnant society remains unchanged. But when the Constitution in turn gives strict definition of power or specific limitations upon it we cannot extend the definition or remove the translation. Precisely because "it is a *constitution* we are expounding," M'Culloch v. Maryland, we ought not to take liberties with it.

Charles Curtis put the point more generally: "Words in legal documents are simply delegations to others of authority to give them meaning by applying them to particular things or occasions. . . . And the more imprecise the words are, the greater is the delegation, simply because then they can be applied or not to more particulars. This is the only important feature of words in legal draftsmanship or interpretation."

This observation seems correct. Yet it is worth noting that the relative precision of a word or clause itself depends both on context and on interpretive conventions, and is often uncertain and contestable. For example, in UNITED STATES v. LOVETT (1946) Justice Frankfurter characterized the BILL OF ATTAINDER clause as among the Constitution's very "specific provisions." Yet he construed that clause to apply to punishments besides death, ignoring the technical eighteenth-century distinction between a bill of attainder, which imposed the death penalty, and a bill of "pains and penalties," which imposed lesser penalties.

The effort to characterize clauses as relatively open or closed confronts a different sort of historical problem as well. The history of interpretation of written constitutions was not extensive in 1787. Marshall's assertion that it is the nature of a constitution "that only its great outlines should be marked" (*McCulloch*) drew more on theory than on practice. But Marshall and his successors practiced this theory. Whatever assumptions the adopters of the original Constitution might have made about the scope of their delegations of authority, the Reconstruction amendments were adopted in the context of decades of "latitudinarian" constitutional interpretation. What bearing should this context have on the interpretation of provisions adopted since the original Constitution?

The intentionalist interpreter's initial task is to situate the provision and documents bearing on it in their original linguistic and social contexts. She can draw on the accumulated knowledge of American social, political, and intellectual history. Ultimately, however, constitutional interpretation is subject to the same limitations that attend all historical inquiry. Quentin Skinner has described the most pervasive of these:

[I]t will never in fact be possible simply to study what any given classic writer has *said* . . . without bringing to bear some of one's own expectations about what he must have been saying. . . . [T]hese models and preconceptions in terms of which we unavoidably organize and adjust our perceptions and thoughts will themselves tend to act as determinants of what we think or perceive. We must classify in order to understand, and we can only classify the unfamiliar in terms of the familiar. The perpetual danger, in our attempts to enlarge our historical understanding, is thus that our expectations about what someone must be saying or doing will themselves determine that we understand the agent to be doing something which he would not—or even could not—himself have accepted as an account of what he *was* doing.

Trying to understand how the adopters intended a provision to apply in their own time and place is, in essence, doing history. But the intentionalist interpreter must take the further step of translating the adopters' intentions into the present. She must decide how the commerce power applies to modes of transportation, communication, and economic relations not imagined—perhaps not imaginable—by the adopters; how the cruel and unusual punishment clause applies to the death penalty in a society that likely apprehends death differently from a society in which death was both more commonplace and more firmly integrated into a religious cosmology. The Court invoked difficulties of this sort when it concluded that the history surrounding the adoption of the Fourteenth Amendment was "inconclusive" with respect to the constitutionality of school DESEGREGATION almost a century later. Noting the vastly different roles of public education in the mid-nineteenth and mid-twentieth centuries, Chief Justice EARL WARREN wrote in BROWN v. BOARD OF EDUCATION (1954): "[W]e cannot turn back the clock to 1868 when the Amendment was adopted. . . . We must consider public education in the light of its full development and its present place in American life throughout the Nation. Only in this way can it be determined if segregation in public schools deprives these plaintiffs of the equal protection of the laws." In sum, even the historian who attempts to meet and understand the adopters on their own ground is engaging in a creative enterprise. To project the adopters into a world they could not have envisioned borders on fantasy.

In an important lecture given in 1968, entitled "Structure and Relationship in Constitutional Law," Professor Charles L. Black, Jr., described a mode of constitutional interpretation based on "inference from the structure and relationships created by the constitution in all its parts or in some principal part." Professor Black observed that in *McCulloch v. Maryland,* "Marshall does not place principal reliance on the [necessary and proper] clause as a ground of decision. . . . [Before] he reaches it he has already decided, on the basis of far more general implications, that Congress possesses the power, not expressly named, of establishing a bank and chartering corporations: . . . [h]e addresses himself to the necessary and proper clause only in response to counsel's arguing its *restrictive* force." Indeed, the second part of *McCulloch,* which held that the Constitution prohibited Maryland from levying a tax on the national bank, rested exclusively on inferences from the structure of the federal system and not at all on the text of the Constitution. Similarly, *Crandall v. Nevada* (1868) was not premised on the PRIVILEGES AND IMMUNITIES clause of either Article IV or the Fourteenth Amendment. Rather, the

Court inferred a right of personal mobility among the states from the structure of the federal system: "[The citizen] has the right to come to the seat of government to assert any claim he may have upon that government, or to transact any business he may have with it . . . and this right is in its nature independent of the will of any State over whose soil he must pass to exercise it."

Citing examples like these, Professor Black argued that interpreters too often have engaged in "Humpty-Dumpty textual manipulation" rather than relying "on the sort of political inference which not only underlies the textual manipulation but is, in a well constructed opinion, usually invoked to support the interpretation of the cryptic text."

Institutional relationships are abstractions from the text and the purposes of provisions—themselves read on a high level of abstraction. The implications of the structures of government are usually vague, often even ambiguous. Thus, while structural inference is an important method of interpretation, it shares the limitations intrinsic to other interpretive strategies. It seldom yields unequivocal answers to the specific questions that arise in the course of constitutional debates.

For the most part, the Supreme Court—the institution that most systematically and authoritatively interprets and articulates the meaning of the Constitution—has construed the language, original history, and structure of the Constitution on a high level of abstraction. It has treated most provisions in the spirit suggested by Chief Justice Marshall in *McCulloch v. Maryland.* This view of the Constitution is partly a political choice, based on the desire to accommodate a venerated and difficult-to-amend historical monument with changing circumstances, attitudes, and needs. But it is no less a consequence of the nature of language and history, which necessarily leave much of the meaning of the Constitution to be determined by its subsequent applications.

Constitutional disputes typically arise against the background of earlier decisions on similar subjects. A complete theory of constitutional interpretation therefore must deal with the role of precedent. Interpreting a judicial precedent is different from interpreting the constitutional provision itself. A precedent consists of a JUDGMENT based on a particular set of facts together with the court's various explanations for the judgment. The precedent must be read, not only in terms of its own social context, but against the background of the precedents it invokes or ignores. Lon Fuller wrote:

In the common law it is not too much to say that the judges are always ready to look behind the words of a precedent to what the previous court was trying to say, or to what it would have said if it could have foreseen the nature of the cases that were later to arise, or if its perception of the relevant factors in the case before it had been more acute. There is, then, a real sense in which the written words of the reported decisions are merely the gateway to something lying behind them that may be called, without any excess of poetic license, "unwritten law."

The American doctrine of STARE DECISIS accords presumptive but not indefeasible authority to precedent. Courts sometimes have overruled earlier decisions to return to what is said to be the original understanding of a provision. They have also overruled precedents that seem inconsistent with contemporary norms. For example, in HARPER v. VIRGINIA STATE BOARD OF ELECTIONS (1966), the Supreme Court overruled a twenty-year-old precedent to invalidate, under the equal protection clause, a state law conditioning the right to vote in state election on payment of an annual POLL TAX of $1.50. After surveying intervening decisions protecting political participation and other interests, Justice WILLIAM O. DOUGLAS concluded: "In determining what lines are unconstitutionally discriminatory, we have never been confined to historic notions of equality, any more than we have restricted due process to a fixed catalogue of what was at a given time deemed to be the limits of fundamental rights. . . . Notions of what constitutes equal treatment for purposes of the Equal Protection clause *do* change."

The process of constitutional adjudication thus has a dynamic of its own. It creates an independent force which, as a DOCTRINE evolves, may compete with the text and original history as well as with older precedents. Whether or not, as Justice JOHN MARSHALL HARLAN argued in dissent, *Harper* was inconsistent with the original understanding of the Fourteenth Amendment, the decision would have been inconceivable without the intervening expansion of doctrine beyond applications contemplated by the adopters of the Fourteenth Amendment.

Disagreements about the propriety of this evolutionary process are rooted in differing theories of constitutional law. To a strict intentionalist like Raoul Berger, the process appears to be simply the accretion of errors, which should be corrected to the extent possible. Others hold that the process properly accommodates the Constitution to changing needs and values. As Justice Holmes wrote in MISSOURI v. HOLLAND (1920):

[W]hen we are dealing with words that are also a constituent act, like the Constitution of the United States, we must realize that they have called into life a being the development of which could not have been foreseen completely by the most gifted of its begetters. It was enough for them to realize or to hope that they had created an organism; it has taken a century and cost their successors much sweat and blood to prove that they created a nation. The case before us must be considered in the light of our entire experience and not merely in that of what was said a hundred years ago. . . . We must consider what this country has become in deciding what the Amendment has reserved.

Chief Justice CHARLES EVANS HUGHES's opinion in *Home Building & Loan* stands as the Court's most explicit assertion of the independent force of precedents and of the changing values they reflect. The Court upheld a law, enacted during the Depression, which postponed a mortgagor's right to foreclose against a defaulting mortgagee. In dissent, Justice Sutherland argued that the CONTRACT CLAUSE, which had been adopted in response to state debtor-relief legislation enacted during the depression following the Revolutionary War, was intended to prohibit precisely this sort of law. Given his intentionalist premise this disposed of the case. Hughes did not dispute Sutherland's account of the original history. Rather, he reviewed the precedents interpreting the contract clause to conclude:

It is manifest . . . that there has been a growing appreciation of public needs and of the necessity of finding ground for a rational compromise between individual rights and public welfare. The settlement and consequent contraction of the public domain, the pressure of a constantly increasing density of population, the interrelation of the activities of our people, and the complexity of our economic interests, have inevitably led to an increased use of the organization of society in order to protect the very bases of individual opportunity. . . . [T]he question is no longer merely that of one party to a contract as against another, but of the use of reasonable means to safeguard the economic structure upon which the good of all depends.

The views articulated by Holmes, Hughes, and Douglas reflect the Court's actual practice in adjudication under the BILL OF RIGHTS, the Fourteenth Amendment, and other provisions deemed relatively open-textured. The process bears more resemblance to COMMON LAW adjudication than to textual exegesis.

In an influential essay, Thomas Grey observed that the American constitutional tradition included practices of nonoriginalist adjudication purportedly based on principles of natural rights or FUNDAMENTAL LAW, or on widely shared and deeply held values not readily inferred from the text of the written Constitution. Several of the Supreme Court's contemporary decisions involving procreation and the family have invoked this tradition, and have given rise to a heated controversy over the legitimacy of adjudication based on "fundamental values."

Originalist and nonoriginalist adjudication are not nearly so distinct as many of the disputants assume. Constitutional provisions differ enormously in their closed- or open-texturedness. Indeed, a provision's texture is not merely a feature of its language or its original history, but of the particular situation in which it is applied. One's approach to a text is determined by tradition and by social outlooks that can change over time. Depending on one's political philosophy, one may bemoan this inevitability, or embrace it. For better or for worse, however, Terrance Sandalow described an important feature of our constitutional tradition when he remarked that "[t]he Constitution has . . . not only been read in light of contemporary circumstances and values; it has been read *so that* the circumstances and values of the present generation might be given expression in constitutional law."

Most disputes about constitutional interpretation and fundamental values concern interpretation in particular institutional contexts. Today's disputes center on the judicial power to review and strike down the acts of legislatures and agencies and are motivated by what ALEXANDER M. BICKEL dubbed the "counter-majoritarian difficulty" of JUDICIAL REVIEW. Urgings of "judicial restraint" or of a more expansive approach to constitutional adjudication tend to reflect differing opinions of the role of the judiciary in a democratic polity and, more crudely, differing views about the substantive outcomes that these strategies yield. The question, say, whether Congress, the Supreme Court, or the states themselves should take primary responsibility for elaborating the equal protection clause is essentially political and cannot be resolved by abstract principles of interpretation. But this observation also cautions against taking interpretive positions based on particular institutional concerns and generalizing them beyond the situations that motivated them.

Constitutional interpretation is as much a process of creation as one of discovery. If this view is commonplace among postrealist academics, it is not often articulated by judges and it probably conflicts with the view of many citizens that constitutional interpretation should reflect the will of the adopters of the Constitution rather than its interpreters.

So-called STRICT CONSTRUCTION is an unsatisfactory response to these concerns. First, the most frequently litigated provisions do not lend themselves to "strict" or unambiguous or literal interpretation. (What are the strict meanings of the privileges or immunities, due process, and equal protection clauses?) Second, attempts to confine provisions to their very narrowest meanings typically produce results so ludicrous that even self-styled strict constructionists unconsciously abandon them in favor of less literal readings of texts and broader conceptualizations of the adopters' intentions. (No interpreter would hold that the First Amendment does not protect posters or songs because they are not "speech," or that the commerce clause does not apply to telecommunications because the adopters could not have foreseen this mode of commerce.) An interpreter must inevitably choose among different levels of abstraction in reading a provision—a choice that cannot itself be guided by any rules. Third, the two modes of strict interpretation— literalism and strict intentionalism—far from being synergistic strategies of interpretation, are often antagonistic. (Although the adopters of the First Amendment surely did not intend to protect obscene speech, the language they adopted does not exclude it.) A strict originalist theory of interpretation must opt either for literalism or for intentionalism, or must have some extraconstitutional principle for mediating between the two.

To reject these strategies is not to shed constraints. The text and history surrounding the adoption of a provision originate a line of doctrine, set its course, and continue to impose limitations. Some interpretations are more plausible than others; some are beyond the pale. And the criteria of plausibility are not merely subjective. Rather, they are intersubjective, constituted by others who are engaged in the same enterprise. Beyond the problem of subjectivity, however, the demographic characteristics of the legal interpretive community gives rise to an equally serious concern: the judiciary and the bar more generally have tended to be white, male, Anglo-Saxon, and well-to-do, and one might well wonder whether their interpretations do not embody parochial views or class interests. The concerns cannot be met by the choice of interpretive strategies, however, but only by addressing the composition and structure of the institutions whose interpretations have the force of law.

Bibliography

ABRAHAM, KENNETH 1981 Three Fallacies of Interpretation: A Comment on Precedent and Judicial Decision. *Arizona Law Review* 23:771–783.

BERGER, RAOUL 1977 *Government by Judiciary: The Transformation of the Fourteenth Amendment.* Cambridge, Mass.: Harvard University Press.

BLACK, CHARLES L., JR. 1969 *Structure and Relationship in Constitutional Law.* Baton Rouge: Louisiana State University Press.

CURTIS, CHARLES 1950 A Better Theory of Legal Interpretation. *Vanderbilt Law Review* 3:407–437.

DWORKIN, RONALD 1981 The Forum of Principle. *New York Law Review* 56:469–518.

ELY, JOHN HART 1980 *Democracy and Distrust.* Cambridge, Mass.: Harvard University Press.

FULLER, LON 1968 *Anatomy of Law.* New York: Praeger.

GREY, THOMAS 1975 Do We Have an Unwritten Constitution? *Stanford Law Review* 27:703–718.

HOLMES, OLIVER W. 1899 The Theory of Interpretation. *Harvard Law Review* 12:417.

MONAGHAN, HENRY 1981 Our Perfect Constitution. *New York University Law Review* 56:353–376.

SANDALOW, TERRANCE 1981 Constitutional Interpretation. *Michigan Law Review* 79:1033–1072.

SKINNER, QUENTIN 1969 Meaning and Understanding in the History of Ideas. *History & Theory* 8:3–53.

SYMPOSIUM 1985 Constitutional Interpretation. *University of Southern California Law Review* 58:551–725.

SYMPOSIUM ON LAW AND LITERATURE. 1982 *Texas Law Review* 60:373–586.

TEN BROEK, JACOBUS 1938–1939 Admissibility and Use by the Supreme Court of Extrinsic Aids in Constitutional Construction. *California Law Review* 26:287–308, 437–454, 664–681; 27:157–181, 399–421.

STRICT CONSTRUCTION

Theodore Eisenberg

This phrase purports to describe a method of CONSTITUTIONAL INTERPRE-TATION. Those using it, however, often are not referring to the same interpretive method. Classically, a strict construction is one that narrowly construes Congress's power under Article I, section 8. But some use strict construction to mean interpretations that limit the situations to which a constitutional provision applies, without regard to the interpretations' effect on the scope of federal power. Despite the existence of these and other definitions, one theme unites many uses of the phrase. Most users employ strict construction to support political positions by portraying them as the result of what at least sounds like a value-neutral interpretive technique. The phrase's political use now outweighs any technical legal significance it may have.

The term's greatest historical importance stems from its use to describe restrictive interpretations of the federal government's constitutional powers. Modern constitutional interpretations render strict construction of federal power a remnant of the past. In the nation's early years, however, the question of strict versus BROAD CONSTRUCTION of federal power was as critical as any question facing the country. The dispute over whether to establish a BANK OF THE UNITED STATES provided the setting for the first debate over the construction to be afforded Congress's powers. THOMAS JEFFERSON and JAMES MADISON, who both opposed the Bank, "strictly construed" the federal government's powers and concluded that Congress lacked power to create the Bank. ALEXANDER HAMILTON, who favored the Bank, advocated a more flexible view of federal power. In disputes over federal power, the phrase would continue to characterize these early Jeffersonian positions opposed by Federalists.

Chief Justice JOHN MARSHALL's reputation as a non-strict-constructionist owes much to his opinion for the Court sustaining the validity of the act creating the second Bank of the United States. In McCULLOCH v. MARYLAND (1819) Marshall endorsed Hamilton's view of Congress's powers in an opinion that included the oft-quoted passage, "Let the end be legitimate, let it be within the scope of the constitution, and all means which are appropriate, which are plainly adapted to that end, which are not prohibited, but consist with the letter and spirit of the constitution, are constitutional." In GIBBONS v. OGDEN (1824), again speaking through Marshall, the Court expressly rejected strict construction of federal power as a proper method of interpretation. It found not "[o]ne sentence in the Constitution . . . that prescribes this rule."

Strict construction becomes a much more complex concept when offered, as it has been, as a method of interpreting the entire Constitution. Strict construction then means interpretations that restrict the situations in which constitutional grants of power, or limitations on them, are deemed applicable. A strict construction simply limits the cases in which the Constitution applies. In this sense, a strict construction need not correspond to a constitutional interpretation that limits federal power. This difference results from the variable structure of constitutional provisions.

Some constitutional provisions are phrased positively in the sense that they confer powers upon Congress, the President, or the courts. Other provisions, such as the FIRST AMENDMENT, are phrased negatively. A strict construction—in the sense of limiting the Constitution's applicability—of the positive powers limits federal authority, as Marshall did in MARBURY V. MADISON (1803), when he construed Article III not to authorize the Supreme Court to issue original writs of MANDAMUS. But strict (that is, narrow) construction of a negative provision such as the First Amendment expands governmental authority. Even if strict construction had become the accepted technique for interpreting grants of power to Congress, it is questionable whether, in a government of limited powers, strict construction would be an appropriate technique for interpreting express constitutional limitations on Congress's power.

When used to interpret the entire Constitution, strict construction fails as a guiding principle in the large class of cases in which one constitutional provision can be interpreted narrowly only by broadly interpreting another provision. DRED SCOTT V. SANDFORD (1857) highlights this problem. *Dred Scott,* which restricted Congress's power to regulate slavery in the territories and assured Chief Justice ROGER B. TANEY's reputation as a strict constructionist, is the Court's most famous strict construction of federal power. Yet, while Taney construed strictly Congress's power, he simultaneously construed broadly constitutional limitations on Congress's authority and the constitutional rights of slaveholders.

A similar problem undermines efforts to embrace strict construction as a politically conservative technique for judicial decision making. The conservative Supreme Court of the late nineteenth and early twentieth centuries did limit Congress's powers by, among other things, invalidating federal statutes as exceeding Congress's power under the commerce clause and by finding, in UNITED STATES V. BUTLER (1936), short-lived limitations on Congress's TAXING AND SPENDING POWER. But in relying on the due process clauses to invalidate many federal and state enactments, the same Court offered broad interpretations of those limitations on government power.

The ambiguity attending strict construction has not deterred many from trying to exploit the concept for political advantage. Even in the early disputes between Federalists and Jeffersonians, when strict construction may have had its clearest meaning, there is a hint of hypocrisy in the reliance placed on strict construction. It is unlikely that insufficient strictness is what really troubled early critics of Marshall's and other Federalists' loose constructions. When it suited their goals, Marshall's critics supported loose construction. For example, to justify an administrative and legislative program imposing an embargo on France and England, President Jefferson interpreted broadly presidential and congressional authority to terminate and influence commerce. And Marshall did not always generously interpret the federal government's powers. At Aaron Burr's treason trial, Marshall strictly, that is to say, narrowly, construed Article III, section 3, the constitutional provision on treason.

Although many have tried to rely on strict constructionism to political advantage, this trend reached its modern peak under President Richard M. Nixon. He referred to strict construction as a characteristic he sought in a Supreme Court appointee. Nixon probably did not primarily mean one who narrowly construed the federal government's powers. He was most dissatisfied with the Supreme Court's CRIMINAL PROCEDURE decisions. In his 1968 campaign, Nixon announced his preference for Supreme Court appointees who would aid the society's peace forces in combating criminals. In this context strict construction was a double negative: limiting the situations in which the Constitution restricted states' criminal procedures. Only coincidentally would such constructions reduce the federal government's role.

Like previous users of the term, Nixon employed strict construction for political advantage, not to facilitate discussion of theories of CONSTITUTIONAL INTERPRETATION. He never articulated his understanding of the phrase, and Justice Harry Blackmun, one of his Supreme Court appointees, disclaimed an understanding of it. Nixon once described Justice Felix Frankfurter as exemplifying what he sought in a Justice, yet Frankfurter delivered nonstrict criminal procedure opinions. In Rochin v. California (1952) he wrote that forcing an emetic into a suspect's stomach to gather recently swallowed evidence shocked the conscience and, therefore, violated the DUE PROCESS CLAUSE of the FOURTEENTH AMENDMENT. And Frankfurter dissented from the Court's decision upholding the admissibility of conversations overheard by means of ELECTRONIC EAVESDROPPING. In addition, in assessing a president's constitutional powers, Nixon was anything but a strict constructionist. The impoundment of funds appropriated by Congress, the invasion of Cambodia, the assertion of EXECUTIVE PRIVILEGE, and many of Nixon's domestic security measures all suggest an expansive, nonstrict view of a president's constitutional authority.

Finally, "strict construction" may have other sensible meanings that do not refer to narrow interpretations. Justice HUGO BLACK may have thought himself to be construing the Constitution strictly when he applied it literally, as in First Amendment cases. Another plausible meaning is strict adherence to the letter and spirit of the Constitution. Under this view, everyone can claim to be a strict constructionist, adhering to what he or she ascertains to be the principles embodied in the Constitution. Strict construction also may characterize a passive judiciary. For example, many believe legislative apportionment to be a POLITICAL QUESTION, a matter of concern only for the legislative and executive branches. A judge who invades the area is deemed active and, therefore, not a strict constructionist. Judge LEARNED HAND may have used strict construction in this sense when he stated that the Supreme Court's failure to define political questions is "a stench in the nostrils of strict constructionists."

Bibliography

BLACK, CHARLES L., JR.   1960   *The People and the Court.* New York: Macmillan.
KELLY, ALFRED H.; HARBISON, WINFRED A., and BELZ, HERMAN   1983   *The American Constitution,* 6th ed. New York: Norton.
KOHLMEIER, LOUIS M., JR.   1972   *God Save This Honorable Court.* New York: Scribner's.
MURPHY, WILLIAM P.   1967   *The Triumph of Nationalism.* Chicago: Quadrangle Books.

BROAD CONSTRUCTION

Dennis J. Mahoney

Broad construction, sometimes called "loose construction," is an approach to CONSTITUTIONAL INTERPRETATION emphasizing a permissive and flexible reading of the Constitution, and especially of the powers of the federal government. Like its opposite, STRICT CONSTRUCTION, the phrase has political, rather than technical or legal, significance.

ALEXANDER HAMILTON advocated broad construction in his 1791 controversy with THOMAS JEFFERSON over the constitutionality of the bill to establish the Bank of the United States. The essence of Hamilton's position, which was accepted by President GEORGE WASHINGTON and endorsed by the Supreme Court in McCULLOCH v. MARYLAND (1819), was the doctrine of IMPLIED POWERS: that the delegated powers implied the power to enact legislation useful in carrying out those powers. The broad constructionists also argued that the NECESSARY AND PROPER CLAUSE empowered Congress to make any law convenient for the execution of any delegated power. Similarly, broad construction justified enactment of the ALIEN AND SEDITION ACTS and expenditures for INTERNAL IMPROVEMENTS.

In his Report on Manufactures (1792) Hamilton advocated a broad construction of the TAXING AND SPENDING POWER that would authorize Congress to spend federal tax money for any purpose connected with the GENERAL WELFARE, whether or not the subject of the appropriation was within Congress's ordinary LEGISLATIVE POWER. Broad construction of the COMMERCE CLAUSE and of the taxing and spending power now forms the constitutional basis for federal regulation of the lives and activities of citizens. Proponents of broad construction argue that the Constitution must be adapted to changing times and conditions. However, a thoroughgoing broad construction is clearly incompatible with the ideas of LIMITED GOVERNMENT and CONSTITUTIONALISM.

The Constitution both grants power to the government and imposes limitations on the exercise of governmental power. Consistent usage would describe the expansive reading of either, and not just of the former, as broad construction. Indeed, President RICHARD M. NIXON frequently criticized the WARREN COURT for its "broad construction" of constitutional provisions guaranteeing the procedural rights of criminal defendants. The more common usage, however, reserves the term for constitutional interpretation permitting a wider scope for governmental activity.

In the late 1970s and the 1980s, broad construction was largely displaced by a new theory of constitutional jurisprudence called "noninterpretivism." Unlike broad construction, which depends upon a relationship between government action and some particular clause of the Constitution, noninterpretivism justifies government action on the basis of values presumed to underlie the constitutional text and to be superior to the actual words in the document.

Bibliography

AGRESTO, JOHN 1984 *The Supreme Court and Constitutional Democracy.* Ithaca, N.Y.: Cornell University Press.

UNWRITTEN CONSTITUTION

Satirios A. Barber

When the American colonists charged that some British colonial policies and practices were unconstitutional, they appealed to what was generally conceived as an unwritten constitutional tradition that combined the practical good sense of English experience with standards of conduct that were simply, or naturally, equitable and right. Though the principles of this constitutional tradition were scattered among state documents, reported cases of the COMMON LAW, treatises, and other writings, their status derived not from having been written or enacted but from their perceived origin in sources like custom, divine will, reason, and nature. These principles were thought superior to acts of Parliament, whose status did depend on their enactment.

While invoking unwritten HIGHER LAW, however, the colonists were implicitly challenging its efficacy. To the charge of TAXATION WITHOUT REPRESENTATION, Parliament responded with the theory of virtual representation. The colonists rejected this DOCTRINE and insisted that as a practical matter responsible government depended on the ballot, not on government's respect for natural justice. Belief in a higher law thus coexisted with a pessimistic view of human nature and a corresponding distrust of government.

Unlike Britain's constitution, the American Constitution was established through RATIFICATION, a form of enactment. As the supreme law of the land this enacted Constitution consigns appeals from its authority to the category of extralegal considerations. But foreclosing the constitutionality of appeals from the highest written law did not depreciate unwritten law as such, for the written or enacted law could still reflect unwritten standards of natural justice and reason whose status did not depend on enactment. This was the claim of those who campaigned for ratification, as was to be expected from the rhetoric typical of public attempts to persuade.

This is not to say that anyone saw the proposed constitution as entirely consistent with the dictates of reason and justice. Slavery and the equal REPRESENTATION in the Senate of small and large states are examples of acknowledged compromises with contingencies that would not bend to principle. Nevertheless, the argument for ratification was full of references to higher norms as standards for evaluating constitutions, as principles behind its rules and institutions, and as objectives of the system as a whole. In THE FEDERALIST #9 and #10, ALEXANDER HAMILTON and JAMES MADISON not only presented the Constitution as an attempt to reconcile democracy with minority rights and the common good, but they also stated that the fate of democracy justly depended on that reconciliation. In *The Federalist* #78 Hamilton defended JUDICIAL REVIEW and recognized the role of judges in "mitigating the severity and confining the operations" of "unjust and partial" enactments. In *The Federalist* #51 Madison said, "Justice is the end of government" and that it "ever will be pursued until it is obtained, or until liberty be lost in the pursuit." And in the same number he described CHECKS AND BALANCES as a "policy of supplying, by opposite and rival interests, the defects of better motives." Taking this statement at face value would require as a prerequisite to a full understanding of the Constitution knowledge of the "better motives" that constituted part of the model for what the Framers wrote.

It is a matter of central importance that appeals to ideas like justice were not expressed as appeals to this or that particular version but to the general idea itself. Aware of the difference, Hamilton urged readers of *The Federalist* #1 to rise above "local prejudices little favorable to the discovery of truth." He recalled the frequent claim that Americans would decide the possibility of rational government for the whole of mankind, a claim that might redouble efforts to rise above parochialism by adding "the inducements of philanthropy to those of patriotism." Equally important, however, was his acknowledgment of the great number and power of "causes which . . . give a false bias to . . . judgement." And he urged "moderation" on those "ever so thoroughly persuaded of their being in the right." This appeal suggests the value of self-critical striving for truth, an attitude more of confidence in progress toward truth than in claims to possess it.

Further indication of the Constitution's dependence on commitments that some theorists believe written constitutions can displace is the fact that properties of the Constitution as a whole influence the interpretation of its parts. In addition to the rhetoric of its PREAMBLE and of its draftsmen, the document reflects a concern for simple justice by virtue of its written character. As written communication to an audience of indefinite composition, size, and duration, the document presupposes that virtually anyone can come to understand what it means. Presupposing a large and lasting community of meaning, it anticipates a community of interests embracing all to whom it would potentially apply or who would accept it as a model.

Because of their content, provisions like the TENTH AMENDMENT and the old fugitive slave clause are at odds with the community of interests presupposed by the Constitution as a whole. They are at odds with themselves by virtue of their enunciation as parts of the whole. This tension justified JOHN MARSHALL's nationalist construction of the Tenth Amendment, ABRAHAM LINCOLN's view that the Constitution had put slavery on the path of ultimate extinction, and the Supreme Court's application of the BILL OF RIGHTS to the states through the INCORPORATION DOCTRINE. Observers have interpreted the acceptance of this kind of construction as a sign that the nation has an unwritten constitution. But therapeutic constructions might as easily indicate the power of a written constitution to undermine the parochial and particularistic aspects of its content, separable as the written word is from the physical presence of its authors and their particular needs and conceptions.

The implications of the Constitution's written character bear on a protracted debate among constitutional theorists over the possibility of limiting the discretion of judges in difficult constitutional cases involving human rights, especially rights to SUBSTANTIVE DUE PROCESS and EQUAL PROTECTION. Many participants in the debate share an academic moral skepticism that finds no meaning in general normative concepts beyond the particular conceptions of historical individuals or communities. They diminish simple justice with quotation marks, and they hold particular conceptions of justice interesting primarily as facts that influence other facts, not as beliefs that can be morally better or worse than other beliefs. Rejecting the object of its quest, they also reject traditional moral philosophy as a method of acquiring knowledge. They treat the beliefs of persons and communities as matters essentially of historical fact, to be established by empirical methods, with some room for conceptual analysis, but not for judgments of right and wrong.

To these commentators, talk of reason and justice is essentially rationalization of personal preference, class interest, community morality, and the like. And because they tend to believe that elected officials have a stronger claim to represent the community, they argue that judicial review often involves the imposition of minority preferences on the majority. In an effort to reconcile judicial review with majoritarianism these theorists have tried to link the meaning of general constitutional norms with the intentions of the Framers, tradition, existing and projected community morality, the institutional prerequisites of democratic decision, and other sources whose content they perceive essentially as matters of fact or uncontroversial inference. The effort has failed largely because each source yields conflicting options, not simple, consistent answers. And when the skeptics make their selections, they inevitably (if covertly and therefore irresponsibly) make normative judgments whose rationality their position would force them to deny.

The failure of these skeptical theorists to extirpate normative judgments from decisions about the meaning of constitutional provisions has strengthened the case for moral philosophy in constitutional inquiry, which, in turn, has exacerbated apprehension of unrestrained judicial power. But renewed concern for natural justice need not threaten hopes for limiting judicial discretion. Those who take seriously the idea of justice as something higher than their particular conceptions will value the self-critical striving for moral and political truth recommended in *The Federalist* #1. This attitude is itself a limitation on discretion of the most objectionable variety because it is the antithesis of willful assertiveness.

Arguments for taking natural justice seriously might begin by reflecting on the apparent power of ordinary political debate to change minds about justice and related ideas. This familiar fact shows that, as ordinary citizens understand it, political life presupposes simple justice. Moral skeptics err in supposing that continuing disagreement about justice proves that debate is pointless or that there is nothing to debate about. If there are moral truths to be known, as is ordinarily presupposed, agreement is not the test of what is right. Holding that agreement is the test may signal that one abandons ordinary presuppositions, but it is not an argument for doing so. Academic inquiry begins with ordinary presuppositions. And though constitutional theorists have not reached agreement (a good thing, for universal consensus would remove the impetus for reflection and improvement), they have been unable to avoid ordinary presuppositions about justice and the value of reasoning in deciding what the Constitution means. Perhaps this is a reason to value self-critical striving for the best constructions to which constitutional language, tradition, and opinion are open.

Bibliography

BREST, PAUL   1981   The Fundamental Rights Controversy: The Essential Contradictions of Normative Constitutional Scholarship. *Yale Law Journal* 90:1063–1109.

GREY, THOMAS C.   1978   Origins of the Unwritten Constitution: Fundamental Law in American Revolutionary Thought. *Stanford Law Review* 30:843–893.

HARRIS, WILLIAM F., II   1982   Bonding Word and Polity: The Logic of American Constitutionalism. *American Political Science Review* 76:34–45.

MOORE, MICHAEL S.   1985   A Natural Law Theory of Interpretation. *Southern California Law Review* 58:277–398.

——————   1982   Moral Reality. *Wisconsin Law Review* 1982:1061–1156.

NATURAL RIGHTS AND THE CONSTITUTION

Walter Berns

The Constitution as it came from the Philadelphia convention contained no bill of rights. Indeed, the word right (or rights) appears only once in it, and there only in the context of Congress's power to promote the progress of science and useful arts "by securing for limited Times to Authors and Inventors the exclusive Right to their respective Writings and Discoveries" (Article 1, section 8). In the view of the Anti-Federalists, the Constitution should have begun with a statement of general principles, or of "admirable maxims," as PATRICK HENRY said in the Virginia ratifying debates, such as the statement in the VIRGINIA DECLARATION OF RIGHTS of 1776: "That all men are by nature equally free and independent, and have certain inherent rights, of which, when they enter a state of society, they cannot by any compact deprive or divest their posterity; namely, the enjoyment of life and liberty, with the means of acquiring and possessing property, and pursuing and obtaining happiness and safety." In short, a bill of rights ought to be affixed to the Constitution containing a statement of natural rights.

The Federalists disagreed. They conceded that the Constitution might properly contain a statement of *civil* rights, and they were instrumental in the adoption of the first ten amendments which we know as the BILL OF RIGHTS, but they were opposed to a general statement of first principles in the text of the Constitution. However true, such a statement, by reminding citizens of the right to abolish government, might serve to undermine government, even a government established on those principles. And, as Publius insisted, the Constitution was based on those principles: "the Constitution is itself, in every rational sense, and to every useful purpose, A BILL OF RIGHTS" (THE FEDERALIST #84). It is a bill of natural rights, not because it contains a compendium of those rights but because it is an expression of the natural right of everyone to govern himself and to specify the terms according to which he agrees to give up his natural freedom by submitting to the rules of civil government. The Constitution emanates from us, "THE PEOPLE of the United States," and here in its first sentence, said Publius, "is a better recognition of popular rights than volumes of those aphorisms which make the principal figure in several of our State bills of rights and which would sound much better in a treatise of ethics than in a constitution of government." Natural rights point or lead to government, a government with the power to secure rights, and only secondarily to limitations on governmental power.

This is not to deny the revolutionary character of natural rights, or perhaps more precisely, of the natural rights teaching. The United States began in a revolution accompanied by an appeal to the natural and unalienable rights of life, liberty, and the pursuit of happiness. But these words of the DECLARATION OF INDEPENDENCE are followed immediately by the statement that "to secure these rights, Governments are instituted among Men." Natural rights point or lead to government in the same way that the Declaration of Independence points or leads to the Constitution: the rights, which are possessed by all men equally by nature (or in the state of nature), require a well-governed civil society for their security.

The link between the state of nature and civil society, or between natural rights and government, is supplied by the laws of nature. The laws of nature in this (modern) sense must be distinguished from the natural law as understood in the Christian tradition, for example. According to Christian teaching, the natural law consists of commands and prohibitions derived from the inclinations (or the natural ordering of the passions and desires), and is enforced, ultimately, by the sanction of divine punishment. According to Hobbes and Locke, however—the principal authors in the school of natural rights—the laws of nature are merely deductions from the rights of nature and ultimately from the right of self-preservation. Because everyone has a natural right to do whatever is necessary to preserve his own life, the state of nature comes to be indistinguishable from the state of war where, in Hobbes's familiar phrase, life is solitary, poor, nasty, brutish, and short; even in Locke's more benign version, and for the same reason, the state of nature is characterized by many unendurable "inconveniences." In short, in the natural condition of man the enjoyment of natural rights is uncertain and human life itself becomes insufferable. What is required for self-preservation is peace, and, as rational beings, men can come to understand "the fundamental law of nature" which is, as Hobbes formulates it, "to seek peace, and follow it." From this is derived the second law of nature, that men enter in a contract with one another according to which they surrender their natural rights to an absolute sovereign who is instituted by the contract and who, from that time forward, represents their rights. More briefly stated, each person must consent to be governed, which he does by laying down his natural right to govern himself. In Locke's version, political society is formed when everyone "has quitted his natural power"—a power he holds as of natural right—and "resigned it up into the hands of the community." In the same way, Americans of 1776 were guided by "the Laws of Nature and of Nature's God" when they declared their independence and constituted themselves as a new political community. Commanding nothing—for these are not laws in the proper sense of commands that must be obeyed—the laws of nature point to government as the way to secure rights, a government that derives its "just powers from the consent of the governed." (See SOCIAL COMPACT THEORY.)

It is important to understand that in the natural rights teaching neither civil society nor government exists by nature. By nature everyone is sovereign with respect to himself. Civil society is an artificial person to which this real person, acting in concert with others, surrenders his natural and sovereign powers, and upon this agreement civil society becomes the sovereign with respect to those who consented to the surrender. It is civil society, in the exercise of this sovereign power, that institutes and empowers government. So it was that "we [became] the People of the United States" in 1776 and, in 1787–1788, that we ordained and established "this CONSTITUTION for the United States of America." The Constitution is the product of the "will" of the sovereign people of the United States (*The Federalist* #78).

The power exercised by this people is almost unlimited. Acting through its majority, the people is free to determine the form of government (for, as the Declaration of Independence indicates, any one of several forms of government—democratic, republican, or even monarchical—may serve to secure rights) as well as the organization of that government and the powers given and withheld from it. It will make these decisions in the light of its purpose, which is to secure the rights of the persons authorizing it. This is why the doctrine of natural rights, if only secondarily, leads or points to limitations on government; and this is why the people of the United States decided to withhold some powers and, guided by the new "science of politics" (*The Federalist* #9), sought to limit power by means of a number of institutional arrangements.

Among the powers withheld was the power to coerce religious opinion. Government can have authority over natural rights, said THOMAS JEFFERSON, "only as we have submitted [that authority] to them, [and] the rights of conscience we never submitted, we could not submit."

Among the institutional arrangements was the SEPARATION OF POWERS, and the scheme of representation made possible by extending "the sphere of society so as to take in a greater variety of parties and interests thus making it less probable that a majority of the whole will have a common motive to invade the rights of other citizens" (*The Federalist* #10). First among these rights, according to Locke, is the property right, for, differing somewhat from Hobbes in this respect, Locke understood the natural right of self-preservation primarily as the right to acquire property. Publius had this in mind when he said that "the first object of government . . . [is] the protection of different and unequal faculties of acquiring property" (*The Federalist* #10). The large (commercial) republic is a means of securing this natural right as well as the natural right of conscience, for, within its spacious boundaries, there will be room for a "multiplicity of [religious] sects" as well as a "multiplicity of [economic] interests" (*The Federalist* #51).

Just as a "respect to the opinions of mankind" required Americans to announce the formation of a people that was assuming its "separate and equal station . . . among the powers of the earth," so a jealous concern for their natural rights required this people to *write* a Constitution in which they not only empowered government but, in various complex ways, limited it.

Bibliography

JAFFA, HARRY V.   1975   *The Conditions of Freedom: Essays in Political Philosophy.* Pages 149–160. Baltimore: Johns Hopkins University Press.

STORING, HERBERT J.   1978   The Constitution and the Bill of Rights. Pages 32–48 in M. Judd Harmon, ed., *Essays on the Constitution of the United States.* Port Washington, N.Y.: Kennikat.

STRAUSS, LEO   1953   *Natural Right and History.* Introduction and chap. 5. Chicago: University of Chicago Press.

FUNDAMENTAL RIGHTS

Henry J. Abraham

Inherent in the Anglo-Saxon heritage of DUE PROCESS OF LAW, the concept of fundamental rights defies facile analysis. Yet it constitutes one of those basic features of democracy that are the test of its presence. As defined by Justice FELIX FRANKFURTER, dissenting in *Solesbee v. Balkcom* (1950), it embraces "a system of rights based on moral principles so deeply embedded in the traditions and feelings of our people as to be deemed fundamental to a civilized society. . . ." The Justice whom Frankfurter succeeded on the high bench, BENJAMIN N. CARDOZO, had spoken in *Snyder v. Massachusetts* (1934) of "principles of justice so rooted in the traditions and conscience of our people as to be deemed fundamental." Three years later, in PALKO V. CONNECTICUT, Cardozo articulated fundamental rights as "implicit in the concept of ORDERED LIBERTY." Because these rights are "fundamental," they have been accorded special protection by the judiciary, which has thus viewed them as PREFERRED FREEDOMS that command particularly STRICT SCRUTINY of their infringement by legislative or executive action. In other words, to pass judicial muster, laws or ordinances affecting fundamental rights must demonstrate a more or less "compelling need," whereas those affecting lesser rights need only be clothed with a RATIONAL BASIS justifying the legislative or executive action at issue.

But which among our rights fall on the "fundamental" and which on the "nonfundamental" side of constitutional protection? The Supreme Court commenced to endeavor to draw a dichotomous line in the turn-of-the-century INSULAR CASES: on the "fundamental" side now fell such rights as those present in the FIRST AMENDMENT (religion, FREEDOMS OF SPEECH, PRESS, ASSEMBLY, and PETITION); on the other side, styled "formal rights," fell such "procedural" rights or guarantees as those embedded in the FOURTH, Fifth, SIXTH, SEVENTH, and Eighth AMENDMENTS, including, for example, TRIAL BY JURY. Justice Cardozo reconfirmed the dichotomy with his *Palko* division, adding to the roster of "fundamental" rights those of assigned counsel to INDIGENT defendants in major criminal trials and the general right to a FAIR TRIAL. He relegated other procedural rights to the nonfundamental sphere, noting that "justice would not perish" in the absence of such "formal rights" at the state level.

Cardozo's dichotomy did not apply to the federal BILL OF RIGHTS, which was wholly enforceable against federal abridgment or denial by the terms of its specific provisions. He used it instead to explain which provisions of the Bill of Rights were, and which were not, made applicable to the states by the FOURTEENTH AMENDMENT. While the "formal" rights, as he explained, do have "value and importance . . . they are not of the essence of a scheme of ordered liberty. To abolish them is not to violate a principle of justice so rooted in the traditions and conscience of our people as to be deemed fundamental. . . . Few would be so narrow as to maintain that a fair and enlightened system of justice would be impossible without them." This dichotomy stood until the 1960s when, through acceleration of the process known as INCORPORATION or "absorption," most of the enumerated safeguards in the Bill of Rights were made applicable to the states by judicial decisions. The Supreme Court's rationale for these decisions was its expanding view of the nature and reach of "fundamental" rights. In practical affect, the incorporation doctrine no longer draws an appreciable distinction between "formal" and "fundamental" rights.

Yet concurrently the WARREN COURT gave new life to the notion that certain fundamental rights should be protected by heightened judicial scrutiny of laws limiting them. This development built on Justice HARLAN FISKE STONE's famed formulation in UNITED STATES v. CAROLENE PRODUCTS CO. (1938). Voting rights and rights concerning marriage, procreation, and family relationships were identified as "fundamental" and clothed with special judicial protection. The Warren Court's other chief category of occasions for strict scrutiny of legislation—that of SUSPECT CLASSIFICATIONS—can also be seen in a similar light. If race is a suspect classification, surely the reason is that no interest in civil society is more fundamental than being treated as a full-fledged member of the community.

In effect, although all but a few of the enumerated rights in the Constitution and its amendments are now regarded as *fundamental,* and thus fully entitled to thorough judicial protection and scrutiny, the Court has embraced a hierarchical or "tiered" formulation. Some fundamental rights thus remain preferred. To what extent that arrangement will stand the test of time and experience will depend chiefly upon the judiciary's perception.

Bibliography

ABRAHAM, HENRY J.   1987   *Freedom and the Court: Civil Rights and Liberties in the United States,* 5th ed. New York: Oxford University Press.

CORTNER, RICHARD C.   1981   *The Supreme Court and the Second Bill of Rights.* Madison: University of Wisconsin Press.

GUNTHER, GERALD   1972   The Supreme Court: 1971 Term; In Search of Evolving Doctrines on a Changing Court: A Model for a Newer Equal Protection. *Harvard Law Review* 86:1–48.

PREFERRED FREEDOMS

Leonard W. Levy

Because First Amendment freedoms rank at the top of the hierarchy of constitutional values, any legislation that explicitly limits those freedoms must be denied the usual presumption of constitutionality and be subjected to strict scrutiny by the judiciary. So went the earliest version of the preferred freedoms doctrine, sometimes called the preferred position or preferred status doctrine. It probably originated in the opinions of Justice Oliver Wendell Holmes, at least implicitly. He believed that a presumption of constitutionality attached to economic regulation, which needed to meet merely a rational basis test, as he explained dissenting in Lochner v. New York (1905). By contrast, in Abrams v. United States (1919) he adopted the clear and present danger test as a constitutional yardstick for legislation such as the Espionage Act of 1917 or state criminal syndicalism statutes, which limited freedom of speech.

Justice Benjamin N. Cardozo first suggested a more general hierarchy of constitutional rights in Palko v. Connecticut (1937), in a major opinion on the incorporation doctrine. He ranked at the top those "fundamental principles of liberty and justice which lie at the base of all our civil and political institutions." He tried to distinguish rights that might be lost without risking the essentials of liberty and justice from rights which he called "the matrix, the indispensable condition, of nearly every other form of freedom." These fundamental rights came to be regarded as the preferred freedoms. A year later Justice Harlan F. Stone, in footnote four of his opinion in United States v. Carolene Products (1938), observed that "legislation which restricts the political processes" might "be subjected to more exacting judicial scrutiny" than other legislation. He suggested, too, that the judiciary might accord particularly searching examination of statutes reflecting "prejudice against discrete and insular minorities."

The First Amendment freedoms initially enjoyed a primacy above all others. Justice William O. Douglas for the Court in Murdock v. Pennsylvania (1943) expressly stated: "Freedom of the press, freedom of speech, freedom of religion are in a preferred position." In the 1940s, despite bitter divisions on the Court over the question whether constitutional rights should be ranked, as well as the question whether the Court should ever deny the presumption of constitutionality, a majority of Justices continued to endorse the doctrine. Justice WILEY B. RUT-LEDGE for the Court gave it its fullest exposition in *Thomas v. Collins* (1945). Justice FELIX FRANKFURTER, who led the opposition to the doctrine, called it "mischievous" in KOVACS V. COOPER (1949); he especially disliked the implication that "any law touching communication" might be "infected with presumptive invalidity." Yet even Frankfurter, in his *Kovacs* opinion, acknowledged that "those liberties . . . which history has established as the indispensable conditions of an open as against a closed society come to the Court with a momentum for respect lacking when appeal is made to liberties which derive merely from shifting economic arrangements."

The deaths of Murphy and Rutledge in 1949 and their replacement by TOM C. CLARK and SHERMAN MINTON shifted the balance of judicial power to the Frankfurter viewpoint. Thereafter little was heard about the doctrine. The WARREN COURT vigorously defended not only CIVIL LIBERTIES but CIVIL RIGHTS and the rights of the criminally accused. The expansion of the incorporation doctrine and of the concept of EQUAL PROTECTION OF THE LAWS in the 1960s produced a new spectrum of FUNDAMENTAL INTERESTS demanding special judicial protection. Free speech, press, and religion continued, nevertheless, to be ranked, at least implicitly, as very special in character and possessing a symbolic "firstness," to use EDMOND CAHN's apt term. Although the Court rarely speaks of a preferred freedoms doctrine today, the substance of the doctrine has been absorbed in the concepts of strict scrutiny, fundamental rights, and selective incorporation.

Bibliography

McKAY, ROBERT B.   1959   The Preference for Freedom. *New York University Law Review* 34:1184–1227.

INCORPORATION DOCTRINE

Leonard W. Levy

According to the incorporation doctrine the FOURTEENTH AMENDMENT incorporates or absorbs the BILL OF RIGHTS, making its guarantees applicable to the states. Whether the Bill of Rights applied to the states, restricting their powers as it did those of the national government, was a question that arose in connection with the framing and ratification of the Fourteenth Amendment. Before 1868 nothing in the Constitution of the United States prevented a state from imprisoning religious heretics or political dissenters, or from abolishing TRIAL BY JURY, or from torturing suspects to extort confessions of guilt. The Bill of Rights limited only the United States, not the states. JAMES MADISON, who framed the amendments that became the Bill of Rights, had included one providing that "no State shall violate the equal rights of conscience, of the FREEDOM OF THE PRESS, or the trial by jury in criminal cases." The Senate defeated that proposal. History, therefore, was on the side of the Supreme Court when it unanimously decided in BARRON V. BALTIMORE (1833) that "the fifth amendment must be understood as restraining the power of the general government, not as applicable to the States," and said that the other amendments composing the Bill of Rights were equally inapplicable to the States.

Thus, a double standard existed in the nation. The Bill of Rights commanded the national government to refrain from enacting certain laws and to respect certain procedures, but it left the states free to do as they wished in relation to the same matters. State constitutions and COMMON LAW practices, rather than the Constitution of the United States, were the sources of restraints on the states with respect to the subjects of the Bill of Rights.

Whether the Fourteenth Amendment was intended to alter this situation is a matter on which the historical record is complex, confusing, and probably inconclusive. Even if history spoke with a loud, clear, and decisive voice, however, it ought not necessarily control judgment on the question whether the Supreme Court should interpret the amendment as incorporating the Bill of Rights. Whatever the framers of the Fourteenth intended, they did not possess ultimate wisdom as to the meaning of their words for subsequent generations. Moreover, the PRIVI-

LEGES AND IMMUNITIES, due process, and EQUAL PROTECTION clauses of section 1 of the amendment are written in language that blocks fixed meanings. Its text must be read as revelations of general purposes that were to be achieved or as expressions of imperishable principles that are comprehensive in character. The principles and purposes, not their framers' original technical understanding, are what was intended to endure. We cannot avoid the influence of history but are not constitutionally obligated to obey history which is merely a guide. The task of CONSTITUTIONAL INTERPRETATION is one of statecraft: to read the text in the light of changing needs in accordance with the noblest ideals of a democratic society.

The Court has, in fact, proved to be adept at reading into the Constitution the policy values that meet its approval, and its freedom to do so is virtually legislative in scope. Regrettably in its first Fourteenth Amendment decision, in the SLAUGHTERHOUSE CASES (1873), the Court unnecessarily emasculated the privileges and immunities clause by ruling that it protected only the privileges and immunities of national CITIZENSHIP but not the privileges and immunities of state citizenship, which included "nearly every CIVIL RIGHT for the establishment and protection of which organized government is instituted." Among the rights deriving from state, not national, citizenship were those referred to by the Bill of Rights as well as other "fundamental" rights. Justice STEPHEN J. FIELD, dissenting, rightly said that the majority's interpretation had rendered the clause "a vain and idle enactment, which accomplished nothing. . . ." The privileges and immunities clause was central to the incorporation issue because to the extent that any of the framers of the amendment intended incorporation, they relied principally on that clause. Notwithstanding the amendment, *Barron v. Baltimore* remained controlling law. The Court simply opposed the revolution in the federal system which the amendment's text suggested. The privileges and immunities of national citizenship after *Slaughterhouse* were those that Congress or the Court could have protected, under the SUPREMACY CLAUSE, with or without the new amendment.

In HURTADO V. CALIFORNIA (1884) the Court initiated a long line of decisions that eroded the traditional procedures associated with due process of law. *Hurtado* was not an incorporation case, because the question it posed was not whether the Fourteenth Amendment incorporated the clause of the Fifth guaranteeing INDICTMENT by GRAND JURY but whether the concept of due process necessarily required indictment in a capital case. In cases arising after *Hurtado,* counsel argued that even if the concept of due process did not mean indictment, or freedom from CRUEL AND UNUSUAL PUNISHMENT, or trial by a twelve-member jury, or the RIGHT AGAINST SELF-INCRIMINATION, the provisions of the Bill of Rights applied to the states through the Fourteenth Amendment; that is, the amendment incorporated them either by the privileges and immunities clause, or by the due process clause's protection of "liberty." In *O'Neil v. Vermont* (1892), that argument was accepted for the first time by three Justices, dissenting; however, only one of them, JOHN MARSHALL HARLAN, steadfastly adhered to it in MAXWELL V. DOW (1900) and TWINING V. NEW JERSEY (1908), when all other Justices rejected it. Harlan, dissenting in *Patterson v. Colorado* (1907), stated "that the privilege of free speech and a free press belong to every citizen of the United States, constitute essential parts of every man's liberty, and are protected against violation by that clause of the Fourteenth Amendment forbidding a state to deprive any person of his liberty without due process of law." The Court casually adopted that view in OBITER DICTUM in GITLOW V. NEW YORK (1925).

Before *Gitlow* the Court had done a good deal of property-minded, not liberty-minded, incorporating. As early as *Hepburn v. Griswold* (1870), it had read the protection of the CONTRACT CLAUSE into the Fifth Amendment's due process clause as a limitation on the powers of Congress, a viewpoint repeated in the SINKING FUND CASES (1879). The Court in 1894 had incorporated the Fifth's JUST COMPENSATION clause into the Fourteenth's due process clause and in 1897 it had incorporated the same clause into the Fourteenth's equal protection clause. In the same decade the Court had accepted SUBSTANTIVE DUE PROCESS, incorporating within the Fourteenth a variety of doctrines that secured property, particularly corporate property, against "unreasonable" rate regulations and reformist labor legislation. By 1915, however, PROCEDURAL DUE PROCESS for persons accused of crime had so shriveled in meaning that Justice OLIVER WENDELL HOLMES, dissenting, was forced to say that "mob law does not become due process of law by securing the assent of a terrorized jury."

The word "liberty" in the due process clause had absorbed all FIRST AMENDMENT guarantees by the time of the decision in EVERSON V. BOARD OF EDUCATION (1947). Incorporation developed much more slowly in the field of criminal justice. POWELL V. ALABAMA (1932) applied to the states the SIXTH AMENDMENT'S RIGHT TO COUNSEL in capital cases, as a "necessary requisite of due process of law." The Court reached a watershed, however, in PALKO V. CONNECTICUT (1937), where it refused to incorporate the ban on DOUBLE JEOPARDY. Justice BENJAMIN N. CARDOZO sought to provide a "rationalizing principle" to explain the selective or piecemeal incorporation process. He repudiated the notion that the Fourteenth Amendment embraced the entire Bill of Rights, because the rights it guaranteed fell into two categories. Some were of such a nature that liberty and justice could not exist if they were sacrificed. These had been brought "within the Fourteenth Amendment by a process of absorption" because they were "of the very essence of a scheme of ORDERED

LIBERTY." In short, they were "fundamental," like the concept of due process. Other rights, however, were not essential to a "fair and enlightened system of justice." First Amendment rights were "the indispensable condition" of nearly every other form of freedom, but jury trials, indictments, immunity against compulsory self-incrimination, and double jeopardy "might be lost, and justice still be done."

The difficulty with *Palko* 's rationalizing scheme was that it was subjective. It offered no principle explaining why some rights were fundamental or essential to ordered liberty and others were not; it measured all rights against some abstract or idealized system, rather than the Anglo-American accusatory system of criminal justice. Selective incorporation also completely lacked historical justification. And it was logically flawed. The Court read the substantive content of the First Amendment into the "liberty" of the due process clause, but that clause permitted the abridgment of liberty with due process of law. On the other hand, selective incorporation, as contrasted with total incorporation, allowed the Court to decide constitutional issues as they arose on a case-by-case basis, and allowed, too, the exclusion from the incorporation doctrine of some rights whose incorporation would wreak havoc in state systems of justice. Grand jury indictment for all felonies and trials by twelve-member juries in civil suits involving more than twenty dollars are among Bill of Rights guarantees that would have that result, if incorporated.

In ADAMSON V. CALIFORNIA (1947) a 5–4 Court rejected the total incorporation theory advanced by the dissenters led by Justice HUGO L. BLACK. Black lambasted the majority's due process standards as grossly subjective; he argued that only the Justices' personal idiosyncrasies could give content to "canons of decency" and "fundamental justice." Black believed that both history and objectivity required resort to the "specifics" of the Bill of Rights. Justices FRANK MURPHY and WILEY RUTLEDGE would have gone further. They accepted total incorporation but observed that due process might require invalidating some state practices "despite the absence of a specific provision in the Bill of Rights." Justice FELIX FRANKFURTER, replying to Black, denied the subjectivity charge and turned it against the dissenters. Murphy's total-incorporation-"plus" was subjective; total incorporation impractically fastened the entire Bill of Rights, with impedimenta, on the states along with the accretions each right had gathered in the United States courts. Selective incorporation on the basis of individual Justices' preferences meant "a merely subjective test" in determining which rights were in and which were out.

Frankfurter also made a logical point long familiar in constitutional jurisprudence. The due process clause of the Fourteenth, which was the vehicle for incorporation, having been copied from the identical clause of the Fifth, could not mean one thing in the latter and something very different in the former. The Fifth itself included a variety of clauses.

To incorporate them into the Fourteenth would mean that those clauses of the Fifth and in the remainder of the Bill of Rights were redundant, or the due process clause, if signifying all the rest, was meaningless or superfluous. The answer to Frankfurter and to those still holding his view is historical, not logical. The history of due process shows that it did mean trial by jury and a cluster of traditional rights of accused persons that the Bill of Rights separately specified. Its framers were in many respects careless draftsmen. They enumerated particular rights associated with due process and then added the due process clause partly for political reasons and partly as a rhetorical flourish—a reinforced guarantee and a genuflection toward traditional usage going back to medieval reenactments of MAGNA CARTA.

Numerous cases of the 1950s showed that the majority's reliance on the concept of due process rather than the "specifics" of the Bill of Rights made for unpredictable and unconvincing results. For that reason the Court resumed selective incorporation in the 1960s, beginning with MAPP V. OHIO (1961) and ending with *Benton v. Maryland* (1969). The Warren Court's "revolution in criminal justice" applied against the states the rights of the Fourth through Eighth Amendments, excepting only indictment, twelve-member civil juries, and bail. IN RE WINSHIP (1970) even held that proof of crime beyond a REASONABLE DOUBT, though not a specific provision of the Bill of Rights, was essential to due process, and various decisions have suggested the Court's readiness to extend to the states the Eighth Amendment's provision against excessive bail.

The specifics of the Bill of Rights, however, have proved to offer only an illusion of objectivity, because its most important clauses, including all that have been incorporated, are inherently ambiguous. Indeed, the only truly specific clauses are the ones that have not been incorporated—indictment by grand jury and civil trials by twelve-member juries. The "specific" injunctions of the Bill of Rights do not exclude exceptions, nor are they self-defining. What is "an ESTABLISHMENT OF RELIGION" and what, given libels, pornography, and perjury, is "the freedom of speech" or "of the press"? These freedoms cannot be abridged, but what is an abridgment? Freedom of religion may not be prohibited; may freedom of religion be abridged by a regulation short of prohibition? What is an "UNREASONABLE" SEARCH, "PROBABLE" CAUSE, or "excessive" bail? What punishment is "cruel and unusual"? Is it really true that a person cannot be compelled to be a witness against himself in a criminal case and that the Sixth Amendment extends to "all" criminal prosecutions? What is a "criminal prosecution," a "SPEEDY TRIAL, or an "impartial" jury? Ambiguity cannot be strictly construed. Neutral principles and specifics turn out to be subjective or provoke subjectivity. Moreover, applying to the states the federal standard does not always turn out as expected. After DUNCAN V. LOUISIANA (1968) extended the trial by jury clause of the Sixth Amendment to the states, the Court decided that a criminal jury of less than twelve (but not less than six) would not violate the Fourteenth Amendment, nor would a non-unanimous jury decision. (See JURY SIZE.) Examples can be multiplied to show that the incorporation doctrine has scarcely diminished the need for judgment and that judgment tends to be personal in character.

On the whole, however, the Court has abolished the double standard by nationalizing the Bill of Rights. The results have been mixed. More than ever justice tends to travel on leaden feet. Swift and certain punishment has always been about as effective a deterrent to crime as our criminal justice system can provide, and the prolongation of the criminal process from arrest to final appeal, which is one result of the incorporation doctrine, adds to the congestion of prosecutorial caseloads and court dockets. However, the fundamental problem is the staggering rise in the number of crimes committed, not the decisions of the Court. Even when the police used truncheons to beat suspects into confessions and searched and seized almost at will, they did not reduce the crime rate. In the long run a democratic society is probably hurt more by lawless conduct on the part of law-enforcement agencies than by the impediments of the incorporation doctrine. In the First Amendment field, the incorporation doctrine has few critics, however vigorously particular First Amendment decisions may be criticized.

Bibliography

ABRAHAM, HENRY J.   1977   *Freedom and the Court,* 3rd ed. Pages 33–105. New York: Oxford University Press.

CORTNER, RICHARD C.   1981   *The Supreme Court and the Second Bill of Rights: The Fourteenth Amendment and the Nationalization of Civil Liberties.* Madison: University of Wisconsin Press.

FRIENDLY, HENRY J.   1967   *Benchmarks.* Pages 235–265. Chicago: University of Chicago Press.

HENKIN, LOUIS   1963   "Selective Incorporation" in the Fourteenth Amendment. *Yale Law Journal* 73:74–88.

NORTH, ARTHUR A.   1966   *The Supreme Court: Judicial Process and Judicial Politics.* Pages 65–133. New York: Appleton-Century-Crofts.

STANDARD OF REVIEW

Kenneth L. Karst

Some constitutional limitations on government are readily susceptible to "interpretation," in the sense of definition and categorization. Once a court categorizes a law as a BILL OF ATTAINDER, for example, it holds the law invalid. Other limitations, however, are expressed in terms that make this sort of interpretation awkward: the FREEDOM OF SPEECH, the EQUAL PROTECTION OF THE LAWS, DUE PROCESS OF LAW. The judicial task in enforcing these open-ended limitations implies an inquiry into the justifications asserted by government for restricting liberty or denying equal treatment. The term "standards of review," in common use since the late 1960s, denotes various degrees of judicial deference to legislative judgments concerning these justifications.

The idea that there might be more than one standard of review was explicitly suggested in Justice HARLAN FISKE STONE's opinion for the Supreme Court in UNITED STATES v. CAROLENE PRODUCTS CO. (1938). Confirming a retreat from the JUDICIAL ACTIVISM that had invalidated a significant number of ECONOMIC REGULATIONS over the preceding four decades, Stone concluded that such a law would be valid if the legislature's purpose were legitimate and if the law could rationally be seen as related to that purpose. Stone added, however, that this permissive RATIONAL BASIS standard might not be appropriate for reviewing laws challenged under certain specific prohibitions of the BILL OF RIGHTS, or laws restricting the political process, or laws directed at DISCRETE AND INSULAR MINORITIES. Such cases, Stone suggested, might call for a diminished presumption of constitutionality, a "more exacting judicial scrutiny."

The WARREN COURT embraced this double standard in several doctrinal areas, most notably in equal protection cases. The permissive rational basis standard continued to govern review of economic regulations, but STRICT SCRUTINY was given to laws discriminating against the exercise of FUNDAMENTAL INTERESTS such as voting or marriage and to laws employing SUSPECT CLASSIFICATIONS such as race. The strict scrutiny standard amounts to an inversion of the presumption of constitutionality: the state must justify its imposition of a racial inequality, for example, by showing that the law is necessary to achieve a COMPELLING STATE INTEREST. Today active judicial review of both the importance of legislative purposes and the necessity of legislative means is employed not only in some types of equal protection cases but also in fields such as the freedom of speech and RELIGIOUS LIBERTY. It has even attended the rebirth of SUBSTANTIVE DUE PROCESS.

Inevitably, however, cracks appeared in this two-tier system of standards of review. The Court used the language of "rational basis" to strike down some laws, and in cases involving SEX DISCRIMINATION it explicitly adopted an intermediate standard for reviewing both legislative ends and means: discrimination based on sex is invalid unless it serves an "important" governmental purpose and is "substantially related" to that purpose. A similar intermediate standard is now part of the required analysis of governmental regulations of COMMERCIAL SPEECH. In practical effect, the Court has created a "sliding scale" of review, varying the intensity of judicial scrutiny of legislation in proportion to the importance of the interests invaded and the likelihood of legislative prejudice against the persons disadvantaged. The process, in other words, is interest-balancing, pure and simple. Justice WILLIAM H. REHNQUIST, writing for the Court in ROSTKER v. GOLDBERG (1981), remarked accurately that the Court's various levels of scrutiny "may all too readily become facile abstractions used to justify a result"—a proposition well illustrated by the *Rostker* opinion itself.

Bibliography

GUNTHER, GERALD 1972 The Supreme Court, 1971 Term—Foreword: In Search of Evolving Doctrine on a Changing Court: A Model for a Newer Equal Protection. *Harvard Law Review* 86:1–48.

FUNDAMENTAL INTERESTS

Kenneth L. Karst

The idea that some interests are fundamental, and thus deserving of a greater measure of constitutional protection than is given to other interests, is an old one. Justice BUSHROD WASHINGTON, sitting on circuit in CORFIELD V. CORYELL (1823), held that the PRIVILEGES AND IMMUNITIES clause of Article IV of the Constitution protected out-of-staters against discriminatory state legislation touching only those privileges that were "in their very nature, fundamental; which belong, of right, to the citizens of all free governments." Washington's list of such interests was limited but significant: free passage through a state; HABEAS CORPUS; the right to sue in state courts; the right to hold and dispose of property; freedom from discriminatory taxation.

Although the *Corfield* doctrine suggested an active role for the federal judiciary in protecting NATURAL RIGHTS against state interference—at least on behalf of citizens of other states—the doctrine was not embraced by the full Supreme Court during Washington's lifetime. If some hoped that the FOURTEENTH AMENDMENT's privileges and immunities clause would breathe new life into the fundamental rights theory, those hopes were disappointed in the SLAUGHTERHOUSE CASES (1873). Rejecting the theory as propounded in two eloquent dissenting opinions, the Court again refused to find any special federal constitutional protection against state invasions of preferred rights.

Within a generation, however, the Court had identified a cluster of preferred rights of property and the FREEDOM OF CONTRACT, to be defended against various forms of ECONOMIC REGULATION. The Court did not use the language of fundamental interests; for doctrinal support it avoided both privileges and immunities clauses, relying instead on a theory of SUBSTANTIVE DUE PROCESS. When this doctrinal development played out in the late 1930s, the Court abandoned its STRICT SCRUTINY of business regulation in favor of a STANDARD OF REVIEW demanding no more than a RATIONAL BASIS for legislative judgments.

Even as the Court adopted its new permissive attitude toward economic regulation, it was laying the groundwork for another round of protections of preferred rights. (See UNITED STATES V. CAROLENE PRODUCTS CO., 1938; SKINNER V. OKLAHOMA, 1942.) When the WARREN COURT set about its expansion of the reach of EQUAL PROTECTION doctrine, it not only followed these precedents but also revived the rhetoric of fundamental interests. A state law discriminating against the exercise of such an interest, the Court held, must be justified as necessary for achieving a COMPELLING STATE INTEREST.

The Warren Court hinted strongly that it would expand the list of fundamental interests demanding strict judicial scrutiny to include all manner of claims to equality. In fact, the Court's holdings placed only a limited number of interests in the "fundamental" category: VOTING RIGHTS and related interests in the electoral process; some limited rights of ACCESS TO THE COURTS; and rights relating to marriage, the family, and other intimate relationships. Even so modest a doctrinal development evoked the strong dissent of Justice JOHN MARSHALL HARLAN: "I know of nothing which entitles this Court to pick out particular human activities, characterize them as 'fundamental,' and give them added protection under an unusually stringent equal protection test."

The BURGER COURT, making Harlan's lament its theme song, called a halt to the expansion of fundamental interests occasioning strict judicial scrutiny under the equal protection clause. However, in cases touching marriage and other close personal relationships, the Court continued to promote the notion of fundamental liberties deserving of special protection—now on a substantive due process theory. (See ABORTION AND THE CONSTITUTION; ILLEGITIMACY; FREEDOM OF INTIMATE ASSOCIATION.) The notion of natural rights as part of our constitutional law is deeply ingrained. Our modern doctrines about fundamental rights are novel only in the particular interests they have termed fundamental.

Bibliography

TRIBE, LAURENCE H.   1978   *American Constitutional Law.* Chaps. 8, 11, 15, and 16. Mineola, N.Y.: Foundation Press. 000 002

SUSPECT CLASSIFICATION

Kenneth L. Karst

Long before the term "suspect classification" gained currency, Justice HARLAN FISKE STONE captured the idea in his opinion for the Supreme Court in UNITED STATES v. CAROLENE PRODUCTS CO. (1938). While insisting on RATIONAL BASIS as the appropriate STANDARD OF REVIEW for cases involving ECONOMIC REGULATION, Stone suggested that "prejudice against DISCRETE AND INSULAR MINORITIES [that is, religious, or national, or racial minorities] may be a special condition, which tends seriously to curtail the operation of those political processes ordinarily to be relied upon to protect minorities, and which may call for a correspondingly more searching judicial inquiry." In modern idiom, to call a legislative classification "suspect" is to suggest the possibility that it resulted from prejudice against the group it burdens, a possibility that justifies strict judicial scrutiny to assure that it is necessary to achieve a COMPELLING STATE INTEREST. In practice, most laws subject to this exacting standard are held invalid.

Irony attends the origins of the expression. Justice HUGO L. BLACK, writing for a majority in *Korematsu v. United States* (1944), one of the JAPANESE AMERICAN CASES, found no denial of EQUAL PROTECTION in an EXECUTIVE ORDER excluding American citizens of Japanese ancestry from the West Coast. Along the way to this extraordinary conclusion, however, he said: "all legal restrictions which curtail the civil rights of a single racial group are immediately suspect. That is not to say that all such restrictions are unconstitutional. It is to say that courts must subject them to the most rigid scrutiny." In *Korematsu* itself, the Court did no such thing; it paid the greatest deference to a "military" judgment that was chiefly political and steeped in racial prejudice. Yet *Korematsu*'s main doctrinal legacy was that racial classifications were suspect.

In one view, this two-stage analysis, first identifying a classification as suspect and then subjecting it to STRICT SCRUTINY, is a roundabout way of addressing the issue of illicit legislative motives. (See LEGISLATION; WASHINGTON v. DAVIS, 1976.) Strict scrutiny is required in order to allay the suspicion that a law was designed to disadvantage a minority that lacked effective power in the legislature. That suspicion is laid to rest only by a showing that the law is well designed to achieve a legitimate purpose that has real importance. In another view, a classification based on race should be subjected to strict scrutiny because the immutable characteristic of race lends itself so well to a system thought dominated by stereotype, which automatically consigns a person to a general category, often implying inferiority. This concern for stigmatic harm is part of the substantive core of the equal protection clause, the principle of equal citizenship; the concern retains vitality even in an era when members of racial minorities have become electoral majorities in many of our major cities.

A number of egalitarian decisions in the later years of the WARREN COURT suggested a wide range of classifications that were candidates for inclusion by the Supreme Court in the "suspect" category: alienage, sex, ILLEGITIMACY, age, indigency. In the event, none of these candidates was accepted fully. Some classifications disadvantaging ALIENS were held "suspect," but many were not. The Court did significantly heighten the standard of review for most cases involving claimed denials of SEX DISCRIMINATION and gave some "bite" to the rational basis standard in cases involving illegitimacy. On the whole, however, the Court's behavior since the late 1970s suggests a determination to limit expansion of the list of suspect classifications, and thus to limit the occasions for active judicial supervision of legislation.

Some racial classifications are adopted as remedies for past societal discrimination based on race. Such an AFFIRMATIVE ACTION program presents neither of the principal dangers that have been said to require strict judicial scrutiny of racial classifications. There is less reason to suspect an illicit motive when a majoritarian body such as a legislature discriminates in favor of a historically disadvantaged minority, and the risk of stigmatic harm to a racial group is much reduced. Thus, varying majorities of the Supreme Court have consistently agreed that the appropriate standard of review for such remedial legislation, including RACIAL QUOTAS, is considerably less exacting than the strictest form of strict scrutiny.

The whole "suspect classifications" idea would seem to have outlived its usefulness. Surely the Supreme Court no longer needs the doctrine to justify its highest levels of intensity of judicial review. In race cases, for example, the Court needs no such locution in order to continue imposing on government a "heavy burden of justification" of laws imposing invidious racial discrimination. Abandonment of the rhetoric of suspect classifications would promote candor, by easing the way for open recognition of the sliding scale of standards of review now serving to cloak the Court's interest balancing. It would also remove a barrier, built into the very language of suspect "classifications," to doctrinal growth in the direction of affirmative governmental responsibility to alleviate those inequalities that prevent the realization of the principle of equal citizenship.

Bibliography

BREST, PAUL A.   1976   The Supreme Court, 1975 Term—Foreword: In Defense of the Antidiscrimination Principle. *Harvard Law Review* 90:1–54.

ELY, JOHN HART   1980   Democracy and Distrust: A Theory of Judicial Review. Cambridge, Mass.: Harvard University Press.

CAROLENE PRODUCTS COMPANY, UNITED STATES v.

Aviam Solfer

Footnote four to Justice HARLAN F. STONE's opinion in UNITED STATES
v. CAROLENE PRODUCTS CO. (1938) undoubtedly is the best known, most
controversial footnote in constitutional law. Stone used it to suggest
categories in which a general presumption in favor of the constitutionality
of legislation might be inappropriate. The issue of if and when particular
constitutional claims warrant special judicial scrutiny has been a core
concern in constitutional theory for nearly fifty years since Stone's three-
paragraph footnote was appended to an otherwise obscure 1938 opinion.

The *Carolene Products* decision, handed down the same day as ERIE
RAILROAD v. TOMPKINS (1938), itself reflected a new perception of the
proper role for federal courts. It articulated a position of great judicial
deference in reviewing most legislation. In his majority opinion, Stone
sought to consolidate developing restraints on judicial intervention in
economic matters, symbolized by WEST COAST HOTEL CO. v. PARRISH
(1937). But in footnote four Stone also went on to suggest that legislation,
if challenged with certain types of constitutional claims, might not merit
the same deference most legislation should enjoy.

Stone's opinion upheld a 1923 federal ban on the interstate shipment
of filled milk. The Court thus reversed a lower federal court and, indirectly, the Illinois Supreme Court, in holding that Congress had power
to label as adulterated a form of skimmed milk in which butterfat was
replaced by coconut milk. Today the decision seems unremarkable; at
the time, however, not only was the result in *Carolene Products* controversial but the theory of variable judicial scrutiny suggested by its footnote
four was new and perhaps daring.

Actually, only three other Justices joined that part of Stone's opinion
which contained the famous footnote, though that illustrious trio consisted of Chief Justice CHARLES EVANS HUGHES, Justice LOUIS D. BRANDEIS,
and Justice OWEN J. ROBERTS. Justice HUGO L. BLACK refused to agree
to the part of Stone's opinion with the footnote because Black wished
to go further than Stone in proclaiming deference to legislative judgments. Justice PIERCE BUTLER concurred only in the result; Justice JAMES

C. McReynolds dissented; and Justices Benjamin N. Cardozo and Stanley F. Reed did not take part.

In fact, the renowned footnote does no more than tentatively mention the possibility of active review in certain realms. The footnote is nonetheless considered a paradigm for special judicial scrutiny of laws discriminating against certain rights or groups. The first paragraph, added at the suggestion of Chief Justice Hughes, is the least controversial. The paragraph hints at special judicial concern when rights explicitly mentioned in the text of the Constitution are at issue. This rights-oriented, interpretivist position involves less of a judicial leap than the possibility, suggested in the rest of the footnote, of additional grounds for judicial refusal or reluctance to defer to judgments of other governmental branches.

The footnote's second paragraph speaks of possible special scrutiny of interference with "those political processes which can ordinarily be expected to bring about repeal of undesirable legislation." To illustrate the ways in which clogged political channels might be grounds for exacting judicial review, Stone cites decisions invalidating restrictions on the right to vote, the dissemination of information, freedom of political association, and peaceable assembly.

The footnote's third and final paragraph has been the most vigorously debated. It suggests that prejudice directed against DISCRETE AND INSULAR MINORITIES may also call for "more searching judicial inquiry." For this proposition Stone cites two commerce clause decisions, McCulloch v. Maryland (1819) and South Carolina State Highway Dept. v. Barnwell Bros. (1938), as well as First Amendment and Fourteenth Amendment decisions invalidating discriminatory laws based on religion, national origin, or race. Judicial and scholarly disagreement since 1938 has focused mainly on two questions. First, even if the category "discrete and insular minorities" seems clearly to include blacks, should any other groups be included? Second, does paragraph three essentially overlap with paragraph two, or does it go beyond protecting groups who suffer particular political disadvantage? The question whether discrimination against particular groups or burdens on certain rights should trigger special judicial sensitivity is a basic problem in constitutional law to this day.

Footnote four thus symbolizes the Court's struggle since the late 1930s to confine an earlier, free-wheeling tradition of judicial intervention premised on FREEDOM OF CONTRACT and SUBSTANTIVE DUE PROCESS, on the one hand, while trying, on the other, to create an acceptable basis for active intervention when judges perceive political disadvantages or racial or other invidious discrimination.

Dozens of Supreme Court decisions and thousands of pages of scholarly commentary since *Carolene Products* have explored this problem. In EQUAL PROTECTION analysis, for example, the approach introduced in footnote four helped produce a two-tiered model of judicial review. Within this model, legislation involving social and economic matters would be sustained if any RATIONAL BASIS for the law could be found, or sometimes even conceived of, by a judge. In sharp contrast, STRICT SCRUTINY applied to classifications based on race, national origin, and, sometimes, alienage. Similarly, judicial identification of a limited number of FUNDAMENTAL RIGHTS, such as VOTING RIGHTS, sometimes seemed to trigger a strict scrutiny described accurately by Gerald Gunther as " 'strict' in theory and fatal in fact."

Though this two-tiered approach prevailed in many decisions of the WARREN COURT, inevitably the system became more flexible. "Intermediate scrutiny" is now explicitly used in SEX DISCRIMINATION cases, for example. The Court continues to wrestle with the problem suggested in footnote four cases involving constitutional claims of discrimination against whites, discrimination against illegitimate children, and total exclusion of some from important benefits such as public education. Parallel with footnote four, the argument today centers on the question whether it is an appropriate constitutional response to relegate individuals who claim discrimination at the hands of the majority to their remedies within the political process. Yet, as new groups claim discriminatory treatment in new legal realms, the meaning of "discrete and insular minorities" grows more problematic. Undeniably, however, the categories suggested in footnote four still channel the debate. A good example is John Hart Ely's *Democracy and Distrust* (1980), an influential book that expands upon footnote four's theme of political participation.

Justice LEWIS H. POWELL recently stated that footnote four contains "perhaps the most far-sighted dictum in our modern judicial heritage." Yet Powell also stressed that, in his view, it is important to remember that footnote four was merely OBITER DICTUM and was intended to be no more. Even so, the tentative words of footnote four must be credited with helping to initiate and to define a new era of constitutional development. The questions raised by footnote four remain central to constitutional thought; controversy premised on this famous footnote shows no sign of abating.

Bibliography

BALL, MILNER S. 1981 Don't Die Don Quixote: A Response and Alternative to Tushnet, Bobbitt, and the Revised Texas Version of Constitutional Law. *Texas Law Review* 59:787–813.

ELY, JOHN HART 1980 *Democracy and Distrust.* Cambridge, Mass.: Harvard University Press.

LUSKY, LOUIS   1982   Footnote Redux: A *Carolene Products* Reminiscence. *Columbia Law Review* 82:1093–1105.
POWELL, LEWIS F., JR.   1982   *Carolene Products* Revisited. *Columbia Law Review* 82:1087–1092.

STRICT SCRUTINY

Kenneth L. Karst

In its modern use, "strict scrutiny" denotes JUDICIAL REVIEW that is active and intense. Although the "constitutional revolution" of the late 1930s aimed at replacing JUDICIAL ACTIVISM with a more restrained review using the RATIONAL BASIS formula, even that revolution's strongest partisans recognized that "a more exacting judicial scrutiny" might be appropriate in some cases. Specific prohibitions of the BILL OF RIGHTS, for example, might call for active judicial defense, and legislation might be entitled to a diminished presumption of validity when it interfered with the political process itself or was directed against DISCRETE AND INSULAR MINORITIES. (See UNITED STATES V. CAROLENE PRODUCTS CO., 1938.) The term "strict scrutiny" appears to have been used first by Justice WILLIAM O. DOUGLAS in his opinion for the Supreme Court in SKINNER V. OKLAHOMA (1942), in a context suggesting special judicial solicitude both for certain rights that were "basic" and for certain persons who seemed the likely victims of legislative prejudice.

Both these concerns informed the WARREN COURT's expansion of the reach of the EQUAL PROTECTION clause. "Strict scrutiny" was required for legislation that discriminated against the exercise of FUNDAMENTAL INTERESTS or employed SUSPECT CLASSIFICATIONS. In practice, as Gerald Gunther put it, the Court's heightened scrutiny was " 'strict' in theory and fatal in fact." The Court took a hard look at both the purposes of the legislature and the means used for achieving them. To pass the test of strict scrutiny, a legislative classification must be "necessary to achieve a COMPELLING STATE INTEREST." Thus the state's objectives must be not merely legitimate but of compelling importance, and the means used must be not merely rationally related to those purposes but necessary to their attainment.

The same demanding standard of review has emerged in other areas of constitutional law. Thus even some "indirect" regulations of the FREEDOM OF SPEECH—that is, regulations that do not purport to regulate message content—must be strictly scrutinized. Similarly, strict scrutiny is appropriate for general legislation whose application is attacked as a violation of the right of free exercise of religion. (See RELIGIOUS LIBERTY.) And in those places where SUBSTANTIVE DUE PROCESS has made a comeback—notably in defense of liberties having to do with marriage and family relations, abortion and contraception, and more generally the FREEDOM OF INTIMATE ASSOCIATION—the same strict judicial scrutiny is the order of the day.

The Court has developed intermediate STANDARDS OF REVIEW falling between the rational basis and strict scrutiny standards. Not every heightening of the intensity of judicial review, in other words, implies strict scrutiny. Most critics of the Supreme Court's modern activism reject not only its employment of the strict scrutiny standard but also its use of any heightened standard of review. For these critics, there is little room in the Constitution for any judicial inquiry into the importance of governmental goals or the utility of governmental means. Some action by the state is forbidden by the Constitution, more or less explicitly. Beyond these prohibitions, say these critics, lie no principled guides to judicial behavior.

Yet strict judicial scrutiny of legislation is almost as old as the Constitution itself. From one season to another, the special objects of the judiciary's protection have varied, but from JOHN MARSHALL's day to our own the courts have always found *some* occasions for "a more exacting judicial scrutiny" of the political branches' handiwork. It is hard to imagine what our country would be like if they had not done so.

Bibliography

GUNTHER, GERALD 1972 The Supreme Court, 1971 Term—Foreword: In Search of Evolving Doctrine on a Changing Court: A Model for a Newer Equal Protection. *Harvard Law Review* 86:1–48.

COMPELLING STATE INTEREST

Kenneth L. Karst

When the Supreme Court concludes that STRICT SCRUTINY is the appropriate STANDARD OF REVIEW, it often expresses its searching examination of the justification of legislation in a formula: the law is invalid unless it is necessary to achieve a "compelling state interest." The inquiry thus touches not only legislative means but also legislative purposes.

Even the permissive RATIONAL BASIS standard of review demands that legislative ends be legitimate. To say that a governmental purpose must be one of compelling importance is plainly to demand more. How much more, however, is something the Court has been unable to say. What we do know is that, once "strict scrutiny" is invoked, only rarely does a law escape invalidation.

Any judicial examination of the importance of a governmental objective implies that a court is weighing interests, engaging in a kind of cost-benefit analysis as a prelude to deciding on the constitutionality of legislation. Yet one would be mistaken to assume that the inquiry follows such a neat, linear, two-stage progression. Given the close correlation between employing the "strict scrutiny" standard and invalidating laws, the very word "scrutiny" may be misleading. A court that has embarked on a search for compelling state interests very likely knows how it intends to decide.

In many a case a court does find a legislative purpose of compelling importance. That is not the end of the "strict scrutiny" inquiry; there remains the question whether the law is necessary to achieve that end. If, for example, there is another way the legislature might have accomplished its purpose, without imposing so great a burden on the constitutionally protected interest in liberty or equality, the availability of that LEAST RESTRICTIVE MEANS negates the necessity for the legislature's choice. The meaning of "strict scrutiny" is that even a compelling state interest must be pursued by means that give constitutional values their maximum protection.

The phrase "compelling state interest" originated in Justice FELIX FRANKFURTER's concurring opinion in *Sweezy v. New Hampshire* (1957), a case involving the privacy of political association: "For a citizen to be made to forego even a part of so basic a liberty as his political autonomy, the subordinating interest of the State must be compelling." The Supreme Court uses some variation on this formula not only in FIRST AMENDMENT cases but also in cases calling for "strict scrutiny" under the EQUAL PROTECTION clause or under the revived forms of SUBSTANTIVE DUE PROCESS. The formula, in short, is much used and little explained. The Court is unable to define "compelling state interest" but knows when it does not see it.

Bibliography

TRIBE, LAURENCE H.   1978   *American Constitutional Law.* Pages 1000–1002. Mineola, N.Y.: Foundation Press.

RATIONAL BASIS

Kenneth L. Karst

The "rational basis" STANDARD OF REVIEW emerged in the late 1930s, as the Supreme Court retreated from its earlier activism in the defense of economic liberties. We owe the phrase to Justice HARLAN FISKE STONE, who used it in two 1938 opinions to signal a new judicial deference to legislative judgments. In UNITED STATES V. CAROLENE PRODUCTS CO. (1938), Stone said that an ECONOMIC REGULATION, challenged as a violation of SUBSTANTIVE DUE PROCESS or of EQUAL PROTECTION, would be upheld unless demonstrated facts should "preclude the assumption that it rests upon some rational basis within the knowledge and experience of the legislators." In *South Carolina State Highway Department v. Barnwell Brothers, Inc.* (1938), Stone proposed "rational basis" as the standard for reviewing STATE REGULATIONS OF COMMERCE. (Later, Stone would accept the necessity for more exacting judicial scrutiny of such laws.) To complete the process, the Court adopted the same deferential posture toward congressional judgments that local activities substantially affected INTERSTATE COMMERCE and thus might be regulated by Congress under the COMMERCE POWER. In all its uses, "rational basis" represents a strong presumption of the constitutionality of legislation.

Yet even so minimal a standard of JUDICIAL REVIEW does, in theory, call for some judicial scrutiny of the rationality of the relationship between legislative means and ends. And that scrutiny of means makes sense only if we assume that the ends themselves are constitutionally required to serve general, public aims; otherwise, every law would be self-justifying, as precisely apt for achieving the advantages and disadvantages it achieves. Although the Court has sometimes suggested in economic regulation cases that even a search for legislative rationality lies beyond the scope of the judicial function, some such judicial scrutiny is required if our courts are to give effect to generalized constitutional guarantees of liberty and equality. Today's assumption, therefore, is that a law depriving a person of liberty or of equal treatment is invalid unless, at a minimum, it is a rational means for achieving a legitimate legislative purpose.

Even so relaxed a standard of review appears to call for a judicial inquiry always beset by uncertainties and often dominated by fictitious assumptions. Hans Linde has demonstrated the unreality attendant on judicial efforts to identify the "purposes" served by a law adopted by legislators with diverse objectives, or objectives only tenuously connected to the public good. Lacking sure guidance as to those "purposes"—which may have changed in the years since the law was adopted—a court must rely on counsel's assertions and its own assumptions. But in its inception the rational basis standard was not so much a mode of inquiry as a formula for validating legislation. Thus, in McGowan v. Maryland (1961), the Supreme Court said, "A statutory discrimination will not be set aside if any state of facts reasonably may be conceived to justify it." Part of the reason why the rational basis standard survives in federal constitutional law is that it is normally taken seriously only in its permissive feature (*United States Railroad Retirement Board v. Fritz*, 1980). A number of state courts, interpreting STATE CONSTITUTIONAL LAW, do take the rational basis standard to require a serious judicial examination of the reasonableness of legislation. And the Supreme Court itself, in its late-1960s forays into the reaches of equal protection doctrine lying beyond racial equality, sometimes labeled legislative classifications as "irrational" even as it insisted that state-imposed inequalities be justified against more exacting standards of review. (See HARPER v. VIRGINIA STATE BOARD OF ELECTIONS, 1966; LEVY v. LOUISIANA, 1968; SHAPIRO v. THOMPSON, 1969.) Since that time, the explicit recognition of different levels of judicial scrutiny of legislation has allowed the Court to reserve the rhetoric of rational basis for occasions thought appropriate for judicial modesty, in particular its review of "economic and social regulation." Some substantive interests call for heightened judicial scrutiny of legislative incursions into them; absent such considerations, the starting point for constitutional analysis remains the rational basis standard.

Bibliography

LINDE, HANS A. 1976 Due Process of Lawmaking. *Nebraska Law Review* 55:197–255.

COMITY, JUDICIAL

Kenneth L. Karst

Comity is the deference paid by the institutions of one government to the acts of another government—not out of compulsion, but in the interest of cooperation, reciprocity, and the stability that grows out of the satisfaction of mutual expectations. When the courts of one nation give effect to foreign laws and the orders of foreign courts, that deference is called judicial comity. (See ACT OF STATE DOCTRINE.)

The states of the United States are, for many purposes, separate sovereignties. A state court, in deciding a case, starts from the assumption that it will apply its own state law. When it applies the law of another state, normally it does so as a matter of comity. (See CHOICE OF LAW, CONSTITUTIONAL LIMITS UPON.) Because comity is not so much a rule as an attitude of accommodation, state courts generally feel free to refuse to apply a law that violates their own state's public policy. In *Nevada v. Hall* (1979) California courts upheld a million-dollar verdict against the State of Nevada in an automobile injury case, rejecting Nevada's claim of SOVEREIGN IMMUNITY; the Supreme Court affirmed, saying that the Constitution left to California's courts the degree of comity they should afford to Nevada law.

A state court's enforcement of the valid judgment of a court of another state is not merely a matter of comity but is required by the FULL FAITH AND CREDIT CLAUSE. Similarly, the SUPREMACY CLAUSE binds state courts to enforce valid federal laws and regulations, along with the valid judgments of federal courts.

Notions of comity have recently taken on increased significance in the federal courts themselves. A federal court may, under some circumstances, stay its proceedings because another action between the same parties is pending in a state court. The Supreme Court in *Fair Assessment of Real Estate Association v. McNary* (1981) discovered in the Tax Injunction Act (1937) a general principle of comity forbidding federal courts not only to enjoin the collection of state taxes but also to award DAMAGES in state tax cases. And comity has been a major consideration in the development of the "equitable restraint" doctrine of YOUNGER v. HARRIS (1971), which generally forbids a federal court to grant an INJUNCTION against the continuation of a pending state criminal prosecution.

INTEREST GROUP LITIGATION

Nathan Hakman

Interest group litigation is sponsored by organizations whose attorneys typically are less interested in specific legal claims than in the constitutional principles that a litigation represents. In contrast, most court cases are pursued for the benefit of the parties directly involved.

In seeking their clients' immediate interests private attorneys sometimes invoke constitutional arguments, but these are incidental to the specific claims of the parties. A sponsored case, however, is often pursued in the name of a litigant even though it is initiated, financed, and supported by an organization seeking its own constitutional goals. Interest groups are particularly attracted to cases involving constitutional principles because the judicial decisions emerging from such cases are relatively insulated from subsequent attacks by legislators and other public officials.

It is arguable, of course, that group-supported litigation has always been in existence. For example, following the WAGNER (NATIONAL LABOR RELATIONS) ACT and other New Deal legislation, litigation was managed, or otherwise assisted, by labor unions, trade associations, stockholder groups, and other business interests. However, the social and economic ferment of the 1960s and 1970s brought interest group litigation into sharper focus. The CIVIL RIGHTS movement and the Vietnam conflict not only produced federal legislation but also stimulated new constitutional demands by litigious organizations representing women, welfare recipients, consumers, and persons resisting military service.

The strategies and tactics of interest group litigants are heavily influenced by SOCIOLOGICAL JURISPRUDENCE and LEGAL REALISM. These philosophies hold that judges, especially Supreme Court Justices, decide controversial cases by choosing among conflicting goals and policies. Such judges do not reach results or write opinions merely by construing statutes, analogizing cases, or analyzing DOCTRINES. Instead, inquiries into judicial decision making have focused on the ways litigation is influenced by the timing of cases and the quality of the constitutional arguments reaching the appellate courts.

Prototypes of interest group litigation are the cases managed by the United States Department of Justice and similar state agencies. Their attorneys select the appropriate government cases to be appealed, and by confessing error or by compromising cases brought against the government, they seek to inhibit the establishment of unfavorable precedents. Also, a federal Legal Service Corporation, independent of the Department of Justice, has become one of the principal sources for funding and supporting litigation aimed at social and economic reform. Consumers, poor people, prisoners, and other low-resource persons have been represented by government-subsidized attorneys in suits against federal and state agencies and private organizations. Besides managing their own cases, government agencies promote private interest group litigation by reimbursing attorneys who participate and intervene for them in administrative proceedings and in court cases involving ADMINISTRATIVE LAW.

Although strategically less favorably situated than government attorneys, those representing private interest groups are also in a position to choose cases for APPEAL and to control the flow of argument in the higher courts. Unlike government litigation, however, the legal requirements for participation in private law suits sometimes prevent an organization from suing on its own, in behalf of its members, or for a similarly situated class of people. This problem has been partially alleviated by Supreme Court decisions liberalizing rules of legal STANDING to permit lawsuits by environmentalists, taxpayers, and other special interests.

Litigation activity by interest groups is visible in constitutional civil cases as well as in the criminal *cause célèbre*. In some of these cases attorneys representing factions of social movements vie for litigation sponsorship. The extensive publicity often connected with such cases, the constitutional issues perceived to be intertwined in the conflict, and the opportunities for fund-raising sometimes result in interest group controversies. For example, in several church–state cases attorneys representing different organizations have quarreled over the management of litigation. In the "Scottsboro" case, involving blacks accused of rape, attorneys representing civil rights organizations and those representing a communist-sponsored legal defense organization disagreed about the use of trial publicity.

Ideological differences among lawyers are occasionally reflected in varying conceptions of litigation strategy. Some attorneys emphasize the importance of a complete trial record raising all possible legal issues while others concentrate on the constitutional issues.

An alternative approach to a single TEST CASE is a litigation program aimed at accumulating a series of favorable decisions changing constitutional law. An incremental approach emphasizes narrow factual issues and specific claims, and groups with large legal staffs and cooperating attorneys are strategically positioned to conduct litigation in this way. Litigation programs of this kind have achieved changes in the constitutional doctrine governing racial SEGREGATION, CRIMINAL PROCEDURE, selective service, religion, and employment.

In politically tinged criminal cases the less provident and unpopular groups are not likely to use incremental litigation; they usually face immediate problems of securing relief for organization leaders and raising money for their causes. For example, in the 1950s when large numbers of cases involving congressional investigations of communism reached the Supreme Court, the lion's share was controlled by lawyers who depended on individual financial contributions to sustain their legal work.

When litigation is controlled by interest groups, constitutional issues are likely to be advanced and developed at the trial level. The "perfecting of a trial record" also gives the adversaries an opportunity to debate broader issues that are likely to be considered on appeal.

The development of a "good" trial record facilitates the preparation of appellate briefs interlaced with statistical and authoritative bibliographical references to social and economic facts supporting particular constitutional arguments. This technique was first used in the early-twentieth-century social legislation cases, and it has been used to illuminate fields ranging from racial equality to abortion. Similar forms of extralegal argument are found in complex court cases involving PUBLIC UTILITY REGULATION and other economic matters. (See BRANDEIS BRIEF.)

Besides expanding the scope of their arguments, interest group attorneys have become increasingly adept at coordinating litigation by discouraging the appeal of inconsistent cases or those with less developed records. They have also been successful in getting publication of sympathetic views in legal, scholarly, and popular journals. Networks of attorneys and other observers have also emerged to monitor court decisions and keep central clearinghouses informed about promising court cases.

Sometimes the immediate concerns of the litigants may conflict with those of the sponsoring interest group. A litigant's claim may be compromised or settled. Legal issues advanced by the parties may be formulated so as to avoid the constitutional issues raised by the sponsor. Also, the trial and appellate preparation may be a labor of love, or the work-product of an attorney who jealously guards his professional prerogatives.

A failure to control a litigation does not necessarily mean that an interest group lacks influence. When the issues defined in court are narrow, or the litigant's attorney has failed to develop the case's constitutional implications, an interest group attorney can still participate as AMICUS CURIAE (friend of the court). Nowhere has this phenomenon been more visible than in the medical school admission case, REGENTS OF THE UNIVERSITY OF CALIFORNIA V. BAKKE (1978). In this case fifty-seven organizations submitted amicus curiae briefs to the Supreme Court. Although some interest group attorneys will refrain from submitting such briefs when a client's attorney adequately has argued the constitutional issues, the filing of such a brief does serve the political function of announcing the group's support for a constitutional argument. Amicus curiae participation usually requires the consent of both parties or the approval of the court, and the influence of either briefs or ORAL ARGUMENTS as amicus remains debatable.

Even though interest group litigation is growing, part of the increase is attributable to government legal services and private foundation philanthropy. If government support is curtailed and private foundations are subjected to closer tax scrutiny, individual contributions and voluntary legal services will be called upon to fill the gap. Such a decline in government support seems likely since some judges and political leaders have expressed concern about government-sponsored litigation directed against public officials. They also criticize lawyers who represent causes rather than clients and overburden the judicial process. Other factors affecting the growth of interest group litigation are the strictness of enforcement of traditional restrictions on the scope of law suits (see INSTITUTIONAL LITIGATION) and the rules governing the award of attorneys' fees to interest group attorneys.

Finally, no description of interest group litigation would be complete without noting that many highly publicized civil cases and "showcase" criminal trials as well as ordinary law cases are financed and carried forward without the participation of organized interest groups. The constitutional and policy arguments advanced by attorneys in these cases, in many instances, are just as likely to advance the development of legal and constitutional doctrine.

Bibliography

COUNCIL FOR PUBLIC INTEREST LAW   1976   *Balancing the Scales of Justice: Financing Public Interest Law in America.* Washington, D.C.: Council on Public Interest Law.

HAKMAN, NATHAN   1966   Lobbying the Supreme Court: An Appraisal of "Political Science Folklore." *Fordham Law Review* 35:15–50.

———   1972   Political Trials in the Legal Order: A Political Scientist's Perspective. *Journal of Public Law* 21:73–126.

KIRCHHEIMER, OTTO   1961   *Political Justice: The Use of Legal Procedure for Political Ends.* Princeton, N.J.: Princeton University Press.

VOSE, CLEMENT E.   1972   *Constitutional Change: Amendment Politics and Supreme Court Litigation Since 1900.* Lexington, Mass.: D. C. Heath.

WEISBROD, BURTON A., HANDLER, JOEL F., and KOMESAR, NEIL K.   1978   *Public Interest Law: An Economical and Institutional Analysis.* Berkeley: University of California Press.

TEST CASE

Clement E. Vose

Whenever a unit of government, or an interest in the private sector, wants a favorable constitutional decision on a point in question, a test case is often organized to gain a ruling from the Supreme Court. The Court has not defined the term, and need not, as there is no judicial criterion for "test case" under the CASES AND CONTROVERSIES clause of Article III. Scholarship on the judicial process provides the best understanding of the term as a strategy employed by different interests, for differing ends. FLETCHER V. PECK (1810) showed that systematically plotting a test case, so framing it as to elicit particular answers based on prediction concerning how the Justices are likely to respond, and then using the judicial decision for political advantage is not a strategy unique to recent CIVIL RIGHTS cases but a durable aspect of constitutional litigation since the early years of the Republic.

Organizers of test cases sometimes look upon victory in the Supreme Court as a secondary goal. For example, the arguments of the National Woman Suffrage Association that women, as citizens, were already enfranchised by terms of the FOURTEENTH AMENDMENT breathed new life into the organization through publicity of test cases. MINOR V. HAPPERSETT (1875) and two other cases failed but they produced national news.

The Department of Justice took little initiative in enforcing new legislation in the nineteenth century, largely because Congress intended enforcement to come through complaints of individuals entitled to sue violators. An example of this is the CIVIL RIGHTS CASES (1883). Individuals challenged about a hundred violations of the CIVIL RIGHTS ACT OF 1875. Eventually, five came to the Supreme Court as test cases, where they were unsuccessfully argued by the SOLICITOR GENERAL. These test cases were not managed; they simply happened as individual blacks complained.

Business interests may bring test cases to prevent enforcement of new regulatory legislation, as in 1917 when David Clark for the Southern Cotton Manufacturers sought to invalidate the KEATING-OWEN ACT which prohibited shipment in INTERSTATE COMMERCE of designated products manufactured in plants employing children. Stephen Wood reports the advice of a Philadelphia lawyer to the manufacturers:

No legal proceeding will lie until the [Keating-Owen] bill is in operation. Some action must be taken under some provision of the bill so that a real and not a moot question is raised. A court, in order to pass upon any phase of it, must have before it an actual case, and if the measure is to be contested, the case should not only be carefully selected in order that the constitutional principle desired to be raised may be clearly presented, but I believe then that when the issue is raised, if possible, a judicial district should be selected in which the judge is a man of known courage. This is no case to try before a weak character [1968: 87–88].

Clark proceeded to raise money, select suitable counsel, identify Judge James Edmund Boyd as courageous, and locate cotton companies in the western district of North Carolina ready to cooperate. After searching for the "perfect combination of factors," Clark worked up four possible test cases to submit to the attorneys in New York. There the *Dagenhart* case was selected as the best. The Dagenharts, a father and two minor sons, and the company "were mere figureheads" whom Clark persuaded to set up the case. First, the company posted notices that under-age employees would be dismissed when the Keating-Owen law went into effect. The attorneys employed by Clark then prepared a complaint for Dagenhart asserting that this threat would deprive him of his VESTED RIGHTS, because he was entitled to the services of his minor sons and the compensation arising from their labors. By moving before the law became effective, the cotton manufacturers put the Department of Justice on the defensive, trapped within the confines of their test case. Judge Boyd, who ruled the Keating-Owen Act invalid under the Fifth and TENTH AMENDMENTS, was upheld by the Supreme Court in 1918 in HAMMER v. DAGENHART.

Success in managing constitutional litigation requires understanding of both substantive law and litigation practice. Following enactment of the WAGNER ACT in 1935, lawyers for the National Labor Relations Board combined these talents in impressive fashion, gaining a stunning triumph from the Supreme Court in *NLRB v. Jones & Laughlin* in March 1937. (See WAGNER ACT CASES.) Against hostile attacks by the National Lawyers' Committee of the American Liberty League, NLRB lawyers carefully developed cases running the gamut of size and type to make the first tests establishing wide congressional power to regulate labor practices in businesses affecting interstate commerce.

NLRB lawyers, even before the Wagner Act was signed, had designed a "master plan" envisioning test cases built around COMMERCE CLAUSE issues stressing the type of industry, characteristics of individual businesses, the degree of actual or threatened obstruction of commerce, and the type of unfair labor practices charged. In Peter Irons's words, this "master plan" gave clear directions for "sifting through their massive case loads in search of ideal test cases, charting a clear path from the picket line to the Supreme Court." The NLRB staff functioned as legal craftsmen, "as much meticulous technicians as partisan advocates," who "winnowed and selected cases with care; scrutinized records with a fine-tooth comb; chose courts with a shopper's discriminating eye; wrote briefs to draw the issues narrowly and precisely."

Although numerous voluntary associations with litigation programs, such as the Anti-Saloon League of America, the National Consumers' League, and the AMERICAN JEWISH CONGRESS, have sponsored test cases as a way of influencing public policy, the organizations most noted for this practice have been the National Association for the Advancement of Colored People (NAACP), formed in 1909, and the NAACP LEGAL DEFENSE FUND, INC., organized in 1939.

Modern test cases by associations, public interest law firms, or lawyers working *pro bono publico* are often cast as CLASS ACTIONS under the FEDERAL RULES OF CIVIL PROCEDURE. Although they may attack conditions that are widespread, these cases rest on particularized explorations of fact, often through discovery and expert testimony. In attacking school segregation in the five cases styled as BROWN V. BOARD OF EDUCATION, the NAACP sought to develop full factual records, building upon the experience of THURGOOD MARSHALL and others as counsel in the earlier white primary cases and racial RESTRICTIVE COVENANT cases. Widespread test cases will continue because both government and private counsel can approach the Supreme Court only by representing particular parties with particular concrete claims.

Bibliography

CORTNER, RICHARD C.   1964   *The Wagner Act Cases.* Pages 106–141. Knoxville: University of Tennessee Press.

FREUND, PAUL A.   1951   *On Understanding the Supreme Court.* Pages 77–116. Boston: Little, Brown.

IRONS, PETER   1982   *The New Deal Lawyers.* Pages 234–289. Princeton, N.J.: Princeton University Press.

KLUGER, RICHARD   1975   *Simple Justice: The History of Brown v. Board of Education and Black America's Struggle for Equality.* Pages 256–540. New York: Vintage Books.

VOSE, CLEMENT E.   1959   *Caucasians Only: The Supreme Court, the NAACP, and the Restrictive Covenant Cases.* Pages 50–73, 151–176. Berkeley: University of California Press.

WOOD, STEPHEN B.   1968   *Constitutional Politics in the Progressive Era.* Pages 81–110. Chicago: University of Chicago Press.

INSTITUTIONAL LITIGATION

Theodore Eisenberg and Stephen C. Yeazell

"Institutional litigation" refers to cases in which the courts, responding to allegations that conditions in some institutions violate the Constitution or CIVIL RIGHTS statutes, become involved in supervising the institutions in question. Loosely used, the term might describe any number of lawsuits, ranging from an assertion of discriminatory employment practices in a CORPORATION to an attack by inmates on the conditions at a state prison. What such apparently diverse cases have in common is the possibility that if the plaintiffs convince the court that a violation of the law has occurred and if the institution proves recalcitrant in remedying the violation, the court may become involved in detailed supervision of the institution over long periods. Though details of such complex suits naturally vary widely, it is the combination of continuous judicial scrutiny and detailed substantive involvement that has characterized institutional litigation.

Laws such as those forbidding discrimination in employment apply to both public and private institutions. Many constitutional provisions, however, guarantee rights only against the government and most institutions to which individuals are involuntarily committed are run by the government. Consequently most of the institutions involved have been public: prisons, mental hospitals, school systems, and the like. Moreover, though the Constitution binds both state and federal courts, the latter tribunals have played the most active role in vindicating constitutional rights. The typical institutional case therefore has involved a federal district court supervising the conduct of a state institution, a setting that has raised constitutional concerns beyond those of the particular substantive law of the case.

From a wide perspective one can trace the roots of institutional litigation to earlier classes of cases: nineteenth-century EQUITY receiverships, bankruptcy reorganizations, antitrust decrees requiring the restructuring of a large industry, even to the efforts of fifteenth-century English chancellors to enforce the duties of trustees to establish and supervise the religious and charitable institutions endowed in a will. Modern institutional cases also have more recent origins in the efforts of the federal judiciary to desegregate schools in the 1950s and 1960s.

Resistance to simple desegregation decrees forced federal courts to become involved in many details of local school administration. As some school boards adjusted their strategies for resistance, courts delved deeper into school board practices, to the point of displacing some traditional school board functions. In GRIFFIN V. SCHOOL BOARD OF PRINCE EDWARD COUNTY (1964) the Supreme Court even suggested that a federal court could order taxes imposed to raise funds to finance a public school system that officials had closed to avoid desegregation.

At about the same time courts were articulating other constitutional rights, including constitutional limitations on prison and mental hospital conditions. In cases such as *Wyatt v. Stickney* (1971) and *Holt v. Sarver* (1969) lower federal courts combined the procedural aggressiveness of the school desegregation cases with the newly developed constitutional rights, enforcing their decrees against recalcitrant officials with INJUNC-TIONS backed by the force of the contempt power. In dozens of institutional cases in the 1970s these same forces triggered widespread court-ordered institutional reform that covered such details of institutional life as cell size, visiting hours, telephone privileges, hygiene, and disciplinary procedures.

Describing institutional litigation and tracing its origins are easier than isolating, much less resolving, the controversies that surround it. Nearly all the issues that arise in public discourse about a federal system and an independent judiciary eventually appear in some discussion of institutional litigation. Perhaps the most central of these issues are questions about the relationship of institutional litigation to (1) the nature of litigation; (2) the judicial capacity to run institutions; (3) the power of the purse; and (4) FEDERALISM.

Some view institutional cases as a form of litigation previously unknown to Anglo-American jurisprudence. In the contrasted traditional vision of litigation, a lawsuit involves two parties who present an isolatable set of facts to a court, which issues a JUDGMENT; the losing party complies with the court's decree, and judicial involvement with the case ends. To the extent that this statement of traditional litigation is accurate, institutional litigation involves a substantial departure. In institutional litigation the set of facts presented to the court often constitutes all of the physical, psychological, and social conditions within the institution. Such widespread allegations prevent the court from addressing any single dispute which, when resolved, will restore the parties to a proper relationship. In several institutional cases, no matter how many disputes the court resolves, additional issues arise with respect to implementation of and compliance with previous orders.

The frequency with which institutional litigation requires courts to address some aspect of institutional life highlights the second central issue—judicial capacity to supervise large public institutions. By training, judges are neither wardens nor hospital administrators. Some critics question whether judges should substitute their judgment about institutional life for that of professional administrators appointed by elected officials. Courts often try to compensate for their inexperience by appointing SPECIAL MASTERS and expert advisory panels and by seeking the views of the defendant administrators. But these tactics may raise further questions about institutional litigation's departure from traditional ideas about litigation. Yet, once a court has concluded that institutional life is constitutionally deficient because of the acts of the regular administrators, it is difficult for courts simply to defer to the judgment of those same persons found to be responsible for the unconstitutional conditions.

In many cases, however, institutional conditions are constitutionally deficient less because of the acts of administrators than because the state has allocated insufficient funds to institutional budgets. Even willing administrators experience difficulty in upgrading conditions at some institutions. A new prison building may be necessary or more staff may need to be hired. When institutional reform may be accomplished only through expenditures of substantial sums, a new issue arises: may courts order the allocation of public funds against the wishes of legislators who presumably reflect their constituents' wishes?

For many observers, this fiscal confrontation reveals the least palatable aspect of institutional litigation—the antimajoritarian judicial usurpation of legislative and executive authority. Courts, self-conscious about express allocative decision making, sometimes disavow authority to order funds raised to carry out institutional reform. And, despite *Griffin*'s OBITER DICTUM about imposing taxes, there is doubt about how far courts may and ought to go in ordering funds raised to satisfy their orders. Yet it is also a commonplace for courts to state that lack of funds is no excuse for failure to comply with the Constitution. Since any public law decision may have important fiscal effects, perhaps institutional cases have been unjustifiably isolated from the rest of the public litigation on this issue. Indeed, if one assumes that, put to the choice between releasing inmates and rectifying the conditions of their institutional confinement, the public and their elected officials would choose the latter, judicially decreed funding may be more in accord with the majority's wishes than any other course of action.

Ironically, institutional cases flourished during the 1970s, while the Supreme Court was emphasizing that federal courts should not interfere with traditional state or local functions. In RIZZO v. GOODE (1976) and O'SHEA v. LITTLETON (1974) the Court rejected systemic attacks on, respectively, a police department and a city's system of criminal justice. In YOUNGER v. HARRIS (1971) and its progeny the Court established prohibitions on federal court interference with state adjudicative proceedings. As a doctrinal matter, the issues in most institutional cases proved distinguishable from the issues in *Rizzo, O'Shea,* and *Younger.* Nevertheless the Court's federalism theme could have been viewed as requiring curtailment of judicial receptivity to institutional litigation. Yet during this period of growing deference to states, the lower federal courts, without Supreme Court disapproval, continued to hear and resolve institutional cases.

Bibliography

CHAYES, ABRAM   1976   The Role of the Judge in Public Law Litigation. *Harvard Law Review* 89:1281–1316.

DIVER, COLIN S.   1979   The Judge as Political Powerbroker: Superintending Structural Change in Public Institutions. *Virginia Law Review* 65:43–106.

EISENBERG, THEODORE and YEAZELL, STEPHEN C.   1980 The Ordinary and the Extraordinary in Institutional Litigation. *Harvard Law Review* 93:465–517.

FISS, OWEN M.   1979   The Supreme Court 1978 Term, Foreword: The Forms of Justice. *Harvard Law Review* 93:1–58.

CLASS ACTION

Stephen C. Yeazell

The class action is a procedural device aggregating the claims or defenses of similarly situated individuals so that they may be tried in a single lawsuit. In recent decades the class action has frequently served as the vehicle by which various groups have asserted constitutional claims. For example, all the minority-race school children in various districts have sued (through their parents) to rectify alleged RACIAL DISCRIMINATION on the part of school authorities; or, to illustrate a nonconstitutional claim, the buyers of home freezers have sued as a group claiming that the dealer had made fraudulent misrepresentations. In both examples the members of the class could have sued separately. The class action pulled these potential individual actions into a single lawsuit making litigation feasible for the members of the class (by permitting a single lawyer to try all their claims together). For the party opposing the class the suit has the advantage of providing a single adjudication of all similar claims and the disadvantage, especially marked in suits for money damages, that the entire potential liability to a large group turns on a single suit.

The class action depends on representation, and that concept draws the Constitution into the picture. In the class action most class members are represented by an active litigant whose success or failure binds the class members. Opinions interpreting the DUE PROCESS clauses of the Constitution (in the Fifth and FOURTEENTH ADMENDMENTS) suggest that normally one may not be bound by the results of litigation to which one is not a party. Yet the class action purports to do just that—to bind the absentee class members to the results of a suit in which they played no active role.

The Supreme Court and the drafters of state and federal class action rules have supplied two solutions to this apparent tension. The Supreme Court's answer came in *Hansberry v. Lee* (1940), in which the justices indicated that class actions could bind absentee class members if the active litigants *adequately represented* the class. If not, the Court reasoned, binding the absentees would deprive them of due process of law.

Adequate representation has two aspects, competence and congruence of interests. All would agree that adequate representation implies some absolute level of competence and diligence on the part of the class representative and attorney. Though few cases have specifically discussed the question, it seems virtually a matter of definition that an adequate representative must pursue the cause with some minimum level of professional skill.

The second aspect of adequate representation presents a more difficult problem, forcing us to decide whether such representation requires the class members to have *agreed* that the action is in their interests, or whether it is possible to define such interests abstractly, without specific consent. Such an abstract definition relies on common intuitions about what would benefit persons in the class's circumstances. In *Hansberry* the Court did not need to decide between these definitions of interest because the attempted class representation failed on either count. Subsequent cases and procedural rules have not clearly resolved the question.

Contemporary procedural rules require that a judge presiding over a class action suit consider initially whether the action is in the class's interest, abstractly considered; that much seems constitutionally required. Beyond that, some rules also require that the absentee members receive individual notice permitting them to exclude themselves from the litigation.

Founded on the constitutional proposition that some form of representation will suffice to bind members of a class, the class suit has come to play an important role in twentieth-century American litigation.

Bibliography

KALVEN, HARRY JR. and ROSENFIELD, MAURICE   1941 The Contemporary Function of the Class Suit. *University of Chicago Law Review* 8:684–721.

WRIGHT, CHARLES A. and MILLER, ARTHUR   1972   *Federal Practice and Procedure*, Vols. 7 & 7A. St. Paul, Minn.: West Publishing Co.

YEAZELL, STEPHEN C.   1980   From Group Litigation to Class Action; Part II: Interest, Class and Representation. *U.C.L.A. Law Review* 28:1067–1121.

LITIGATION STRATEGY

Burt Neuborne

Litigation strategy in constitutional cases is shaped by a single animating principle—a desire to increase the likelihood that a black-robed bureaucrat called a judge will act on behalf of a politically vulnerable applicant to alter or set aside the act of a popularly accountable official. Although the degree of tension that exists between democratic political theory and constitutional litigation varies widely depending on the nature of the case and the attributes of the forum—a police brutality case litigated before an elected state judge poses no threat to democratic decision making; an EQUAL PROTECTION challenge to an act of Congress argued before an appointed, life-tenured, federal judge poses a more direct conflict—constitutional cases generally involve persons who are unable to secure redress through more conventional appeals to the political process. Litigation strategy in constitutional cases is designed to increase the potential that a judicial forum will rule in favor of such politically disfavored plaintiffs.

Sustained constitutional litigation in the United States has involved many sets of litigants, including abolitionists versus slaveholders in the period prior to the Civil War; radical reconstructionists versus southern revisionists in the period immediately following the Civil War; business CORPORATIONS versus populist reformers during the first third of the twentieth century; and civil libertarians versus majoritarians during the modern era. Although the political goals of the participants have varied widely, the strategic choices of the contestants have remained remarkably stable, involving five areas: choice of forum; selection of parties; articulation of theories of recovery; choice of tactics; and articulation of anti-democratic apologia.

Choice of forum is the most important strategic decision for a constitutional litigator. In choosing a forum, a constitutional litigator must choose between state and federal court; between a judge and jury; and sometimes between one judge and another. The outcome of many, if not most, constitutional cases turns as much on the wisdom of those strategic choices as on the intrinsic merits of the cases.

Because a constitutional plaintiff is generally seeking to trump a decision that enjoys the imprimatur of democratic decision making, the institutional capacity of the forum to render sustained anti- (or, at least, counter-) majoritarian doctrine is critical to the success of any constitutional litigation campaign. Judges who are themselves elected by the political majority or who are otherwise closely tied to the political process are least likely to enunciate sustained countermajoritarian doctrine. Judges who enjoy maximum political insulation are, on the other hand, in a position to ignore the short-term political consequences of their unpopular decisions. It would, for example, have been impossible for elected judges to have effectively enforced the fugitive slave clause in the pre-Civil War North on behalf of southern slaveholders, or the equal protection clause in the post-World War II South on behalf of black schoolchildren seeking an integrated education.

The search for an insulated judge in constitutional cases has generally led politically vulnerable plaintiffs—whether slaveholders, business corporations, or CIVIL RIGHTS activists—to seek a federal judicial forum, for federal judges are appointed and enjoy life tenure. Much of the procedural infighting that characterizes constitutional litigation revolves around attempts by plaintiffs to force claims into insulated federal forums and by defendants to deflect them to more politically accountable state courts.

The search for an insulated forum has led many constitutional litigators to view juries with suspicion. Not surprisingly, a principal litigation strategy of the abolitionist bar was to choreograph disputes about alleged fugitive slaves before free state juries in the hope that juries would decline to enforce the Fugitive Slave Act. (See FUGITIVE SLAVERY.) Modern civil rights lawyers have experienced analogous difficulty in persuading juries to return verdicts in favor of unpalatable plaintiffs whose rights may have been violated by a popularly responsible official.

Finally, the choice of forum involves a decision about the identity of the judge or, in less polite terms, judge-shopping. The identity of the judge in a constitutional case is extremely important for two reasons, one obvious and one less well understood. The obvious reason for judge-shopping involves the judge's politics. Because constitutional cases often turn on a clash of values and because the urgency with which a judge views a constitutional case may well depend on his or her view of the relative importance of the conflicting values, the same case may be decided differently by equally competent judges with differing value systems.

The less obvious reason why judge-shopping is important in constitutional cases involves the judge's technical competence. Victory for the plaintiff in constitutional cases depends upon persuading a judge that constitutional doctrine requires the overturning of a presumptively valid decision by another government official. Unless a judge is equipped to understand and evaluate complex argumentation about the meaning of ambiguous textual provisions and judicial PRECEDENT, it will be impossible to persuade the judge that doctrinal factors compel a decision for the plaintiff. Because the inertial advantage in constitutional cases almost always favors government defendants—failure to persuade the judge to act results in perpetuation of the challenged status quo—the inability of a judge to grapple with complex argumentation generally works to the disadvantage of a constitutional plaintiff.

In addition to care in selecting a forum, constitutional litigators expend a good deal of energy on the choice of a plaintiff, seeking to project the most sympathetic and appealing fact pattern. Because the judge's view of the equities may play a substantial role in the outcome of a constitutional case, the capacity of a constitutional plaintiff to evoke sympathy can be crucial. Constitutional lawyers have learned, moreover, that courts respond most favorably to fact patterns that emerge naturally from the interrelationship between a constitutional plaintiff and the government, but balk at being asked to decide artificially constructed TEST CASES.

A difficult decision constitutional litigators face in selecting a plaintiff is whether to bring the case as an individual action involving only named individuals or as a CLASS ACTION on behalf of all similarly situated persons. Militating in favor of class action status is its increased impact. A single class action can provide relief to thousands of people. Class actions, however, have drawbacks. Against the prospect of increased impact must be weighed the risk of loss, for members of a losing class are generally bound by the loss. Moreover, class actions can act as red flags to judges who would be sensitive to the claims of an individual plaintiff but who are reluctant to become involved in litigation seeking institutional change.

The selection of a defendant in a constitutional case also requires careful thought. Most important, the defendant must be capable of providing adequate relief. If injunctive relief is sought, the defendant must be sufficiently senior in the bureaucratic hierarchy to be able to promulgate and implement the changes sought by the action. At the same time, of course, the defendant must be sufficiently involved in the factual dispute giving rise to the lawsuit to justify naming him as an adverse party. If DAMAGES are sought, the defendant must have a sufficiently "deep pocket" to pay the judgment. A damage award against a judgment-proof defendant is hardly worth the effort.

One method of dealing with both the need for a high-ranking defendant and the quest for financial solvency is the naming of an entity-defendant such as the City of New York or the United States in addition to the individual defendants. The extremely complicated interplay between rules limiting the extent to which government entities can be sued in constitutional cases and plaintiffs' interest in suing government entities poses one of the serious tactical dilemmas in constitutional litigation.

A final—and less empirically verifiable—concern in selecting a defendant flows from what may be called the "Redneck-Mandarin dichotomy," which seeks to match a defendant and a judge from different educational and social backgrounds in the hope that the judge will be less constrained in exercising vigorous review powers. Although such an assumption is highly speculative, many constitutional litigators believe, for example, that they perceive a difference between many judges' willingness to exercise vigorous review of the actions of low-ranking police officers and the same judges' willingness to review the decisions of police commissioners.

Given the difficulty of overcoming the inertial advantage enjoyed by the government in constitutional cases, strategic considerations often play a role in the articulation of plaintiff's theory of recovery. It is often advisable to proceed by incremental stages and to develop alternatives to the primary constitutional theory. Thus, for example, litigation aimed at the OVERRULING of the SEPARATE BUT EQUAL DOCTRINE enunciated by PLESSY V. FERGUSON (1896) proceeded by carefully calibrated constitutional steps designed to develop sufficient momentum to make the final decision in BROWN V. BOARD OF EDUCATION (1954) possible. It is, however, extremely difficult to execute a sustained litigation campaign over time, for the factors of chance and changing tides of legal analysis are difficult to predict. On the other hand, asking for too much too soon in the absence of a carefully laid doctrinal foundation places an intolerable degree of pressure on even a sympathetic judge.

In an effort to lessen the tension between constitutional litigation and democratic political theory, litigators often seek to articulate a process-based alternative to their principal substantive theory. Thus, litigators attacking FIRST AMENDMENT violations often invite the court to seize upon a narrower, process-based claim such as VAGUENESS or OVERBREADTH as the basis for invalidating a statute, rather than confront the substantive question of the legislature's power to enact it at all. Similarly, constitutional litigators often seek to link their constitutional theories with non-constitutional claims, such as a claim based on a statute or a COMMON LAW tort. Posing alternative theories of recovery provides a judge with a less dramatic means of protecting a constitutional value while providing effective relief to the plaintiff. Of course, many such alternative theories of recovery are subject to modification by the legislature, but the short-term result is often indistinguishable from success of the constitutional claim.

Although much litigation strategy depends on a perception of the degree to which constitutional law is shaped by value judgments, constitutional lawyers also recognize the extent to which constitutional litigation shapes community values. The process of bringing a constitutional lawsuit is educational as well as remedial. It seeks to expose the judge to a set of facts and a legal reality that would ordinarily be far from his or her consciousness. It seeks to inform the public of the existence of a social problem that, even if not ultimately amenable to constitutional resolution, requires increased public attention. Viewed as a part of the process by which the interests of the politically powerless can be protected in a democracy, constitutional litigation provides a mechanism not only for classic remedial action but for a sharpening of the underlying social issues for ultimate political resolution. Thus, for example, although under current legal standards it is difficult to establish a violation of the constitutional right of a minority community to receive equal municipal services (discriminatory purpose, not merely disparate effect, must be proven), constitutional litigation provides a forum for the dramatization of unequal treatment as a first step to a political resolution. Similarly, although only the most optimistic believed that courts would actually stop the VIETNAM WAR because it was supposedly carried on in violation of Article 1, section 8, of the Constitution, the repeated presentation of the issue both shaped public perception of the war and helped pave the way for the passage of the War Powers Resolution which attempted to deal with the legal issue of undeclared war.

Two major constraints limit the use of constitutional litigation as an educational vehicle. First is the ethical obligation to refrain from presenting frivolous or inappropriate claims to a court. Judicial attention is a scarce national resource which must be rationed, and lawyers must be prudent in presenting claims that cannot win. In the absence of a good faith belief in the legal—as opposed to the moral—soundness of a claim, it should not be presented to a court. Moreover, even if a claim is sufficiently substantial to satisfy ethical considerations, tactical considerations often argue against presenting a weak claim for adjudication. Losing a constitutional case risks the enunciation of dangerous precedent and acts to legitimate the challenged activity. Thus, although constitutional litigation plays an educational as well as a remedial role, its educational role should be a by-product of a bona fide attempt to secure a legal remedy.

A significant dilemma in planning and executing litigation strategy in constitutional cases is posed by the potential for conflict between the best interest of a plaintiff and the furtherance of the cause that precipitated the case into court. For example, a plaintiff who has gone to court to vindicate a principle and who poses a powerful TEST CASE may be confronted with a settlement offer which, while advantageous to the plaintiff, leaves the legal issue unresolved. Constitutional lawyers, while recognizing this conflict, generally resolve it in favor of the plaintiff and recommend acceptance to their clients, who then make the final decision. Despite the recognition that the interest of the client in a constitutional case should predominate over the advancement of the cause, a disturbing tendency exists on the part of both bench and bar to use a constitutional plaintiff as a convenient vehicle to trigger the enunciation of norms that may benefit society as a whole but which do little for the parties before the Court. William Marbury never did get his commission. (See MARBURY V. MADISON.)

Once a constitutional case is underway, three recurring tactical issues arise. Should immediate relief be sought, usually in the form of a preliminary INJUNCTION? Should the case be pursued as an abstract issue of law or should substantial resources be expended in developing the facts? And how broad a remedy should be sought? It is impossible to formulate even a general rule governing these three issues, except that attorneys with weak cases rarely seek preliminary injunctions and that issues of law should not be presented to a potentially hostile court in the absence of clearly established fact, given that a judge's freedom of action is greatest in determining the facts on an ambiguous record.

A parallel tactical issue defendants in a constitutional case face is whether to move to dismiss—and, thus, to assume the truth of the facts alleged in the complaint for the purposes of the motion—or to force plaintiffs to prove their facts by going to trial. Surprisingly, most defendants, in an effort to save time and resources, attempt dismissal motions, which require courts to rule on the theoretical validity of plaintiff's case without requiring plaintiff to establish the facts. Much constitutional law has been made in denying motions to dismiss and thus creating important legal precedents in cases where plaintiffs might have experienced difficulty in proving their allegations.

Finally, in presenting a constitutional case to a judge, a constitutional litigator will often seek to place it within one of three categories posing the least tension with democratic political theory in order to free the judge to exercise vigorous review. If the case involves a member of a DISCRETE AND INSULAR MINORITY, constitutional litigators will stress the inability of unpopular or disadvantaged minority groups to protect themselves within the traditional political process, thus invoking the special responsibility of courts to act as a bulwark against majoritarian overreaching. If the case involves significant political values, constitutional litigators will stress the responsibility of courts to guarantee the proper functioning of the democratic process. It is not antidemocratic, they argue, for a court to prevent the majority from refusing to permit the democratic process to function properly. If the case involves a "fundamental" value, like marriage or REPRODUCTIVE AUTONOMY, constitutional litigators will argue that the importance of such values warrants increased judicial protection. This third category involves the most controversial exercises of judicial power, because the selection of "fundamental" values appears subjective.

Ultimately, litigation strategy in constitutional cases, even at its most sophisticated, can exert only a relatively weak influence on the outcome.

The adjudication of issues that impinge on deeply held values and in many other systems would be relegated solely to the political process is an inherently unpredictable phenomenon. No other area of law fits Tolstoy's vision of history so well as the claim of constitutional lawyers to be able to influence the ocean on which they most often bob like corks.

Bibliography

COVER, ROBERT M.   1975   *Justice Accused: Anti-Slavery and the Judicial Process.* New Haven, Conn.: Yale University Press.

GREENBERG, JACK   1977   *Judicial Process and Social Change: Constitutional Litigation.* St. Paul, Minn.: West Publishing Co.

KLUGER, RICHARD   1975   *Simple Justice.* New York: Knopf.

NEUBORNE, BURT   1977   The Myth of Parity. *Harvard Law Review* 90:1105.

SUPREME COURT PRACTICE

Eugene Gressman

The SUPREME COURT is the only judicial body created by the Constitution. Article III, Section 1, specifies that "The JUDICIAL POWER OF THE UNITED STATES, shall be vested in one supreme Court, and in such inferior Courts as the Congress may from time to time ordain and establish." The judges of that "one supreme Court," like the judges of the inferior courts created by Congress, are to hold their offices "during GOOD BEHAVIOUR" and to suffer no diminution of compensation during their continuance in office. Supreme Court Justices can be impeached, however. And it is not constitutionally clear that their "good Behaviour" term of office is the equivalent of a life term, as generally thought.

In practice, this "one supreme Court" has always acted as a unitary body. That means that the Court never divides into panels or groups of Justices for purposes of resolving matters submitted to the Court. All petitions and briefs are circulated to, and considered by, all participating Justices; and all Court decisions are rendered on behalf of the Court as a unit of nine Justices.

Article III of the Constitution, in establishing the judicial institution known as the Supreme Court, vests in the Court two basic kinds of jurisdiction: ORIGINAL JURISDICTION and APPELLATE JURISDICTION. The Court's original jurisdiction is its power to decide certain cases and controversies in the first instance. Its appellate jurisdiction is its power to review certain cases and controversies decided in the first instance by lower courts.

In COHENS V. VIRGINIA (1821), Chief Justice JOHN MARSHALL stated that the Court "must decide" a case before it that is properly within one of these two areas of jurisdiction, and that the Court has "no more right to decline the exercise of jurisdiction which is given, than to usurp that which is not given . . . [either of which] would be treason to the Constitution." But in the Court's judicial world, Marshall's proposition is no longer universally true, if it ever was. The modern need to control and limit the voluminous number of cases clamoring for review has forced the Court to resist demands that every facet of the Court's vested jurisdiction be exercised. Limitations of time and human energy simply do not permit the luxury of resolving every dispute that comes before the Court. Notions of judicial prudence and sound discretion, given these limitations, have thus become dominant in the Court's selection of those relatively few cases it feels it can afford to review in a plenary fashion and to resolve the merits. Such factors are evident in the Court's control of both its original docket and its appellate docket.

Section 2 of Article III specifies that the Supreme Court "shall have original jurisdiction" in all cases "affecting Ambassadors, other public Ministers and Consuls, and those in which a State shall be Party." Compared with cases on the appellate docket, cases on the original docket are quite few in number. Indeed, cases involving ambassadors, ministers, and consuls have never been common and have virtually disappeared from the original docket. The typical original case has thus become that in which a state is the plaintiff or defendant; most frequent are suits between two or more states over boundaries and water rights, suits that cannot appropriately be handled by any other tribunal. States have also sued each other over state financial obligations, use of natural resources, multistate domiciliary and escheat problems, breaches of contracts between states, and various kinds of injuries to the public health and welfare of the complaining state.

States can also invoke the Court's original jurisdiction to sue private nonresident citizens, or ALIENS, for alleged injuries to the sovereign interests of the complaining state. And a state may bring such suits on behalf of all its citizens to protect the economy and natural resources of the state, as well as the health and welfare of the citizens. The ELEVENTH AMENDMENT bars an original action against a defendant state brought by a private plaintiff who is a citizen of another state; and the sovereign immunity principle recognized by that Amendment also bars such an action by a citizen of the defendant state. Because that amendment does not apply to the federal sovereign as plaintiff, the United States can bring an original action in the Supreme Court against a defendant state. All cases brought by a state against a private party defendant, however, fall within the nonexclusive category of the Court's original jurisdiction; such suits can alternatively be brought in some other federal or state court. The Court in recent years has sought to reduce its original docket workload by rejecting some nonexclusive causes of action and requiring the parties to proceed in an available alternative forum.

Original cases often involve factual disputes. In processing such cases, the Court considers itself the equivalent of a federal trial court, though with significant differences. The Court's rules and procedures in this respect are not very specific, and practices may vary from case to case. The case starts with a motion for leave to file a complaint, a requirement that permits the Court to consider and resolve jurisdictional and prudential objections. If the Court denies the motion for leave to file, the case terminates. If the motion is granted, the complaint is ordered filed, the defendant files an answer, and in most instances a trial ensues.

The Justices themselves do not conduct trials in original cases. Instead, they appoint a member of the bar or a retired lower court judge to serve as a special master. The special master then takes evidence, hears witnesses, makes fact-findings, and recommends legal conclusions. But all rulings, findings, and conclusions of the special master are subject to review by the Court. That review occurs after parties aggrieved by the special master's actions have filed exceptions thereto; all parties then brief and orally argue the exceptions before the entire Court, which decides the case by written opinion. A complicated case may require more than one hearing before the special master and more than one opinion by the Court, prolonging the case for years.

The Court itself has admitted that it is "ill-equipped for the task of factfinding and so forced, in original cases, awkwardly to play the role of factfinder without actually presiding over the introduction of evidence." Original cases take away valuable time and attention from the Court's main mission, the exercise of its appellate jurisdiction, where the Court serves as the prime overseer of important matters of federal constitutional and statutory law. The Court is thus increasingly disposed to construe its original jurisdiction narrowly, exercising that jurisdiction only where the parties cannot secure an initial resolution of their controversy in another tribunal. If there is such an alternative proceeding, the Court prefers to REMAND the parties to the lower court and to deal with any important issues in the case on review of the lower court's determination.

The Court's appellate jurisdiction is also defined and vested by Article III, Section 2. That jurisdiction extends to all categories of CASES AND CONTROVERSIES, decided in the first instance by lower federal courts or state courts, that fall within the JUDICIAL POWER OF THE UNITED STATES. Those categories include: cases arising under the Constitution, laws, and treaties of the United States; cases affecting ambassadors, ministers, and consuls; cases of ADMIRALTY AND MARITIME JURISDICTION; controversies to which the United States is a party; controversies between two or more states; and controversies between a state and citizens of another state, between citizens of different states, between citizens of the same state claiming lands under grants of different states, or between a state or its citizens and foreign states or citizens. The Court's appellate jurisdiction extends "both as to Law and Fact, with such Exceptions, and under such Regulations as the Congress shall make."

The exceptions clause in Section 2 contains within it a constitutional enigma, as yet unsolved. The problem is the extent of Congress's power to control and limit the Supreme Court's appellate jurisdiction. The Court has never held that its appellate jurisdiction is coterminous with the Section 2 categories of judicial power. Consistently since *Wiscart v.*

Dauchy (1796) the Court has said, albeit often by way of OBITER DICTUM, that it can exercise appellate jurisdiction only to the extent permitted by acts of Congress, and that a legislative denial of jurisdiction may be implied from a failure by Congress to make an affirmative grant of jurisdiction. The Court, in other words, assumes that its appellate jurisdiction comes from statutes, not directly from Section 2 of Article III. The assumption is that Congress cannot add to the constitutional definitions of appellate jurisdiction, but that Congress can subtract from or make exceptions to those definitions.

It is clear that Congress has made broad statutory grants of jurisdiction to the Court, though not to the full extent permitted by Section 2. These affirmative grants have always been sufficient to permit the Court to fulfill its essential function of interpreting and applying the Constitution and of insuring the supremacy of federal law. So far, the statutory omissions and limitations have not hobbled the performance of that function.

At the same time, periodic proposals have been made in Congress to use the exceptions clause to legislate certain exclusions from the appellate jurisdiction previously granted by Congress. Such proposals usually spring from displeasure with Court decisions dealing with specific constitutional matters. The proponents would simply excise those areas of appellate jurisdiction that permit the Court to render the objectionable decisions. Many commentators contend that the exceptions clause was not designed to authorize Congress to strip the Court of power to perform its essential function of overseeing the development of constitutional doctrines and guarantees. Objections are also raised that such legislative excisions are mere subterfuges for overruling constitutional rights established by the Court, a most serious infringement of the separation of powers doctrine. Because no jurisdictional excisions of this broad nature have been enacted, the Court has yet to speak to this constitutional conundrum. (See JUDICIAL SYSTEM.)

Whatever the outer limits of the exceptions clause, Congress since 1789 has vested in the Court broad appellate power to review lower court decisions that fall within the constitutional "case or controversy" categories. Statutes permit the Court to review virtually all decisions of lower federal appellate courts, as well as a limited number of decisions of federal trial courts. And Congress has from the start given the Court jurisdiction to review decisions of the highest state courts that deal with federal constitutional, treaty, or statutory matters.

An ingredient of most jurisdictional statutes are legislative directions as to the mode by which the Court's appellate powers are to be invoked. In modern times, most lower court decisions are made reviewable by way of WRIT OF CERTIORARI or, in a declining number of specialized instances, by way of APPEAL. Congress permits the Court to issue its own extraordinary writs, such as HABEAS CORPUS or MANDAMUS, and to review certain matters not otherwise reviewable on certiorari or appeal; and there is a rarely used authorization for lower federal appellate court CERTIFICATION of difficult questions to be answered by the Supreme Court.

At COMMON LAW, the term "certiorari" means an original writ commanding lower court judges or officers to certify and transfer the record of the lower court proceedings in a case under review by a higher court. In the Supreme Court lexicon, the common law meaning of the term has been modified and expanded. Certiorari refers generally to the entire process of discretionary review by the Supreme Court of a lower court decision. Such review is sought by filing a petition for writ of certiorari. That document sets forth in short order the reasons why the questions presented by the decision below are so nationally important that the Court should review the case and resolve those questions on the merits. In most cases, the record in the court below is not routinely filed in the Court along with the petition.

Each Justice, after reviewing the petition for certiorari, the brief in opposition, and the opinion below, makes his or her own subjective assessment as to the appropriateness of plenary review by the entire Court. Such review is granted only if at least four Justices vote to grant the petition, a practice known as the RULE OF FOUR. If the petition is granted, a formal order to that effect is entered; copies of the order are sent to the parties and to the court below, which is then requested to transmit a certified copy of the record. But at no time does any writ of certiorari issue from the Court. The parties proceed thereafter to brief and argue orally the questions presented in the petition.

An appeal, on the other hand, refers to a theoretically obligatory type of review by the Supreme Court. That means that once the appeal is properly filed and docketed, the Court must somehow consider and dispose of the case on its merits. There is said to be no discretion to refuse to make such a decision on the merits of the appeal, which serves to distinguish an appeal from a certiorari case.

To invoke the Court's review powers by way of appeal, the aggrieved party first files a short notice of appeal in the lower court and then dockets the appeal in the Supreme Court by filing a document entitled "jurisdictional statement." Apart from the different title, a jurisdictional statement is remarkably like a petition for writ of certiorari. Like a petition, the jurisdictional statement sets forth briefly the reasons why the issues are so substantial, or important, "as to require plenary consideration, with briefs on the merits and oral argument, for their resolution." The Rule of Four is followed in considering whether to grant plenary consideration of an appeal. Such a grant takes the form of an order to the effect that "probable jurisdiction is noted," although if there remains any question as to whether the case complies with the technical jurisdictional requirements of an appeal, the order is changed to read: "further consideration of the question of jurisdiction is postponed to the hearing of the case on the merits." The appeal then follows the pattern of a certiorari case with respect to obtaining the record from the lower court(s), briefing the questions presented, and arguing orally before the Court.

As if to underscore the similarity between a jurisdictional statement and a petition for writ of certiorari, Congress has directed the Court, in situations where a party has "improvidently" taken an appeal "where the proper mode of review is by petition for certiorari," to consider and act on the jurisdictional statement as if it were a petition for writ of certiorari, and then either granting or denying certiorari. Thus a party cannot be prejudiced by seeking the wrong mode of Supreme Court review.

There is, however, one historical and confusing difference in the Court's summary disposition of certiorari cases and appeals, a difference springing from the notion that the Court is obliged to dispose of all appeals on their merits. When a petition for writ of certiorari is denied, the order denying the petition has no precedential value. It means only that fewer than four Justices, or perhaps none at all, want to hear and decide the merits of the questions presented. That is the end of the case.

But when fewer than four Justices wish to hear an appeal in a plenary manner, the long-held theory is that the Court is still compelled to dispose of the appeal on the merits of the questions presented. To comply with this theory, which is judge-made and not dictated by Congress, the Court has constructed a number of one-line orders, any one of which can be used to dismiss or dispose of the appeal without further briefing or oral argument. A typical order of this nature, used particularly in appeals from state court decisions, reads: "the appeal is dismissed for want of a substantial FEDERAL QUESTION." Such summary orders, which are devoid of explanation of the insubstantiality of the question involved, consistently have been held to be precedents. The Court has said that they must be understood and followed by state and lower federal courts.

In 1978, all nine Justices publicly conceded to the Congress that, while these summary dispositions of appeals are decisions on the merits, experience has shown that they "often are uncertain guides to the courts bound to follow them and not infrequently create more confusion than clarity." The Justices accordingly asked Congress to eliminate virtually all appeals, thereby recognizing formally that the Court's appellate jurisdiction is almost wholly discretionary. Congress has yet to respond.

At the start in 1789 and for a century thereafter, the Court was authorized to exercise only mandatory jurisdiction, either by way of appeal or a closely related process known as WRIT OF ERROR. But as the nation expanded and matured, litigation proliferated. It became evident toward the end of the nineteenth century that the Court could not keep up with its growing docket if it had to continue resolving the merits of every case that was filed. Gradually, Congress began to withdraw some of this mandatory jurisdiction from the Court, replacing it with discretionary jurisdiction by way of certiorari. But it was not until 1925 that Congress decreed a major shift toward discretionary review powers. At that time the dockets of the Court were so clogged with mandatory appeals and writs of error that litigants had to wait two and three years to have their cases decided. In the JUDICIARY ACT OF 1925, written largely at the suggestion of the Court, Congress transferred large segments of appellate jurisdiction from the obligatory to the discretionary category. Fully eighty percent of the Court's docket thereafter was of the certiorari variety.

But the 1925 transfer proved insufficient. During the 1970s, Congress eliminated many of the remaining appeals that could be taken from lower federal courts, leaving only a handful within the federal sector of Supreme Court jurisdiction. The largest pocket of mandatory appeals left untouched consists of appeals from state court decisions validating state statutes in the face of federal constitutional challenges. The caseload explosions in the 1970s and 1980s, which saw the Court's annual case filings rising near the 5,000 mark, created pressure to eliminate all significant remnants of mandatory appeal jurisdiction.

Nearly one-half of these filed cases are petitions and applications filed by prisoners, petitions that are often frivolous and thus quickly disposed of. But from the overall pool of some 5,000 cases the Justices select about 150 cases each term for plenary review and resolution. The Justices feel that time limitations do not permit them to dispose of many more than 150 important and complex controversies, although they do manage to dispose of another 200 or so cases in a summary fashion, without briefs or oral arguments. In any event, the number of cases granted full review has hovered around the 150 mark for many of the last fifty years. This constancy is largely the product of the discretion and the docket control inherent in the certiorari jurisdiction. Without discretion to deny review to more than ninety-five percent of the certiorari petitions filed each year, the Court's ability to function efficiently would soon cease.

The procedures by which the Court achieves this docket control and makes this vital selection of cases for plenary review are simple but not well understood by the public. And some of the processes change as workloads increase and issues tend to become more difficult of resolution. As of the 1980s, the procedures may be summarized as follows:

By law, the Supreme Court begins its annual TERM, or working session, on the first Monday in October. Known as the October Term, this session officially runs for a full year, eliminating the prior practice of convening special sessions during the summer to hear urgent matters. But for most administrative purposes, each term continues for about nine months, October through June, or until all cases considered ready for disposition have been resolved. At that point, the Court normally recesses without formally adjourning until the following October.

The Court usually disposes of requests for review, hears oral arguments, and issues written opinions only during the nine-month working portion of the term. But the Court never closes for purposes of accepting new cases, as well as briefs and motions in pending cases. That means that filing time requirements are never waived during the summer recess; parties must respect those requirements in all seasons. In most civil cases, certiorari petitions and jurisdictional statements must be filed within ninety days from the entry of judgment, or from the denial of rehearing, in the court below. This filing period is only sixty days in criminal cases, federal or state.

As soon as opposing parties have filed briefs or motions in response to a certiorari petition or jurisdictional statement, these documents are circulated to all nine Justices. These circulations occur on a weekly basis all year round. The circulated cases are then scheduled by the Court's clerk for disposition by the Justices at the next appropriate CONFERENCE. Cases circulated during the summer recess accumulate for consideration at a lengthy conference held just before the opening of the new October term. Cases circulated during term time are considered at a conference held about two weeks after a given weekly circulation.

The massive numbers of case filings make it impossible for every Justice personally to examine these thousands of documents, although some may try. Most are aided in this task by law CLERKS, each Justice being entitled to employ four. The clerks often have the task of reading these documents and reducing them to short memoranda for the convenience of their respective Justices. In recent years, a number of Justices have used a "cert pool" system, whereby law clerk resources in several chambers are pooled to produce memoranda for the joint use of all the participating Justices. But whether a Justice reads all these matters or is assisted by law clerk memoranda, the ultimate discretionary judgments made respecting the grant or denial of review are necessarily those of each Justice. Law clerks simply do not make critical judgments or cast votes.

Law clerks are selected personally by each Justice, a practice dating back to 1882 when Justice HORACE GRAY first employed a top Harvard Law School graduate. In modern times, clerks are invariably selected from among recent law school graduates with superior academic records.

And many Justices require that their clerks also have clerked for lower court judges. The clerks normally stay with their Justices for one term only, though some have served longer. Many law clerks have gone on to distinguished legal careers of their own. Three of them have become Supreme Court Justices: Justices BYRON R. WHITE, WILLIAM H. REHN-QUIST, and JOHN PAUL STEVENS.

An important element of each Justice's workload is to act in the capacity of Circuit Justice, a vestigial remnant of the earlier circuit-riding tasks. For this purpose, each Justice is assigned one or more federal judicial circuits, which divide the nation into twelve geographical areas. The Justice assigned to a particular circuit handles a variety of preliminary motions and applications in cases originating in the area covered by the circuit. Included are such matters as applications for stays of lower court judgments pending action on a petition for certiorari, applications in criminal cases for bail or release pending such action, and applications to extend the time for filing certiorari or appeal cases. Law clerks frequently assist in processing these applications, and on occasion an application may be disposed of by a written "in chambers" opinion of the Circuit Justice.

The Court no longer discusses every certiorari petition at conference. The excessive number of petitions makes it necessary and appropriate to curtail collegial discussion of petitions at the formal conferences of the Justices. At present, the Chief Justice circulates a "discuss list," a list of cases in a given weekly circulation deemed worthy of discussion and formal voting at conference. All appeals are discussed at conference, but rarely more than thirty percent of the certiorari cases are listed for discussion. Any Justice may add an omitted case to the list, however. Review is then automatically denied to any unlisted case, without conference consideration.

Decisions whether to grant or deny review of cases on the "discuss list" are reached at one of the periodic secret conferences. During term time, conferences are normally held each Friday during the weeks when oral arguments are heard, and on the Friday just before the commencement of each two-week oral argument period. Conferences can be held on other days as well. Only the Justices are present at these conferences; no law clerks or secretaries are permitted to attend.

Conferences are held in a well-appointed room adjacent to the Chief Justice's chambers, which are to the rear of the courtroom. The conference begins with exchanges of handshakes among the Justices, a custom originating in 1888. Coffee is available from a silver urn. The typical conference begins with discussion and disposition of the "discuss list" cases, appeals being considered first. The Chief Justice leads the discussion of each case, followed by each associate Justice in order of seniority. Any formal voting takes place in reverse order of seniority. Then, if there are argued cases to be decided, a similar order of discussion and voting is followed. Argued cases, however, may be discussed at other conferences scheduled immediately after a day or two of oral arguments, thus making the Friday conferences less lengthy.

Using the Rule of Four at these conferences, the Court selects from the pool of "discuss list" cases those that it will review and resolve on the merits, following full briefs and oral argument. A few cases, however, may be granted review and then resolved immediately in a summary manner without briefs or oral argument, by way of a PER CURIAM written opinion. Such summary disposition has been much criticized by those who lose their cases without being fully heard, but the practice has been codified in the Court's rules. The important point is that it is the cases that are selected at these conferences for plenary review that account for the 150 or so cases at the core of the Court's workload each term.

The cases thus selected for full review reflect issues that, in the Justices' view, are of national significance. It is not enough that the issues are important to the parties to the case; they must be generally important. But the Court rarely if ever explains why review is denied, or why the issues were not deemed important enough to warrant plenary attention. There are occasional written explanatory dissents from the denial of review, but these can only express the views of a minority. Review is granted only when four or more Justices are subjectively convinced that there are special and important reasons for reviewing the questions presented, which may or may not involve a conflict among lower courts as to how to resolve such questions. It bears emphasis that the exercise of this kind of discretionary judgment enables the Court to control its docket and to limit the extent of its plenary workload.

When a "discuss list" case is granted review, the petitioning party has forty-five days in which to file a brief on the merits, together with a printed record appendix. The opposing party then has thirty days to file a brief on the merits. Briefs of intervening parties and AMICI CURIAE, if there are any in a given case, are filed during these periods. When all briefs are in, the case is ready to be scheduled for oral argument.

Oral argument before the Justices occurs only on Monday, Tuesday, and Wednesday of a scheduled week of argument, leaving the other weekdays available for work and conferences. Usually, fourteen weeks of oral argument are scheduled, in two-week segments from October through April. One hour of argument is allowed in most cases, one-half hour for each side. Arguments start promptly at 10 A.M. and end at 3 P.M., with a lunch adjournment from noon to 1 P.M. The Justices are well prepared, having read the briefs. Some may also be aided by "bench memos" prepared by their law clerks, memoranda that outline the critical facts and the opposing arguments. Counsel arguing a case may thus expect sharp and penetrating questions from the bench; and counsel are warned by the Court's rules not to read arguments from a prepared text.

Sometime during the week in which a particular case has been argued, the Court meets in secret conference to decide the merits of that case. With the Chief Justice presiding and leading the discussion, the normal pattern of collegial discussion and voting takes place. But the vote reached at conference is necessarily tentative and subject to change as work begins on opinion writing. Shortly after the vote is taken, the case is assigned to one of the Justices to draft an opinion for the Court. The assignment is made by the senior Justice in the majority, if the vote is split. Normally, the assignment is made by the Chief Justice, unless he is in dissent.

The Justice assigned to write an opinion for the Court then begins work on a draft. This is essentially a lonely task. Following the conference discussion, there is little time for further collegial consultation among the Justices in the preparation of an opinion. Depending upon the work patterns of a particular Justice, the law clerks may engage in much of the research and analysis that underlie scholarly opinions; some clerks may be assigned the task of producing drafts of an opinion, while some Justices may do all the drafting themselves. Since 1981, drafting of opinions has been mechanically made easier by the installation of word processors in each Justice's chambers.

Once the draft of the majority opinion has been completed, it is circulated to all other members of the Court. The other Justices may suggest various changes or additions to the draft. To become an opinion of the Court, the draft opinion must attract the adherence and agreement of a majority of five Justices, which sometimes requires the author of the draft to accept modifications suggested by another Justice as the price of the latter's adherence. One or more of the Justices who cannot accept the reasoning or the result of the draft opinion then may produce their own drafts of CONCURRING or DISSENTING OPINIONS. The circulation of these separate opinion drafts may in turn cause the author of the majority draft to make further changes by way of answer to arguments made in a draft concurrence or dissent. Thus nothing is truly final until the collegial exchange of opinions is complete, the votes are set in concrete, and the result is considered ready for public announcement. Even then, there are cases in which the Court cannot reach a majority censensus, resulting in simply an announcement of the judgment of the Court accompanied by a number of PLURALITY, concurring, and dissenting opinions. The difficulty sometimes encountered in reaching a clear-cut majority result, while distressing to the bar and the lower courts, is generally reflective of the difficulty and complexity of some of the momentous issues that reach the Court.

The opinions and judgments of the Court in argued cases are announced publicly in the courtroom. At one time, opinions were uniformly announced on what became known as Opinion Monday. But the Court found that too many opinions announced on a Monday, particularly toward the end of a term, made it difficult for the press to give adequate media coverage to important Court rulings. The Court now announces opinions on any day it sits, thereby spreading out opinion announcements. In weeks in which oral arguments are scheduled for three days, the practice is to announce opinions only on a Tuesday or Wednesday, leaving Monday for the announcement of summary orders. Opinions may still be announced on a Monday, particularly if no oral arguments are scheduled for that day. After all oral arguments have been heard, usually by the end of April, opinions can be announced on any given Monday, when the Court sits to announce summary orders, or on any other day of the week that the Court wishes to sit solely to announce opinions.

The practices regarding the announcement of opinions in open court change from time to time. At one time, many opinions were read by the authors in full or in substantial part. More recently the Justices have tended merely to give short summaries save in the most important cases; in some less important cases only the result is announced. All opinions and orders are made available to the public and the news media a few moments after the courtroom announcements. Eventually, opinions and orders appear in bound volumes known as the United States Reports.

When the Court first convened in February of 1790, one of its first actions was to prescribe qualifications for lawyers wishing to practice before the Court. The original rule, in language very like that of the present rule, established two requirements: the attorney must have been admitted to practice in a state supreme court "for three years past," and the attorney's "private and professional character" must appear to be good.

Nearly 200,000 attorneys have been admitted to the Supreme Court bar since the Court was established. In recent times, as many as 6,000 have been admitted in a year. Prior to 1970, an attorney could be admitted only on motion of a sponsor in open court, before all the Justices. But the Court found that so much time was taken in listening to these routine motions and admissions and that it was often so expensive for a lawyer to travel to Washington from afar just to engage in this briefest of ceremonies, that an alternative "mail-order" procedure should be made available. Most attorneys today are admitted by mail, although some prefer to follow the earlier practice of being admitted in open court.

The modern Supreme Court bar has no formal structure or leadership. It is largely a heterogeneous collection of individual lawyers located in all parts of the nation. Many members of the bar never practice before the Court, and even fewer ever have the opportunity to argue orally. Most private practitioners who do have occasion to argue orally do so on a "once-in-a-lifetime" basis. Those who appear with some regularity before the Court are usually connected with an organization or governmental group specializing in Supreme Court litigation, such as the office of the SOLICITOR GENERAL of the United States. Gone are the days when private legal giants, such as DANIEL WEBSTER, were repeatedly employed specially by litigants to present oral arguments before the Court.

While a lay litigant may prepare and file petitions and briefs on the litigant's own behalf, without the aid of a member of the bar, the complexities and subtleties of modern practice make such self-help increasingly inadvisable. Only in the rarest of circumstances will the Court permit a lay litigant to present oral argument. Those imprisoned have frequently filed their own petitions for certiorari, seeking some sort of review of their criminal convictions. Indeed, about half of the nearly 5,000 case filings per year can be ascribed to prisoner petitions. The Court catalogues these petitions on its IN FORMA PAUPERIS docket but gives them the same careful treatment it gives petitions filed on behalf of clients who can afford to pay filing and printing costs.

The Court will, on application by an impecunious litigant or prisoner, appoint a member of the Court's bar to prepare briefs on the merits and to present oral arguments, once review has been granted in the case. But the Court will not appoint a lawyer to aid in preparing and filing a petition for certiorari or jurisdictional statement. Legal aid programs operating in most lower courts usually insure that a lawyer appointed or volunteering to represent a prisoner in the lower courts will be available to file such documents in the Supreme Court.

Such are the basic processes and procedures that enable the Court to perform its historic missions. As the Court approaches its third century, the Justices are deeply concerned with the Court's growing workload and the resulting effect upon the quality of its decision making. The Court's internal and external procedures have been streamlined and perfected about as much as possible. Some restructuring of its jurisdiction and functions seems necessary. Yet despite these perceived shortcomings, the Court has managed to maintain its prime role in the evolving history of the American legal system. The Court's effective performance of that role is due in no small part to the procedures and rules established for those who practice before it.

Bibliography

STERN, ROBERT L.; GRESSMAN, EUGENE; and SHAPIRO, STEPHEN M. 1986 *Supreme Court Practice,* 6th ed. Washington, D.C.: Bureau of National Affairs.

LEGISLATIVE FACTS

Kenneth L. Karst

The growth of American constitutional doctrine has been influenced, from the beginning, by the traditions of the Anglo-American COMMON LAW. Judges make constitutional law, as they make other kinds of law, partly on the basis of factual premises. Sometimes these premises are merely assumed, but sometimes they are developed with the aid of counsel. However they may be determined, the facts on which a court's lawmaking is premised are called "legislative facts." In modern usage they are sometimes contrasted with "adjudicative facts," the facts of the particular case before the court.

Not all constitutional questions concern the validity of legislation. In the 1970s and 1980s, for example, the Supreme Court went through a period of reappraisal of the EXCLUSIONARY RULE, which excludes from a criminal case some types of EVIDENCE obtained in violation of the Constitution. One factual issue repeatedly raised during this reconsideration was whether the rule actually served to deter police misconduct. In considering that question, the Court was not second-guessing the judgment of a legislature. Yet the question was properly regarded as one of legislative fact; its resolution would provide one of the premises for the Court's constitutional lawmaking.

More frequently, however, the courts consider issues of legislative fact in reviewing the constitutionality of legislation. In many cases, particularly when the laws under review are acts of Congress, the legislature itself has already given consideration to the same fact questions. Congress sometimes writes its own factual findings into the text of a law, explicitly declaring the actual basis for the legislation. In such cases the courts typically defer to the congressional versions of reality. Similar legislative findings are only infrequently written into the enactments of state and local legislative bodies, but even there the practice has recently increased. It seems unlikely, however, that judges, especially federal judges, will pay the same degree of deference to those legislative findings.

The courts' treatment of issues of legislative fact is thus seen as a function of the STANDARD OF REVIEW used to test a law's validity. When a court uses the most permissive form of the RATIONAL BASIS standard, it asks only whether the legislature could rationally conclude that the law under review was an appropriate means for achieving a legitimate legislative objective. The BRANDEIS BRIEF was invented for use in just such cases, presenting evidence to show that a legislature's factual premises were not irrational. When the standard of review is heightened— for example, when the courts invoke the rhetoric of STRICT SCRUTINY— arguments addressed to questions of legislative fact can be expected to come from both the challengers and the defenders of legislation. A court's fact-finding task in such a case is apt to be more complicated; the complication is implicit in any standard of review more demanding than the "rational basis" standard, any real interest-balancing by the courts. Arguments about the proper judicial approach to the factual premises for legislation are, in fact, arguments about the proper role of the judiciary in the governmental system. (See JUDICIAL REVIEW; JUDICIAL ACTIVISM AND JUDICIAL RESTRAINT.)

The technique of the Brandeis brief was invented for the occasion of the Supreme Court's consideration of MULLER V. OREGON (1908), upholding a law regulating women's working hours, and has been in fairly frequent use ever since. Increasingly, however, counsel have sought to present evidence on issues of legislative fact to trial courts. An early example was SOUTHERN PACIFIC CO. V. ARIZONA (1945), in which the Supreme Court struck down a law limiting the length of railroad trains. For five and a half months the trial judge heard evidence filling some 3,000 pages in the record; he made findings of legislative fact covering 148 printed pages. Justice HUGO L. BLACK, dissenting, complained that this procedure made the judiciary into a "super-legislature," but courts cannot escape from this kind of factual inquiry unless they adopt Justice Black's permissive views and abandon most constitutional limits on STATE REGULATION OF COMMERCE.

Nor are such trials of legislative fact limited to issues lying within the competence of people like safety engineers. When the California school finance case, SERRANO V. PRIEST (1972), was remanded for trial, the court took six months of expert testimony centered on a single question: Does differential spending on education produce differences in educational quality? (The court's unsurprising answer: Yes.)

As the *Serrano* and *Southern Pacific* cases show, proving legislative facts at trial is considerably more costly than filing a Brandeis brief. It permits cross-examination, however, and sharpens the focus for evidentiary offerings. Even when appellate review seems certain, the trial court's sorting and evaluation of a complex record can aid the appellate court greatly. Expert testimony, the staple of such a trial, typically rests on the sort of opinion and hearsay about which nonexperts ordinarily would not be permitted to testify. Legislative facts, of course, are tried to the judge and not to a jury; furthermore, questions of legislative fact, by definition, touch a great many "cases" not in court that will be "decided" by the precedent made in the court's constitutional ruling. Just as a constitutional case is an especially appropriate occasion for hearing the views of an AMICUS CURIAE, the widest latitude should be allowed to the parties (and to an amicus) to present evidence broadly relevant to the lawmaking issues before the court.

Ultimately there is no assurance that counsel's efforts to educate a court about the factual setting for constitutional lawmaking will improve the lawmaking itself. Yet our courts, with the Supreme Court's encouragement, continue to invite counsel to make these efforts. One of America's traditional faiths, which judges share with the rest of us, is a belief in the value of education.

Bibliography

FREUND, PAUL A.   1951   *On Understanding the Supreme Court.* Boston: Little, Brown.
KARST, KENNETH L.   1960   Legislative Facts in Constitutional Litigation. *Supreme Court Review* 1960:75–112.

SOCIAL SCIENCE IN CONSTITUTIONAL LITIGATION

Hans Zeisel and David Kaye

All litigation, including constitutional litigation, resolves issues of law and fact. Social science research can help to clarify the facts on which a case may turn; and it can help the resolution of legal issues by laying before the courts data and analyses that bear on the choice of an appropriate legal rule.

Legal lore has it that the rise of social science in the law began with the BRANDEIS BRIEF, in which LOUIS D. BRANDEIS, special counsel for the state of Oregon, successfully bolstered the state's claim in MULLER V. OREGON (1908) that its statute limiting the working hours for women was constitutional. Although in theory the state merely had to show that such a regulation was not unreasonable, previous decisions had struck down laws regulating working hours of other employees as unreasonable invasions of the liberty of contract. The brief supported the reasonableness of the law in part by showing that a great many American states and even more countries abroad had similar statutes. It was an effective if modest social science effort.

More sophisticated techniques are to be found in contemporary constitutional litigation. Sampling, the most powerful tool of social science research, is now firmly established as an appropriate means of gathering EVIDENCE. If the survey was conducted without bias and if the technical requirements are met, a sample may be accepted as a reasonably accurate representation of the sampled universe. For instance, in support of a motion for change of VENUE in a criminal case, a sample survey measures the extent and depth of pretrial prejudice in the community. If a voluminous body of communications is at issue, sampling may be combined with a technique called content analysis. Thus, when the constitutionality of the work of the House Committee on Un-American Activities was litigated, a sample of the committee's public hearings was examined. This approach yielded a numerical statement of the frequency with which the committee asked its witnesses questions that transcended its constitutional authority. Similar content analysis has sometimes been used in support of a motion for change of venue, documenting the charge that a substantial part of the pretrial publicity originated in the prosecutor's office.

Proof of racial or other discrimination in jury selection, employment, and other contexts frequently employs sampling and subsequent statistical analysis. Such proof involves an analysis of the differences between the actual outcome of the selection process and the outcome that would have been expected if discrimination had no role in the process.

In *United States v. Hazelwood School District* (1977), for instance, the Supreme Court made its own probability computations to determine whether excluding the metropolitan area from the labor market in which a suburban school district hired its teachers would substantially weaken the government's statistical proof that the district had engaged in discrimination. Although the Court's statistical performance in *Hazelwood* was flawed in certain respects, similar methods in proving discrimination have become accepted in both federal and state courts.

Of particular interest are the cases in which the judicial system itself is charged with discrimination. The two main targets here are the administration of the death penalty and the selection of jurors. Evidence has been mounting, and finally has drawn the attention of the Supreme Court, that the death penalty is administered with bias, discriminating against black offenders who killed white victims. The major technical problem in distilling this evidence is to assure comparability of the homicides under analysis.

In the jury selection area, the statistical analysis of discrimination has had more impact. Despite substantial efforts in this direction, the lower courts have rejected these efforts. In *Castandeda v. Partida* (1977), for instance, the Court used a standard statistical formula to compute the probability that the disparity between the proportion of Mexican-Americans serving on GRAND JURIES and their proportion in the county population could have arisen if grand jurors had been selected at random. The majority found the probability to be so minute (about one in a number with 140 zeros) that the discrepancy was sufficient to establish discrimination even though there were problems with the data used to estimate these proportions and even though the majority of jury commissioners were themselves Mexican-Americans.

In the trial of Dr. Benjamin Spock and others accused of conspiring to obstruct the draft, the alleged discrimination involved female jurors. The allegation of bias in that case was directed not against the system but against the particular judge who consistently selected juries with significantly fewer women than those of his colleagues, although all drew from the same pool of potential jurors.

At times experimental social science research is offered to aid a court in assessing the consequences of its legal options or in ascertaining facts relevant to the choice of these options. When the Supreme Court in BROWN v. BOARD OF EDUCATION (1954) held that segregated education was inherently unequal, the Court quoted with approval a lower court's finding that school segregation with the sanction of law produced feelings of inferiority among black children, affecting their motivation to learn. The Court remarked that its conclusion was "amply supported by modern authority." That authority, cited in a footnote, consisted of seven items. Five, such as Gunnar Myrdal's *American Dilemma,* dealt generally with problems of black education. Two bore more directly on the issue: a statement by thirty-two leading social scientists and an experiment conducted by the psychologist Kenneth Clark. Clark had given sixteen black children in a South Carolina elementary school a sheet of paper on which two dolls were drawn, identical in every respect except that the one was black, the other white. The children were asked, "Which doll would you like to play with?" "Which is the nice and which the bad doll?" "Which doll looks like you yourself?" Ten of the children liked the white doll best; eleven called the black doll the "bad" one; seven of the black children, when asked which doll was like themselves, picked the white one. From these answers and earlier research, Clark concluded "that these children . . . like other human beings who are subjected to an obviously inferior status in the society in which they live, have been definitely harmed in the development of their personalities. . . ."

Later, scholars disputed both the evidentiary power of that study and the weight the Justices had attached to it. The study, obviously limited in size and structure, today would hardly survive cross-examination. Most likely its major function was to buttress a position the Justices had reached on their own.

Social science research has provided more solid evidence in litigation over the constitutionality of juries with fewer than twelve members. In the two decisions that affirmed the legality of such juries, the Court cited a number of empirical studies purporting to show that these modifications did not affect the quality of the verdicts rendered by the smaller juries. Subsequently these studies were severely criticized, and five years later BALLEW v. GEORGIA held five-member criminal juries unconstitutional. Justice HARRY A. BLACKMUN's opinion repeatedly cited these critical views.

Most social science operations suffer from some imperfection, partly because their subject matter is so complex, and partly because of methodological flaws. Even if such imperfections are minor, courts may hesitate to accept social science findings that threaten to dislodge established rules. One type of effort to compensate for imperfection is "triangulation"—the confluence of evidence from independent studies that approach the same problem from different angles. An example is the series of studies of "death qualified" juries.

At one time, a New York statute allowed New York City to try murder and other crimes of public notoriety before specially selected BLUE RIBBON JURIES, whose members, among other qualifications, were required to have no objection to the death penalty. When the Court was asked to declare these juries unconstitutional because of alleged bias in favor of the prosecution, it declined by a bare majority on the ground that there was no proof of such bias. Speculation as to how such proof might be established led to the first study which found that jurors who were in favor of the death penalty were indeed more likely to convict, not only in capital trials, but generally. Six other studies followed, with different approaches; each replicated the result.

Witherspoon v. Illinois (1968), decided halfway through these studies, did not reach the issue. Although the Court agreed that merely having scruples about the death penalty was not sufficient cause for eliminating jurors, it dismissed the first few research findings, indicating that the exclusion of jurors with scruples against the death penalty would bias the jury in favor of conviction, as "too tentative and fragmentary." Subsequent efforts to convince other courts that the post-*Witherspoon* juries, too, were biased in favor of convicting defendants failed until 1983 and 1984 when two federal district courts in HABEAS CORPUS proceedings accepted the evidence provided in these studies and invalidated the convictions. Although the federal Courts of Appeals have divided on this issue and the Supreme Court has agreed to review one of these cases, these two decisions mark a preliminary acceptance of proof by triangulation.

The role of social science research in litigation is bound to grow in spite of deep-seated hesitancy on the part of the courts to look at statistical evidence. It is difficult to predict how fast and where the use of social science techniques will increase in constitutional litigation. Much will depend on the resourcefulness of social scientists in developing new research and the initiative of attorneys in presenting evidence that can sharpen the perception of litigated facts and aid courts in judging the consequences of their legal options.

Bibliography

BALDUS, D. and COLE, J. 1980 *Statistical Proof of Discrimination.* Colorado Springs, Colo.: Shepard's.

CAHN, EDMOND 1962 A Dangerous Myth in the School Segregation Cases. In Kenneth Clark, ed., *Confronting Injustice.* Pages 329–345. Boston: Little, Brown.

KAYE, DAVID 1980 And Then There Were Twelve: Statistical Reasoning, the Supreme Court, and the Size of the Jury. *California Law Review* 68:1004–1043.

——— 1982 Statistical Evidence of Discrimination. *Journal of the American Statistical Association* 77:773–783.

LEMPERT, RICHARD O. 1975 Uncovering "Nondiscernible" Differences: Empirical Research and the Jury-Size Cases. *Michigan Law Review* 73: 643–708.

LOH, WALLACE D. 1984 *Social Research in the Judicial Process: Cases, Readings and Text.* New York: Russell Sage Foundation.

SAKS, MICHAEL J. 1974 Ignorance of Science Is No Excuse. *Trial* 10:18–20.

WALBERT, DAVID 1971 The Effect of Jury Size on the Probability of Conviction: An Evaluation of *Williams v. Florida. Case Western Law Review* 22:529–554.

ZEISEL, HANS 1971 And Then There Were None: The Diminution of the Federal Jury. *University of Chicago Law Review* 38:710–724.

——— 1980 Reflections on Experimental Techniques in the Law. *Journal of Legal Studies* 2:107–124.

——— 1968 *Some Data on Juror Attitudes Towards Capital Punishment.* Chicago: University of Chicago Center for Studies in Criminal Justice.

——— 1985 *Say It with Figures,* 6th ed. Chap. 14. New York: Harper & Row.

——— and DIAMOND, SHARI 1974 "Convincing Empirical Evidence" on the Six-Member Jury. *University of Chicago Law Review* 41:281–295.

PRECEDENT

Kenneth L. Karst

In MARBURY v. MADISON (1803) Chief Justice JOHN MARSHALL rested the legitimacy of JUDICIAL REVIEW of the constitutionality of legislation on the necessity for courts to "state what the law is" in particular cases. The implicit assumption is that the Constitution is law, and that the content of constitutional law is determinate—that it can be known and applied by judges. From the time of the nation's founding, lawyers and judges trained in the processes of the COMMON LAW have assumed that the law of the Constitution is to be found not only in the text of the document and the expectations of the Framers but also in judicial precedent: the opinions of judges on "what the law is," written in the course of deciding earlier cases. (See STARE DECISIS.)

Inevitably, issues that burned brightly for the Framers of the Constitution and of its various amendments have receded from politics into history. The broad language of much of the Constitution's text leaves open a wide range of choices concerning interpretation. As the body of judicial precedent has grown, it has taken on a life of its own; the very term "constitutional law," for most lawyers today, primarily calls to mind the interpretations of the Constitution contained in the Supreme Court's opinions. For a lawyer writing a brief, or a judge writing an opinion, the natural style of argumentation is the common law style, with appeals to one or another "authority" among the competing analogies offered by a large and still growing body of precedent.

The same considerations that support reliance on precedent in common law decisions apply in constitutional adjudications: the need for stability in the law and for evenhanded treatment of litigants. Yet adherence to precedent has also been called the control of the living by the dead. Earlier interpretations of the Constitution, when they seem to have little relevance to the conditions of society and government here and now, do give way. As Chief Justice EARL WARREN wrote in BROWN v. BOARD OF EDUCATION (1954), "In approaching [the problem of school SEGREGATION], we cannot turn the clock back to 1868 when the [FOURTEENTH] AMENDMENT was adopted, or even to 1896 when PLESSY [v. FERGUSON] was written. We must consider public education in the light of its full development and its present place in American life. . . ." Justice OLIVER WENDELL HOLMES put the matter more pungently: "It is revolting to have no better reason for a rule of law than that so it was laid down in the time of Henry IV."

Although the Supreme Court decides only those issues that come to it in the ordinary course of litigation, the Court has a large measure of control over its own doctrinal agenda. The selection of about 150 cases for review each year (out of more than 4,000 cases brought to the Court) is influenced most of all by the Justices' views of the importance of the issues presented. (See CERTIORARI, WRIT OF.) And when the Court does break new doctrinal ground, it invites further litigation to explore the area thus opened. For example, scores of lawsuits were filed all over the country once the Court had established the precedent, in BAKER V. CARR (1962), that the problem of legislative REAPPORTIONMENT was one that the courts could properly address. The Justices see themselves, and are seen by the Court's commentators, as being in the business of developing constitutional DOCTRINE through the system of precedent. The decision of particular litigants' cases today appears to be important mainly as an instrument to those lawmaking ends. The theory of *Marbury v. Madison,* in other words, has been turned upside down.

Lower court judges pay meticulous attention to Supreme Court opinions as their main source of guidance for decision in constitutional cases. Supreme Court Justices themselves, however, give precedent a force that is weaker in constitutional cases than in other areas of the law. In a famous expression of this view, Justice LOUIS D. BRANDEIS, dissenting in *Burnet v. Coronado Oil & Gas Co.* (1932), said, "in cases involving the Federal Constitution, where correction through legislative action is practically impossible, this court has often overruled its earlier decisions. The court bows to the lessons of experience and the force of better reasoning, recognizing that the process of trial and error, so fruitful in the physical sciences, is appropriate also in the judicial function."

Although this sentiment is widely shared, Justices often are prepared to defer to their reading of precedent even when they disagree with the conclusions that produced the earlier decisions. Justice JOHN MAR-SHALL HARLAN, for example, regularly accepted the authoritative force of WARREN COURT opinions from which he had dissented vigorously. The Court as an institution occasionally takes the same course, making clear that it is following the specific dictates of an earlier decision because of the interest in stability of the law, even though that decision may be out of line with more recent doctrinal developments.

The Supreme Court is regularly criticized, both from within the Court and from the outside, for failing to follow precedent. But a thoroughgoing consistency of decision cannot be expected, given the combination of three characteristics of the Court's decisional process. First, the Court is a collegiate body, with the nine Justices exercising individual judgment on each case. Second, the body of precedent is now enormous, with the result that in most cases decided by the Court there are arguable precedents for several alternative doctrinal approaches, and even for reaching opposing results. Indeed, the system for selecting cases for review guarantees that the court will regularly face hard cases—cases that are difficult because they can plausibly be decided in more than one way. Finally, deference to precedent itself may mean that issues will be decided differently, depending on the order in which they come before the Court. The Court's decision in *In re Griffiths* (1973), that a state cannot constitutionally limit the practice of law to United States citizens, is still a good precedent; yet, if the case had come up in 1983, almost certainly it would have been decided differently. (See ALIENS.)

The result of this process is an increasingly fragmented Supreme Court, with more PLURALITY OPINIONS and more statements by individual Justices of their own separate views in CONCURRING OPINIONS and dissents—thus presenting an even greater range of materials on which Justices can draw in deciding the next case. In these circumstances, it is not surprising that some plurality opinions, such as that in MOORE v. CITY OF EAST CLEVELAND (1977), are regularly cited as if they had a precedent value equal to that of OPINIONS OF THE COURT.

The range of decisional choice offered to a Supreme Court Justice by this process is so wide as to call into the question the idea of principled decision on which the legitimacy of judicial review is commonly assumed to rest. Yet the hard cases that fill the Supreme Court's docket—the very cases that make constitutional law and thus fill the casebooks that law students study—do not typify the functioning of constitutional law. A great many controversies of constitutional dimension never get to court, because the law seems clear, on the basis of precedent; similarly, many cases that do get to court are easily decided in the lower courts. Although we celebrate the memory of our creative Justices—Justices who are remembered for setting precedent, not following it—the body of constitutional law remains remarkably stable. In a stable society it could not be otherwise. As Holmes himself said in another context, "historic continuity with the past is not a duty, it is only a necessity."

Bibliography

EASTERBROOK, FRANK H.   1982   Ways of Criticizing the Court. *Harvard Law Review* 95:802–832.
LEVI, EDWARD H.   1949   *An Introduction to Legal Reasoning.* Chicago: University of Chicago Press.
LLEWELLYN, KARL N.   1960   *The Common Law Tradition.* Boston: Little, Brown.
MONAGHAN, HENRY P.   1979   Taking Supreme Court Opinions Seriously. *Maryland Law Review* 39:1–26.

RETROACTIVITY OF JUDICIAL DECISIONS

Paul Bender

LEGISLATION ordinarily does not apply retroactively to conduct occurring prior to its adoption but only to actions taking place after enactment. Indeed, the potential unfairness of some retroactive legislation is so great that certain forms of legislative retroactivity are specifically prohibited by the Constitution. The EX POST FACTO clauses of the Constitution prohibit retroactive criminal penalties, and the CONTRACT CLAUSE limits state legislation that would impair the obligation of pre-existing contracts. In addition, certain other fundamentally unfair forms of legislative retroactivity may violate constitutional due process guarantees.

Judicial decisions, on the other hand, ordinarily *are* retroactive in application. To some extent, such retroactivity is a consequence of the nature and function of the judicial decision-making process. Traditional lawsuits and criminal prosecutions concern the legal consequences of acts that have already taken place. If judicial decisions in such cases are to adjudicate the issues between the parties, those decisions necessarily must apply to prior events. The retroactive effect of judicial decisions, however, commonly extends beyond application to the particular parties involved in a case. To the extent that a judicial decision constitutes a new legal precedent, it will ordinarily be applied to all undecided cases that are subsequently litigated, regardless of whether the relevant events occurred before or after the new precedent was announced.

Although traditional judicial decisions are, in theory, completely retrospective in nature, two sets of legal doctrines place important practical limits on the actual breadth of decisional retroactivity. Statutes of limitations, which require suits to be brought within some specified period of time after the relevant events occur, limit the retrospective application of new precedents to the length of the prescribed limitations period; and the doctrines of RES JUDICATA and collateral estoppel prevent the relitigation of cases and issues that have been finally decided before the new precedent is announced. In addition, as in the case of retroactive legislation, there are some circumstances of fundamental unfairness in which constitutional principles may prevent the retroactive use of judicial decisions. By analogy to the constitutional prohibition of ex post facto laws, for example, the Supreme Court in *Bowie v. City of Columbia* (1964) held it unconstitutional to apply a new expansive judicial interpretation of a criminal statute to prior conduct.

The principal theoretical basis supporting the broad traditional retroactivity of judicial decisions is the abstract idea that courts (unlike legislatures) do not make, but merely find, the law. This theory in effect denies the existence of retroactivity; under the theory the events in question were always subject to the newly announced rule, although that rule had not been authoritatively articulated.

The theory that judicial decisions do not make law does not always reflect reality. Perhaps the clearest example of apparent judicial lawmaking is a court's overruling of an earlier judicial decision regarding the meaning of the COMMON LAW, a statute, or a constitutional provision. Even when no earlier decision is overruled, judicial decisions or interpretations may announce genuinely new principles. When judicial decisions thus create new law, it is plausible to argue that the new principles should not be given the retroactive effect normally accorded to judicial decisions, but should instead be treated more like new legislation and given prospective effect only. These arguments are strongest when individuals or governments have relied (perhaps irrevocably) upon earlier decisions in shaping their conduct. In such circumstances, retroactive application may cause unanticipated and harmful results.

In response to these and similar considerations, some courts have used the practice of PROSPECTIVE OVERRULING of prior decisions. Such a court, in overruling a precedent upon which substantial reliance may have been placed, may announce in OBITER DICTUM its intention to reject the old doctrine for the future, but nevertheless apply the old rule to the case at hand and to other conduct prior to the new decision. Alternatively, the court may apply the new rule to the parties before it, thus making the announcement of the new rule HOLDING rather than "dictum," but may otherwise reserve the rule for future application. In *Great Northern Railway Company v. Sunburst Oil and Refining Company* (1932) the Supreme Court held that the Constitution permits either of these forms of prospective overruling. The *Sunburst* decision gave constitutional approval to prospective judicial overruling of common law precedents and of decisions interpreting statutes. Such prospective overruling has primarily been used in two kinds of cases: new interpretations of statutes relating to property and contract rights, and the overruling of doctrines of municipal and charitable immunity from tort liability.

The most prominent and controversial recent issue concerning prospective overruling, however, has involved the retroactivity of new Supreme Court decisions enlarging the constitutional rights of defendents in criminal proceedings. During the 1950s and 1960s, the Court significantly broadened the rights of criminal defendants with respect to unconstitutional SEARCHES AND SEIZURES, POLICE INTERROGATION AND CONFES-

SIONS, the scope of the RIGHT AGAINST SELF-INCRIMINATION, and the inadmissibility of unconstitutionally obtained evidence. The Court has ruled that some of these new constitutional interpretations should not be given general retrospective application.

The extent of the possible retroactive application of new doctrines affecting the constitutionality of criminal convictions is greater than in most other areas of law because of the potential availability of post-conviction relief to prisoners whose convictions might be effectively challenged if the newly announced rules were applicable to prior convictions. Petitions for HABEAS CORPUS are not subject to statutes of limitations or to the ordinary operation of the doctrine of *res judicata*. Thus, in 1961, when the Supreme Court decided in MAPP v. OHIO that the Constitution prohibits states from basing criminal convictions upon EVIDENCE obtained in violation of the FOURTH and FOURTEENTH AMENDMENTS, full retroactivity of that decision would have permitted a great many prisoners to challenge their convictions, no matter when their trials had occurred. Because the *Mapp* decision was based upon the interpretation of constitutional provisions dating from 1791 and 1868, the theoretical arguments for full retroactivity were strong. However, *Mapp* overruled the opinion of the Court in WOLF v. COLORADO (1949), which had held, directly contrary to *Mapp*, that the states were free to use unconstitutionally obtained evidence in most circumstances. Although police could hardly have legitimately relied upon *Wolf* in engaging in unconstitutional searches, state prosecutors and courts might have relied upon *Wolf* in using unconstitutionally obtained evidence. The primary reason given by the Court for the *Mapp* decision, moreover, was to deter police misconduct; the *Mapp* EXCLUSIONARY RULE is not a safeguard against conviction of the innocent. Retroactive application of *Mapp* to nullify pre-existing convictions would thus arguably contribute little to the main purpose of the *Mapp* rule while permitting guilty defendants to escape their just punishment. Similar issues have surrounded the potential retroactivity of other new Supreme Court decisions enlarging the constitutional rights of criminal defendants.

The Supreme Court has resolved these retroactivity issues by employing a test focusing on three main criteria: whether the purpose of the new rule would be furthered by its retroactive application; the extent of the reliance by law enforcement authorities and courts on prior decisions and understandings; and the likely effect of retroactive application on the administration of justice. Using this approach the Court held, in *Linkletter v. Walker (1965)*, that the *Mapp* decision would be applied to trials and direct APPEALS pending at the time of the *Mapp* decision, but not to state court convictions where the appeal process had been completed prior to announcement of the *Mapp* opinion. The same rule of general nonretroactivity has been applied to new constitutional interpretations prohibiting comment on a defendant's failure to take the witness stand at trial; establishing the MIRANDA RULES for police warnings to persons interrogated; prohibiting WIRETAPPING without judicial SEARCH WARRANTS; and limiting the permissible scope of SEARCHES INCIDENT TO ARRESTS. On the other hand, full retroactivity has been accorded to new decisions requiring provision of free counsel for INDIGENTS in criminal trials; requiring proof beyond a REASONABLE DOUBT in state criminal proceedings; and broadening the definition of constitutionally prohibited DOUBLE JEOPARDY. In general, rules designed to protect innocent persons from conviction have been given full retroactive application, while rules primarily intended to correct police and prosecutorial abuses that do not implicate guilt have been given limited retroactivity. The practical significance of these retroactivity decisions has been diminished in recent years by Supreme Court decisions that limit the availability of post-conviction relief to incarcerated persons (for example, STONE V. POWELL, 1976) and by the current Supreme Court's general opposition to continued expansion of defendants' constitutional rights in criminal proceedings.

Bibliography

FIELD, OLIVER P.   1935   *The Effect of an Unconstitutional Statute.* Minneapolis: University of Minnesota Press.

COMMENTATORS ON THE CONSTITUTION

Maxwell Bloomfield

The first important analysis of the Constitution appeared during the ratification contests of 1787 and 1788. ALEXANDER HAMILTON and JAMES MADISON, who had participated in the CONSTITUTIONAL CONVENTION, collaborated with JOHN JAY on THE FEDERALIST (1788), a series of essays defending the proposed new plan of government. Appealing to the rationalistic temper of the eighteenth century, they justified the creation of a strong central government on logical and philosophical grounds, and developed a model of CONSTITUTIONALISM that relied upon structural CHECKS AND BALANCES to promote harmony within the system. Ultimate SOVEREIGNTY, they argued, inhered in the American people; the Constitution, as an instrument of the popular will, defined and limited the powers of both the national government and the states. *The Federalist* provided valuable insights into the thinking of the Founding Fathers and established the guidelines for further constitutional commentary down to the Civil War.

Between 1789 and 1860 two major groups of commentators emerged in response to recurring political crises and sectional tensions. Legally trained publicists from New England and the middle states espoused a national will theory of government to justify the expansion of federal power, while southern lawyers and statesmen formed a state compact school of constitutional interpretation that championed decentralization and state sovereignty. Each group approached constitutional issues in a formal and mechanistic way, and relied upon close textual analysis to support its position.

The nationalists argued that the American people, acting in a collective national capacity, had divided sovereign power between the nation and the states and established the Constitution as the supreme LAW OF THE LAND. Under the resulting federal system, the states retained control of their internal affairs but were subordinate to the general government in all important national concerns, including taxation, INTERSTATE COMMERCE, and FOREIGN AFFAIRS. The Constitution, moreover, created a permanent union, whose basic features could be changed only by resort to a prescribed AMENDING PROCESS. Although several nationalists conceded that the Constitution had originated in a compact of the people of the

266

several states, they insisted that such a compact, once executed, was inviolate, and could not be modified thereafter by the parties. Such was the message of NATHANIEL CHIPMAN's *Sketches of the Principles of Government* (1793) and William Alexander Duer's *Lectures on Constitutional Jurisprudence* (1843).

Other advocates of national supremacy rejected contractual assumptions altogether, and moved toward an organic theory of the Union. Nathan Dane, in *A General Abridgment and Digest of American Law* (1829), contended that the states had never been truly sovereign, because they owed their independence from British rule to the actions of the CONTINENTAL CONGRESS, a national body that represented the American people. The people, not the states, had ratified the Constitution through the exercise of majority will; therefore, any state efforts to nullify federal law or to withdraw from the Union amounted to illegal and revolutionary acts. JAMES KENT's *Commentaries on American Law* (1826–1830) and Timothy Walker's *Introduction to American Law* (1837) further noted that the Constitution provided for the peaceful resolution of federal–state disputes through the Supreme Court's power of JUDICIAL REVIEW.

In attacking the compact model of constitutionalism, these commentators stressed the noncontractual language of the PREAMBLE and the SUPREMACY CLAUSE. A similar preoccupation with formal textual analysis characterized JOSEPH STORY's *Commentaries on the Constitution of the United States* (1833), the most influential and authoritative statement of the nationalist position. Story, an associate Justice of the Supreme Court, interpreted the Constitution on a line-by-line basis, in light of the nationalistic jurisprudence of JOHN MARSHALL. Like Marshall, he insisted that the powers of the federal government had to be construed broadly, as the Framers had intended. On both theoretical and pragmatic grounds, Story defended the power of the Supreme Court to strike down unconstitutional state laws. Yet he also emphasized the limits of national authority, noting that the states retained control over matters of internal police that affected the daily lives of their citizens. Although Congress alone could regulate interstate commerce, for example, state legislatures might pass health and safety measures that indirectly affected such commerce. By focusing upon questions of terminology and classification, Story sought to demonstrate the stability of the federal system and to place the Constitution above partisan politics.

Nationalist historians described the formation of the Union in similarly legalistic and reverential terms. GEORGE TICKNOR CURTIS's *History of the Origin, Formation, and Adoption of the Constitution of the United States* (1854–1858), the first work to deal exclusively with a constitutional topic, quoted at length from the journals of the Continental Congress and other public records, but largely ignored surrounding political and economic circumstances. For Curtis and other romantic nationalists, the

/

Founding Fathers were disinterested and divinely inspired patriots, who enjoyed the full confidence and support of the American people. Only RICHARD HILDRETH's *History of the United States of America* (1849–1852) presented a contrary view. Hildreth stressed the importance of conflicting economic groups in the new nation and pointed out that the Constitution had been ratified by conventions representing only a minority of American voters.

Although state compact theorists shared the prevailing belief in a fixed and beneficent Constitution, they deplored what they perceived as the aggrandizing tendencies of the national government. St. George Tucker's "View of the Constitution of the United States," appended to his edition of WILLIAM BLACKSTONE's *Commentaries* (1803), established the basic premises of the southern constitutional argument. The states and their respective citizens, Tucker contended, had entered into a compact—the Constitution—and had delegated some of their sovereign powers to the resulting federal government for specific and limited purposes. Because the Union remained subordinate to its creators, the states, and depended upon their cooperation for its continued existence, all positive grants of national power had to be construed strictly. If the federal government overstepped its constitutional powers, Tucker suggested that individuals might look to the state or federal courts for redress, while violations of STATES' RIGHTS would be answered by appropriate action from the state legislatures.

Later commentators refined Tucker's ideas and fashioned new remedies for the protection of state rights. The Philadelphia lawyer WILLIAM RAWLE introduced the possibility of peaceable SECESSION through the action of state CONSTITUTIONAL CONVENTIONS in *A View of the Constitution of the United States* (1825). Rawle's reasoning was hypothetical: because the people of each state had agreed to form a permanent union of representative republics, they could withdraw from their compact only by adopting a new state constitution based upon nonrepublican principles. A more realistic assessment of the nature and consequences of secession appeared in HENRY ST. GEORGE TUCKER's *Lectures on Constitutional Law* (1843). In Tucker's view, secession provided the only mode of resistance available to a state after a controversial federal law had been upheld by the judiciary. Secession was a revolutionary measure, however, because the Constitution had established the courts as the permanent umpires of federal–state relations.

Advocates of NULLIFICATION proposed a more extreme version of the state sovereignty argument, whose origins went back to JOHN TAYLOR of Caroline's *Construction Construed; and Constitutions Vindicated* (1820) and *New Views of the Constitution of the United States* (1823). Unlike the southern moderates, Taylor insisted that sovereignty was indivisible and inhered exclusively in the states. Each "state nation" thus retained the power to construe the terms of the federal compact for itself, and to interpose its authority at any time to protect its citizens against the consolidating tendencies of the federal government. Whenever a federal law violated the Constitution, asserted Abel Parker Upshur in *A Brief Inquiry into the Nature and Character of Our Federal Government* (1840), a state might summon its citizens to a special convention and declare the act null and void within its borders.

As the influence of the slaveholding South continued to decline in national politics, some commentators sought to preserve the Union by adding still more checks and balances to the constitutional structure. In *A Disquisition on Government* and *A Discourse on the Constitution and Government of the United States* (1851), JOHN C. CALHOUN called for amendments that would establish a dual executive and base REPRESENTATION upon broad interest groups, any one of which might block the enactment of undesirable congressional legislation. ALEXANDER H. STEPHENS's *A Constitutional View of the Late War Between the States* (1868–1870) and JEFFERSON DAVIS's *The Rise and Fall of the Confederate Government* (1881) confirmed the mechanistic cast of southern constitutional thought, as they summed up the case for secession in its final form. With the defeat of the Confederacy, the secessionist option ceased to exist, and later commentators treated the issue as a historical footnote. During the 1950s conservative Southerners tried unsuccessfully to circumvent federal CIVIL RIGHTS policy by reviving the idea of INTERPOSITION in such works as William Old's *The Segregation Issue: Suggestions Regarding the Maintenance of State Autonomy* (1955).

For Civil War Unionists the exercise of sweeping WAR POWERS by the President and Congress provoked vigorous constitutional debate. Conservative publicists, committed to a restrictive view of federal power, insisted that no departure from prewar constitutional norms was permissible, despite the wartime emergency. Former Supreme Court Justice BENJAMIN R. CURTIS charged in *Executive Power* (1862) that President ABRAHAM LINCOLN had acted illegally in authorizing the military to arrest and imprison suspected disloyal civilians in areas removed from a war zone. Joel Parker's *The War Powers of Congress, and of the President* (1863) denounced the EMANCIPATION PROCLAMATION and related CONFISCATION ACTS for impairing property rights and revolutionizing federal–state relations.

A rival group of Lincolnian pragmatists defended the actions of federal authorities by appealing to an organic theory of constitutional development. Evolving national values and practices had shaped the Constitution far more than abstract legal rules, asserted FRANCIS LIEBER in *What Is Our Constitution—League, Pact, or Government?* (1861). The Founding Fathers had not anticipated the problem of secession; therefore, the Lincoln administration might, in conformity with natural law principles, take whatever measures it deemed necessary to preserve the nation. Sidney George Fisher's *The Trial of the Constitution* (1862) discovered new sources of federal power in the doctrine of popular sovereignty and other unwritten democratic dogmas. Charging that adherence to the checks and balances of the formal Constitution had immobilized the government in practice, Fisher urged Congress to create a new constitutional tradition by transforming itself into an American parliament immediately responsive to the popular will. William Whiting, solicitor of the War Department, contended that existent constitutional provisions authorized the federal government to pursue almost any wartime policy it chose. In *The War Powers of the President and the Legislative Powers of Congress in Relation to Rebellion, Treason, and Slavery* (1862), Whiting looked to the GENERAL WELFARE CLAUSE and other statements of broad national purpose to legitimize controversial Union measures.

The leading commentators of the late nineteenth century carried forward an organic view of the Constitution, but linked it to a laissez-faire ideology that sharply restrained the exercise of governmental power at all levels. Influenced by the conservative Darwinism of Herbert Spencer and William Graham Sumner, these economic libertarians feared legislative innovation and called upon the judiciary to preserve the fundamental economic rights of the individual against arbitrary state action. In *A Treatise on the Constitutional Limitations Which Rest upon the Legislative Power of the States of the American Union* (1868), THOMAS MCINTYRE COOLEY argued that a libertarian tradition stretching back to MAGNA CARTA protected private property from harmful regulation, even in the absence of specific constitutional guarantees. By appealing to these historic liberties, Cooley sought to broaden the scope of the DUE PROCESS clause, transforming it into a substantive restraint upon economic legislation. JOHN FORREST DILLON's *A Treatise on Municipal Corporations* (1872) discovered implied limits to the taxing power. Taxes could only be levied for a PUBLIC PURPOSE, Dillon maintained, and could not benefit one social class at the expense of another. CHRISTOPHER G. TIEDEMAN took an equally restrictive view of state and federal POLICE POWER in *A Treatise on the Limitations of Police Power in the United States* (1886), condemning usury laws and efforts to control wages and prices.

In the area of civil rights, commentators opposed "paternalistic" legislation and insisted that the Civil War had not destroyed the traditional division of power between the nation and the states. Amendments must conform to the general principles underlying the Constitution, asserted John Norton Pomeroy in *An Introduction to the Constitutional Law of the United States* (1868); and these principles included FEDERALISM, as defined by the Founding Fathers. Despite the broad language of the FOURTEENTH AMENDMENT, therefore, Congress lacked power to remedy most civil rights violations, which remained subject to state control. JOHN RANDOLPH

TUCKER's *The Constitution of the United States* (1899) warned that federal attacks on customary racial practices in the South would undermine local institutions and create a dangerous centralization of power in the national government. The racist assumptions shared by most libertarians surfaced clearly in John Ordronaux's *Constitutional Legislation in the United States* (1891). Noting that national progress depended upon "race instincts," Ordronaux suggested that blacks, Orientals, and other non-Aryans were unfit for the full responsibilities of democratic CITIZENSHIP.

Constitutional historians of the late nineteenth century used a Darwinian model of struggle and survival to explain the rise of the American nation. HERMANN VON HOLST, the first scholar to make systematic use of the records of congressional debates, combined antislavery moralism with a laissez-faire attitude toward northern business in his ponderous *Constitutional and Political History of the United States* (1876–1892). Equally moralistic and libertarian was JAMES SCHOULER's *History of the United States under the Constitution* (1880–1913). In the growth of republican institutions and the triumph of Union arms Schouler discerned the unfolding of a divine plan. From a Social Darwinist perspective, William A. Dunning's *The Constitution of the United States in Civil War and Reconstruction, 1860–1867* (1885) and JOHN W. BURGESS's *Reconstruction and the Constitution, 1866–1876* (1902) criticized federal policymakers for enfranchising blacks at the expense of their Anglo-Saxon superiors.

In its mature form libertarian theory created a twilight zone on the borders of the federal system, within which neither the national government not the states could act. While the TENTH AMENDMENT prevented Congress from regulating local economic activities, state legislatures found their police powers circumscribed by the restrictive principles defined by Cooley and his associates. These extraconstitutional restraints also limited the federal government when it sought to exercise its express powers over taxation and commerce. Twentieth-century economic and racial conservatives have continued to defend the libertarian viewpoint and to protest the expansion of federal regulatory power. In *Neither Purse Nor Sword* (1936), James M. Beck and Merle Thorpe condemned early New Deal legislation for violating property rights and invading the reserved powers of the states. Charles J. Bloch's *States' Rights—The Law of the Land* (1958), written in the aftermath of the *Brown* decision, charged that the VINSON COURT and WARREN COURT had subverted the meaning of the Fourteenth Amendment in civil rights cases, and called upon Congress to revitalize the Tenth Amendment, "the cornerstone of the Republic."

As the excesses of a period of industrial growth threatened the welfare of workers and consumers, however, other commentators condemned the laissez-faire model of constitutionalism as archaic and unsuited to the needs of a modern democracy. Impressed by the empiricism of the emerging social sciences, these democratic instrumentalists approached constitutional questions from a pragmatic and reformist perspective. Although they did not deny the existence of fundamental principles, they argued that these principles needed to be adapted to changing environmental conditions. Through intelligent social planning, they maintained, federal and state lawmakers might control an expanding economy in accordance with the popular will.

Mechanistic eighteenth-century concepts, such as SEPARATION OF POWERS, impaired the efficiency of modern government, charged WOODROW WILSON in *Congressional Government* (1885) and *Constitutional Government in the United States* (1908). Constitutional grants of power to the national government established only "general lines of definition," he added, and should be broadly construed by the courts in response to developing societal needs. In a similar vein, WESTEL W. WILLOUGHBY's *The Constitutional Law of the United States* (1910) and FRANK J. GOODNOW's *Social Reform and the Constitution* (1911) criticized judges for obstructing progressive reforms through their continued adherence to laissez-faire idealism.

The advent of the welfare state in the 1930s magnified disagreements between libertarians and instrumentalists, and provoked a major confrontation between President FRANKLIN D. ROOSEVELT and the Supreme Court. EDWARD S. CORWIN, the most influential constitutional commentator of the time, applauded the programs of the early New Deal for establishing a new COOPERATIVE FEDERALISM. In *The Twilight of the Supreme Court* (1934), Corwin urged the Justices to uphold legislative policymaking in economic matters, and pointed to the nationalistic decisions of John Marshall as appropriate precedents. When judicial intransigence persisted, according to Attorney General ROBERT H. JACKSON in *The Struggle for Judicial Supremacy* (1941), the administration adopted a court-packing plan as the only apparent means of restoring the full constitutional powers of the national government. Although the plan failed, a majority of Justices began to redefine congressional power in more liberal terms. Corwin welcomed the Court's belated acceptance of sweeping federal regulation in *Constitutional Revolution, Ltd.* (1941), and correctly predicted that the Justices would thereafter focus their review power on protection of CIVIL LIBERTIES and the rights of minorities.

Instrumentalist historians tended to seek the causes of constitutional change in underlying social and economic developments. CHARLES A. BEARD's pathbreaking study, *An Economic Interpretation of the Constitution of the United States* (1913), encouraged Progressive reformers by demythologizing the work of the Philadelphia Convention. Using previously neglected Treasury and census records, Beard presented the Founding Fathers as a conspiratorial elite who had devised an undemocratic Constitution to protect their property from the attacks of popular legislative majorities. In *American Constitutional Development* (1943) CARL BRENT SWISHER drew upon other nontraditional sources to explain, and justify, the emergence of the positive state. With comparable erudition WILLIAM W. CROSSKEY's *Politics and the Constitution in the History of the United States* (1953) used linguistic analysis to demonstrate the legitimacy of New Deal regulatory measures. After an exhaustive inquiry into the eighteenth-century meaning of "commerce" and other key words, Crosskey concluded that the Framers had intended to create a unitary, centralized system in which "the American people could, through Congress, deal with any subject they wished, on a simple, straightforward, nation-wide basis."

Although the instrumentalists emphasized the need to adapt the Constitution to changing socioeconomic conditions, they remained committed to the RULE OF LAW and acknowledged the binding force of constitutional norms. This moderate position failed to satisfy a small group of radical empiricists, who argued that written codes were meaningless in themselves and merely served to rationalize the political decisions of legislators and judges. "The language of the Constitution is immaterial since it represents current myths and folklore rather than rules," asserted THURMAN W. ARNOLD in *The Folklore of Capitalism* (1937). "Out of it are spun the contradictory ideals of governmental morality." Howard L. McBain's *The Living Constitution: A Consideration of the Realities and Legends of Our Fundamental Law* (1927) similarly contended that law had no life of its own, but depended for its substance on the unpredictable actions of men. Because the American people believed the fiction of a government of law, they had grown politically apathetic, charged J. ALLEN SMITH in *The Growth and Decadence of Constitutional Government* (1930). Although constitutionalism had been designed to limit arbitrary power, he noted, it protected an irresponsible governing elite from popular scrutiny and control.

The empiricists were more successful in diagnosing ills than in prescribing remedies. Because they stressed the determining influence of ideology and personality upon decision making, they could find no satisfactory way to limit the discretionary power of public officials. The scope of administrative discretion must necessarily broaden as society grows more complex, contended William B. Munro in *The Invisible Government* (1928). He welcomed the trend, which promised to give government agencies greater flexibility in dealing with contemporary problems. Yet unrestrained power might also encourage irresponsible behavior, such as judges so often displayed in reviewing legislative measures. Both LOUIS B. BOUDIN's *Government by Judiciary* (1932) and Fred Rodell's *Nine Men: A Political History of the Supreme Court of the United States from 1790 to 1955* (1955) reduced jurisprudence to politics, and charged that judges wrote their conservative policy preferences into law under the guise of legal principles. The only remedy they could suggest, however, was the appointment to the bench of liberals who would promote the public welfare in a more enlightened, albeit equally subjective, fashion.

During the past quarter-century commentators, preeminently ALEX-ANDER M. BICKEL, have continued to debate the nature and scope of JUDICIAL REVIEW, in the context of the Supreme Court's enlarged role as guardian of individual and minority rights. The timely aspects of such recent studies attest to the constructive role that commentators have historically played in the shaping of American constitutional law. Responsive to changing trends in social and political thought, they have often helped to redefine and clarify the terms of constitutional discourse. As Corwin once quipped, "If judges make law, so do commentators."

Bibliography

BAUER, ELIZABETH K.   1952   *Commentaries on the Constitution, 1790–1860.* New York: Columbia University Press.

BELZ, HERMAN   1971   The Realist Critique of Constitutionalism in the Era of Reform. *American Journal of Legal History* 15:288–306.

HYMAN, HAROLD M.   1973   *A More Perfect Union: The Impact of the Civil War and Reconstruction on the Constitution.* New York: Knopf.

KONEFSKY, ALFRED S.   1981   Men of Great and Little Faith: Generations of Constitutional Scholars. *Buffalo Law Review* 30:365–384.

LARSEN, CHARLES E.   1959   Nationalism and States' Rights in Commentaries on the Constitution after the Civil War. *American Journal of Legal History* 3:360–369.

MURPHY, PAUL L.   1963   Time to Reclaim: The Current Challenge of American Constitutional History. *American Historical Review* 69:64–79.

NEWTON, ROBERT E.   1965   Edward S. Corwin and American Constitutional Law. *Journal of Public Law* 14:198–212.

LEGAL REALISM

Wilfrid E. Rumble

Legal realism was the most significant movement that emerged within American jurisprudence during the 1920s and 1930s. Numerous factors conditioned this development, including pragmatism, SOCIOLOGICAL JURISPRUDENCE, and certain ideas of Justice OLIVER WENDELL HOLMES. The legal realists were not, however, an organized or highly unified group of thinkers. Their concepts had diverse sources, their work branched out in many directions, and their responses to particular issues often varied. The substantial differences between Judge JEROME N. FRANK and Karl N. Llewellyn illustrate these tendencies. Even so, these men and the other realists shared a number of distinctive attitudes and ideas.

The term "legal realism" signifies the basic thrust of the movement, which was to uncover and to explain legal realities. This effort reflects the allegation that some of the most cherished beliefs of lawyers are myths or fictions. The major purpose of the realists' provocative criticisms of these beliefs was not, however, to undermine the American legal system. Rather, it was to facilitate development of an accurate understanding of the nature, interpretation, operation, and effects of law. The realists insisted that achievement of this goal was essential for intelligent reform of legal rules, doctrines, and practices.

This outlook contributed to the realists' intense dissatisfaction with prevailing modes of legal education and scholarship. Both were under the spell of the case method pioneered by Christopher Columbus Langdell, the influential dean of the Harvard Law School from 1870 to 1895. He conceived of legal science as a small number of fundamental principles derived from study of relatively few cases. This conception was anathema to the realists, most of whom taught at leading American law schools. Their objective was to reform and to supplement, however, rather than to discard, the case method. The changes they advocated included focus on the *behavior* of judges and other officials, on their actual *decisions* rather than broad precepts. This emphasis was essential for the understanding of "real" instead of mere "paper" rules. The realists also urged the broadening of legal education to embrace not only the law on the books but also its administration and social impact. The development of this approach required a much closer integration of law and the social sciences than was traditional.

Some of these ideas were an outgrowth of major themes of ROSCOE

POUND's sociological jurisprudence. Still, the realists tended to develop criticisms of legal orthodoxies more radical than Pound's. This tendency is apparent from both the fact-skepticism of Judge Frank and the rule-skepticism of virtually all of the realists. The first of these doctrines stresses the difficulty of predicting findings of fact by judges or jurors, while the second emphasizes the limitations of legal rules. Rule-skepticism takes various forms, one of which is the conception of law as the past or future decisions of judges or other officials. Legal rules are descriptive or predictive rather than prescriptive generalizations about their behavior. This idea stems from Justice Holmes's predictive conception of law, which is one reason for the large shadow he cast over the realist movement.

Rule-skepticism also signifies distrust of the assumption that traditional legal rules or principles are the most influential determinant of judicial decisions. Numerous considerations explain this distrust, the degree of which varied among the realists. The most important factors were: a conviction of the possibility of widely different interpretations of established legal rules and principles; a belief in the existence of competing precedents, each of which could justify conflicting decisions in most cases; an awareness of the ambiguity inherent in legal language; a perception of the rapidity of socioeconomic change; and a study of the teachings of modern psychology. This last factor also influenced the realists' critique of judicial opinions. They attacked the syllogistic reasoning of judges on the ground that it failed to explain their choice of premises, which was all-important. This failure meant that opinions were often misleading rationalizations of decisions, the real reasons for which were unstated.

Rule-skepticism is the basis of some of the most important ideas of the legal realists. Their rejection of the conventional belief that judges do or should interpret rather than make law is a significant example. That belief is untenable because judicial legislation is unavoidable. Judges frequently must choose between competing decisions or interpretations, each of which is consistent with at least some precedents, rules, or principles. Although these generalizations limit judicial freedom, judges retain a substantial amount of room to maneuver.

This analysis underlies the realists' pragmatic approach to the evaluation of law, which emphasizes its practical results or effects. Rule-skepticism also influenced their de-emphasis of legal doctrine for the purpose of explaining and predicting judicial decisions. Instead, the realists stressed the importance of such factors as the personality, attitudes, or policies of judges. A similar emphasis characterized the behavioral jurisprudence developed largely by political scientists after World War II.

Although most of the realists did not specialize in constitutional law, their ideas facilitate understanding of the decisions of the Supreme

Court. The Justices frequently must choose between conflicting interpretations of the Constitution, each of which has some legal basis. Their choices depend most basically upon their values, which may vary among Justices and may change over time. These variations help to explain disagreements among the Justices as well as changes in constitutional doctrine. Realism was also a formative influence on the legal philosophy of Justice WILLIAM O. DOUGLAS.

Despite the influence of the realists on American legal thought, the reaction to their ideas has not been uniform. In fact, large numbers of lawyers expressed varying degrees of dissatisfaction with the realist movement from its inception. If some of the concepts of the realists are unsatisfactory, others are enduring contributions to the study of law and the judicial process. Legal realism therefore warrants close scrutiny by students of constitutional law and judicial behavior.

Bibliography

FRANK, JEROME 1949 *Law and the Modern Mind.* New York: Coward-McCann.
LLEWELLYN, KARL N. 1962 *Jurisprudence: Realism in Theory and Practice.* Chicago: University of Chicago Press.
RUMBLE, WILFRID E. 1968 *American Legal Realism: Skepticism, Reform, and the Judicial Process.* Ithaca, N.Y.: Cornell University Press.
TWINING, WILLIAM 1973 *Karl Llewellyn and the Realist Movement.* London: Weidenfeld & Nicolson.

The Jurisdiction of the Federal Courts

JUDICIAL POWER OF THE UNITED STATES

David P. Currie

"[T]he legislative, executive, and judicial powers, of every well constructed government," said JOHN MARSHALL in OSBORN v. BANK OF THE UNITED STATES (1824), "are co-extensive with each other; . . . [t]he executive department may constitutionally execute every law which the Legislature may constitutionally make, and the judicial department may receive from the legislature the power of construing every such law." The ARTICLES OF CONFEDERATION fell far short of this model. Not only was there no federal executive with authority to enforce congressional measures against individuals, but, apart from a cumbersome procedure for resolving interstate disputes, Congress was authorized to establish courts only for the trial of crimes committed at sea and for the determination of "appeals in all cases of captures." The remedy for these shortcomings was one of the major accomplishments of the Constitution adopted in 1789. As Article II gave the country a President with the obligation to "take care that the Laws be faithfully executed," Article III provided for a system of federal courts that more than satisfied Marshall's conditions for a "well constructed government."

Article III consists of three brief sections. The first describes the tribunals that are to exercise federal judicial power and prescribes the tenure and compensation of their judges. The second lists the types of disputes that may be entrusted to federal courts, specifies which of these matters are to be determined by the SUPREME COURT in the first instance, and guarantees TRIAL BY JURY in criminal cases. The third defines and limits the crime of TREASON.

"The judicial Power of the United States," Article III declares, "shall be vested in one Supreme Court, and in such inferior Courts as the Congress may from time to time ordain and establish." The text itself indicates that the Supreme Court was the only tribunal the Constitution required to be established, and the debates of the CONSTITUTIONAL CONVENTION demonstrate that the latter words embodied a deliberate compromise.

In fact, however, Congress created additional courts at the very beginning, in the JUDICIARY ACT OF 1789. Since 1911 the basic system has consisted of the UNITED STATES DISTRICT COURTS—at least one in every state—in which most cases are first tried; a number of regional appellate courts now called the UNITED STATES COURTS OF APPEALS; and the Supreme Court itself, which functions largely as a court of last resort. From time to time, moreover, Congress has created specialized courts with JURISDICTION to determine controversies involving relatively limited subjects. All this lies well within Congress's broad discretion under Article III to determine what lower courts to create and how to allocate judicial business among them. Specialization at the highest level, however, seems precluded; Congress can no more divide the powers of "one Supreme Court" among two or more bodies than abolish it altogether.

"The Judges, both of the supreme and inferior Courts," section 1 continues, "shall hold their Offices during GOOD BEHAVIOUR and shall, at stated Times, receive for their Services, a Compensation, which shall not be diminished during their Continuance in Office." Under the second section of Article II the judges have always been appointed by the President subject to Senate confirmation; under the fourth section of that article they may be removed from office on IMPEACHMENT and conviction of "Treason, Bribery, or other high Crimes and Misdemeanors." The central purpose of the tenure and salary provisions, as ALEXANDER HAMILTON explained in THE FEDERALIST #78, was to assure judicial independence.

The Supreme Court has repeatedly enforced the tenure and salary provisions. In Ex PARTE MILLIGAN (1867), for example, the Court held even the Civil War no excuse for submitting civilians to military trials in states where the civil courts were open, and in *O'Donoghue v. United States* (1933), it held that the Great Depression did not justify reducing judicial salaries.

On a number of occasions, however, the Court has permitted matters within the judicial power to be determined by LEGISLATIVE COURTS whose judges do not possess tenure and salary guarantees. State courts may decide Article III cases, as the Framers of the Constitution clearly contemplated; the tenure and salary provisions do not apply to the TERRITORIES or to the DISTRICT OF COLUMBIA, where there is no SEPARATION OF POWERS requirement; Article III did not abolish the traditional COURT-MARTIAL for military offenses; federal magistrates may make initial decisions in Article III cases provided they are subject to unlimited reexamination by tenured judges.

Early in the twentieth century the Supreme Court appeared to give judicial blessing to the numerous quasi-judicial bodies that have grown up since the creation of the Interstate Commerce Commission in 1887, although scholars have debated heatedly whether there is any satisfactory way to distinguish them from the nontenured trial courts plainly forbidden by Article III. That these developments did not mean the effective end of the tenure and salary requirements, however, was made clear in 1982, when the Court in NORTHERN PIPE LINE CONSTRUCTION CO. v. MARATHON PIPE LINE CO. invalidated a statute empowering judges with temporary commissions to exercise virtually the entire jurisdiction of the district courts in BANKRUPTCY cases. Where to draw this line promises to be a continuing problem.

The power to be vested in federal courts is the "judicial power," and the various categories of matters that fall within this power are all described as CASES OR CONTROVERSIES—"Cases," for example, "arising under this Constitution," and "Controversies to which the United States shall be a Party." From the beginning the Supreme Court has taken this language as a limitation: federal courts may not resolve anything but "cases" and "controversies," and those terms embrace only judicial functions.

Thus, for example, when President GEORGE WASHINGTON asked the Justices for legal advice respecting the United States' neutrality during hostilities between England and France, they declined to act "extra-judicially"; and when Congress directed them to advise the war secretary concerning veterans' pensions, five Justices sitting on circuit refused, saying the authority conferred was "not of a judicial nature" (HAYBURN'S CASE, 1792). Washington's request for advice did not begin to resemble the ordinary lawsuit, but later decisions have invoked the "case" or "controversy" limitation to exclude federal court consideration of matters far less remote from the normal judicial function. The essential requirement, the Court has emphasized, is a live and actual dispute between adversary parties with a real stake in the outcome.

One dimension of this principle is the doctrine of RIPENESS or prematurity: the courts are not to give advice on the mere possibility that it might be of use in the future. Occasionally the Court has appeared to require a person to violate a law in order to test its constitutionality—causing one commentator to remark that "the only way to determine whether the subject is a mushroom or a toadstool, is to eat it." The DECLARATORY JUDGMENT ACT, passed to mitigate this hardship, has generally been applied to allow preenforcement challenges when the intentions of the parties are sufficiently firm, and it has been held consistent with the "Case" or "Controversy" requirement.

At the opposite end of the spectrum is the MOOTNESS doctrine, which ordinarily forbids litigation after death or other changed circumstances deprive the issue of any further impact on the parties. A series of debatable decisions essentially dating from *Moore v. Ogilvie* (1969), however, has relaxed the mootness DOCTRINE, especially in CLASS ACTIONS, so as to permit persons with no remaining interest to continue litigating issues deemed "capable of repetition, yet evading review."

The "case or controversy" requirement has also been held to forbid the decision of COLLUSIVE SUITS, and to preclude the courts from exercising the discretion of an administrator, as by reviewing de novo the decision to grant a broadcasting license. The most important remaining element of that requirement, however, is the constitutional dimension of the doctrine of STANDING to sue.

While standing has been aptly characterized as one of the most confused areas of federal law, its constitutional component was simply stated in *Warth v. Seldin* (1975): "[t]he Article III power exists only to redress or otherwise to protect against injury to the complaining party." Injury in this context is hardly self-defining, but it plainly requires something more than intellectual or emotional "interest in a problem." This principle puts under a serious cloud the periodic congressional attempts to authorize "any person" to obtain judicial relief against violations of environmental or other laws. On the other hand, other aspects of the standing doctrine are not of constitutional dimension and thus do not preclude Congress from conferring standing on anyone injured by governmental action.

One of the principal points of contention of the law of standing has been the right of federal taxpayers to challenge the constitutionality of federal spending programs. When a taxpayer attacked expenditures for maternal health on the ground that they exceeded the powers granted Congress by Article I, the Court in FROTHINGHAM V. MELLON (1923) found no standing: "the taxpayer's interest in the moneys of the treasury . . . is shared with millions of others, is comparatively minute and indeterminable, and the effect upon future taxation, of any payment out of the funds, so remote, fluctuating, and uncertain, that no basis is afforded for an appeal to the preventive powers of a court of EQUITY."

Although the apparent reference to equitable discretion made it uncertain that the Court was saying taxpayer suits were not "cases or controversies" within Article III, the remainder of the passage suggests that the taxpayer could not show the constitutionally required injury because it was uncertain that a victory would mean reduced taxes. Nevertheless, in FLAST V. COHEN (1968) the Court allowed a federal taxpayer to challenge expenditures for church-related education as an ESTABLISHMENT OF RELIGION in violation of the FIRST AMENDMENT. Unlike the taxpayer in *Frothingham*, who "was attempting to assert the States' interest in their legislative prerogatives," the plaintiff in *Flast* asserted "a federal taxpayer's interest in being free of taxing and spending in contravention of specific constitutional limitations," for one purpose of the establishment clause was to prevent taxation for religious ends. Whether the distinction was of constitutional scope the Court did not say; interestingly, the taxpayer opinions have tended to avoid entirely the traditional constitutional inquiry into the existence of an injury that will be redressed if the plaintiff's claim prevails.

Underlying the constitutional "case or controversy" limitation are a variety of policy concerns. The first group relates to reducing the risk of erroneous decisions. Concrete facts enable judges to understand the practical impact of their holdings; adverse parties help to assure that arguments on both sides will be considered; as argued by FELIX FRANKFURTER, "the ADVISORY OPINION deprives CONSTITUTIONAL INTERPRETATION of the judgment of the legislature upon facts." A second group of reasons focuses upon strengthening the Court's institutional position. Lawmaking by appointed judges is least difficult to reconcile with democratic principles when it is the inevitable by-product of the stock business of judging; the courts should not squander their power of moral suasion or multiply conflicts with other branches by deciding unnecessary legal questions. Third, and of considerable importance, is a concern for the separation of powers. The courts are not to exercise a general superintendence over the activities of the other branches.

The costs of the "case or controversy" limitation include the delay, uncertainty, and disruption incident to determining the constitutionality of legislation only in the course of subsequent litigation, and the danger that some legislative and executive actions may escape JUDICIAL REVIEW entirely. Whether the latter is cause for concern has much to do with one's perception of the function and importance of judicial review itself; it seems reasonable to expect that perception to influence the definition of a "case" or "controversy."

In addition to restricting federal courts to the decision of "cases" and "controversies" of a judicial nature, section 2 of Article III enumerates those categories of "cases" and "controversies" to which the "judicial Power shall extend." As the former limitation serves the interests of separating federal powers, the latter serves those of FEDERALISM. In accord with the spirit of the TENTH AMENDMENT the Supreme Court has held that Congress may not give the federal courts jurisdiction over disputes of types not listed in Article III. John Marshall set the tone in cutting down to constitutional size a statute providing for jurisdiction over cases involving ALIENS in HODGSON V. BOWERBANK in 1809: "Turn to the article of the constitution of the United States, for the statutes cannot extend the jurisdiction beyond the limits of the constitution."

Article III's provision that federal judicial power "shall extend to" certain classes of cases and controversies has generally been taken to mean that it shall embrace nothing else. From the text alone one might think it even more plain that federal courts *must* be given jurisdiction over all the matters listed, for section 1 commands that the federal judicial power "shall be vested" in federal courts. Indeed, Justice JOSEPH STORY suggested just such an interpretation in MARTIN V. HUNTER'S LESSEE in 1816. This conclusion, however, was unnecessary to the decision, contrary to the understanding of the First Congress, and inconsistent with both earlier and later decisions of the Supreme Court.

Article III, in other words, has been read to mean only that Congress may confer jurisdiction over the enumerated cases, not that it must do so. This arguably unnatural construction has been defended by reference to the limited list of controversies over which the Supreme Court has original jurisdiction, the explicit congressional power to make exceptions to the Supreme Court's appellate authority, and the compromise at the Constitutional Convention permitting Congress not to establish inferior courts at all.

This is not to say, however, that Congress has unfettered authority to deny the courts jurisdiction, for all powers of Congress are subject to limitations found elsewhere in the Constitution. A statute depriving the courts of authority to determine cases filed by members of a particular racial group, for instance, would be of highly doubtful vitality under the modern interpretation of the Fifth Amendment DUE PROCESS clause, and one part of Marshall's reasoning in MARBURY v. MADISON (1803) supports an argument that closing all federal and state courts to free-speech claims would defeat the substantive right itself. Proposals to remove entire categories of constitutional litigation from the ken of one or more federal courts often follow controversial judicial decisions. Out of respect for the tradition of CHECKS AND BALANCES, however, such bills are seldom enacted; we have so far been spared the constitutional trauma of determining the extent to which they may validly be adopted.

The cases and controversies within federal judicial power fall into two categories: those in which jurisdiction is based upon the nature of the dispute and those in which it is based upon the identity of the parties. In the first category are three kinds of disputes: those "arising under this Constitution, the Laws of the United States, and Treaties made, or which shall be made, under their Authority"; those "of ADMI-RALTY AND MARITIME JURISDICTION"; and those involving competing land claims "under Grants of different States." The provision last quoted is of minor importance; the second formed the staple business of the district courts throughout their early history; the first fulfills Marshall's condition for a "well constructed government" and is by any measure the most critical ingredient of federal jurisdiction today.

The provision for jurisdiction in cases arising under the Constitution and other federal laws has two essential purposes: to promote uniformity in the interpretation of federal law, and to assure the vindication of federal rights. The First Congress sought to accomplish the second of these goals by providing, in section 25 of the 1789 Judiciary Act, for Supreme Court review of state-court decisions denying federal rights; the additional uniformity attendant upon review of state decisions *uphold-ing* federal claims was not provided until 1914. In sustaining section 25, the opinion in *Martin v. Hunter's Lessee* demonstrated the difficulty of achieving Article III's purpose without Supreme Court review of state courts: while plaintiffs might be authorized to file federal claims directly in federal courts and defendants to remove state court actions to federal courts on the basis of federal defenses, it was not easy to see how a state court opposing removal "could. . . be compelled to relinquish the jurisdiction" without some federal court reviewing the state court decision.

Conversely, although Congress failed to give federal trial courts general jurisdiction of federal question cases until 1875, Marshall made clear as early as 1824, in *Osborn v. Bank of the United States*, that it had power to do so. Supreme Court review alone was no more an adequate protection for federal rights, Marshall argued, than was exclusive reliance on litigation beginning in federal trial courts. As the latter would leave claimants without remedy against a recalcitrant state court, the former would give a state tribunal the critical power to shape the factual record beyond assurance of federal appellate correction.

The *Osborn* opinion also settled that jurisdiction of a federal trial court over a case arising under federal law was not defeated by the presence of additional issues dependent upon state law. In a companion case, indeed, the Court upheld jurisdiction over a suit by the national bank on notes whose validity and interpretation were understood to depend in substantial part upon nonfederal law: it was enough that the plaintiff derived its existence and its right to contract from the act of Congress incorporating it. The courts have not followed this broad approach, however, in determining whether FEDERAL QUESTION JURISDIC-TION lies under general *statutory* provisions; when the federal ingredient of a claim is remote from the actual controversy, as in a dispute over ownership of land whose title is remotely derived from a federal land grant, the district courts lack statutory jurisdiction.

In the contract dispute discussed in *Osborn*, federal and state law were bound together in the resolution of a single claim; in such a case, as HENRY HART and Herbert Wechsler said, "a federal trial court would . . . be unable to function as a court at all" if its jurisdiction did not extend to state as well as federal matters. In the interest of "judicial economy," however, as the Supreme Court put it in *United Mine Workers v. Gibbs* (1966), jurisdiction over a case arising under federal law embraces not only a plaintiff's federal claim but also any claims under state law based on the same facts. This so-called PENDENT JURISDICTION doctrine, however, is inapplicable when the Supreme Court reviews a state court decision. With one exception, in such a case the Court may review only federal and not state questions, as the Court held in *Murdock v. Memphis* (1875); for to reverse a state court in the interpretation of its own law would be a major incursion into state prerogatives not required by the purposes for which Supreme Court review was provided.

A corollary of the *Murdock* principle is that a state court decision respecting state law often precludes the Supreme Court from reviewing even federal questions in the same case. If a state court concludes, for example, that a state law offends both federal and state constitutions, the Supreme Court cannot reverse the state law holding; thus, however it may decide the federal issue, it cannot alter the outcome of the case. This independent and ADEQUATE STATE GROUND for the state court decision means there is no longer a live case or controversy between the parties over the federal question. In light of this relation between state and federal issues, *Martin* itself announced the sole exception to the *Murdock* rule: when the state court has interpreted state law in such a way as to frustrate the federal right itself—as by holding that a contract allegedly impaired in violation of the CONTRACT CLAUSE never existed— a complete absence of power to review the state question would mean the Court's authority to protect federal rights "may be evaded at pleasure."

"The most bigoted idolizers of state authority," wrote Alexander Hamilton in *The Federalist* #80, "have not thus far shown a disposition to deny the National Judiciary the cognizance of maritime causes"; for such cases "so generally depend upon the law of nations, and so commonly affect the rights of foreigners, that they fall within the considerations which are relative to the public peace." Jurisdiction over what Article III refers to as "Cases of admiralty, and maritime Jurisdiction" has been vested by statute in the district courts since 1789. Today federal admiralty jurisdiction extends, as the Court stated in another context in *The Daniel Ball* (1871), to all waters forming part of "a continued highway over which commerce is or may be carried on with other states or foreign countries."

Not everything occurring on navigable waters, however, is a proper subject of admiralty jurisdiction; in denying jurisdiction of claims arising out of an airplane crash in Lake Erie, the Supreme Court made clear that the case must "bear a significant relationship to traditional maritime activity . . . involving navigation and commerce on navigable waters." Conversely, the relation of an activity to maritime concerns may bring it within admiralty cognizance even if it occurs on land. Marine insurance contracts, for example, are within the jurisdiction although both made and to be performed on land. Similarly, the Court has acquiesced in Congress's provision for jurisdiction over land damage caused by vessels on navigable waters.

Because an additional purpose of federal judicial power over maritime cases is understood to have been to provide a uniform law to govern the shipping industry, the Supreme Court also held in *Southern Pacific Company v. Jensen* (1917) that Article III empowers the federal courts to develop a "general maritime law" binding even on state courts, and that Congress may supplement this law with statutes under its authority to adopt laws "necessary and proper" to the powers of the courts. Indeed the Court has held that this aspect of the judicial power, like the legislative authority conferred by the commerce clause of Article I, has an implicit limiting effect upon state law. Not only does state law that contradicts federal law yield under the SUPREMACY CLAUSE, but, as the Court said in rejecting the application of a state workers' compensation law to long-shoremen in the case last cited, no state law is valid if it "interferes with the proper harmony and uniformity" of the general maritime law "in its international and interstate relations."

The remaining authorization of federal court jurisdiction protects parties whose fortunes the Framers were for various reasons unwilling to leave wholly at the mercy of state courts. Many of these categories involve government litigation: "Controversies to which the United States shall be a Party; . . . between two or more States; between a State and Citizens of another State, . . . and between a State, or the Citizens thereof, and foreign States, Citizens or Subjects." A federal forum for the national government itself protects against possible state hostility; federal jurisdiction over interstate conflicts provides not only a neutral forum but also a safeguard against what Hamilton in *The Federalist* #80 called "dissentions and private wars"; that "the union will undoubtedly be answerable to foreign powers, for the conduct of its members," was an additional reason for jurisdiction over disputes involving foreign countries as well as the related jurisdiction over "Cases affecting Ambassadors, other public Ministers and Consuls."

The most interesting issue concerning these provisions has been that of SOVEREIGN IMMUNITY. In CHISHOLM v. GEORGIA (1793), ignoring the assurances of prominent Framers like James Madison and Alexander Hamilton as well as the common law tradition that the king could not be sued without his consent, the Supreme Court relied largely on the text of Article III to hold that the power over "Controversies . . . between a State and Citizens of another State" included those in which the state was an unwilling defendant. Obviously, as the Justices pointed out, this was true of the parallel authority over "Controversies . . . between two or more States," and Justice JAMES WILSON added his understanding that the English tradition was a mere formality, since consent to sue was given as a matter of course.

Whether this decision was right or wrong as an original matter, within five years it was repudiated by adoption of the ELEVENTH AMEND-MENT, which provides that "[t]he Judicial power of the United States shall not be construed to extend to any suit in law or equity, commenced or prosecuted against one of the United States by Citizens or Subjects of any Foreign State." Notably, the amendment does not mention admiralty cases, suits by foreign countries, suits against a state by its own citizens under federal law, or suits against the United States. Nevertheless the Supreme Court, taking the amendment as casting doubt on the reasoning underlying *Chisholm,* has denied jurisdiction in all of these instances. The best explanation has been that, although not excepted by the amendment, they are outside the power conferred by Article III itself. One state may still sue another, however, and the United States may sue a state. The Court has found such jurisdiction "essential to the peace of the Union" and "inherent in the constitutional plan." Why this is not equally true of a suit by a state against the United States has never been satisfactorily explained.

At least since the 1824 decision in *Osborn v. Bank of the United States,* however, both the Eleventh Amendment and its related immunities have been construed to allow certain actions against state or federal officers even though the effect of the litigation is the same as if the government itself had been named defendant. The theoretical explanation that the officer cannot be acting for the state when he does what the Constitution forbids is inconsistent with the substantive conclusion, often reached in the same cases, that his action is attributable to the state for purposes of the FOURTEENTH AMENDMENT. A more principled explanation is that suits against officers are necessary if the Constitution is to be enforced at all; the response is that those who wrote the amendment could not have intended to allow it to be reduced to a hollow shell.

In any event, the *Osborn* exception has not been held to embrace all suits against government officers. At one time it was said generally that an officer could be prevented from acting but could not be ordered to take affirmative action such as paying off a government obligation, for if he was not acting for the state he had no authority to reach into its treasury. The simplicity of this distinction was shattered, however, by opinions acknowledging the availability of a WRIT OF MANDAMUS to compel an officer to perform a nondiscretionary duty. The more recent formulation in EDELMAN v. JORDAN (1974), which essentially distinguishes between prospective and retrospective relief, seems difficult to reconcile with the language of the Constitution, with its apparent purposes, or with the fiction created to support the *Osborn* rule.

Even when the government is itself a party, it may consent to be sued, and the books are filled with a confusing and incomplete array of statutes allowing suits against the United States. Some judges and scholars have argued that suits against consenting states are inconsistent with the language of the amendment, which declares them outside the judicial power; the Court's persuasive explanation has been that, like venue and personal jurisdiction, immunity is a privilege waivable by the party it protects (*Clark v. Barnard,* 1883). More debatable was the Court's decision in *Parden v. Terminal Railway* (1964) that a state had "waived" its immunity by operating a railroad after passage of a federal statute making "every" interstate railway liable for injuries to its employees; in *Edelman v. Jordan,* retreating from this conclusion, the Court emphasized that "[c]onstructive consent is not a doctrine commonly associated with the surrender of constitutional rights." Still later, however, in FITZPATRICK V. BITZER (1976) the Court held that Congress had power to override a state's immunity in legislating to enforce the Fourteenth Amendment, although it has never suggested that that amendment allowed Congress to ignore other constitutional limitations, such as the BILL OF RIGHTS.

The two remaining categories of disputes within federal judicial power are "controversies . . . between Citizens of different States" and between state citizens and "Citizens or Subjects" of "foreign States." Once again the reasons for federal jurisdiction are generally said to be the avoidance of state-court bias and of interstate or international friction. In contrast not only to the admiralty cases but also to those between states, federal jurisdiction based solely on the diverse citizenship of the parties does not carry with it authority to make substantive law. Absent a federal statute, the Court held in ERIE RAILROAD V. TOMPKINS (1938), "the law to be applied . . . is the law of the State." Later cases such as *Textile Workers Union v. Lincoln Mills* (1957) have qualified the effect though not the principle of this decision by finding in silent statutes implicit authorization to the federal courts to make law. An occasional decision has upheld FEDERAL COMMON LAW, without the pretense of statutory authority, on matters mysteriously found to be "intrinsically federal"; an example was the Court's refusal in *Banco Nacional de Cuba v. Sabbatino* (1964) to look behind official acts of foreign governments. (See ACT OF STATE DOCTRINE.)

In early decisions the Supreme Court took a narrow view of what constituted a controversy between citizens of different states for purposes of the statute implementing this provision of Article III. More recently, however, the Court has generously interpreted the power of Congress to confer DIVERSITY JURISDICTION on the federal courts. And as early as the mid-nineteenth century, recognizing that corporations can be the beneficiaries or victims of state court prejudice without regard to the citizenship of those who compose them, the Court effectively began to treat corporations as citizens by employing the transparent fiction of conclusively presuming that the individuals whose citizenship was determinative were citizens of the state of incorporation.

The best known decision involving the diversity jurisdiction was DRED SCOTT V. SANDFORD (1857), in which three Justices took the position that a black American descended from slaves could never be a state citizen for diversity purposes because he could not be a citizen of the United States. Questionable enough at the time, this conclusion was repudiated by the Fourteenth Amendment's provision that all persons born in this country are citizens of the United States "and of the state wherein they reside." Nevertheless the courts have held that only American citizens are "Citizens of . . . States" within Article III, and conversely that only foreign nationals are "Citizens or Subjects" of "foreign States."

"In all Cases involving Ambassadors, other public Ministers and Consuls, and those in which a state shall be Party," Article III, Section 2 provides, "the supreme Court shall have ORIGINAL JURISDICTION. In all the other Cases before mentioned, the supreme Court shall have APPELLATE JURISDICTION, both as to Law and Fact, with such Exceptions, and under such Regulations as the Congress shall make."

Original jurisdiction is the power to determine a dispute in the first instance; appellate jurisdiction, the power to review a decision already made. *Marbury v. Madison* (1803) held that Congress had no power to give the Supreme Court original jurisdiction of a case to which neither a diplomat nor a state was a party; a contrary result, Chief Justice Marshall argued, would make the constitutional distribution between original and appellate jurisdiction "mere surplusage." This reasoning is not especially convincing, and the converse is not true; in COHENS v. VIRGINIA in 1821 Marshall himself conceded that Congress could give the Court appellate jurisdiction over cases for which Article III provided original jurisdiction. *Cohens* also held that the Supreme Court had original authority not over all Article III cases in which a state happened to be a party but only over those "in which jurisdiction is given, because a state is a party," and thus not over a federal question case between a state and one of its own citizens. Inconsistently, however, the Court allowed the United States to sue a State in the Supreme Court in *United States v. Texas* (1892).

Marbury's implicit conclusion that the exceptions clause quoted above does not allow Congress to tamper with the original jurisdiction strongly suggests that the enumeration of original cases is a minimum as well as a maximum, and the Court has described as "extremely doubtful" the proposition that Congress may deprive it of original power over state or diplomat cases; yet the Court has concluded that it has discretion not to entertain cases within its original jurisdiction.

Unlike the original jurisdiction provision, that giving the Court appellate authority in "all the other" Article III cases contains an explicit escape valve: "with such Exceptions . . . as the Congress shall make." In *The Federalist* #81, Hamilton explained that this clause permitted Congress to limit review of facts decided by juries, but he did not say this was its sole objective. From the beginning Congress has denied the Court jurisdiction over entire classes of controversies within the constitutional reach of appellate power—such as federal criminal cases, most of which were excluded from appellate cognizance for many years even if constitutional issues were presented. The Court itself accepted this particular limitation as early as *United States v. More* (1805), without questioning its constitutionality. Moreover, when Congress repealed a statute under which a pending case attacking the Reconstruction Act had been filed, the Court in EX PARTE McCARDLE (1869) meekly dismissed the case, observing that "the power to make exceptions to the appellate jurisdiction of this court is given by express words."

As the *McCardle* opinion noted, however, other avenues remained available for taking similar cases to the Supreme Court, and three years later the Court made clear in *United States v. Klein* (1872) that Congress could not under the guise of limiting jurisdiction effectively dictate the result of a case by directing dismissal if the Court should find for the plaintiff. Respected commentators have contended that the Supreme Court must retain appellate authority over certain constitutional questions, arguing that the exceptions clause cannot have been intended, in Henry Hart's words, to "destroy the essential role of the Supreme Court in the constitutional plan." The persuasiveness of this position depends on one's perceptions of the function of judicial review. (See JUDICIAL SYSTEM.)

In order for the Court in *Marbury v. Madison* to dismiss an action that it found Congress had authorized, it had first to conclude that it had the right to refuse to obey an unconstitutional act of Congress. Marshall's argument that this power was "essentially attached to a written constitution" is contradicted by much European experience; and his assertion that choosing between the Constitution and a statute was an inescapable aspect of deciding cases begged the question, for the Constitution might have required the courts to accept Congress's determination that a statute was valid. For the same reason one may object to his reliance on Article VI's requirement that judges swear to support the Constitution: one does not offend that oath by enforcing an unconstitutional statute if that is what the Constitution requires.

The SUPREMACY CLAUSE of Article VI is no better support; the contrasting reference to "Treaties made, or which shall be made" in the same clause strongly suggests that the phrase "laws . . . which shall be made in Pursuance of" the Constitution, also invoked by Marshall, was meant to deny supremacy to acts adopted under the Articles of Confederation, not to those that were invalid. Most promising of the provisions brought forward in *Marbury* was Article III's extension of judicial power to "Cases . . . arising under this Constitution"; as Marshall said, it could scarcely have been "the intention of those who gave this power, to say that in using it the constitution should not be looked into." Yet even here the case is not airtight. For while Article III provides for jurisdiction in constitutional cases, it is Article VI that prescribes the force to be given the Constitution; and while the latter article plainly gives the Constitution precedence over conflicting *state* laws, it appears to place *federal* statutes on a par with the Constitution itself.

Nevertheless the *Marbury* decision should be regarded as neither a surprise nor a usurpation. Though Marshall did not say so, judicial review had a substantial history before *Marbury,* and despite occasional scholarly denials it seems clear that most of the Framers expected that the courts would refuse to enforce unconstitutional acts of Congress. Moreover, there is force to Marshall's argument that a denial of this power would effectively undermine the express written limitations on congressional power; the natural reluctance to assume that the Framers meant to leave the fox in charge of the chickens lends credence to the conclusion that judicial review is implicit in the power to decide constitutional cases or in the substantive constitutional limitations themselves.

In fact the *Marbury* opinion espouses two distinct theories of judicial review that have opposite implications for a number of related issues, some of which have been discussed above. If, as Marshall at one point seemed to suggest, judicial review is only an incidental by-product of the need to resolve pending cases, it is no cause for constitutional concern if Congress eliminates the Supreme Court's jurisdiction over First Amendment cases, or if no one has standing to attack a federal spending program. If, on the other hand, as argued elsewhere in *Marbury,* judicial review is essential to a plan of constitutional checks and balances, one may take a more restrictive view of Congress's power to make exceptions to the appellate jurisdiction, and perhaps a broader view of what constitutes a case or controversy as well.

Dissenting from the assertion of judicial authority over legislative reapportionment cases in BAKER v. CARR (1962), Justice Felix Frankfurter argued for a broad exception to judicial review of both federal and state actions: even unconstitutional acts could not be set aside if they presented POLITICAL QUESTIONS. Some have attempted to trace this notion to *Marbury* itself, where the Court did say that "[q]uestions in their nature political" were beyond judicial ken. The context suggests, however, that Marshall meant only that the Court would respect actions taken by other branches of government within their legitimate authority, and Louis Henkin has shown that most later decisions using "political question" language can be so explained.

The Court itself, however, spoke in *Baker* of a general "political question" doctrine preventing decision of the merits when, among other things, there was "a lack of judicially discoverable and manageable standards for resolving" a "political" issue. A number of lower courts relied on such a doctrine in refusing to decide the legality of the VIETNAM WAR. While the doctrine as so conceived appears at cross-purposes with the checks-and-balances aspect of *Marbury,* nothing in that decision bars a finding that a particular constitutional provision either gives absolute discretion to a nonjudicial branch (such as the power to recognize foreign governments) or makes an exception to Article III's grant of the judicial power itself (as, arguably, in the case of impeachment).

In most respects, then, Article III amply satisfies Marshall's conditions for a "well constructed government." Though the governmental immunities associated with the Eleventh Amendment may seem anachronistic today, unsympathetic judicial interpretation has blunted their interference with the enforcement of federal law. Decisions since the 1950s have generally rejected Justice Frankfurter's broad conception of the political question. Thus with rare exceptions the federal judiciary, as Marshall insisted, may be given authority to construe every federal law; and the extension of judicial power to controversies between citizens of different states means that the federal courts may often be given power to apply state law as well. Though increased mobility has led to serious efforts to repeal the statutory basis for the diversity jurisdiction, it served an important function in the past and conceivably may become more important in the future. Moreover, the Framers were farsighted enough to assure federal judges the independence necessary to do their appointed job. The weakest point in the system is the arguable authority of Congress to take away all or a substantial part of the Supreme Court's appellate power in constitutional cases; for such an authority undermines other elements of the system of checks and balances that the Framers so carefully constructed.

Bibliography

BICKEL, ALEXANDER   1962   *The Least Dangerous Branch*. Pages 111–199. Indianapolis: Bobbs-Merrill.

BORCHARD, EDWIN   1928   *Hearings on H.R. 5623 before the Subcommittee of the Senate Committee on the Judiciary*. 70th Cong., 1st Sess., pp. 75–76.

FARRAND, MAX (ED.)   1911   *Records of the Federal Convention of 1787*. Vol. 1, pp. 119–129. New Haven, Conn.: Yale University Press.

HART, HENRY and WECHSLER, HERBERT   1973   *The Federal Courts and the Federal System*. Pages 309–418, 833–1103. Mineola, N.Y.: Foundation Press.

HENKIN, LOUIS   1976   Is There a "Political Question" Doctrine? *Yale Law Journal* 85:597–625.

JURISDICTION

Stephen C. Yeazell

Jurisdiction is a magical and protean term. In American law it refers to the power of legislatures, the competence of courts to deal with certain types of cases, the allocation of cases between state and federal courts, the power of both state and federal courts over defendants who have only peripheral attachments to the locale of the court, and the territory in which a unit of government exercises its power. Not surprisingly the word shifts its meanings as it moves among these quite different tasks.

The term's confusing spread of meanings has its roots in the English medieval experience. What modern observers would think of as political power accompanied the grant of property; the landlord was lord of more than land; he exercised powers of justice over the people who tilled that soil. Yet that jurisdiction also had limits: above it stood the powers of the monarch, who at least in theory had the power and responsibility to see that the lords rendered justice. Thus the word emerged from the Middle Ages carrying several meanings: the power to make law, the power to adjudicate cases, and, loosely, the territory within which that power was exercised.

We use all three senses today. We speak, for example, of legislative jurisdiction, meaning legislative power, generally allocated by state and federal constitutions. Thus the earliest opinion of the Supreme Court applying the limits of SUBSTANTIVE DUE PROCESS to state economic regulation, in ALLEGEYER V. LOUISIANA (1897), said that the state had exceeded its territorial jurisdiction. Territorial considerations aside, any decision holding a law unconstitutional can be described as a holding that the legislative body has transgressed the limits of its jurisdiction—its lawful authority. The courts have employed this rhetoric especially in defining a state's jurisdiction to tax.

We use the extended, territorial sense of the term when we write of a fugitive's having fled a jurisdiction, or when lawyers ask about which jurisdiction's law applies. Article IV, section 3, of the Constitution uses the term in this sense when it prohibits creation of a new state within the jurisdiction of an existing state without the latter's consent.

The most distinctively legal, though not exclusively constitutional, sense of the term refers to the authority of a court to decide a matter or to issue an order—its subject matter jurisdiction. Some state courts are courts of so-called general jurisdiction, competent to decide all cases within the ordinary bounds of the law. Other state courts are courts of limited jurisdiction, empowered only to decide specified types of cases or to grant only specified forms of relief. A municipal court, for example, may have jurisdiction to award damages only up to a limited dollar amount and may have no jurisdiction at all to grant an IN-JUNCTION.

In constitutional law jurisdiction has two special meanings, both involving civil cases. One flows from the limitation of the subject matter jurisdiction of the federal constitutional courts in Article III of the Constitution; the other grows from the due process clauses of the Fifth and FOURTEENTH AMENDMENTS.

Fundamental to the constitutional scheme is the proposition that each branch of the federal government must share powers and observe limits not only in regard to the other two branches of government but also in regard to the states. Article III and many statutes thus limit the subject matter jurisdiction of the federal courts to certain types of cases; that article, for example, ordinarily would prohibit a federal court from deciding a case between two citizens of the same state in which no question of federal or maritime law was involved. Because the limitations of Article III describe a fundamental division of authority between state and federal governments, the federal courts have been scrupulous, some would say zealous, not to overstep those subject matter boundaries. Thus even though no party to a lawsuit evinces the least concern about it, a federal court has an independent duty to investigate the basis for its subject matter jurisdiction and to dismiss the suit if jurisdiction is lacking. Such dismissals, like the jurisdictional rules that require them, protect the interests of the state court systems, to which the litigation must go if the federal courts cannot hear it.

The Constitution also limits the powers of the federal government and the states over individual citizens. State courts, for example, must observe a limitation that flows from the Fourteenth Amendment's due process clause. Since *Pennoyer v. Neff* (1878) the Supreme Court has insisted that, regardless of the kind of case involved, the defendant have some connection with the state in which the suit occurs. Over the past century the Court has remolded the basis and expanded the range of personal jurisdiction—changes that, some have suggested, have come in response to an increasingly mobile population and an economy increasingly national in scope. The Court has sometimes based the requirement of personal jurisdiction on the state's lack of power over persons not within its borders—thus harking back to the territorial sense of the term; more recently it has tended to speak less of territorial power and more of unfair inconvenience to a defendant forced to litigate in a distant forum. Whether it has grounded the requirements in FEDERALISM or in fairness to the defendant, however, the Court has insisted that such connections exist in order for a judgment of a court to be entitled to FULL FAITH AND CREDIT.

Whether similar constitutional restrictions on personal jurisdiction apply to federal courts is a more obscure matter. Because the federal government is sovereign throughout the United States, notions of geographical territoriality play no role, and only the inconvenience to the defendant would be at issue in such a case. In a number of instances involving the national economy, such as federal securities law cases, Congress has provided for nationwide personal jurisdiction in the federal courts, and such grants of power have been upheld, presumably because any harm to the defendant is outweighed by the need for a nationally available system of courts supervising the national economy. The outer limits of congressional power have not been tested, for in most cases either venue statutes (controlling the districts in which civil suits may be brought) or the FEDERAL RULES OF CIVIL PROCEDURE limit federal courts to essentially the same reach of personal jurisdiction that a state court would have.

Unlike subject matter jurisdiction, personal jurisdiction can be waived by those entitled to its protection: the Supreme Court has repeatedly held that either by prior agreement or by the simple failure to raise the issue at an early stage of litigation defendants may lose their opportunity to challenge the court's power to decide the case. COLLATERAL ATTACK on a judgment on the ground that the court lacked personal jurisdiction is available only to a defendant who did not appear in the original suit.

Article III's limits on the subject matter jurisdiction of federal courts allocate cases as between state and federal courts; the due process limitations in personal jurisdiction allocate cases between a court, either state or federal, in a particular place and courts in other places more convenient to the defendant. Though both doctrines in their more technical aspects are quintessential lawyer's law, their roots lie in the Constitution's allocations of governmental power and in a tradition of individualism. The same origins underlie the idea of jurisdiction as the limitations on the power of various branches of government. Ultimately all the uses of "jurisdiction" derive from the medieval Western tradition that distinguished between power and justice, making the ability to dispense the latter a function of allocations of the former.

Bibliography

BATOR, PAUL M.; MISHKIN, PAUL J.; SHAPIRO, DAVID L.; and WECHSLER, HERBERT   1973   Hart and Wechsler's The Federal Courts and the Federal System. Mineoloa, N.Y.: Foundation Press.

HAZARD, GEOFFREY C.   1965   A General Theory of State-Court Jurisdiction. *Supreme Court Review* 1965:241–289.

MEHREN, ARTHUR T. VON, and TRAUTMAN, DONALD 1966   Jurisdiction to Adjudicate: A Suggested Analysis. *Harvard Law Review* 79:1121–1179.

JUDICIARY ACT OF 1789

Paul M. Bator

Article III of the Constitution constitutes an authorizing charter for a system of national courts to exercise the JUDICIAL POWER OF THE UNITED STATES, but is not self-executing, needing legislation to bring it to life. Accordingly, the First Congress, in its twentieth enactment, turned to the creation of a JUDICIAL SYSTEM for the new nation. Its work—the First Judiciary Act, approved September 24, 1789—has ever since been celebrated as "a great law." The statute, obeying a constitutional command, constituted a SUPREME COURT. It created the office of Attorney General of the United States. It devised a judicial organization that was destined to survive for a century. And, by providing for Supreme Court review of state court judgments involving issues of federal law, it created a profoundly significant instrument for consolidating and protecting national power.

But it is the decision of the First Congress to take up the constitutional option to establish a system of federal courts "inferior" to the Supreme Court that has been characterized as the act's "transcendent achievement." The Constitution does not require the creation of inferior courts. Nevertheless, the decision to do so came swiftly, actuated by the unanimously shared view that an effective maritime commerce—trading lifeblood for the thirteen states—needed a dependable nationwide body of maritime law, and by a consensus that the most reliable method to assure its development would be to entrust it to a distinctive body of national courts. (Far more controversy surrounded the view, also finding expression in the act, that national courts were needed to assure out-of-state litigants protection against parochial prejudices.)

The act thus created a system of federal courts of original (trial) jurisdiction, establishing a tradition that has survived without interruption to this day. On the other hand, the act gave these courts the authority to adjudicate only a small fraction of the CASES AND CONTROVERSIES encompassed by the federal judicial power, attesting to the clear contemporaneous understanding of the Constitution that it is for Congress to determine which, if any, of the cases, within the federal judicial power should be adjudicated in the first instance in a federal tribunal.

The first section of the act provided for a Supreme Court, consisting of a Chief Justice and five associates. Below this, the act created a curious bifurcated system. The country was divided into districts generally coterminous with state boundaries (Massachusetts and Virginia each had two districts), each with a district court manned by a district judge. In addition, the act divided the country into three circuits, in each of which another trial court, called a CIRCUIT COURT—manned not by its own judges but by two Supreme Court Justices and a district judge—was to sit twice a year in each district within the circuit. These circuit courts, in addition, received a limited APPELLATE JURISDICTION to review district court decisions. The system of circuit courts set up in 1789, with its requirement that Supreme Court Justices sit on circuit as trial judges, persisted for more than a century; it proved to be the weakest architectural feature of the first Judiciary Act.

The act exploited only a fraction of the constitutional potential for original federal court jurisdiction. Significantly, the constitutional grant of federal judicial power over cases arising under the Constitution and laws of the United States (FEDERAL QUESTION JURISDICTION) was largely unused and remained so until 1875. (A notable exception was section 14, the All Writs Act, which, among other matters, authorized Supreme Court Justices and district judges to "grant writs of HABEAS CORPUS" to inquire into the legality of federal detentions.) The act made important use, however, of the power to locate litigation affecting out-of-staters in the new national courts. Thus, the circuit courts were given CONCURRENT JURISDICTION with the state courts over civil cases involving more than $500 "between a citizen of the State where the suit is brought, and a citizen of another State," as well as over civil cases involving more than $500 in which an ALIEN was a party.

The most important grant of jurisdiction to the new district courts gave them "exclusive original cognizance of all civil causes of ADMIRALTY AND MARITIME JURISDICTION," subject to a savings clause preserving COMMON LAW remedies.

The litigation interests of the national government were given narrow recognition in the First Judiciary Act. The circuit courts were given power to adjudicate civil cases involving more than $500 in which the United States were "plaintiffs or petitioners" (suits against the United States were not contemplated); the district courts had power to adjudicate suits at common law involving $100 brought by the United States. The act gave the district courts exclusive original cognizance over certain seizures, penalties, and forfeitures. And, finally, Congress provided for the then tiny criminal business of the national government by giving the circuit courts "exclusive cognizance of all crimes and offenses cognizable under the authority of the United States," subject to a concurrent jurisdiction in the district courts to try certain minor criminal offenses.

The circuit courts were given the authority to review final decisions of the district courts in civil and admiralty cases involving more than $50 or $300, respectively. In addition, the first Judiciary Act originated the device, in continuous use ever since, of providing for pretrial removal of certain cases from state to federal court (for example, removal in civil cases to a circuit court by alien defendants and by out-of-staters sued in the plaintiff's home-state court).

The framers of the first Judiciary Act, notwithstanding the later established DOCTRINE that the ORIGINAL JURISDICTION of the Supreme Court does not depend on legislative grant, specified in section 13 what this original jurisdiction was to be; the listing nearly (but not completely) exhausted the constitutional grant, encompassing controversies between states, between a state and a citizen of another state, and suits involving foreign diplomats. Setting another lasting precedent, the act designated only a portion of the original jurisdiction of the Supreme Court as exclusive jurisdiction. In his opinion for the Court in MARBURY V. MADISON (1803), Chief Justice JOHN MARSHALL read section B to give the Supreme Court original jurisdiction over certain cases that Article III had not expressly placed within the Court's original jurisdiction. Accordingly, the Court held this narrow provision of the 1789 act unconstitutional.

Not all lower federal court decisions were made reviewable. For instance, no provision at all was made for review of federal criminal cases (which remained, in the large, unreviewable for a century). The act authorized the Supreme Court to review final judgments in civil cases decided by the circuit courts if the matter in dispute exceeded $2,000.

In its celebrated section 25, Congress asserted the constitutional authority—sustained in MARTIN V. HUNTER'S LESSEE (1816) and COHENS V. VIRGINIA (1821)—to give the Supreme Court authority to review certain final judgments or decisions in the "highest" state court in which a decision "could be had" (language that survives to this day). Significantly, this authority did not encompass all cases involving issues of federal law: review was limited to cases where a state court had *rejected* a claim of right or immunity under federal law. (This limitation eventually proved to create an unacceptable institutional gap and was eliminated by the Judiciary Act of 1914.) A seminal feature of section 25 was its specification that Supreme Court review is limited to the question of federal law in the case.

The first Judiciary Act originated a fundamental structural feature of our legal topography in its section 34, called the Rules of Decision Act, providing (in language that still survives) that, except where federal law otherwise requires, the laws of the several states shall be regarded as "rules of decision" in trials at common law in the federal courts "in cases where they apply." Interpretations of this delphic provision— including the reversal from SWIFT V. TYSON (1842) to ERIE RAILROAD V. TOMPKINS (1938)—have had a significant impact on our judicial

FEDERALISM. In addition, the act contained elaborate boilerplate with respect to many matters no longer of current interest, (for example, the exact days for court sessions, quorums, clerks, forms of oaths, bail).

The first Judiciary Act, passed by a Congress many of whose members had participated in the framing of the Constitution, has had a lasting effect, not only on the shape of the federal judicial system but on our thought about the constitutional and structural premises on which that system is based. Created by great statesmen, it set on foot an enterprise that 200 years later still bears its imprint.

Bibliography

FRANKFURTER, FELIX and LANDIS, JAMES M.   1928   *The Business of the Supreme Court: A Study of the Federal Judicial System.* New York: Macmillan.

GOEBEL, JULIUS   1971   *History of the Supreme Court of the United States: Antecedents and Beginnings to 1801.* Pages 457–508. New York: Macmillan.

WARREN, CHARLES   1923   New Light on the History of the Federal Judiciary Act of 1789. *Harvard Law Review* 37:49–132.

CIRCUIT COURTS

Kermit L. Hall

The JUDICIARY ACT OF 1789 fashioned a decentralized circuit court system. The boundaries of the three circuits coincided with the boundaries of the states they encompassed, a practice that opened them to state and sectional political influences and legal practices. The act assigned two Supreme Court Justices to each circuit to hold court along with a district judge in the state where the circuit court met. (After 1794, a single Justice and a district judge were a quorum.) The circuit-riding provision brought federal authority and national political views to the new and distant states, but also compelled the Justices to imbibe local political sentiments and legal practices.

For a century questions about the administrative efficiency, constitutional roles, and political responsibilities of these courts provoked heated debate. In the JUDICIARY ACT OF 1801, Federalists sought to replace the Justices with an independent six-person circuit court judiciary, but one year later the new Jeffersonian Republican majority in Congress eliminated the circuit judgeships and restored the Justices to circuit duties, although they left the number of circuits at six. (See JUDICIARY ACTS OF 1802.) Subsequent territorial expansion prompted the addition of new circuits and new Justices until both reached nine in the Judiciary Act of 1837. Slave state interests opposed further expansion because they feared the loss of their five-to-four majority on the high court. Congress in 1855 did create a special circuit court and judgeship for the Northern District of California to expedite land litigation.

Significant structural and jurisdictional changes accompanied the Civil War and Reconstruction. The Judiciary Act of 1869 established a separate circuit court judiciary and assigned one judge to each of the nine new circuits that stretched from coast to coast. Justices retained circuit-riding duties although the 1869 act and subsequent legislation required less frequent attendance.

Historically, these courts had exercised ORIGINAL and APPELLATE JURISDICTION in cases involving the criminal law of the United States, in other areas where particular statutes granted jurisdiction, and in cases resting on diversity of citizenship. The Judiciary Act of 1869 strengthened the appellate responsibilities of the circuit courts by denying litigants access to the Supreme Court unless the amount in controversy exceeded $5,000. The Jurisdiction and Removal Act of 1875 established a general

FEDERAL QUESTION JURISDICTION and made it possible for, among others, interstate CORPORATIONS to seek the friendly forum of the federal as opposed to the state courts. The 1875 measure also transferred some of the original jurisdiction of the circuit courts to the district courts. However, because the circuit courts were given increased appellate responsibilities, along with only modest adjustments in staffing, their dockets became congested. The resulting delay in appeals, combined with similar congestion in the Supreme Court, persuaded Congress in 1891 to establish the Circuit Courts of Appeals which became the nation's principal intermediate federal appellate courts. (See CIRCUIT COURTS OF APPEALS ACT.) Although the old circuit courts became anachronisms, Congress delayed abolishing them until 1911.

Throughout the nineteenth century Supreme Court Justices held ambivalent attitudes toward circuit duty. The Justices complained about the rigors of circuit travel and the loss of time from responsibilities in the nation's capital, but most of them recognized that circuit judging offered a unique constitutional forum free from the immediate scrutiny of their brethren on the Court. "It is only as a Circuit Judge that the Chief Justice or any other Justice of the Supreme Court has, individually, any considerable power," Chief Justice SALMON P. CHASE observed in 1868.

Circuit court judges contributed to the nationalization of American law and the economy. Justice JOSEPH STORY, in the First Circuit, for example, broadly defined the federal ADMIRALTY AND MARITIME JURISDICTION. In perhaps the most important circuit court decision of the nineteenth century, Story held, in *De Lovio v. Boit* (1815), that this jurisdiction extended to all maritime contracts, including insurance policies, and to all torts and injuries committed on the high seas and in ports and harbors within the ebb and flow of the tide. This decision, coupled with Story's opinion eight years later in *Chamberlain v. Chandler* (1823), expanded federal control over admiralty and maritime-related economic activity and added certainty to contracts involving shipping and commerce.

The circuit courts extended national constitutional protection to property, contract, and corporate rights. Justice WILLIAM PATERSON's 1795 decision on circuit in VAN HORNE'S LESSEE V. DORRANCE was the first significant statement in the federal courts on behalf of VESTED RIGHTS. But in 1830 Justice HENRY BALDWIN anticipated by seven years the PUBLIC USE doctrine later embraced by the Supreme Court. In *Bonaparte v. Camden & A. R. Co.* he held that state legislatures could take private property only for public use, and that creation of a monopoly by a public charter voided its public nature. As new forms of corporate property emerged in the post-Civil War era, the circuit courts offered protection through the CONTRACT CLAUSE. In the early and frequently cited case of *Gray v. Davis* (1871) a circuit court held, and the Supreme Court subsequently affirmed, that a legislative act incorporating a railroad constituted a contract between the state and the company, and a state constitutional provision annulling that charter violated the contract clause.

The circuit courts' most dramatic nationalizing role involved commercial jurisprudence. Through their DIVERSITY JURISDICTION the circuit courts used SWIFT V. TYSON (1842) to build a FEDERAL COMMON LAW of commerce, thus encouraging business flexibility, facilitating investment security, and reducing costs to corporations. After the Civil War these courts eased limitations on the formation and operation of corporations in foreign states (*In Re Spain,* 1891), supported bondholders' rights, allowed forum shopping (*Osgood v. The Chicago, Danville, and Vincennes R. R. Co.,* 1875), and favored employers in fellow-servant liability cases.

Ambivalence, contradiction, and frustration typified circuit court decisions involving civil and political rights. In 1823 Justice BUSHROD WASHINGTON, in CORFIELD V. CORYELL, held that the PRIVILEGES AND IMMUNITIES clause guaranteed equal treatment of out-of-state citizens as to those privileges and immunities that belonged of right to citizens of all free governments, and which had at all times been enjoyed by citizens of the several states. After 1866 some circuit judges attempted to expand this narrow interpretation. Justice JOSEPH P. BRADLEY held, in *Live-Stock Dealers' & Butchers' Ass'n v. Crescent City Live-Stock Landing & Slaughter-House Co.* (1870), that the FOURTEENTH AMENDMENT protected the privileges and immunities of whites and blacks as national citizens against STATE ACTION. In 1871 the Circuit Court for the Southern District of Alabama, in *United States v. Hall,* decided that under the Fourteenth Amendment Congress had the power to protect by appropriate legislation all rights in the first eight amendments. And in *Ho Ah Kow v. Nunan* (1879) Justice STEPHEN J. FIELD struck down as CRUEL AND UNUSUAL PUNISHMENT, based on the Eighth Amendment and the EQUAL PROTECTION clause of the Fourteenth Amendment, a San Francisco ordinance that required Chinese prisoners to have their hair cut to a length of one inch from their scalps.

These attempts to nationalize civil rights had little immediate impact. The Supreme Court in 1873 rejected Bradley's reading of the Fourteenth Amendment, and in 1871 the Circuit Court for the District of South Carolina in *United States v. Crosby* concluded that the right of a person to be secure in his or her home was not a right, privilege, or immunity granted by the Constitution. Neither the Supreme Court nor any other circuit court adopted the theory of congressional power to enforce the Fourteenth Amendment set forth in *Hall.* Justice Field's *Nunan* opinion was most frequently cited in dissenting rather than majority opinions.

Political rights under the FIFTEENTH AMENDMENT fared only slightly better. In *United States v. Given* (1873) the Circuit Court for the District of Delaware held that the Fifteenth Amendment did not limit congressional action to cases where states had denied or abridged the right to vote by legislation. In the same year, however, Justice WARD HUNT, in *United States v. Anthony*, concluded that the right or privilege of voting arose under state constitutions and that the states might restrict it to males.

Despite a regional structure and diverse personnel, these circuit courts placed national over state interests, reinforced the supremacy of federal power, promoted national economic development, and enhanced the position of interstate corporations. However, in matters of civil and political rights they not only disagreed about the scope of federal powers but also confronted a Supreme Court wedded to a traditional state-centered foundation for these rights.

Bibliography

FRANKFURTER, FELIX and LANDIS, JAMES M.   1927   *The Business of the Supreme Court: A Study in the Federal Judicial System.* Pages 3–86. New York: Macmillan.

HALL, KERMIT L.   1975   The Civil War Era as a Crucible for Nationalizing the Lower Federal Courts. *Prologue: The Journal of the National Archives* 7:177–186.

SWISHER, CARL B.   1974   *The Taney Period, 1836–1864.* Volume IV of *The Oliver Wendell Holmes Devise History of the Supreme Court of the United States.* Pages 248–292. New York: Macmillan.

JUSTICIABILITY

Jonathan Varat

Federal judges do not establish legal norms at will or on demand, but only when deciding cases that are justiciable, that is, appropriate for federal court decision. What makes a case justiciable is thus itself an important threshold question, because it determines whether a federal court will exercise its power to formulate and apply substantive law, rather than leaving the issues in the case to be resolved by political or other means. Hence, when the Supreme Court fashions the criteria of justiciability for itself and the lower federal courts, it effectively defines the nature and scope of the JUDICIAL POWER OF THE UNITED STATES— the power to make decisions in accordance with law.

Most justiciability issues arise when litigants who are primarily motivated to vindicate public rights seek to contest the validity of government behavior, especially on constitutional grounds. Such public interest suits are usually designed not so much to redress traditional personal grievances as to vindicate fundamental principles. Commonly the plaintiffs seek DECLARATORY JUDGMENTS or INJUNCTIONS to prevent government officials from carrying on objectionable practices that affect a wide segment of the population. These actions often test and illustrate the degree to which federal judges, particularly Supreme Court Justices, view their power of constitutional oversight as warranted only by the necessity to resolve traditional legal disputes or, instead, by a broader judicial mission to ensure government observance of the Constitution.

In demarcating the federal judicial function, the law of justiciability comprises a complex of subtle doctrines, including STANDING, RIPENESS, MOOTNESS, ADVISORY OPINIONS, and POLITICAL QUESTIONS, among others. The Supreme Court has derived that law from two sources: Article III, which limits federal judicial power to the decision of CASES AND CONTROVERSIES, and nonconstitutional "prudential" rules of the Court's own creation. Both Article III and the rules of prudence incorporate notions of the attributes or qualities of litigation that make the legal issues presented appropriate for judicial determination. The difference between the two is that if Congress wants to have the federal courts entertain public actions, it may override the Court's prudential barriers, but not the constitutional limits of "case" and "controversy."

Three primary, and often mutually reinforcing, conceptions of appropriateness shape the many manifestations of justiciability. One concerns judicial capability. It centers on making federal court adjudication competent, informed, necessary, and efficacious. In this conception, a judicial decision is proper only when adversely affected parties litigate live issues of current personal consequence in a lawsuit whose format assures adversary argument and judicial capacity to devise meaningful remedies. The second conception of appropriateness concerns fairness. It promotes judicial solicitude for parties and interests not represented in the lawsuit, whose rights might be compromised unfairly by a substantive decision rendered without their participation. The third conception concerns the proper institutional and political role in our democracy of the appointed, electorally unaccountable federal judiciary. It cautions federal courts to be sure of the need for imposing restraints, especially constitutional restraints, on other, particularly more representative, government officials.

Whether the policies underlying justiciability doctrine are (or should be) applied in a principled, consistent fashion, depending on the form and characteristics of litigation alone, as the Supreme Court professes, or whether the Court does (or should) manipulate them for pragmatic reasons, is a subject of major controversy among the Court's commentators. Inevitably, the Court has discretion to adjust the degree to which these imprecise and flexible policies must be satisfied in particular cases, given individual variations in the configuration of lawsuits and the inherently relative nature of judgments about judicial capability, litigant need, and the propriety of JUDICIAL ACTIVISM AND RESTRAINT. Assessments of the information and circumstances needed for intelligent, effective adjudication will vary with the levels of generality at which issues are posed and with judicial willingness to act under conditions of uncertainty. Appraisals frequently diverge concerning hardship to, and representation of, present and absent parties who will be affected by rendering or withholding decision. Perhaps most dramatically, Justices differ in their evaluations of the relative importance of judicial control of government behavior and the freedom of politically accountable officials to formulate policy without judicial interference.

In view of the latitude and variation in the Court's self-conscious definition of federal judicial power, it is not surprising that justiciability is a sophisticated, controversial, and difficult field, or that many decisions provoke the skepticism that justiciability DOCTRINE has been manipulated to avoid decision of some issues and advance the decision of others. The Court certainly considers (and is willing to articulate) the degree of concrete focus and clarity with which issues are presented, and how pressing is the need for judicial protection of the litigants. The Court may also consider (but almost certainly will not articulate) a number of the following factors: how substantial, difficult, and controversial the issues are; whether a decision would likely legitimate government action or hold it unconstitutional; how important the Court believes the principle it would announce is and whether the principle could be expected to command public and government acceptance; the possibility of nonjudicial resolution; whether a decision would contribute to or cut off public debate; the expected general public reaction to a decision; the Justices' own constitutional priorities; and a host of other practical considerations that may implicate the Court's capacity to establish and enforce important constitutional principles.

Such judgments appear to have influenced a number of notable justiciability rulings in diverse ways. For example, in *Poe v. Ullman* (1961) the Court held a declaratory judgment challenge to Connecticut's contraception ban nonjusticiable because the statute was not being enforced, but later held the ban unconstitutional in the context of a criminal prosecution. By contrast, in a declaratory judgment challenge to an unenforced prohibition on teaching evolution, the Court, in EPPERSON v. ARKANSAS (1968), held the case justiciable and the prohibition unconstitutional without awaiting a prosecution. Similarly, the Court twice dismissed a seemingly justiciable appeal challenging Virginia's ban on MISCEGENATION, as applied to an annulment proceeding, within a few years of declaring public school segregation unconstitutional in 1954, but in 1967, following the CIVIL RIGHTS advances of the early 1960s, held the law unconstitutional on appeal of a criminal conviction. Moreover, although the Court has deferred decision in some cases where it ultimately held state statutes unconstitutional, it also occasionally appears to have lowered justiciability barriers and rushed to uphold the constitutionality of important federal legislation (the Tennessee Valley Authority and nuclear liability limitation statutes) or to invalidate it when Congress wanted constitutional assistance with ongoing legislative reform (the FEDERAL ELECTION CAMPAIGN ACT).

Perhaps the Court is inclined to insist on a greater showing of justiciability where it expects to hold governmental action unconstitutional than where it expects to uphold the action, in part because of a substantive presumption of the constitutionality of government conduct. Yet any generalization about the relations between justiciability and the Court's substantive views is hazardous, given the many factors and subtle judgments that may be weighed in any given case. What seems certain is that decisions on questions of justiciability will always be influenced by visions of the judicial role and will be difficult to comprehend without understanding those visions.

Bibliography

BICKEL, ALEXANDER M. 1962 *The Least Dangerous Branch: The Supreme Court at the Bar of Politics.* Chap. 4. Indianapolis: Bobbs-Merrill.
GUNTHER, GERALD 1964 The Subtle Vices of the "Passive Virtues": A Com-

ment on Principle and Expediency in Judicial Review. *Columbia Law Review* 64:1–25.

VARAT, JONATHAN D.   1980   Variable Justiciability and the *Duke Power* Case. *Texas Law Review* 58:273–327.

WRIGHT, CHARLES A.; MILLER, ARTHUR R.; and COOPER, EDWARD H. 1984   *Federal Practice and Procedure.* Vol. 13:278–293. St. Paul, Minn.: West Publishing Co.

CASES AND CONTROVERSIES

Jonathan Varat

Article III of the Constitution vests the JUDICIAL POWER OF THE UNITED STATES in one constitutionally mandated Supreme Court and such subordinate federal courts as Congress may choose to establish. Federal judges are appointed for life with salaries that cannot be diminished, but they may exercise their independent and politically unaccountable power only to resolve "cases" and "controversies" of the kinds designated by Article III, the most important of which are cases arising under the Constitution and other federal law. The scope of the federal judicial power thus depends in large measure on the Supreme Court's interpretations of the "case" and "controversy" limitation applicable to the Court itself and to other Article III tribunals.

That limitation not only inhibits Article III courts from arrogating too much power unto themselves; it also prevents Congress from compelling or authorizing decisions by federal courts in nonjudicial proceedings and precludes Supreme Court review of state court decisions in proceedings that are not considered "cases" or "controversies" under Article III. The limitation thus simultaneously confines federal judges and reinforces their ability to resist nonjudicial tasks pressed on them by others.

The linkage between independence and circumscribed power is a continuously important theme in "case" or "controversy" jurisprudence, as is the connection between "case" or "controversy" jurisprudence and the power of JUDICIAL REVIEW of government acts for constitutionality—a power that MARBURY V. MADISON (1803) justified primarily by the need to apply the Constitution as relevant law to decide a "case." During the CONSTITUTIONAL CONVENTION OF 1787, EDMUND RANDOLPH proposed that the President and members of the federal judiciary be joined in a council of revision to veto legislative excesses. The presidential VETO POWER was adopted instead, partly to keep the judiciary out of the legislative process and partly to insure that the judges would decide cases independently, without bias in favor of legislation they had helped to formulate. Similar concerns led the convention to reject CHARLES PINCKNEY's proposal to have the Supreme Court provide ADVISORY OPINIONS at the request of Congress or the President. Finally, in response to JAMES MADISON's doubts about extending the federal judicial power to expound the Constitution too broadly, the Convention made explicit its under-standing that the power extended only to "cases of a Judiciary nature." The Framers understood that the judicial power of constitutional gover-nance would expand if the concept of "case" or "controversy" did.

What constitutes an Article III "case," of a "judiciary nature," is hardly self-evident. No definition was articulated when the language was adopted, but only an apparent intent to circumscribe the federal judicial function, and to insure that it be performed independently of the other branches. In this century, Justice FELIX FRANKFURTER suggested that Article III precluded federal courts from deciding legal questions except in the kinds of proceedings entertained by the English and colonial courts at the time of the Constitution's adoption. But the willingness of English courts to give advisory opinions then—a practice clearly incon-sistent with convention history and the Court's steadfast policy since 1793—refutes the suggestion. Moreover, from the outset the SEPARATION OF POWERS aspect of the "case" or "controversy" limitation has differenti-ated CONSTITUTIONAL COURTS (courts constituted under Article III) from others. Most fundamentally, however, the indeterminate historical con-tours of "cases" or "controversies" inevitably had to accommodate changes in the forms of litigation authorized by Congress, in the legal and social environment that accompanied the nation's industrial growth and the rise of the regulatory and welfare state, and in the place of the federal judiciary in our national life.

After two centuries of elaboration, the essential characteristics of Article III controversies remain imprecise and subject to change. Yet underlying the various manifestations of "case" or "controversy" doctrine are three core requirements: affected parties standing in an adverse relationship to each other, actual or threatened events that provoke a live legal dispute, and the courts' ability to render final and meaningful judgments. These criteria—concerning, respectively, the litigants, the facts, and judicial efficacy—have both independent and interrelated sig-nificance.

As to litigants, only parties injured by a defendant's behavior have constitutional STANDING to sue. COLLUSIVE SUITS are barred because the parties' interests are not adverse.

As to extant factual circumstances, advisory opinions are banned. This limitation not only bars direct requests for legal rulings on hypotheti-cal facts but also requires dismissal of unripe or moot cases, because, respectively, they are not yet live, or they once were but have ceased to be by virtue of subsequent events. The parties' future or past adversari-ness cannot substitute for actual, current adversariness. Disputes that have not yet begun or have already ended are treated as having no more present need for decision than purely hypothetical disputes. (See RIPENESS; MOOTNESS).

The desire to preserve federal judicial power as an independent, effective, and binding force of legal obligation is reflected both in the finality rule, which bars decision if the judgment rendered would be subject to revision by another branch of government, and in the rule denying standing unless a judgment would likely redress the plaintiff's injury. These two rules are the clearest instances of judicial self-limitation to insure that when the federal courts do act, their judgments will be potent. To exercise judicial power ineffectively or as merely a preliminary gesture would risk undermining compliance with court decrees generally or lessening official and public acceptance of the binding nature of judicial decisions, especially unpopular constitutional judgments. Here the link between the limitations on judicial power and that power's independence and effectiveness is at its strongest.

Historically, congressional attempts to expand the use of Article III judicial power have caused the greatest difficulty, largely because the federal courts are charged simultaneously with enforcing valid federal law as an arm of the national government and with restraining unconstitutional behavior of the coequal branches of that government. The enforcement role induces judicial receptivity to extensive congressional use of the federal courts, especially in a time of expansion of both the federal government's functions and the use of litigation to resolve public disputes. The courts' checking function, however, cautions judicial resistance to congressional efforts to enlarge the scope of "cases" or "controversies" for fear of losing the strength, independence, or finality needed to resist unconstitutional action by the political branches.

The early emphasis of "case" or "controversy" jurisprudence was on consolidating the judiciary's independence and effective power. The Supreme Court's refusal in 1793 to give President GEORGE WASHINGTON legal advice on the interpretation of treaties with France—the founding precedent for the ban on advisory opinions—rested largely on the desire to preserve the federal judiciary as a check on Congress and the executive when actual disputes arose. Similarly, HAYBURN'S CASE (1792) established that federal courts would not determine which Revolutionary War veterans were entitled to disability pensions so long as the secretary of war had the final say on their entitlement: Congress could employ the federal judicial power only if the decisions of federal courts had binding effect. In the mid-nineteenth century the concern for maintaining judicial efficacy went beyond finality of substantive judgment to finality of remedy. The Supreme Court refused to accept appeals from the Court of Claims, which Congress had established to hear monetary claims against the United States, because the statutory scheme forbade payment until the Court certified its judgments to the treasury secretary for presentation to Congress, which would then have to appropriate funds. The Court concluded that Congress could not invoke Article III judicial power if the judges lacked independent authority to enforce their judgments as well as render them.

Preserving judicial authority remains an important desideratum in the twentieth century, but the growing pervasiveness of federal law as a means of government regulation—often accompanied by litigant and congressional pressure to increase access to the federal courts—inevitably has accentuated the law-declaring enforcement role of the federal judiciary and tended to expand the "case" or "controversy" realm. MUSKRAT v. UNITED STATES (1911) cited the courts' inability to execute a judgment as a reason to reject Congress's authorization of a TEST CASE to secure a ruling on the constitutionality of specific statutes it had passed. Similarly, the Court initially doubted the federal courts' power to give DECLARATORY JUDGMENTS. Yet, by the late 1930s, the Supreme Court had upheld both its own power to review state declaratory judgment actions and the federal DECLARATORY JUDGMENT ACT of 1934. The declaratory judgment remedy authorizes federal courts to decide controversies before legal rights are actually violated. The judge normally enters no coercive order, but confines the remedy to a binding declaration of rights. So long as the controversy is a live one, between adverse parties, and the decision to afford a binding remedy rests wholly with the judiciary, the advisory opinion and finality objections pose no obstacles. A controversy brought to court too early may fail Article III ripeness criteria, but the declaratory remedy itself does not preclude the existence of a "case" or "controversy."

Congress has succeeded in expanding the reach of federal judicial power not only by creating new remedies for the federal courts to administer but also by creating new substantive rights for them to enforce. The Supreme Court maintains as a fundamental "case" or "controversy" requirement that a suing party, to have standing, must have suffered some distinctive "injury in fact." The injury must be particularized, not diffuse; citizen or taxpayer frustration with alleged government illegality is insufficient by itself. In theory, Congress cannot dispense with this requirement and authorize suits by individuals who are not injured. Congress may, however, increase the potential for an injury that will satisfy Article III, simply by legislating protection of new rights, the violation of which amounts to a constitutional "injury in fact." For example, Trafficante v. Metropolitan Life Insurance Company (1972) held that a federal CIVIL RIGHTS ban on housing discrimination could be enforced not only by persons refused housing but also by current tenants claiming loss of desired interracial associations; the Court interpreted the statute to create a legally protected interest in integrated housing. To a point, then, Article III "cases" or "controversies" expand correspondingly with the need to enforce new federal legislation. Yet the scope of congressional power to transform diffuse harm into cognizable Article III injury remains uncertain and apparently stops short of providing everyone a judicially enforceable generalized right to be free of illegal governmental behavior, without regard to more individualized effects.

The historically approved image is that federal judges decide politically significant public law issues only to resolve controversies taking the form of private litigation. Over the years, however, this picture has had to accommodate not only congressional creation of enforceable rights and remedies but also the modern realities of public forms of litigation such as the CLASS ACTION, the participation of organized public interest lawyers, and lawsuits aimed at reforming government structures and practices. (See INSTITUTIONAL LITIGATION.) Public law adjudication, especially constitutional adjudication, is certainly the most important function of the federal courts. The inclination to stretch the boundaries of "cases" or "controversies" to provide desired legal guidance on important social problems, although it has varied among federal judges and courts of different eras, increases in response to congressional authorization and the perception of social need. Offsetting that impulse, however, are two countervailing considerations. First, the judges realize that the more public the issues raised, the more democratically appropriate is a political rather than a judicial resolution. Second, they understand the importance of a litigation context that does not threaten judicial credibility, finality, or independence; that presents a realistic need for decision; and that provides adequate information and legal standards for confident, well-advised decision making. These competing considerations will continue to shape the meaning of "cases" and "controversies," setting the limits of the federal judicial function in ways that preserve the courts' checking and enforcement roles in the face of changes in the forms and objectives of litigation, in the dimensions of federal law, and in the expectations of government officials and members of the public.

Bibliography

BRILMAYER, LEA 1979 The Jurisprudence of Article III: Perspectives on the "Case or Controversy" Requirement. *Harvard Law Review* 93:297–321.

MONAGHAN, HENRY P. 1973 Constitutional Adjudication: The Who and When. *Yale Law Journal* 82:1363–1397.

RADCLIFFE, JAMES E. 1978 *The Case-or-Controversy Provision.* University Park: Pennsylvania State University Press.

TUSHNET, MARK V. 1980 The Sociology of Article III: A Response to Professor Brilmayer. *Harvard Law Review* 93:1698–1733.

ADVISORY OPINION

Jonathan Varat

Article III of the Constitution extends the JUDICIAL POWER OF THE UNITED STATES only to the decision of CASES OR CONTROVERSIES. Since 1793, when the Supreme Court declined, in the absence of a concrete dispute, to give legal advice to President GEORGE WASHINGTON on the correct interpretation of treaties with France and Britain, the Court has refused steadfastly to issue advisory opinions, finding them inconsistent with Article III. This refusal is required whether the request seeks advice on interpretation of existing law or on the constitutionality of pending LEGISLATION or anticipated action. The Justices' view is that the federal courts function not as lawyers giving advice but as judges limited to deciding cases presented by adverse parties with a real, not a hypothetical, dispute, one that is subject to judicial resolution and the granting of meaningful relief. The Court held in *Aetna Life Insurance Co. v. Haworth* (1937) that the prohibition against advisory opinions does not preclude declaratory relief, but there must be a concrete controversy between parties of adverse legal positions which a DECLARATORY JUDGMENT can settle.

If doubts exist about the constitutionality of a proposed government policy or the legality of a contemplated application of current law, an advisory opinion could prevent the interim harm that adoption and application of law subsequently found invalid would cause. Moreover, advisory opinions could save time, money, and effort in deliberation and enforcement by clarifying legal limitations before invalid action is taken. Clearing away unlawful options could also contribute to the quality and focus of public debate and accountability.

The rule against advisory opinions responds to different considerations, however. It limits workload, but the dominant concerns involve judicial competence to decide issues in an advisory context and the place of the federal judiciary in a regime characterized by SEPARATION OF POWERS. Fear that decision before a dispute arises would be premature and unwise, that is, made without relevant facts stemming from application of law or other experience and without the benefit of perspectives presented by already affected parties, combined with concern that the advisory opinion may prejudge unfairly the decision of later concrete cases raising the same questions, induces judges to avoid making nonessential and potentially vulnerable decisions that might weaken judicial legitimacy. In addition, the prevailing belief views advisory opinions as likely to stifle rather than clarify the deliberative process, to distort the obligations of legislative or executive officials to evaluate legal questions independently, thereby blurring accountability, and to deprive experimental proposals of an opportunity to prove themselves before being reviewed for the legality of their actual effects.

Bibliography

FRANKFURTER, FELIX   1924   Note on Advisory Opinions. *Harvard Law Review* 37:1002–1009.

STANDING

Jonathan Varat

In the United States, unelected, life-tenured federal judges may decide legal issues only when they are asked to do so by appropriate litigants. Such litigants are said to have standing to raise certain legal claims, including constitutional claims, in the federal courts.

A litigant's standing depends on two sets of criteria, one constitutionally required and one not, each ostensibly having three parts. The constitutional criteria derive from Article III's job description for federal judges, which permits them to declare law only when such a declaration is necessary to decide CASES AND CONTROVERSIES. These criteria center on the notion of an injured person's asking a court for a remedy against the responsible party, and each criterion corresponds to one of the three participants—to the plaintiff, the defendant, and the court, respectively. The plaintiff must assert that he suffered a cognizable personal injury; that the defendant's conduct caused the injury; and that the court's judgment is substantially likely to relieve it. The three nonconstitutional criteria for standing are "prudential" rules, self-imposed by the courts for their own governance, rules which Congress can eliminate if it chooses. These criteria, too, serve to diminish the frequency of substantive pronouncements by federal judges, but they focus on the legal basis of the suit, not on the plaintiff's actual injury. The first nonconstitutional criterion concerns representation: to secure judicial relief, injured litigants normally must assert that the injurious conduct violated their own legal rights, not the rights of third parties. The second assumes that government violations of everyone's undifferentiated legal rights are best left to political, not judicial, response: no one has standing if his or her legal position asserts "only the generalized interest of all citizens in constitutional governance." The third "prudential" criterion for standing seeks assurance that the law invoked plausibly protects the legal interest allegedly invaded: whatever interest is asserted must be "arguably within the zone of interests to be protected or regulated by the statute or constitutional guarantee in question."

Standing issues rarely surface in traditional suits, but federal courts applying these guidelines frequently deny standing to "public interest" plaintiffs anxious to challenge the legality of government behavior. The aim is not only to prevent federal judges from proclaiming law unless such declarations are needed to resolve concrete disputes, but also to promote proper conditions for intelligent adjudication (including adversary presentation of the facts and legal arguments) and to foster adequate representation of affected interests. When litigants ask federal courts to restrict the constitutional authority of politically accountable public officials, moreover, apprehension about unwise or excessive judicial intervention heightens, and the standing limitations may be applied with particular force.

Collectively, the Supreme Court's standing criteria often overlap; they are applied flexibly—sometimes inconsistently—to give the Supreme Court considerable discretion to exercise or withhold its power to declare law. The way that discretion is exercised reflects any particular Court's ideology of JUDICIAL ACTIVISM AND RESTRAINT and the substantive, constitutional rights it is either eager or reluctant to enforce.

The refinements of standing doctrine illustrate this flexibility and discretion. The core requirement of cognizable personal injury, for example, demands that the plaintiff have suffered injury to an interest deemed deserving of judicial protection. Over time, the Court has expanded the category of judicially acknowledged injuries beyond economic harm to include reputational, environmental, aesthetic, associational, informational, organizational, and voter harms, among others. Because of its vision of constrained judicial power in a representative democracy, however, the Court steadfastly forbids TAXPAYERS' SUITS and citizens' suits asserting purely ideological harm, particularly the harms of frustration, distress, or apprehension born of unlawful government conduct. Resting on lack of cognizable injury, the ban on citizen standing thus appears constitutionally compelled, although it effectively duplicates the non-constitutional barrier to asserting generalized grievances, which appears to rest on the absence of a cognizable legal interest. Less diffuse, but in ALLEN v. WRIGHT (1984) nonetheless held an insufficiently personal injury, is the feeling of stigma arising from discrimination directed, not personally, but against other members of the plaintiff's race. If the type of injury is judicially approved and the plaintiff personally suffered it, however, the fact that many others have suffered it will not negate standing. For example, in UNITED STATES v. SCRAP (1973) a student activist group was deemed to have standing based on widespread environmental injury.

Flexibility also characterizes the Court's degree of insistence on the remaining constitutional criteria. The closeness of the causal link between defendant's conduct and plaintiff's injury has varied from *United States v. SCRAP,* which accepted a loose connection between the Interstate Commerce Commission's approval of freight rate increases for scrap materials and increased trash problems in national parks, to *Allen v. Wright* (1984), which found too attenuated a seemingly closer link between the Internal Revenue Service's allegedly inadequate enforcement of the law requiring denial of tax exemptions to racially discriminatory private schools and "white flight" in public school districts undergoing DESEGREGATION. Similarly, insistence that judicial relief be substantially likely to redress plaintiff's injury has varied from *Linda R. S. v. Richard D.* (1973), where mothers of illegitimate children seeking to force prosecution of the fathers for nonsupport were denied standing because a court order supposedly would result only in jailing the fathers, not in increased support, to *Duke Power Co. v. Carolina Environmental Study Group* (1978), where neighbors of nuclear power plants, seeking relief from present injury caused by normal plant operation, were granted standing to contest (unsuccessfully) the constitutional validity of a federal statute limiting recovery of DAMAGES for potential nuclear disasters, despite considerable uncertainty that a legal victory for the plaintiffs would stop the plants' normal operations.

Of the nonconstitutional criteria, only the usual prohibition against representing third-party rights needs elaboration, primarily because of its different forms and its significant exceptions. When a personally injured plaintiff seeks to argue that the injurious conduct violated the legal rights of others, the prohibition, beyond serving the usual objectives of standing, serves also to protect nonlitigants who may not wish to assert their own rights or would do so differently (and perhaps more effectively) if they became litigants. Major exceptions to that prohibition respond to this policy by allowing representation, even of constitutional rights, when the Court concludes that the absent third parties would benefit rather than suffer from a substantive decision. One important example of this exception is the case in which third parties would have difficulty asserting their own rights, as in NAACP v. ALABAMA (1958), where the CIVIL RIGHTS group was permitted to assert its members' right to remain anonymous. Another example is the case in which the disputed conduct affects special plaintiff–third party relationships in ways suggesting that the plaintiff and third-party interests coincide. Under this exception doctors can represent patient rights to abortion, private schools can represent parent rights to choose private education, and sellers can represent the rights of young consumers to buy beer or contraceptives.

The Court generally denies standing when persons constitutionally subject to regulation urge that the regulation would be unconstitutional in application to others. This rule preserves legislative policy in cases where the law is applied constitutionally. Again, however, there is an exception, invoked most often in FIRST AMENDMENT challenges of VAGUENESS and OVERBREADTH, when the law's very existence would significantly inhibit others from exercising important constitutional rights and thus deter them from mounting their own challenge.

A final example is the case in which uninjured representatives seek to champion the legal rights of injured persons they represent outside of litigation. Thus, associations, not injured themselves, may sue on behalf of their members' injuries, provided that the members would have standing, the associations seek to protect interests germane to their purposes, and the claims and requested relief do not require individual member participation. And a state, which normally lacks standing as *parens patriae* to represent the claims of individual citizens, or even of all its citizens in opposition to the federal government, may represent its citizens when the injury alleged substantially affects the state's general population, especially if suit by individual citizens seems unlikely.

Like other JUSTICIABILITY doctrines, standing rules often thwart attempts to induce federal courts to make or reform constitutional or other law. How often the rules have that result will depend not only on the articulated criteria of standing but also on the Supreme Court's receptivity to the substance of the underlying claims and its judgment of the desirability and likelihood of political solutions.

Bibliography

NICHOL, GENE R., JR.   1984   Rethinking Standing. *California Law Review* 72:68–102.

SCOTT, KENNETH E.   1973   Standing in the Supreme Court: A Functional Analysis. *Harvard Law Review* 86:645–692.

VINING, JOSEPH   1978   *Legal Identity: The Coming of Age of Public Law.* New Haven, Conn.: Yale University Press.

MOOTNESS

Jonathan Varat

Article III's CASE OR CONTROVERSY restriction precludes federal courts from declaring law except in the context of litigation by parties with a personal stake in a live dispute that judicial decision can affect. They may not resolve moot questions—questions whose resolution can no longer affect the litigants' dispute because events after the commencement of litigation have obviated the need for judicial intervention. However live the issues once were, however much the parties (and the public) may desire a declaration of law, and however far the litigation may have progressed when the mooting events occur, Article III requires dismissal of the lawsuit. Common examples include a criminal defendant's death during appeal of a jail sentence, enactment of a new statute superseding one whose enforcement the plaintiff seeks to enjoin, or full satisfaction of a party's litigation demands.

Other cases exhibit less certainty that the substantive issues raised no longer need judicial action to forestall anticipated harm. In these cases, mootness questions are more troublesome. They inevitably introduce discretion to exercise or withhold judgment, discretion potentially influenced by the substantive issues' public importance. Thus, in DeFunis v. Odegaard (1974) a divided Supreme Court refused to decide the constitutionality of a race-conscious AFFIRMATIVE ACTION program for law school admissions when it appeared fairly certain that the challenger, who had only become a student through lower court victories, would be graduated irrespective of the lawsuit's outcome.

Several DOCTRINES reveal mootness to be a matter of degree. First, when changed circumstances moot the main dispute, but adjudication could produce collateral consequences, the issue is not moot, as when a prisoner's sentence expires before his appeal is decided, but the conviction might subject him to other civil or criminal penalties. Second, cases where defendants voluntarily agree to refrain from challenged behavior are not moot absent proof that they are unlikely to resume the behavior. This rule protects plaintiffs by preventing defendants from manipulating the mootness doctrine to avoid adverse decisions. Third, issues are not moot, despite passage of the immediate problem, when they are "capable of repetition, yet evading review," that is, when they arise sporadically, do not persist long enough to be reviewed before ceasing each time, and are reasonably likely to threaten the challengers again. Suits challenging ELECTION rules, where the immediate election passes before judicial resolution but the rules probably would affect the challengers in subsequent elections, or litigation challenging an abortion restriction that necessarily can apply to a woman only during the term of pregnancy are important instances where an unbending application of the mootness doctrine might deny judicial protection to persons periodically subject to harm. Finally, the Court generously allows a CLASS ACTION to continue, despite developments eliminating any need to protect the party bringing the lawsuit on behalf of the class, if the case is not moot as to other members of the class.

These refinements give federal courts some flexibility either to reach issues of their choice without pressing necessity to protect the parties or to decline to rule by insisting on a higher degree of probability that the threat of harm continues. Like other JUSTICIABILITY doctrines, mootness is not only a constitutional doctrine itself but a somewhat pliable tool of constitutional governance.

Bibliography

NOTE   1974   The Mootness Doctrine in the Supreme Court. *Harvard Law Review* 88:373.

RIPENESS

Jonathan Varat

People who anticipate harm occasionally attack a law's constitutionality before it is applied to them, or even before the law takes effect. A federal court may decline to decide such a case for lack of ripeness if it is unclear that adjudication is needed to protect the challengers, or if information sufficient to permit intelligent resolution is not yet available. A matter of timing and degree, ripeness is grounded both in Article III's CASE OR CONTROVERSY requirement and the federal courts' reluctance to issue constitutional decisions needlessly or prematurely. Delaying decision may cause interim hardship and allow unconstitutional harm to occur, but further developments may narrow the issues, or produce important information, or even establish that no decision is needed.

The Supreme Court's ripeness decisions display varying sensitivity to these sometimes conflicting factors. Normally, a court is more likely to defer resolution of fact-dependent issues, like those based on a particular application of a law, than it is to defer adjudication of strictly legal issues. A single case may present some issues ripe for adjudication, but others not ripe. Ripeness decisions mainly respond, however, to the degree of contingency or uncertainty of the law's expected effect on the challenger.

Where leeway exists, the court may be influenced by determining whose interests a quicker decision would serve. Thus, when federal civil servants fearing dismissal for violation of the HATCH ACT asked that the political activities they were contemplating be declared constitutionally protected in *United Public Workers v. Mitchell* (1947), the Court found the case unripe absent enforcement of the act against some particular employee behavior. Similarly, a challenge to IMMIGRATION policy was held unripe in *International Longshoremen's Union v. Boyd* (1954) despite a strong indication that, without a ruling, resident ALIENS risked jeopardizing their right to return to the United States. With little doubt that the laws would be applied, the challengers nonetheless were forced to act at their peril. By contrast, when a delay in decision has threatened to frustrate government policy, the Court has resolved anticipatory challenges to laws whose future application appeared inevitable, including legislation restructuring some of the nation's railroads in the *Regional Rail Reorganization Act Cases* (1974) and the FEDERAL ELECTION CAMPAIGN ACTS in BUCKLEY v. VALEO (1976).

Sensitivity to the government's interest in quick resolution even led the Court to uphold a federal statute limiting aggregate operator liability for nuclear power plant explosions in *Duke Power Co. v. Carolina Environmental Study Group, Inc.* (1978), despite evidence that explosions are unlikely and serious doubt that this statute would ever be applied. Because injury to the asserted right of unlimited recovery for nuclear disaster was unlikely to occur soon, if at all, the constitutional issues did not seem ripe; yet the Court concluded that the case was ripe, because the normal operation of nearby nuclear plants (whose development the statute had facilitated) threatened imminent pollution—even though the suit had not questioned the pollution's legality.

As the *Duke Power* case illustrates, the inherent policy choice in ripeness decisions—between finding constitutional adjudication premature and finding prevention of harm or validation of government policy timely—embodies important perceptions of judicial role in a regime characterized by the SEPARATION OF POWERS.

Bibliography

WRIGHT, CHARLES A.; MILLER, ARTHUR R.; and COOPER, EDWARD H.
    1984   *Federal Practice and Procedure.* Vol. 13A:112–214. St. Paul, Minn.: West
    Publishing Co.

ELEVENTH AMENDMENT

Clyde E. Jacobs

The Eleventh Amendment of the Constitution provides that "the JUDICIAL POWER OF THE UNITED STATES shall not be construed to extend to any suit in law or EQUITY, commenced or prosecuted against one of the United States by citizens of another State, or by citizens or subjects of a foreign State." Congress submitted this amendment, on votes of twenty-three to two in the Senate and eighty-one to nine in the House of Representatives, for ratification in March 1794. By February 1795, the legislatures of three-fourths of the states had ratified, but, because of delays in certification of this action, adoption of the amendment was not proclaimed until 1798.

According to traditional theory the purpose of the amendment was to correct an erroneous interpretation of the Constitution by the Supreme Court. Impetus for the amendment undoubtedly was the unpopular decision in CHISHOLM V. GEORGIA (1793)—one of seven early suits instituted against a state by citizens of other states or by ALIENS. In *Chisholm* the Court, voting 4–1, held that the judicial power of the United States and the JURISDICTION of the Court reached such suits under the provision in Article III extending the federal judicial power to "Controversies between a State and Citizens of another State . . . and between a State . . . and foreign States, Citizens or Subjects."

Although the language of Article III is broad enough to support the *Chisholm* holding, proponents of the theory that the amendment was adopted to correct an error in constitutional interpretation have argued that (1) the doctrine of SOVEREIGN IMMUNITY, exempting the sovereign from unconsented suits, was part of the COMMON LAW heritage at the time the Constitution was adopted, and hence implicitly qualified some delegations of judicial power in Article III; and (2) an understanding to that effect emerged during the ratification debates.

Existence of an implicit common law qualification upon the various delegations of federal judicial power is doubtful, however. While the supposition that the immunity doctrine was already incorporated into American law appears sound, at least some state immunity surely was surrendered under the Constitution. The purpose behind the various delegations of judicial power to the United States was to create a judiciary competent to decide all cases "involving the National peace and harmony." Surrender—rather than retention—of state immunity is consonant with that objective. Nor is the argument that the ratification debates evidenced an understanding that the states would be immune from suit persuasive. While ALEXANDER HAMILTON, JAMES MADISON, and JOHN MARSHALL offered assurances to that effect in reply to Anti-Federalist objections, these objections were not quieted; and other leading Federalists, including EDMUND RANDOLPH and JAMES WILSON—members of the Committee of Detail where most provisions of Article III were drafted—took the contrary view.

While some proponents of the Eleventh Amendment probably understood it to be corrective, the broad support enlisted for its adoption can be better explained in terms of diverse perceptions and objectives. These ranged from the desire of STATES' RIGHTS advocates to repudiate the extravagant nationalism manifested by Federalist justices in their *Chisholm* opinions, to Federalist perceptions that the amendment effected only a relatively insignificant restriction upon part of the DIVERSITY JURISDICTION of the federal judiciary. Experience was accumulating that suit against a state in the Supreme Court was cumbersome and unnecessary for the maintenance of federal supremacy. Moreover, assumption of a major portion of state indebtedness and rapid liquidation of the remainder had allayed a Federalist concern that partially accounted for the original grant of federal judicial power.

Judicial construction of the amendment has been shaped by the view that as a corrective measure, it restored common law sovereign immunity as an implicit qualification upon some grants of judicial power in Article III. As interpreted, the amendment bars any suit against a state, including those raising federal questions, instituted by private plaintiffs, regardless of CITIZENSHIP (*Hans v. Louisiana,* 1890), as well as by foreign states (*Monaco v. Mississippi,* 1934) in federal court. In general, only where another state or the United States is plaintiff, is a state subject to unconsented suit in federal court (*Virginia v. West Virginia,* 1907; (*United States v. Mississippi,* 1965). The amendment does not affect Article III rights of a state to institute suits in federal courts, nor does it preclude appeals by private plaintiffs in actions commenced by a state. (See COHENS v. VIRGINIA, 1821.)

Although the amendment literally limits the federal judicial power—which, by general rule, may not be modified by consent of the parties—as shorthand for the doctrine of sovereign immunity, it has always been interpreted to permit exercises of Article III powers upon a state's waiver of immunity from suit in federal court. Such waivers ordinarily must be explicit (EDELMAN v. JORDAN, 1974); however, implied and imputed waivers, although exceptional, are not unknown (*Parden v. Terminal Railway,* 1964).

The amendment imposes an absolute bar against unconsented suits commenced in federal court by private plaintiffs against state governments and their agencies. To this generalization, there is a single but increasingly important exception. Congress, pursuant to its enforcement powers under the FOURTEENTH AMENDMENT, may create federal causes of action against the states and thereby deprive them of immunity (FITZPATRICK V. BITZER, 1976). Whether such authority can be inferred from other powers delegated to the national government has not been settled.

The exemption from suit enjoyed by the states under the amendment does not extend to their political subdivisions nor, in general, to governmental corporations (*Lincoln County v. Luning*, 1890). Of paramount importance in restricting the impact of the amendment is the availability of relief in suits instituted against state officers for acts performed or threatened under color of unconstitutional state legislation. The issues whether and to what extent the amendment bars suits against state officers for official acts have occasioned more litigation under the amendment than any others, and the course traversed by the Court from OSBORN V. BANK OF THE UNITED STATES (1824) through *In re Ayers* (1887) to EX PARTE YOUNG (1908) was tortuous. In some early cases the amendment was held applicable only to suits in which a state was a defendant of record, but this rule was never firmly established. Later cases turned on whether a suit against a state officer was substantially a suit against the state itself. In *Ayers* the Court held that a suit against a state officer is a suit against the state unless the officer's act, if stripped of its official character, constitutes a private wrong; but this rigorous test was abandoned in *Ex parte Young*, a landmark case which, despite its unpopularity at the time, fixed the law for the future. While adhering to the general rule that a suit against a state officer is barred by the amendment if it is substantially against the state itself, the Court adopted the fiction that mere institution of state judicial proceedings by a state officer pursuant to an allegedly unconstitutional statute is a wrong for which federal equitable relief is available. The theoretical difficulties posed by this formulation are grave and many, but in facilitating direct access to the federal courts to test the validity of state legislation, *Young* is of transcendent importance in maintaining federal supremacy and the RULE OF LAW. Adopted as the instrument of judicial protection of the rights of property and enterprise, the *Young* principle today does the same essential service in the protection of personal rights and liberties. Even so, not every act of a state may be reached through suit against its officers. Where such suits are adjudged to be against the state itself—actions affecting the public treasury for past wrongs and those seeking to dispossess the state of property—the Eleventh Amendment remains a bar (*Edelman v. Jordan*, 1974).

Bibliography

JACOBS, CLYDE E.   1972   *The Eleventh Amendment and Sovereign Immunity.* Westport, Conn.: Greenwood Press.

NOWAK, JOHN E.   1975   The Scope of Congressional Power to Create Causes of Action Against State Governments and the History of the Eleventh and Fourteenth Amendments. *Columbia Law Review* 75:1413–1469.

SOVEREIGN IMMUNITY

Clyde E. Jacobs

At COMMON LAW the sovereign, although subject to the law, was immune from the JURISDICTION of its own courts. The English doctrine of sovereign immunity was established at an early time, probably in the thirteenth century; but long before the American Revolution the jurisdictional exemption of the sovereign, though remaining theoretically absolute, was riddled with exceptions. Judicial process against the sovereign was available through petition of right and other procedures resting upon waiver of immunity, and subordinate officers could be sued for damages attributable to official acts and were subject to process by prerogative writ.

Because sovereign immunity was part of the common law heritage existing when the Constitution was adopted, the courts later embraced the doctrine as an implicit limitation upon their jurisdiction. Hence, some provisions of Article III of the Constitution were interpreted as subject to this qualification. The immunity of the United States, first acknowledged by the Supreme Court in *United States v. McLemore* (1846), became a complete exemption, protecting the federal government and its agencies from unconsented suit in any court by any plaintiff. State immunity was initially rejected by the Court in CHISHOLM v. GEORGIA (1793), but that unpopular HOLDING was quickly reversed by the ELEVENTH AMENDMENT. The amendment, in juxtaposition with Article III, was subsequently construed to immunize the states from unconsented suits by private plaintiffs and by foreign governments in federal court.

The states, however, are not immune from suit by either the United States or other states. As a matter of state law, states commonly have claimed immunity from suit by private plaintiffs in state court. The power of Congress to lift the states' common law immunity seems restricted only by the limitations of the JUDICIAL POWER OF THE UNITED STATES as defined in Article III, the general limitations of congressional power, and—arguably—some core notion of state sovereignty. (See NATIONAL LEAGUE OF CITIES v. USERY, 1976.)

The immunity doctrine is in tension with the RULE OF LAW, and pragmatic justifications for its perpetuation are unpersuasive. By means of statutes waiving immunity and through judicial interpretation, the ambit of the exemption has been drastically reduced. Congressional legislation creating the COURT OF CLAIMS in 1855 and later enactments, such as the Tucker Act (1887) and the FEDERAL TORT CLAIMS ACT (1946), subject the United States to suit on many kinds of claims. The states, by state constitutional provision or statute, have abolished completely or restricted their own immunity—often in state judicial proceedings only, less commonly in federal court actions. Moreover, as a practical matter, the impact of the doctrine is significantly restricted by differentiating suits against public officers for official acts done or threatened pursuant to unconstitutional or legally deficient authorization from suits against the government itself. Although the courts permit state and federal officers to assert sovereign immunity where the suit against them is adjudged to be substantially against the government itself, such cases are generally limited to suits seeking damages or restitution for past acts where judgment will expend itself upon the public treasury, those seeking to dispossess the government of property, and some suits seeking specific performance. As a consequence of these developments, sovereign immunity has become a narrow and ill-defined jurisdictional bar, whose contemporary legitimacy and utility are doubtful.

Bibliography

DAVIS, KENNETH C.   1970 Supp.   *Administrative Law Treatise.* Pages 895–940. St. Paul, Minn.: West Publishing Co.

HOLDSWORTH, SIR WILLIAM S.   1944   *A History of English Law.* Vol. 9 of 15. London: Methuen.

ABSTENTION DOCTRINE

Martha A. Field

All the abstention doctrines refer to circumstances in which federal courts, having JURISDICTION over a case under a congressional enactment, nonetheless may defer to state tribunals as decision makers. Federal courts may not abstain simply because they believe that particular cases, on their facts, would more appropriately be heard in state courts; they have a general obligation to exercise jurisdiction in cases Congress has placed before them. Abstention is justified only in exceptional circumstances, and then only when it falls within a particular abstention doctrine.

There are several abstention doctrines; they differ in their consequences and in their requirements. *Colorado River Water Conservation District v. United States* (1976) suggests a general doctrine that federal courts have power to defer in favor of ongoing state proceedings raising the same or closely related issues. This type of deference to ongoing proceedings often is not identified as abstention at all, and courts have not spelled out its requirements other than general discretion.

When a federal court does defer under this doctrine, it stays federal proceedings pending completion of the state proceedings. If the state does not proceed expeditiously, or if issues remain for decision, the federal court can reenter the case. When it does not abstain and both state and federal forums exercise their CONCURRENT JURISDICTION over a dispute, the JUDGMENT that controls is the first to become final. Federal courts deferring in favor of ongoing state proceedings avoid this wasteful race to judgment, but the price paid is that the federal plaintiff may lose the federal forum she has chosen and to which federal law entitles her.

In reconciling the competing interests, federal courts are much more likely to defer to prior state proceedings, in which the state plaintiff has won the race to the courthouse, than they are when the federal suit was first filed.

Deference, even to previously commenced state proceedings involving the same parties as the federal suit, is by no means automatic; it is discretionary—justified by the court's INHERENT POWER to control its docket in the interests of efficiency and fairness—and the Supreme Court has said that it is to be invoked sparingly. In *Colorado River Water Conservation District v. United States* the Court stated that the inherent problems in duplicative proceedings are not sufficient to justify deference to the state courts because of "the virtually unflagging obligation of the federal courts to exercise the jurisdiction given them."

This doctrine permitting deference serves as a backdrop to other doctrines that the Supreme Court more consistently calls "abstention." The most important of these today is the doctrine of YOUNGER V. HARRIS (1971). The doctrine started as a principle against enjoining state criminal prosecutions, but it has grown enormously. It has been expanded to bar not only suits for federal injunction but also suits for federal declaratory judgment concerning the constitutionality of an enactment involved in a pending prosecution; and today some believe it goes so far as to bar a federal damage action against state officials that might decide issues that would interfere with a state prosecution. Moreover, the doctrine has grown to protect state civil proceedings as well as criminal ones. Most remarkably, as the Court held in *Hicks v. Miranda* (1975), the doctrine now allows abstention even if the federal action is first filed, so long as the state commences prosecution "before any proceedings of substance on the merits" have occurred in federal court. That rule effectively deters federal suit; a federal plaintiff who wins the race to the courthouse may simply provoke his own criminal prosecution. These developments together have turned *Younger* into a doctrine that permits federal courts to dismiss federal constitutional challenges to state criminal prosecution (or quasi-criminal) enactments whenever a state criminal prosecution (or other enforcement proceeding) provides a forum for the federal constitutional issue. The state forum in theory must be an adequate one, but courts applying the doctrine often overlook this aspect of the inquiry.

Courts abstaining under the *Younger* doctrine generally dismiss the federal suit rather than retaining jurisdiction. Federal plaintiffs who are left to defend state proceedings generally cannot return to federal court for adjudication of the federal or any other issues, and the state court's decision on the constitutional issue and others may control future litigation through collateral estoppel. Litigants do, of course, retain the possibility of Supreme Court review of the federal issues they raise in state court, but the chances that the Supreme Court will hear such cases are slim.

The *Younger* doctrine therefore often deprives the federal plaintiff of any federal forum—prior, concurrent, or subsequent to the state proceeding against him—for his CIVIL RIGHTS action against state officials. This contradicts the apparent purpose of SECTION 1983, TITLE 42, UNITED STATES CODE and its jurisdictional counterpart (section 1343, Title 28) that such a forum be available. Some of those convicted in state criminal prosecutions may later raise federal issues in federal HABEAS CORPUS proceedings, but ACCESS to habeas corpus is itself increasingly limited. (See STONE V. POWELL, 1976; WAINWRIGHT V. SYKES, 1977.)

The *Younger* doctrine does have exceptions. If the federal court finds state courts inadequate on the facts of the particular case (because of what the Court in *Younger* termed "bad faith, harassment, or any other unusual circumstance that would call for equitable relief"), it will exercise its jurisdiction. But this approach turns around the usual rule that it takes exceptional circumstances to decline jurisdiction, not to justify its exercise. To avoid this conflict with the usual rules allowing Congress, not the courts, to determine the appropriate cases for federal jurisdiction, *Younger* abstention should be cut back, at least by limiting it to cases in which state proceedings began before the federal one. Such an approach would assimilate *Younger* abstention to the general doctrine of deference to ongoing state proceedings, discussed above.

In the meantime the expanded version of the *Younger* doctrine has largely displaced what had been the key form of abstention, formulated in RAILROAD COMMISSION OF TEXAS v. PULLMAN COMPANY (1941). *Pullman* abstention applies to cases involving federal constitutional challenges to state law. It allows (but does not require) federal judges to refrain from deciding highly uncertain questions of state law when resolution of the questions may avoid or affect the federal constitutional issue.

Pullman today is the only abstention doctrine in which deference to state courts is limited to state law issues. When the federal court abstains under the *Pullman* doctrine, it holds the case while the parties seek declaratory relief on the state law issues in state court. Unless the parties voluntarily submit federal along with state issues to the state court, they have a right to return to federal court after the state adjudication is completed, for decision of the federal issues and for federal factfinding. In this respect *Pullman* abstention is a narrower intrusion on federal court jurisdiction than the *Younger* doctrine is, although the cost of shuttling back and forth from state to federal court dissuades many federal plaintiffs from retaining their federal forum. *Pullman* also differs from *Younger* because the federal plaintiff generally initiates the proceedings in state court, and they are declaratory judgment proceedings rather than criminal prosecutions or civil enforcement proceedings.

As *Younger* has expanded to include some civil enforcement proceedings and to allow abstention in favor of later-filed state proceedings, it has reduced the area for *Pullman* abstention. Both doctrines typically apply to constitutional litigation against state officials. In many cases where *Pullman* abstention could be at issue, *Younger* is operative because a state enforcement proceeding against the federal plaintiff is a possibility as long as the federal plaintiff has violated the law she challenges. If, however, the federal plaintiff has not violated the enactment she challenges, *Younger* abstention cannot apply, for the state is unable to bring a prosecution or civil enforcement proceeding against her and thereby displace the federal forum. *Pullman,* therefore, is the applicable doctrine for pre-violation suits and for challenges to state enactments that do not involve state enforcement proceedings. Many of those cases, however, will be dismissed before abstention is considered; where the plaintiff has not violated the enactment she complains of, she may have trouble showing that her controversy is justiciable. (See RIPENESS.)

While *Pullman* abstention has therefore become less and less important, a new area has recently been created for a *Pullman* -like abstention. PENNHURST STATE SCHOOL V. HALDERMAN (1984), restricting federal courts' pendent jurisdiction, requires federal litigants in suits against state governments to use state courts to pursue any related state causes of action they do not wish to forfeit. *Pennhurst* thus creates the equivalent of a mandatory *Pullman* abstention category—where state courts must be given certain state law questions to adjudicate even while a federal court exercises jurisdiction over the rest of the case. This new category is not, however, dependent upon uncertainty in state law.

Another abstention doctrine, administrative abstention, was first articulated in *Burford v. Sun Oil Company* (1943). The *Burford* doctrine allows a federal court with jurisdiction of a case to dismiss in favor of state court adjudication, ongoing or not. Like *Younger* abstention, *Burford* abstention displaces federal jurisdiction; if abstention is ordered, state courts adjudicate all issues, subject only to Supreme Court review. The Court has never clearly explained which cases are eligible for administrative abstention. The doctrine is typically employed when a state administrative process has dealt with a controversy in the first instance and the litigant then asks a federal district court to exercise either its federal question or diversity jurisdiction to review that administrative interpretation. The federal court's ability to abstain under this doctrine may be limited to situations in which state statutes concentrate JUDICIAL REVIEW of the administrative process in a particular state court so that it becomes "an integral part of the regulatory process," as the Court said in *Alabama Public Service Commission v. Southern Railway* (1951), or to situations involving complex factual issues. There is no requirement that legal issues, state or federal, be unclear for this abstention to be ordered, or that the case contain any federal issues.

Burford abstention does not apply when state administrative remedies have been skipped altogether and the litigant has sued first in federal court. The only issue then is whether state administrative remedies must be exhausted. There is no overlap between *Burford* and the *Younger* or *Pullman* abstention doctrines, because exhaustion of administrative remedies has not been required in suits under section 1983, which today includes all constitutional litigation. The Court recently affirmed this exception to the exhaustion requirement in PATSY V. BOARD OF REGENTS (1982). If the Court were to modify the section 1983 exception to the exhaustion requirement, retreat from the *Burford* doctrine would seem to follow. Otherwise, *Burford* would mandate state judicial review after deference to state administrative proceedings, so federal jurisdiction would be altogether unavailable in section 1983 cases whenever an administrative agency was available.

A final minor category of abstention, which seems to have been limited to EMINENT DOMAIN cases involving unclear state issues, is reflected in *Louisiana Light & Power Company v. Thibodaux* (1959). In contexts other than eminent domain, abstention is not proper simply to clarify difficult state law issues. (In states that provide for certification, however, a federal court without more can certify difficult state issues to the state supreme court.)

All these theories of abstention are judge-made rules, without any statutory authority; they avoid jurisdiction in cases where Congress has given it. By contrast, Congress itself has provided for deference to state processes in narrow categories of cases, most notably cases involving INJUNCTIONS against state rate orders and tax collections. And in the Anti-Injunction Act, Congress has generally prohibited federal injunctions against state proceedings. This prohibition is limited by explicit statutory exceptions, however, and by some judge-made exceptions, and since the area outside the prohibition also is limited, by the judge-made abstention doctrines, the statute apparently has little effect.

Bibliography

FIELD, MARTHA A.   1974   Abstention in Constitutional Cases: The Scope of the Pullman Abstention Doctrine. *University of Pennsylvania Law Review* 122:1071–1087.

——— 1981   The Uncertain Nature of Federal Jurisdiction. *William & Mary Law Review* 22:683–724.

FISS, OWEN   1977   Dombrowksi. *Yale Law Journal* 86:1103–1164.

LAYCOCK, DOUGLAS   1977   Federal Interference with State Prosecutions: The Need for Prospective Relief. *Supreme Court Review* 1977:193–238.

ORIGINAL JURISDICTION

Kenneth L. Karst

The original jurisdiction of a court (as distinguished from APPELLATE JURISDICTION) is its power to hear and decide a case from the beginning. In the federal court system, the district courts originally hear the overwhelming majority of cases. Most discussion and litigation concerning the JURISDICTION OF FEDERAL COURTS centers on the district courts' original JURISDICTION. Yet the term "original jurisdiction" is heard most frequently in discussion and litigation concerning the jurisdiction of the Supreme Court.

The Constitution itself establishes the Supreme Court's original jurisdiction. After setting out the types of cases subject to the JUDICIAL POWER OF THE UNITED STATES, Article III distributes the Supreme Court's jurisdiction over them: "In all cases affecting ambassadors, other public ministers and consuls, and those in which a state shall be a party, the Supreme Court shall have original jurisdiction. In all other cases mentioned, the Supreme Court shall have appellate jurisdiction. . . ."

From the beginning, Congress has given the district courts CONCURRENT JURISDICTION over some of the cases within the Supreme Court's original jurisdiction, offering plaintiffs the option of commencing suit in either court. The Supreme Court has given this practice its stamp of constitutional approval. Furthermore, because the Court is hardpressed by a crowded docket, it has sought ways of shunting cases to other courts. Thus, even when a case does fall within the Court's original jurisdiction, the court has conferred on itself the discretion to deny the plaintiff leave to file an original action. Typically the Court decides only three or four original jurisdiction cases each year, conserving its institutional energies for its main task: guiding the development of federal law by exercising its appellate jurisdiction.

Congress, however, cannot constitutionally diminish the Court's original jurisdiction. Nor can Congress expand that jurisdiction; the dubious reading of Article III in MARBURY v. MADISON (1803) remains firmly entrenched. However, the Supreme Court does entertain some actions that have an "original" look to them, even though Article III does not list them as original jurisdiction cases: HABEAS CORPUS is an example; so are the common law WRITS OF MANDAMUS and PROHIBITION. The Court hears such cases only when they can be characterized as "appellate," calling for Supreme Court supervision of actions by lower courts.

Of the two types of original jurisdiction cases specified in Article III, the state-as-party case has produced all but a tiny handful of the cases originally decided by the Supreme Court. Officers of foreign governments enjoy a broad diplomatic immunity from suit in our courts, and, for motives no doubt similarly diplomatic, they have not brought suits in the Supreme Court. (The "ambassadors" and others mentioned in Article III, of course, are those of foreign governments, not our own.)

The state-as-party cases present obvious problems of SOVEREIGN IMMUNITY. The ELEVENTH AMENDMENT applies to original actions in the Supreme Court; indeed, the amendment was adopted in response to just such a case, CHISHOLM v. GEORGIA (1793). Thus a state can no more be sued by the citizen of another state in the Supreme Court than in a district court. However, when one state sues another, or when the United States or a foreign government sues a state, there is no bar to the Court's jurisdiction.

The spectacle of nine Justices of the Supreme Court jointly presiding over a trial has a certain Hollywood allure, but the Court consistently avoids such proceedings. The SEVENTH AMENDMENT commands TRIAL BY JURY in any common law action, and at first the Supreme Court did hold a few jury trials. The last one, however, took place in the 1790s. Since that time the Court has always managed to identify some feature of an original case that makes it a suit in EQUITY; thus jury trial is inappropriate, and findings of fact can be turned over to a SPECIAL MASTER, whose report is reviewed by the Court only as to questions of law.

The source of the substantive law applied in original actions between states is FEDERAL COMMON LAW, an amalgam of the ANGLO-AMERICAN COMMON LAW, policies derived from congressional statutes, and international law principles. Thus far no state has defied the Supreme Court sufficiently to test the Court's means of enforcing its decrees, but some states have dragged out their compliance for enough years to test the patience of the most saintly Justice.

Bibliography

NOTE 1959 The Original Jurisdiction of the United States Supreme Court. *Stanford Law Review* 11:665–719.

APPELLATE JURISDICTION

Kenneth L. Karst

A court's appellate jurisdiction is its power to review the actions of another body, usually a lower court. The appellate jurisdiction of our federal courts lies within the control of Congress. Article III of the Constitution, after establishing the Supreme Court's ORIGINAL JURISDICTION over certain cases, gives the Court appellate jurisdiction over all other types of cases within "the JUDICIAL POWER OF THE UNITED STATES," but empowers Congress to make "exceptions and regulations" governing that jurisdiction. In the JUDICIARY ACT OF 1789 Congress did not, formally, make exceptions to the Supreme Court's appellate jurisdiction; rather it purported to *grant* the Court jurisdiction to hear various types of cases on WRIT OF ERROR. The assumption has been that such an affirmative grant of appellate jurisdiction over specified types of cases is, by implication, an "exception," excluding the Court from taking appellate jurisdiction over cases not mentioned.

The Supreme Court itself accepted this line of reasoning in Ex PARTE MCCARDLE (1869), stating that without a statutory grant of appellate jurisdiction it had no power to hear a case. Read broadly, this holding empowers Congress to undermine JUDICIAL REVIEW by withdrawing the Supreme Court's most important functions. Some commentators argue that Congress, in controlling the Supreme Court's appellate jurisdiction, is constitutionally bound to respect the Court's essential role in a system of SEPARATION OF POWERS. Other writers, however, reject this view, and the Supreme Court has been presented with no modern occasion to face the issue. (See JUDICIAL SYSTEM.)

Whatever the Constitution may ultimately require, Congress has acted on the assumption that it need not extend the Supreme Court's appellate jurisdiction to occupy the whole of the judicial power established by Article III. Until 1925, for example, the Court's appellate review of civil cases was limited by a requirement of a certain dollar amount in controversy. For the first century of the Court's existence, it had no general appellate jurisdiction over federal criminal cases, but reviewed such a case only on writ of HABEAS CORPUS or upon a lower court's certification of a division of opinion on an issue of law. Until 1914, the Supreme Court could review state court decisions only when they *denied* claims of federal right, not when they validated those claims. Although all these major limitations on the Court's appellate jurisdiction have now been eliminated, the halls of Congress perennially ring with calls for removing the Court's power over cases involving such emotion-charged subjects as SUBVERSIVE ACTIVITIES, school prayers, or ABORTION.

From the beginning the Supreme Court has reviewed cases coming from the lower federal courts and the state courts. The latter jurisdiction has been the source of political controversy, not only in its exercise but in its very existence. In a doctrinal sense, the power of Congress to establish the Court's appellate jurisdiction over state court decisions was settled early, in MARTIN v. HUNTER'S LESSEE (1816). In the realm of practical politics, the issue was settled when any serious thoughts of INTERPOSITION or NULLIFICATION were laid to rest by the outcome of the Civil War. (Ironically, the CONFEDERATE CONSTITUTION had provided a similar appellate jurisdiction for the Confederacy's own supreme court.) By the late 1950s, when the Court confronted intense opposition to school DESEGREGATION, its appellate jurisdiction was firmly entrenched; southern efforts to curb the Court failed miserably.

The Supreme Court's review of state court decisions is limited to issues of federal law. Even federal questions will not be decided by the Court if the state court's judgment rests on an ADEQUATE STATE GROUND. By congressional statute the Court is instructed to review only FINAL JUDGMENTS of state courts, but this limitation is now riddled with judge-made exceptions. The Court does, however, obey strictly its statutory instruction to review the decision of only the highest state court in which judgment is available in a given case. As THOMPSON v. LOUISVILLE (1960) shows, even a justice of the peace may constitute that "highest court" if state law provides no APPEAL from the justice's decision.

When the Supreme Court reviews a state court decision, all the jurisdictional limitations on the federal courts come into play. For example, although a state court may routinely confer STANDING on any state taxpayer to challenge state governmental action, the Supreme Court can take appellate jurisdiction only if the taxpayer satisfies the federal standards for standing.

Of the 4,000 cases brought to the Court in a typical year, only about 150 will be decided with full opinion. A large number of state criminal convictions raise substantial issues of federal constitutional law, but they largely go unreviewed in the Supreme Court. The WARREN COURT sought to provide a substitute federal remedy, facilitating access for state prisoners to federal habeas corpus. In the 1970s, however, the BURGER COURT drastically limited that access; in practical terms, a great many state convictions now escape review of their federal constitutional issues in any federal forum.

Final judgments of the federal district courts are normally reviewed in the courts of appeals, although direct appeal to the Supreme Court is available in a very few categories of cases. Usually, then, a case brought to the Supreme Court has already been the subject of one appeal. The Court thus can husband its resources for its main appellate functions: nourishing the development of a coherent body of federal law, and promoting that law's uniformity and supremacy.

For the Supreme Court's first century, its appellate jurisdiction was mostly obligatory; when Congress authorized a writ of error, the Court had no discretion to decline. The Court's second century has seen a progressive increase in the use of the discretionary WRIT OF CERTIORARI as a means of invoking Supreme Court review, with a corresponding decline in statutory entitlements to review on appeal. Today the Court has a high degree of discretion to choose which cases it will decide. Some observers think this discretion weakens the theoretical foundation of judicial review, expressed in MARBURY v. MADISON (1803). The Court there based its power to hold an act of Congress unconstitutional on the necessity to decide a case. If the Court has discretion whether to decide, the necessity disappears, and thus (so the argument goes) judicial review's legitimacy. Ultimately, that legitimacy may come to depend, both theoretically and politically, on the very power of congressional control so often seen as a threat to the Supreme Court's appellate jurisdiction.

Bibliography

BATOR, PAUL M., MISHKIN, PAUL J., SHAPIRO, DAVID L., and WECHSLER, HERBERT, EDS. 1973 *The Federal Courts and the Federal System,* 2nd ed. Chaps. 5, 11. Mineola, N.Y.: Foundation Press.

ADEQUATE STATE GROUNDS

Kenneth L. Karst

Although most decisions of state courts falling within the Supreme Court's APPELLATE JURISDICTION involve questions of both state and federal law, the Supreme Court limits its review of such cases to the FEDERAL QUESTIONS. Moreover, the Court will not even decide the federal questions raised by such a case if the decision below rests on a ground of state law that is adequate to support the judgment and is independent of any federal issue. This rule applies to grounds based on both state substantive law and state procedures.

In its substantive-ground aspect, the rule not only protects the state courts' authority as the final arbiters of state law but also bolsters the principle forbidding federal courts to give ADVISORY OPINIONS. If the Supreme Court were to review the federal issues presented by a decision resting independently on an adequate state ground, the Court's pronouncements on the federal issues would be advisory only, having no effect on the resolution of the case. It has been assumed that ordinarily no federal policy dictates Supreme Court review of a decision resting on an independent state substantive ground; the winner in the state court typically is the same party who has asserted the federal claim. The point is exemplified by a state court decision invalidating a state statute on both state and federal constitutional grounds. This assumption, however, is a hindrance to Justices bent on contracting the reach of particular constitutional guarantees. In *Michigan v. Long* (1983) the BURGER COURT announced that when the independence of a state court's judgment from federal law is in doubt, the Court will assume that the judgment does not rest independently on state law. To insulate a decision from Supreme Court review now requires a plain statement by the state court of the independence of its state law ground.

Obviously, the highest state court retains considerable control over the reviewability of many of its decisions in the Supreme Court. If the state court chooses to rest decision only on grounds of federal law, as the California court did in REGENTS OF THE UNIVERSITY OF CALIFORNIA v. BAKKE (1978), the case is reviewable by the Supreme Court. Correspondingly, the state court can avoid review by the Supreme Court by resting solely on a state-law ground, or by explicitly resting on *both* a state and a federal ground. In the latter case, the state court's pronouncements on federal law are unreviewable. Recently, several state supreme courts (Alaska, California, Massachusetts, New Jersey, and Oregon) have used these devices to make important contributions to the development of both state and federal constitutional law.

When the state court's decision rests on a procedural ground, the usual effect is to cut off a party's right to claim a federal right, because of some procedural default. The Supreme Court generally insists that federal questions be raised in the state courts according to the dictates of state procedure. However, when the state procedural ground itself violates the federal Constitution (and thus is not "independent" of a federal claim), the Supreme Court will consider the federal issues in the case even though state procedure was not precisely followed. Another exception is exemplified in NAACP v. ALABAMA (1964). There the Court reviewed the NAACP's federal claims although the state court had refused to hear them on the transparently phony ground that they had been presented in a brief that departed from the prescribed format. The adequate state ground rule protects judicial federalism, not shamming designed to defeat the claims of federal right.

A similar rule limits the availability of federal HABEAS CORPUS relief for state prisoners. (See FAY v. NOIA, 1963; WAINWRIGHT v. SYKES, 1977.)

Bibliography

FALK, JEROME B., JR.   1973   The Supreme Court of California, 1971–1972—Foreword: The State Constitution: A More Than "Adequate" Nonfederal Ground. *California Law Review* 61:273–286.